S0-AJM-872

WITHDRAWN

**Recent Titles in
Contributions in Military Studies**

Beyond Glasnost: Soviet Reform and Security Issues
David T. Twining, editor

For King and Kaiser! The Making of the Prussian Army Officer, 1860–1914
Steven E. Clemente

The U.S. Navy, the Mediterranean, and the Cold War, 1945–1947
Edward J. Sheehy

The Soviet Military and the Future
Stephen J. Blank and Jacob W. Kipp, editors

Soviet Military Doctrine from Lenin to Gorbachev, 1915–1991
Willard C. Frank and Philip S. Gillette, editors

Soviet Military Reform in the Twentieth Century: Three Case Studies
Raymond J. Swider, Jr.

The Laws of Land Warfare: A Guide to U.S. Army Manuals
Donald A. Wells

Raiders or Elite Infantry? The Changing Role of the U.S. Army Rangers from Dieppe
to Grenada
David W. Hogan, Jr.

The U.S. Military
John E. Peters

Unconventional Conflicts in a New Security Era: Lessons from Malaya and Vietnam
Sam C. Sarkesian

"Mad Jack": The Biography of Captain John Percival, USN, 1779–1862
David F. Long

Military Helicopter Doctrines of the Major Powers, 1945–1992: Making Decisions
about Air-Land Warfare
Matthew Allen

Joint Military Operations

A SHORT HISTORY

Roger A. Beaumont

Contributions in Military Studies,
Number 139

GREENWOOD PRESS
Westport, Connecticut • London

Library of Congress Cataloging-in-Publication Data

Beaumont, Roger A.
    Joint military operations : a short history / Roger A. Beaumont.
       p.   cm. — (Contributions in military studies, ISSN 0883–6884
; no. 139)
    Includes bibliographical references and index.
    ISBN 0–313–26744–8
    1. Unified operations (Military science)—History. I. Title.
II. Series.
    U260.B43   1993
    355.4′22—dc20   92–36227

British Library Cataloguing in Publication Data is available.

Copyright © 1993 by Roger A. Beaumont

All rights reserved. No portion of this book may be
reproduced, by any process or technique, without the
express written consent of the publisher.

Library of Congress Catalog Card Number: 92–36227
ISBN: 0–313–26744–8
ISSN: 0883–6884

First published in 1993

Greenwood Press, 88 Post Road West, Westport, CT 06881
An imprint of Greenwood Publishing Group, Inc.

Printed in the United States of America

The paper used in this book complies with the
Permanent Paper Standard issued by the National
Information Standards Organization (Z39.48–1984).

10 9 8 7 6 5 4 3 2 1

U
260
.B43
1993

To
the Suderlands
Nancy   •   Otto
Brenda   •   Heidi

Contents

Maps   ix

Acknowledgments   xi

Introduction   xiii

1 Varieties of Jointness: From Ancient to Modern   1

2 Dark and Swift Narrows: World War I   41

3 Backwaters and Rivulets: Jointness Between the World Wars   65

4 The Cresting Torrent: Jointness in World War II   85

5 Fitful Ebb and Flow: Jointness from 1943 to 1991   127

6 Patterns and Paradoxes: The Central Problem of Friction   185

Appendix 1: Principal Events Relating to Jointness in the U.S. Defense Nexus, 1943–1946   199

Appendix 2: Some Official Definitions Related to Jointness   201

Select Bibliography   203

Index   215

Maps

U.S. Assault Landing at Vera Cruz, Mexico, March 9, 1847   18

Western Theater of Operations, American Civil War, 1862   22

Approach to Vicksburg and Siege, American Civil War, 1863   24

U.S. Landings in Cuba, June 1898   33

Allied Landings on Gallipoli Peninsula, April and August 1915   49

German Landings on Oesel Island, October 1917   56

Franco-Spanish Assault Against Rif Rebels' Headquarters (Alhucemas, Morocco), September 1925   79

Major Allied Joint Operations in Western Europe and the Mediterranean, 1940–45   91

Major Allied Joint Operations in Asia and the Pacific, 1937–45   98

UN Forces Assault Landing at Inchon, South Korea, September 15, 1950   142

Anglo-French-Israeli Attacks on Egypt, October–November 1956   160

Acknowledgments

I am grateful for support of my research and writing to: the United States Naval Academy Secretary of Navy Fellows Program, and especially Nancy Gorum, program coordinator, 1989–90; to Dr. Michael Halbig, dean of administration at the USNA; and at Texas A&M, to Associate Dean Charles Johnson, College of Liberal Arts; Dr. Larry Hill, head, Department of History; to Drs. Arthur Blair and Frank Vandiver, of the Mosher Defense Institute; and last but not least, Dr. Lee Peddicord, head of the Engineering Program at Texas A&M.

For encouragement and counsel, I am very much obliged to Dr. Roger Spiller of the Combat Studies Institute; to Col. William Griffith, U.S. Army, retired; to Professors Robert Love and Jack Huston of the U.S. Naval Academy History Department faculty; to the midshipmen in my classes there in 1989–90, and to the cadets at Texas A&M over the years since 1974, for a great many insights; to Professors Joseph Dawson of the Military Studies Institute and Arnold Krammer of the History Department; to John Robertson of the Political Science Department, all at Texas A&M; and to David Fulghum, military editor, *Aviation Week and Space Technology*.

I am also very much in the special debt of Mildred Vasan, of Greenwood Press, for her special encouragement and patience; of my wife, Penny, for her warm support and ready ear; of my daughter Anne, for her cheeriness, sympathy, and patience as I clambered up some of the steepest slopes in 1989–90; and of Dr. Craig Symonds, then History Department chairman at the Naval Academy.

This enterprise lies on a foundation laid by many others as well, including the staffs of the libraries at the University of Texas, the U.S. Naval Academy, the Library of Congress, and the British Public Record Office at Kew, and to those who met my demands unstintingly in the Texas A&M Sterling C. Evans Library Inter-Library Loan Branch in the spring and summer of 1989: Rachel

Robbins, Susan Scott, Susie Kelly, Karen Charba, Andrew Seville, and Janie Kelly.

And last but not least, I am most appreciative of the word-processing and decrypting of my editorial scrawlings to Laura De Sola, Nicole Pottberg, and Gloria Johnson of the Texas A&M Engineering Program, and Jude Swank and Daisy Jones of the Texas A&M History Department.

Introduction

This study arose from my longstanding interest in organizational dynamics, born first of experiences in the army and private business, then focused increasingly while at the Center for Advanced Study in Organization Science at the University of Wisconsin-Milwaukee, headed by Bernard James, and while working on my dissertation, a study of modern military elite forces, under the direction of Robin Higham at Kansas State University. While studying command and staff processes and other problems in military organization, I was struck by how uneven discipline was in military hierarchies, and by the wide polarity between conflict and accommodation. I also noticed how debates over jointness in U.S. defense circles resembled those over command-and-control and special operations, in the sense that perception varied widely in regard to definitions.[1] It was clear that a basic historical survey of jointness was in order. In seeking to remedy that, I tried to keep a wide range of readers in view, including those generally interested in military problems, as well as historians, policymakers, and practitioners, military and otherwise. I strove to strike a balance between detail and impressionism, recognizing that, for many, the references will be more useful than the text. Since no two analysts of jointness, as with any complex phenomenon, are likely to select and emphasize the same elements, I have tried to touch on as wide a range of cases as possible, while recognizing how close that has often come to making lists and lapsing into short-hand.

Before setting forth the course of joint operations, the question of basic terms must be dealt with. Through most of military and naval history, until the coming of heavier-than-air flight, such undertakings were viewed as land-sea, army-navy, conjunct or amphibious operations, assault landings, and raids. Some confusion arises from British usage of the terms ''joint'' and ''combined'' to describe interallied and interservice operations respectively, while the converse is true in the United States. Hence the reference to Combined Operations, the British organization formed in World War II to develop doctrine for and carry out what Americans call joint operations—and the unavoidable conflict of terms in the bibliography, since American practice prevails throughout this study.

Even though the coming of air power and other technologies complicated matters substantially, no universal terms as widely accepted as "amphibious" have emerged that are routinely used to describe air-sea or air-land as opposed to strictly naval-military/land-sea joint operations of the traditional kind. Several have made attempts. Admiral Sir Reginald Custance, for example, referred to military aviation linked to ground and sea operations as "Aery," and "triphibious" was used occasionally in World War II. A glance at Appendix 2 will give some sense of recent usage.[2] In any event, this study attempts to show how long the lineage of joint operations is. Since the limits of space force any such effort to be selective, I have dealt with the complex and closely linked matter of alliances, coalitions, and interoperability only tangentially.

Jointness and opposition to it have arisen from human emotions and relationships at their most elemental and intimate, and from allegiances and antipathies. It became increasingly clear to me as I progressed why von Clausewitz saw tact as the crucial but all-too-scarce antidote to friction in war. Although jointness has often been defined in specific and mechanistic terms related to a particular operational context, such as amphibious operations or air-sea-rescue, the interplay of psychological and political forces conforms both to von Clausewitz's view of war as a continuation of politics by other means and to Marx's dictum that "all acts are political acts." Nevertheless, defense analysts have paid far more attention to civil-military and political-military relations, perhaps due to the fact that jointness usually falls into a mix of domains, that is, military-military, intra-military or military-naval-air relations, or combinations thereof. Even though jointness is a more intricate dynamic—like war itself—than is often suggested in popular culture or military history, it has often been fuzzily defined in doctrine, planning and operations. Paradoxically, armed services, branches, and corps tenaciously guard their borders, while looking with disfavor upon subelements *within* their structures that strive for autonomy, perhaps due to the fact that soldiers, sailors, and airmen are possessed of a very strong sense of boundary and combativeness. Ironically, senior leaders who resisted jointness among or between the armed services often favored fusion within their services, and fostered such concepts as "combined fleets," "task forces," and "combined arms." Other such paradoxes will be noted along the way, but this one leads to a basic tenet: Fusion is seen as good by those able to control it.

As I began this study, I quickly found that jointness is a subject that sets many teeth on edge, and I encountered filtering, discrepancies, undocumented anecdotes, and the like. A gap between official reports, memoirs, and histories and what "really happened" was often suggested to me, but not always with substantiation. Beyond the imperfections of human memory, defensive arguments, willful distortion, and purging of records lies the problem that in the heat of action in complex systems, exactly what happens or how people do what they do, let alone why, is very rarely set down in detail or accurately recalled.[3]

In the course of research and analysis, I also gained a sense of why jointness has rarely been treated clinically. In peacetime, the bewildering maze of operational detail, legislation, doctrine, technology, personalities, factions, and formal organizations has made jointness many things to many people. Since as a subset of war, jointness in combat lies in the realm of chaos, it is no more tractable to numerical reductionism, logical formats or formulae than the arts, sculpture, or the weather. Like schools of thought in art, the intensity of partisanship on issues of jointness has sometimes approached the level of emotion held toward foes in war, for it touches closely on the critical bonding and cohesion that lie at the heart of military institutions, and their predisposition to see the world in "them-us" terms. The strong motives and emotions lying behind the bland language of white papers, orders, or "flimsies" often shine through only faintly, if at all.

Another basic law or paradox of jointness should be noted at the outset. Many have found interservice tension often greater at high echelons than at the cutting edge. Why? Obviously, those in battle find it easier to transcend the parochial concerns so salient in peacetime bureaucratic infighting. As jointness came to the fore in major modern wars, most of those serving "for the duration of hostilities" were less committed than careerists to protecting the institutional "turf" interests of their service than to getting the job done and the war over. In World War II, jointness flowered as the armed services of the major warring nations were virtually swamped by masses of "Christmas help," and higher echelons grappled with a torrent of plans, contracts, and administrative details. The boundaries between the services blurred (but did not dissolve) in the U.S. forces, at least to the point that a tribute was paid to the Navy in the Army benefit show, "This is the Army," in 1943, reflecting, at least, how much interservice tension, visible in several early failures in the war, had gone out of public favor. And Williamson Murray has noted how there was less bickering between the Luftwaffe and Nazi ground forces at middle and lower levels than in the Allied forces.[4] Certainly, the hostility among and within groups pursuing common goals in war or in preparation has its counterparts in other human organizational settings, such as religion, business, and sports. Such tensions can have a positive effect, as Strachey noted in observing: "that group mentality involves a strengthening of primitive attitudes of mind in the individual . . . [is not] altogether a bad thing. For such attitudes have great value . . . [for example,] encouraging in each feelings of pride in and devotion to his group which . . . may enable him to behave in an altruistic way."[5]

For good or ill, military organizations are wracked by the unique tension between risking danger to gain a stated goal and the instinct of self-preservation. To offset the latter, military training, socialization, and discipline are deliberately made crude and harsh, and shared ordeals used to bond and develop a sense of uniqueness within the small group. Such "tribalism" (which Elting Morison deemed "limited parochial identification") is the bedrock of military and naval structure. Nor has the intellectualizing of such processes had much effect, even upon those socialized to such values. Writers caught in the toils of such allegiance have been visible from Sophocles, to "Sergeant Shakespeare," and more recently, Ernest Hemingway, Robert Graves, Ernest Jünger, William Manchester, and Norman Mailer. That is not to suggest that the effects are positive and functional, for camaraderie and esprit can be seen at a high level among pirates, mutineers, and terrorists. In a special paradox of war, bonding and the resultant alignment of allegiance and morale toward group maintenance and preservation may run counter to the performance of mission and purpose, as dramatized in "Twelve O'Clock High."

Also, paradoxically, the boundaries of jointness sit at right angles to those drawn between friend and foe. Although internecine struggles in wartime have become proverbial, the sharp distinction between armies and navies that has fed such feuding was not always so throughout history, and in the West dates from the seventeenth century. As will be seen, in the Classical age and through the long series of Mediterranean maritime empires, a functional partnership of land and sea forces, born of geography and pragmatism, was usually taken for granted, as was the subordination of the sea forces to land forces much of the time—but not always. While recent hostility toward jointness may arise from modern concepts of organizational separateness, the expansion of military and naval systems in war and crisis has often erased boundaries erected in peacetime during bitter competition for scarce resources. In a sense, reduced funding and manpower, and the low sense of urgency of peacetime create a figurative desert in dry years in which vegetation is sparse and widely spaced. In war, rain comes to the desert, wild diversity bursts forth, and separation of individual species is lost amid dazzling and crowded blooming. To stretch that metaphor, jointness throughout history has been much like latent seeds in the desert's dry cycle, blossoming and shrivelling cyclically, returning to dormancy when resources shrink in the wake of war. Analogies of coolness and heating or of compression and expansion suggest the same cyclic pattern, which led Louis Morton to conclude that "perhaps . . . the supreme lesson of the Pacific war . . . [is] that true unity of command can be achieved only on the field of battle."[6] I found little that suggests otherwise.

Inasmuch as jointness resembles partisan politics at their most intense, I sought to strike a balance in respect to judgment and evidence. All of what I have cited is available for scrutiny by scholars and critics, and much of it will be easily accessible to general readers. Those who labor further in this vineyard, as I hope they will, may develop other perspectives. Revisions and responses might well lead me to change some of my views and conclusions, since rigidity is not a key to wisdom in this complex domain. I began this under a sense that the time was well past for someone to turn down this trail. While the path proved longer and more winding than I expected, traveling it proved far more rewarding than I expected.

NOTES

1. I am obliged to Andrew Marshall for this insight.

2. For ranges of definitions related to jointness, see *Joint Chiefs of Staff, Official Dictionary of Military Terms* (Cambridge: Hemisphere Publishing Corp., 1981); n.a., *The Joint Staff Officer's Guide* (Norfolk: Armed Forces Staff College, 1988), and *Federal Register* 52:182 (September 21, 1987): 35417–419.

3. Elizabeth Loftus, *Memory* (Reading, Mass.: Addison Wesley, 1980).

4. Williamson Murray, "The Luftwaffe Experience, 1939–1941," in B.F. Cooling, *Case Studies in Close Air Support* (Washington, D.C.: U.S. Government Printing Office, 1990).

5. Alex Strachey, *The Unconscious Motive of War: A Psychoanalytical Contribution* (New York: Universities Press, 1957), p. 193.

6. Louis Morton, "Pacific Command: A Study in Interservice Relation," in *The Harmon Memorial Lectures in Military History, 1957–1987* (Washington, D.C.: Office of Air Force History, 1988), p. 152.

_____ Chapter 1 _____

Varieties of Jointness:
From Ancient to Modern

Lord Byron's vision of the sea unscarred by ten thousand fleets' passing suggests how often the tortuous coastal waters and passages around Europe and Asia have been the scene of wars. Such broad allusions, metaphors, and impressions are appropriate not only for the poet but also for the historian who does not wish to be caught up in a vast litany of expeditions and battles. A compendium of even brief descriptions of pre-modern maritime campaigns and clashes would be a vast work since, for over four millennia, geography and technology forced most naval expeditions around Eurasia to conform in essence to the spirit of modern jointness, as they carried and convoyed armies and supplies, shielded and conducted assault landings and raids, or supported sieges. The list of major maritime powers that held sway in various parts of the Mediterranean alone over that time is long indeed, and includes Phoenicians, Cretans, Egyptians, Athenians, Spartans, Persians, Carthaginians, Romans, Byzantines, the Knights of Malta and Rhodes, Cypriots, Turks, Crusaders, Normans, Venetians, Genoese, French, British, Spanish, Austrians, Barbary pirates, Italians, Americans, and Russians.[1] Almost all naval battles until the air age were fought close to shore, linked to the progress and clash of armies, and frequently decided by fights between ship-borne infantry at sea. Such undertakings were sometimes impulsive, and sometimes planned and executed in a scale and complexity that would evoke admiration from current students of "operational art."

Because the civilizations of ancient Eurasia arose along rivers and adjacent seacoasts and relied on ships for trade and to extend and protect their power, much of the warfare in antiquity was littoral. Although tactics encompassed land and sea elements pragmatically, sailors were generally not held in high esteem. Over the milennia that galley warfare predominated in the Mediterranean, the function and prestige of admirals and standing navies was unevenly defined, perhaps due to the fact that over much of the history of galley warfare, rowing was seen as the task of slaves and convicts. (No clear distinction was made in classical Greece between the roles of generals and admirals.) Even though some citizens, like Sophocles, served in navies in wartime and were proud of it, others, including Xenophon and Plato, slighted Athens' naval-maritime enterprises and schemes. In any case, few admirals gained historical importance to the degree that generals did, let alone enduring fame, partly due to the fact that generals usually commanded afloat. Until the appearance of guns at sea, soldiers aboard ship sometimes served as rowers and crew members as well as providing the main combatant force in ship-to-ship combat; hence the frequent use of the term "marines" by historians of the ancient world. Jointness yielded prestige unevenly. Marines of the Imperial Roman Army were given higher status than sailors, as were elite light infantry in the navies of Athens, Hellenistic Egypt, Rhodes, and the Roman Republic, and later, in the fleets of Byzantium and Venice.[2] With the rise of feudalism, the prestige of land warriors was further heightened due to the fact that aristocratic status derived from feudal obligation and consequent land tenure, even in Anatolia and amongst the Vikings as they became Frankified and Russified.

Even though most military-naval operations in the Mediterranean, and in the Baltic as well, were shaped by narrow seas, straits, gulfs, and by convoluted coasts, and oared galleys dominated naval warfare for many centuries, few precise details of ship types and tactics survived. Although clearly depicted variants of galleasses and galleys were in naval service in the Mediterranean well into the nineteenth century, earlier records offer only frustrating traces of the evolution of naval architecture. Since the vague references found in accounts of classical, medieval, and early modern warfare assume a knowledge on the part of the reader that faded with time, naval and maritime historians are faced with frustratingly vague and schematic tracings on vases, monumental sculptures, and tombs depicting Cretan and Egyptian oared sailing ships, Greek *triremes* and *pentakonters*, Roman *biremes, triremes,* and *quinqueremes,* and Byzantine *dromons.*

MARINES IN THE CLASSICAL AGE

As precise description of ships is rare, so are surviving data on projectile weapons, which, along with the composition and method of use of "Greek fire," remain subject of speculation and debate. Nevertheless, strong links between land and sea warfare are clear enough. References abound to marines,[3] to riverine and coastal warfare and to the superimposing of land tactics into naval settings. Battles sometimes spilled over from sea to land when fleets became crowded against a shore, or they became contests between skill in ship-handling on one side and the quality of marines on the other.[4] References to incursions and raids dot the chronicles of Egypt, which suffered seaborne invasion by Cretan sea kings, Achaeans, Ptolemy, and ultimately, the Romans. In 1200 B.C., the Egyptians repelled an invasion of ''sea-peoples'' whose ships' decks were crowded ''from bow to stern'' with warriors serving as marines.[5] In Greece, from the heroic melées of the second millennium B.C. portrayed by Homer onward, the Hellenes, with their hunger for elegant ordering, refined their land-sea war tactics—as did the Persians. Amphibious operations, major and minor, were common in the Persian Wars and in subsequent struggles between the Greek city-states. Best-known of the many coastal raids of classical warfare is Marathon, at the beginning of the Persian War in 490 B.C., where Athenian militia overwhelmed a Persian landing force on a beach, fighting amidst its grounded ships, which may have included special craft for landing cavalry.

Athenian Triumphs and Failures

In shattering the Persian fleet in the Battle of Salamis in the Saronic Gulf near Athens in 480 B.C., the Athenians and their allies used their *hoplites*—lightly armored infantry—as marines.[6] Their sturdy ships maneuvered deftly in the narrow waters of the Bay of Salamis, ramming hulls and shattering oar banks, then grappling to allow their troops to overwhelm ship after ship of the larger but more cumbersome and congested Persian fleet. Most of the Persian crews could only look on helplessly as doom approached. With small losses, the Greeks destroyed or captured half of the Persians' and their allies' fleets, while the rest fled, then launched an amphibious landing by forces under Aristides that ''mopped up'' Persian elements left behind on the island at the mouth of the Gulf.

In subsequent sea-fights, the Greeks shifted to the use of projectile weapons and refined their ramming tactics that aimed at shearing oar banks. While the sailors of antiquity sought to use favorable weather to advantage, and to use tides, shoals, or reefs to harry their foes, like the practitioners of amphibious operations in modern times, they often suffered from sudden major storms.

The Peloponnesian War of the fifth century B.C. between Athens and Sparta and various allies was marked not only by many amphibious raids but also by several major enterprises. Armies often marched along constricted littorals with mountains on one flank and escorting fleets on the other, as Persians had when they moved south to and then beyond Thermopylae. In the early and middle phases of the conflict, Athens was dominant at sea and Sparta on land, with, as Donald Kagan noted, ''the Athenians count[ing] . . . on their usual advantage as a sea power'' for ''surprise attack in the unexpected place.''[7] Ultimately, those tables turned and the conflict ended with Sparta triumphant, although some judged the Persians the real victors, since their support of the Spartan fleet's buildup gave Persia naval dominance in the Aegean.

That war also saw the zenith and nadir of Athenian grand plans hinging on jointness, as an undertaking that yielded great success led to greater failure later. In 425 B.C., on the islet of Sphacteria near Pylos, a small-scale amphibious double envelopment before daybreak by Athenian forces captured a battalion of

Spartiate elite troops. Public enthusiasm over the unexpected windfall trans-
formed a tactical accident into an inspiring precedent, buoying up Alcibiades'
plans to conquer Syracuse on Sicily.[8] The subsequent grand expedition, however,
led to what Chester Starr judged as both the "greatest" such operation of the
war—and "one of the most poorly conceived amphibious operations ever attempted in history," resulting in the loss of 50,000 Athenians and 200 ships.[9]

The Roman Ascendancy

During the Punic Wars between the mid-third to mid-second century B.C.,
Rome persevered through many natural disasters and defeats to vanquish and,
finally, obliterate its chief maritime rival, the Phoenician colony of Carthage.
Amphibious landings and major naval expeditions marked those struggles—
several on Sicily, in Spain in 218 B.C., and in North Africa in 256 and 204 B.C.
At the outset, the Romans sent infantry to sea in large numbers, seeking to come
to close quarters with their foe. The Carthaginians' initially successful mobile
and evasive tactics resembled those of the Greek city-states, since they sometimes
employed Greek mercenaries. After the Romans increased reliance on ship-borne
infantry and shifted away from emulating Greek maneuver-and-ram tactics, their
marine-based tactics prevailed off the Aegetes Islands in 248 B.C., as the Romans
smashed a Carthaginian fleet on its way to lift a siege that lacked a marine
contingent since it expected to pick one up before engaging in battle.[10] The
Romans, consummate engineers and ever-determined to close with their infantry,
developed the *corvus,* a long, thin gangplank with a spike affixed at the far end,
which when dropped upon an enemy ship's deck, held it fast, allowing Roman
troops, often from several ships at once, to swarm aboard and do their grisly
work.[11] They also devised giant tongs for grappling, scythes for cutting enemy
rigging, large castles at bow and stern to protect archers and catapults, and, by
the time of the Civil Wars, were using some sort of belt armor to protect ships'
waterlines against ramming.

Like previous wielders of maritime power in the Mediterranean, the Romans
understood that amphibious operations offered a special advantage in carrying
out strategic surprise since ships moved faster than armies. Awareness of this
was evident, for example, in the major amphibious incursion under Quintus
Metullus in 68 B.C. that squashed a Cretan revolt. The best-known Roman
amphibious operations, however, came in the next decade when Julius Caesar
landed in Britain in 55 B.C. Initially repulsed by the Britons, his forces gained
a foothold when, under supporting fire from catapults, they were spurred on by
the bravery of a Xth Legion standard bearer who leaped into the surf and shamed
his hesitant comrades into following him ashore. The Romans' half-millennium
lodgment in Brittania was firmly founded two generations later, in A.D. 43, when
a 50,000-man expedition landed in Kent, followed by the Emperor Claudius the
next year, who came with elephants and major forces.

In the first century B.C., many major operations in the Civil Wars that led to the founding of the Roman Empire hinged on jointness, including Pompey's anti-pirate campaigns, Caesar's expedition to Egypt, major troop movements, and, as a climax, the naval battle at Actium in 31 B.C. that shattered the dreams of Marc Antony and Cleopatra. The Roman approach to maritime and naval matters, as to much else, was flavored with blunt pragmatism, sometimes tinged with ferocity and cruelty, as they seized the edges of the Mediterranean basin and then moved inland. While the army was the main instrument of that encroachment, close fusion with the navy was visible in many instances. Up to the founding of the empire on the eve of the Christian era, fleets had been formed on an *ad hoc* basis and commanded by generals. Octavian had been impressed by the vital role played by seapower in both Pompey's suppression of the Cicilian pirates and in the Civil Wars, especially in Caesar's crossing of the Upper Adriatic, and in the great sea-battle at Actium. Octavian, after assuming the title Augustus, as the first emperor, created standing naval forces. The squadrons that patrolled Italian waters and the Rhine and Danube flotillas were initially established out of the army's structure, and some 700 ships of Pompey Sextus' navy.[12] The Augustan fleet of some 30,000 men, not including provincial detachments, had its two major bases at Cape Misenum near Naples and at Ravenna, and runner systems that carried dispatches from those ports to Rome.[13] Claudius later established naval detachments throughout the Empire, and the navy served for about four centuries as a kind of constabulary and signal service, securing lines of communication, transport and supply, and suppressing pirates—but fighting no major sea battles. As in the old imperial system, the navy's general duties included carrying despatches, accompanying the army in frontier campaigns where topography allowed, and, as depicted on Trajan's column, rooting out piracy.

Although usually ranked lower in status than the army and under its control, the fleets sometimes emerged into special prominence, especially when they helped bring an emperor to power. Some historians have argued that at least until the massive naval decline in the late third century, the Romans navalmaritime network was as crucial a component in the functioning of their empire as its much-vaunted road network. In any event, the transporting of troops during civil wars and power struggles as well as in frontier uprisings and riverine campaigns were important enough to warrant permanent maintenance. Yvon Garlan, noting the higher status of marines than either army rank-and-file or sailors, observed that "the naval policy of Rome was to avoid the need of having one."[14]

The Byzantine Succession

As the vigor of the mother empire in the West ebbed and its fleets were swept away by barbarian engulfments by the fifth century, the Byzantines assumed the naval mantle of Rome, as what John Guilmartin has called the "symbiotic relationship between the seaside fortress and the war galley" began.[15] A persistent pattern of amphibious warfare in the classical and early modern periods can be glimpsed both clearly and faintly throughout the centuries. Although the destruction of Byzantine records and an apparent lack of chroniclers make much of the course of sea warfare from the early eighth to the early eleventh century invisible, accounts of Belisarius' verve and cunning in clearing much of the east coast of Italy and parts of Sicily of barbarians in the sixth century are rich with references to amphibious operations, blockades, and sieges, and such stratagems as hoisting archers to the masthead during approaches to fortified seawalls.[16]

Unfortunately, as an historian of Byzantium noted, aside from data regarding organization and basing structure,[17] some basic principles, and brief and vague glimpses of battles and involvement in politics, there is "no professional record of the functions of naval warfare in Byzantium" to match the detailed record of land warfare.[18] Weak or fading evidence, however, proves neither a plateau nor a trough in technical developments. The endurance of its empire suggests that Byzantium cannot have wholly abandoned naval enterprise as part of its intricate system of defenses. The general descriptions of events that have survived mention the presence of Byzantine fleets and armies in Syria, Africa, south Italy, the Aegean, and Middle East, as well as lists of bases and the extermination of Cretan pirates in A.D. 961—all indicating substantial vigor. Beyond the dimension of established naval forces lie the faint traces of privateers, that is, the conversion of civilian vessels to naval purpose in wartime, whose depredations ashore over the centuries were often undistinguishable in effect to the victims from those of pirates, Scandinavian sea raiders, and North African corsairs who scourged much of the European littoral.

The Vikings

From the seventh century onward, other forces steadily wore away the outworks and then broke into the bastions of Rome and Byzantium. As Islam expanded on land and at sea, by the early eighth century, the Arabs, having seized all of North Africa, were moving into Spain and crowding in on the mainland and island frontiers of Byzantium in Asia Minor and in the eastern Mediterranean and Aegean seas. Another human wave lapped and then crashed against Europe in the form of those highly effective practitioners of jointness— the Vikings. At first, their raids were seasonal and occasional; hence the prayer that implied a pattern of intermittent violence: *A furore Normanorum libera nos Domine*—God free us from the Northmen's fury. Like other tribes on the move in the twilight of Rome, they ultimately occupied territories that they had at first only raided and terrified. The initial destructive phase brought fierce-masked oarsmen and light cavalry to the gates of Byzantium and into the courtyards of Irish monasteries. By the tenth century, their *drakkars*—dragon-prowed, flat-bottomed ships—had penetrated rivers and fens and breasted Atlantic combers, planting a great arc of Viking settlements from Labrador to Kiev. Later, in a somewhat more constructive mode, their descendants established Norman colonies and kingdoms and blended their culture with that of their subjects and neighbors in France, Sicily, Greenland, Iceland, England, Ireland, and Russia.

The Vikings' method of war was the essence of jointness. They carried horses in their ships, not for mounted combat, but for scouting, transport, and baggage, and in sea fights, like the Romans, they relied on infantry afloat. They eschewed ramming, and lashed their ships together, the crews sometimes clambering across vast clusters to mass at the points of heaviest fighting.[19] Their methods were steadily refined in organization and increased in scale, so that in 1066, in the Norman conquest of England, William of Normandy's fleet of 700 ships carried 12,000 men and a sizable number of horses—although his array fought on foot at Hastings. The Normans in the Mediterranean apparently drew upon the Byzantines' techniques, and hired their ships and crews as well as they shaped their assault tactics around armored cavalrymen who spearheaded amphibious landings in their conquest of Sicily, methods that may have served as a model for William's forces.[20]

Byzantine Renaissance and Decline

Byzantium had long stood against these mighty tides that surged afar and sometimes dashed against its walls. In the late ninth century, after the fleets of the Western Empire had wholly vanished, two centuries of naval decline in the East were dramatically reversed by Emperor Nicephorus Phocas. The exploits of his admirals, Hadrian, Nazar, and Ooryphus, in defeating the fleets of Crete, Syria, and Egypt led to a rise in the social status of sailors in the imperial hierarchy as well. As the power of the home fleet, drawn from the lower strata of Byzantine urban society,[21] came to stand in political balance against that of the mainland Asian feudal lords, a corps of naval guards and galleys assumed praetorian duties alongside the Imperial Life Guards of the army, a flowering of naval eminence that marked the final flourish of Byzantine glory.[22]

Forces eroding the eastern empire's naval supremacy came both from within and afar. In the late eleventh century, even before gunpowder blunted the tactical edge of the Byzantines' massive vessels and their "Greek fire," the Italian maritime states of Venice, Pisa, and Genoa began to crowd in on the eastern empire. Friction between Byzantium and the West mounted during the Crusades, leading to the siege and sack of Constantinople in the Fourth Crusade in 1204 by western crusaders in a series of major amphibious landings. The alliance with the Genoese, who had surpassed their competitors, was a symptom of Byzantine decline. Although a token naval resurgence took place in the early 1300s in the face of the Seljuk Turk threat, the great city was finally brought down in the Ottoman siege and sack of 1453.

Over the next two centuries, well after guns appeared, galleys with crews of archers as their main armament remained the mainstay of navies in the Mediterranean,[23] with patterns of crewing and equipage of Byzantine *dromons* of the tenth century[24] not varying widely from those of Venetian ships 500 years later.[25]

At the same time, amphibious raids and assault landings tactics underwent refinement, including development of horse transports with landing ramps and
towers for assaulting fortifications mounted on groups of ships lashed together.[26]
In the fourteenth and fifteenth centuries, during the Anglo-French Hundred Years
War, English kings, most notably Edward III and Henry V, had transported what
were by the standards of the age sizable armies to France. Many dozens of joint
expeditions marked the course of wars of nationalism and mercantilism from the
fifteenth to the early nineteenth century.

GUNPOWDER VERSUS GALLEYS: THE DECLINE OF
MARINE-BASED TACTICS

The mounting of large guns on warships, which took place on a major scale
in the sixteenth century in northwest Europe, extended in stages into the Mediterranean. John Guilmartin has noted how, although a kind of jointness was
initially induced by putting landlubber gunners aboard ship, design changes
wrought by increasing weight of ordnance and ammunition ultimately undercut
the war galleys' "amphibious capability, perhaps their most important strategic
and tactical characteristic."[27] Warship design shifted away from the galley form
and, in the case of the sailing ships, from lumbering forts with light guns, to
more maneuverable types with more and heavier guns on and below the main
deck, firing through ports. That trend was marked in the contrast between the
Battle of Lepanto in 1571, and in the thwarting of the Spanish Armada in 1588.
The Turks and various Christian powers grappled in the Mediterranean throughout the sixteenth century, for example, on Cyprus in 1527, at Tunis in 1541,
on Rhodes in 1552, and on Malta in 1565. In the climactic clash of oar-powered
navies at Lepanto, the Christian fleet under Don Juan of Austria broke Ottoman
naval power in the Mediterranean. In a confused series of close combats, much
in the spirit of classical sea-battles like Salamis, Don Juan's force inflicted 30,000
casualties on the Turks and destroyed or captured 200 of their ships.

The Spanish Armada was a wholly different weapon system. The mixed
composition of that fleet reflected the transition underway in stages from galleys
and galleasses—sailing vessels with large banks of oars—to square-rigged, oar-
less sailing ships up to a thousand tons. The large sterns and forecastles providing
"high ground" and protection for marines that marked the first variants had,
during the sixteenth century, become less prominent, and they were eventually
smoothed into the hull to lower the center of gravity and cut wind drag. The
increase in the weight and number of cannon had reduced the need for specially
designated fighting men aboard, and by the eighteenth century, marines, although
maintained in all major navies, had become more and more auxiliary in function,
serving as boarding and landing parties, providing harassing fire from the rigging,
and aiding ships' officers in maintaining discipline.

Increases in speed, seaworthiness, and size of sailing vessels led to a growth
in the scale and to sophistication of joint operations in the middle and late 1500s,

evident in Spanish successes at Tunis in 1535, 1541, and 1573, and Malta in 1565, and at Lisbon in 1580. In their major expedition against Terceira in the Azores in 1583, an armada of almost 100 ships landed a force of 15,000. In Ireland, in 1594, English forces took Enniskillen Castle by combining bases of fire and amphibious incursions in a careful plan that reflected a high state of what would be referred to in today's terms as "operational art."[28] These presaged major undertakings by both adversaries. A series of English counter-raids and landings included the major raid against Cadiz that put off the Armada's sailing two years, and the depredations of the "Sea Dogs" in America, while four abortive Spanish amphibious expeditions were launched against England and Ireland from 1586 to 1601. The most famous of these, the Great Armada of 1588, was originally proposed on a scale gigantic for the times—560 ships bearing some 35,000 soldiers. Ultimately pared to 137 vessels, its mission was to convey the main invasion force of 30,000 troops under the Duke of Parma, poised to lunge across the Channel at night in barges, to establish a beachhead, then to drive into Kent and Sussex—not far in essence from German SEALION plans in 1940.[29] Its failure is well known, although its harrying and destruction and the Great Wind that scattered it long lay closer to folklore than to objective reportage.[30] Subsequent Spanish enterprises and English counterthrusts are less well known. The expedition of 1596 bent on Ireland was also shattered by a tempest, as was a nearly successful descent on the West Country in 1597, the latter, unlike the others, having prepared and sailed without detection by English agents. Such harrying and destruction of expeditions by storms, seen so often in the ancient world, was a pattern that persisted throughout the modern Age of Sail, from the shattering of Charles V's forces in their attempt on Algiers in 1541 and of the Spanish armadas in the late sixteenth century to the crippling of the French expedition to Ireland in 1796 and the scattering of Napoleon's expedition to Egypt in 1798.

The basic problem that all joint expeditions faced was maintaining the naval strength required to protect the line of supply and communications between the home country and the zone of operations, maintaining it at all times, no matter what an enemy or weather might bring against it. As Churchill said of the Nazis' task in invading Britain in World War II, "a very considerable undertaking."

THE RISE OF THE MERCANTILIST EMPIRES

Since the late medieval period, maritime trading networks had been extended around the periphery of Europe. In the mid-fifteenth century, as the Hanseatic League ebbed, Constantinople fell, and as the Renaissance began to flower, the Italian maritime states' power was cresting. At the same time, the Portuguese had begun their sea-march round Africa to the Indies, setting the pace for a widespread surge of imperial maritime enterprise that was ultimately brought to the highest level of success by the British mercantile elites. More and more, over the next two centuries, technical evolution altered the exercise of sea power.

Increasingly complex building methods, ship-handling based on the mastery of evolving sail square-rigged systems, gunnery, navigational techniques, and cartography all required both literacy and proficiency in mathematics, leading in the mid-eighteenth century to the consequent emergence of a distinct naval profession.

As the rivalries of Europe were projected across the world, combined, joint, and special operations abounded. As great battle fleets were being built, empires grew and commerce expanded as a function of the rise of mercantilism and intense commercial and imperial rivalry heated by nationalism. At the lower end of the spectrum of warfare, raiding and amphibious landings become more frequent. At the very onset of the three-and-a-half century struggle, first involving Spain, Holland, France, and Portugal, and, later, Germany, Japan, Russia and the United States, something much like modern special operations in concept and method had appeared in the various undertakings of Drake, Frobisher, Hawkins, and the "sea dogs," who engaged in sabotage and raids as well as the major raid on Cadiz.[31]

While the wars of empire afar were increasingly fought by colonists, subject peoples and mercenaries, large standing armies became the major instruments and symbols of power in Europe. The Thirty Years' War, the English Civil War and the military reforms during the reign of Louis XIV fixed the attention and ambitions of European ruling elites upon a highly geometric pattern of land warfare. As French kings, ministers, and masters of the greatest superpower of that age fixated on northern France, the Rhineland, and Germany as the crucial chessboard of war, they frequently held back the relative driblets of resources that could have yielded massive returns, or overlooked opportunities in distant realms which their rivals did not.

It was not only the French who mismanaged the mechanics of imperial defense. Since a mercantilist mother country required protection of its capital and major cities with warehouses, manufacturers, and markets, problems at a distance often appeared less urgent. At several points during the seventy years of colonial wars in North America, from 1689 to 1759, the British colonists undertook expensive preparations for major joint operations, and waited for ships, troops, and support promised by the mother country, of which some came late and others too late or not at all. Some of those expeditions, like the taking of Acadia and Louisbourg, succeeded, while others, like the tragic Cartagena expedition of 1745, failed.

In peace treaties, such gains and remote territory were often traded off at a discount as the result of battles won and lost in Europe. The major problems of sending troops and fleets overseas also discouraged taking a larger view. Food rotted, water grew foul, and regiments literally disintegrated within weeks of arrival in tropical settings due to disease. While an exchange of messages within Europe might take hours or days, contact with some distant imperial outposts took weeks or months. It is not surprising that some reasonable people saw dispatching scarce resources to far-off places to carry out operations under uncertain conditions out of immediate control as a gamble or as costly adventuring.

The swing between a focused continental strategy to a dispersed maritime strategy was reflected in oscillations in British strategy until World War II between the options of fielding large armies on the continent and committing smaller armies and fleets in distant imperial campaigns.

The path of the initial excursions of colonial-imperial powers was marked out by forts in Siberia, South and North America, and India. In naval circles, until the mid-nineteenth century, it was generally accepted that, as Nelson suggested, "a ship can not fight a fort." While there were exceptions, they were few. Such an undertaking was a very risky proposition, and the caution stood as a guideline, with some exceptions, for another two generations. In a parallel vein, until the coming of railroads, the greater speed of ships carrying troops as compared with that of armies marching raised the possibility that a sizeable force might land quickly and stealthily, out of the range of forts' guns, and overwhelm local forces, or seize a major town quickly and conduct a rapid siege, or surprise a garrison, then strengthen fortifications against a riposte. That had been the case in the Dutch raids up the Thames in the reign of Charles II and in the British seizure of Gibraltar in 1703.

JOINTNESS IN THE WARS OF EMPIRE

In the 1750s, jointness was affected by basic changes in the world-view of those who controlled military and naval forces. The Industrial Revolution was changing the face of Britain while the Enlightenment in France altered the intellectual and political life of Europe against the backdrop of global struggles for imperial dominance. The increase in joint operations in those wars was matched by a rising sense of military and naval professionalism that generated attempts to bend the phenomenology of "conjunct operations" closer to a science than to a haphazard art.

Many of those joint operations were British undertakings that often failed,[32] but when such risky ventures paid off, dividends were rich indeed,[33] as in the "special operations" against Cadiz that delayed the Armada's preparations in 1586 and the assault landing that captured Gibraltar in 1703. The ascendancy of Swedish military and naval power in the mid-seventeenth century led to a series of conflicts in the Baltic in which joint expeditions and raids were a principal operational mode, including war with Denmark in the 1790s, and with Russia, the Great Northern War of 1700–21, and those of 1741–42 and 1788–90.

Pitt and Ligonier

Pitt the Elder is generally credited with the special breadth of view as prime minister that, by mixing continental and peripheral strategies artfully, produced the British victories of the late 1750s in India and Canada, which laid the cornerstones of the modern British empire.[34] At the same time, Sir John Ligonier, chief of staff of the British Army (and later its first commander-in-chief) framed a strategy much like the one Churchill and his advisers shaped for Britain after the fall of France in 1940 in World War II. Ligonier saw that Britain, as the dominant sea power, could force the French, who controlled the continent, to disperse troops to defend their coasts, and that was not possible everywhere. Britain also needed land defense forces, but far fewer, so that British raids on the French coast could divert French forces to watch and fend off attacks, thus hampering their building up of an invasion force. As Ligonier's biographer suggested: "French manpower was engaged and pinned on the Continent while mixed army and naval task forces operated offensively in the continents and islands across the great sea."[35] Half a century later, Napoleon caught the essence of the dilemma posed by Britain's uncommitted amphibious potential in observing that "with 30,000 men in transports at the Downs, the English can paralyze 300,000 of my Army and that will reduce us to the rank of a second-class power."[36]

When the meshing of British and land power led to major success in the mid-eighteenth century, as in British expeditions to Havana, Quebec, the West Indies, and Manila, the quality of joint doctrine and tactics was often very high.[37] The various navies of the time had worked out systems and procedures for command-and-control, boat-handling, maintaining unit cohesion in the transit ashore, combat loading, logistics and naval gunfire support, landing craft design, and production.

Molyneux and Wolfe

By the mid-eighteenth century, the term "amphibious" had come into use, and Thomas Molyneux's treatise, *Conjunct Expeditions*, listed seventy such enterprises mounted by or against England since the reign of Elizabeth I.[38] His book appeared at a critical time, following the failure of a major British expedition against the French stronghold at Rochefort in 1757, a debacle that confounded Ligonier's strategic hopes. Lack of cooperation between the naval and army commanders was seen as the main cause of that failure. According to a pre-World War II (but post-Gallipoli) biographer of General James Wolfe, the Rochefort fiasco also imparted an "amphibious strain" to Wolfe's thinking on the eve of his being given command in North America. If so, it was hardly a bolt-of-lightning inspiration,[39] for not only was Wolfe a reconnaissance officer in the Rochefort expedition, but his father had served in the failed Cartagena expedition of 1745 while a colonel of Marines. That sad enterprise, which broke the health of George Washington's brother, had also been marred by interservice command friction and floundering.

While there is no detailed transcript of their discussions while crossing the Atlantic, the accord between Wolfe and his naval counterpart, Admiral Charles Saunders, well-noted at the time, was the antithesis of the "want of experience and unanimity" noted by Molyneux and many others as a chronic cause of joint operational failure.[40] Thus Bernard Fergusson saw Wolfe and Saunders as ''fully in each other's minds'' while directing the series of joint operations that invested Quebec and led to the decisive battle in 1759 that ended French rule in Canada.[41]

Many elements that characterized subsequent successful major joint operations were evident at Quebec: a careful application of method in ''setting the stage''; thorough, systematic naval blockade; close collaboration of the principals; a willingness to gamble; and boldness. The course of those operations are well known to some—the landing of the army at night, the fleet's slipping past major enemy defenses, the landing under uncertain conditions, and the use of a primitive path to ascend and deploy against a well-sited enemy. The pitched battle on the Plains of Abraham, the gigantic political rewards that crowned the success and Wolfe's death are known to many more.

Although Molyneux's treatise did not break the historical pattern of a counterpoint of success and failure, *Conjunct Expeditions* remained useful over the next century in its details and caught the essence of jointness. Close rapport between commanders in joint operations remained a problem. As a first lord of the admiralty observed in considering tiffs between commanders in the expeditions against Minorca in 1798 and Cadiz in 1800–01, ''Cordiality and good understanding . . . are essential to the conducting with energy and effect any conjunct operation.''[42]

BRITISH JOINT OPERATIONS IN NORTH AMERICA

In 1788, with French forces arriving in North America to augment the armies of the American rebellion, France and Spain mounted a major expedition against Britain that was confounded by bad weather. Although sluggish reaction and confusion on both sides may have been due to the superannuation of the commanders involved, a general pattern of failure of French conjunct expeditions over the next generation had been set.[43] While British joint operations from Rochefort to Gallipoli followed a somewhat random pattern of success and failure, that was less true of the political effects of those undertakings. Several British joint expeditions in the late eighteenth and early nineteenth centuries became well known to many Americans, including the blocking or delaying of British thrusts down Lake Champlain in 1776, 1777, and 1814, and the repulse of major British invasion attempts at Charleston in 1776 and at New Orleans in 1815. On the other side of the ledger lay Howe's move to Head of Elk, far up Chesapeake Bay, in 1777, Arnold's Rhode Island depredations, and the seizures of Charleston and Savannah late in the Revolutionary War, and of Washington in 1814. Nevertheless, the negative effects of the British failure at Fort McHenry and Baltimore and at New Orleans and even such ''successes'' as their retaliatory burning of public buildings in Washington for American excesses at York in the final balance outweighed the impact of their triumphs.

Dunkirk, 1793

A generation later, Pitt the Younger had neither the good fortune nor skill of his father when, as prime minister, he presided over a scheme to carry out a major landing on the French coast near Dunkirk in 1793.[44] Various historians have blamed Pitt, Henry Dundas, the home secretary, and Lord Grenville, all of whom stuck an oar into the affair, each out of stroke with the others. Not only were the unpleasant political results of the failed joint operation substantial, but it also demonstrated that the tendency of high political authorities to reach down the military-naval chain of command that has been ascribed to electronic communications well predated such technology.

The botching of the Dunkirk expedition at every level was especially perplexing, since both the successful and the failed joint operations of a generation earlier were well known in government and military-naval circles. The Dunkirk failure drove home the fact that success is not necessarily passed on by example, by awareness of the past in a general sense, or even by more systematic attempts to preserve "lessons learned." It also reflected how vagueness in policy and intent could yield sharp penalties, for it was not the pursuit of a clear-cut strategic goal that drove the expedition, but a reaction to alarming events and a somewhat vague desire of the government to prepare the British public for protecting Holland against France.

At the outset, it did not seem too great a risk. The revolutionary regime in France had stunned the world by guillotining Louis XVI in January. It was now squeezed by converging German and Austrian forces and wracked internally by the Reign of Terror and the turbulence of mass mobilization. Whatever the British might have gained by quick action in the early summer was lost. The advantage that Ligonier stressed of keeping a standing amphibious force and conducting hit-and-run raids had been ignored. Week after week, delays in massing artillery and ships held up departure of the British expedition, while a leak to the press in August vaporized all traces of surprise left at that point. After the force landed, commanders failed to detect the approach of the French, while the Army and Navy operated independently, their commanders lacking the rapport that had marked earlier success. After the French massed over 40,000 troops whose ardor compensated for their lack of military skill, on September 6th, at Hondschoote, Houchard's Army of the North, although suffering heavy losses, drove the Duke of York from the field and captured his heavy guns. With the chance to crush the French revolutionary government lost, the sluggish British operations allowed the regime to suppress the reaction against the Terror, and to shift its forces to capitalize on Austrian-Prussian tensions. The French now conducted joint operations. Their aggressive use of gunboats was followed by a series of heavy attacks, forcing the British forces scattered along the Channel coast of France to withdraw from the area while losing a quarter of their forces. In 1794, the shock power of the *levée en masse* and British ineptitude led to further debacles in the Low Countries and abandonment of Holland to the French.

Another ''conjunct expedition'' failed in July of that year when an amphibious assault by exiled Frenchmen at Quiberon in Brittany was shattered by Revolutionary forces. Accompanying British units were pulled out, and yet another attempt was repulsed in late autumn, when a small force that landed in Poitou to take advantage of a flare-up of the revolt in the Vendée was forced to turn back after the insurgents were defeated.

JOINT OPERATIONS IN THE NAPOLEONIC ERA

The vast tapestry of the Napoleonic Wars was dotted by dozens of joint amphibious operations. While most were minor raids, major expeditions were mounted in South America, the Far East, the Caribbean, Egypt, and the West Indies, and around the periphery of Europe, in the Baltic, Belgium, northwest, western and southern France, Spain, and Portugal. Most failed in their purpose, but such successes as Abercromby's thwarting of Napoleon on the Nile in 1800 and the lodgement of Wellington's army at Mondego Bay in Portugal in 1808 served to offset the deficits on Britain's strategic ledger sheet.[45]

And those were many. In early September 1789, a small Russian army joined a British contingent of almost 30,000 under the Duke of York that had landed on the northwest coast of the Netherlands. The subsequent campaign led to three battles—a loss, a victory, and another loss—and several opportunities missed due to weak inter-Allied rapport, and was much like the Dunkirk expedition in its final result. With his principal strategic goal—the capture of Holland's navy—gained, York, having lost almost 10,000 as prisoners, recognized that he could not push French forces out of the Netherlands. After signing an agreement with the French for return of the Allied POWs, York withdrew from the second of three failed English expeditions to Holland in its war with Revolutionary France and Napoleon.

The Antwerp expedition stood in sharp contrast with the British amphibious assault landing at Aboukir in Egypt in 1800, which quashed Napoleon's dreams of a neo-Alexandrian Near Eastern empire. The enterprise was carefully planned, and practice landings at Marmorice sharpened the edge of naval gunfire support and worked out problems of maintaining unit integrity. The cliché that joint operations hinged on the rapport of commanders was also disproved. Soundness of plans and rigor of training yielded victory over superior enemy forces, even though the commander of the 18,000-man Anglo-Turkish force, General Sir Ralph Abercromby, was killed and his deputy, Major-General John Moore, was wounded.[46]

Napoleon's abortive excursion to the Middle East was only one of several French joint operations that met with defeat. The expedition to Haiti in 1801 by General LeClerc began with a successful assault landing but ended three years later in withdrawal of the remnants of the original force of 25,000. A quarter of the forty-three ships of an abortive expedition to Ireland in 1796 were lost to bad weather or captured by the British, and two years later, over 1,000 French troops were captured at Killala Bay while supporting French naval forces were defeated at sea. In 1814, a French expedition bent on recapturing Guadeloupe in the West Indies was defeated.

In 1806–07, Britain's exercise of maritime strategic flexibility surged after Nelson's victory at Trafalgar, taking the form of amphibious operations, raids, and naval battles around the world, again with mixed results. In January, Capetown fell after an assault landing; in February, French naval forces in the West Indies were overcome in the Battle of Santo Domingo; in March, a small French squadron off the coast of India surrendered; in June and July, an amphibious force operating on the Calabrian coast of Italy, supporting insurgents opposing Napoleon's brother, Joseph, won a victory at Maida, then pulled back to Sicily. At the same time, two British attempts to occupy Buenos Aires were thwarted by local militia, as was a British naval raid on Constantinople in early 1807. In September of that year, Sir Arthur Wellesley, soon to be the Duke of Wellington, commanded army elements in an amphibious landing at Copenhagen in joint operations that led to the capture of Denmark's navy.

The British Walcheren expedition in the late summer of 1809 was aimed at scourging the Scheldt estuary and seizing Antwerp. An army of 35,000, commanded by Lieutenant General the Earl of Chatham (Pitt the Younger), and a fleet of 245 warships and some 400 transports occupied Walcheren Island and took Flushing, in the course of which a naval brigade served ashore. A cautiousness in the Councils of War, an epidemic of malaria, and the preoccupation of Chatham with his health all led to the loss of another major opportunity.[47]

The British predisposition to joint operations was visible in the final phase of the Napoleonic Wars. In late February 1814, an amphibious "left hook" by British forces at Bayonne in western France forced Marshal Soult to retreat to Toulouse, which fell to Wellington just before Bonaparte abdicated. Across the Atlantic, the War of 1812 was also moving to conclusion. In late 1814 and early 1815, with Napoleon defeated and U.S. naval power shattered, the British were free to exercise their dominance at sea. As small raids were carried out along the coast, the blockade tightened, and in mid-August, a 5,000-man British force landed on the Patuxent River, brushed aside thin defenses, briefly occupied Washington, D.C., and re-embarked at the end of the month. After landing again near Baltimore in mid-September, the British approach to the city was thwarted by well dug-in militia, and the British commander, Major General Robert Ross was killed.

After the Royal Navy failed to reduce Fort McHenry, the force withdrew, and in mid-December, a larger British joint expedition based out of Jamaica sailed to New Orleans. Some 7,500 Peninsular veterans under Major General Sir Edward Pakenham, the Duke of Wellington's brother-in-law, launched two close-order assaults against the well-entrenched defenders commanded by Major General Andrew Jackson. After a third of their forces became casualties and the three senior British officers were killed, they fell back and re-embarked a week later. American losses were reported as seven killed and six wounded. An energetic defense by the American garrison of Fort St. Philip at the mouth of the Mississippi prevented the Royal Navy from unhinging Jackson's defenses. Wellington's attribution of British failure at New Orleans to Providence overlooked the fact that it had also resulted from breaches of security, a shortage of landing craft, the greed of some commanders and speculators, major disagreement between Army and Navy leaders, and bureaucratic delay on the part of the admiralty.[48]

JOINT OPERATIONS IN THE EARLY NINETEENTH CENTURY

Vera Cruz

The scale of joint expeditions fell off after the Napoleonic Wars, and most such undertakings throughout the nineteenth century were small, of short duration, and categorized as "port-forcing" or "punitive" in the lexicon of imperialism. Occasionally, they were sizeable, for example, the French invasion of Algeria in 1830, with 500 ships and 37,000 troops, and the British landing at Ismailia in Egypt in 1882 of 25,000 troops. A high level of practice in joint operations was displayed by American forces near Vera Cruz in Mexico in early March 1847. Although rapport between land and naval commanders was high, jointness was not visible at all points during the preparations. In late October 1846, a detailed plan was prepared by General Winfield Scott, at the direction of the Secretary of War, for a landing by 10,000 men. Two days later, a somewhat similar plan arrived that had been drawn up by Zachary Taylor, the major victorious commander in the field at that point. Taylor suggested holding his gains in the north while moving against the Mexican capital from the east. Scott then raised the number of troops to 15,000 and requested 141 flatboats for the landing, which were finished by late November. He did not, however, recognize that the undertaking would be fully joint, that is, a landing in the face of the enemy, until he conducted a reconnaissance at Vera Cruz in early March.[49]

The initial plan called for troops to be transferred to warships well away from the zone of action, then moved to the assault beaches in forty-man groups under command of a naval captain, in boats (built especially for the operations under Scott's orders) that were nested aboard ship in groups of three, with seats inserted just prior to lowering. Towed to the assault area, under the command of naval ratings and junior officers, each boat held half a company of troops—forty men—carrying basic loads of ammunition and three days' "iron rations." After the boat divisions, commanded by naval lieutenants, proceeded to the ships that marked the line of departure, the vast formation, carefully arrayed to maintain unit integrity and interspersed with sixty gunboats, was to move into the shore.

As preparation began in earnest, lack of interservice coordination was reflected in the delay of eight warships and in major snarls in the assembling of transport and supply vessels in the gulf. Bureaucratic confusion, delay, and poor rapport

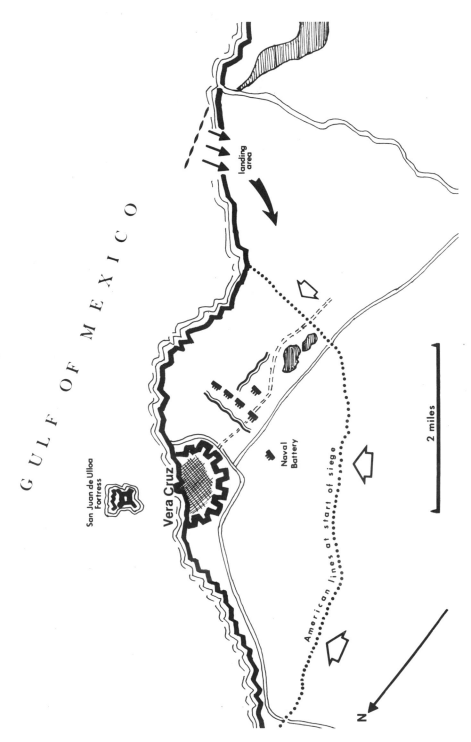

GULF OF MEXICO

San Juan de Ulloa Fortress

Vera Cruz

landing area

Naval Battery

American lines at start of siege

N

2 miles

U.S. Assault Landing at Vera Cruz, Mexico, March 9, 1847

were paralleled by intra-service political tensions between generals Scott and Taylor. Both had presidential ambitions, which President James K. Polk was concerned about. At the same time, Commodore Matthew Perry aspired to assume naval command in the main theater of war, the Gulf of Mexico. Commodore David Conner, soon to be relieved, put the best face on matters by offering Scott enthusiastic support, including a battalion of seamen and Marines for the landing force if he desired it.

As the Vera Cruz landing approached, when it was revealed in a Cabinet meeting that several ships required for the operation were not yet in the Gulf of Mexico, Polk realized that his assumptions of ongoing cooperation between the secretaries of the army and navy were incorrect. That seemed all the stranger, inasmuch as the undertaking had arisen from discussions among the president, the service secretaries, and the paymaster general and chief of ordnance and hydrography the previous October, and it was frequently discussed in Cabinet meetings thereafter.[50]

The landing went much according to plan—but not completely. As the fleet's guns opened fire on the landing area, a detachment of Mexican lancers departed. The marking of boats and ships with large numerals and much else in the details of preparation conformed to the spirit and the letter of Molyneux's treatise,[51] but well-laid plans went awry when the landing force encountered an unexpected current. Amid crowding and chaos, General Worth, commanding the first wave of regulars, ordered the boats bearing regimental colors to unfurl them and to serve as rallying points. Although a far less than tidy formation resulted, the expedient served its purpose, and some 8,000 American troops were ashore by twilight.[52] When, in classic fashion, heavy weather intruded for three days, the individual combat rations proved vital, as did the priority loading scheme, which allowed quick replenishment after the weather lifted.

The storm also frustrated the Army's attempts to take the fortress of San Juan de Ulloa, since the delay in the arrival of the Army's siege ordnance left Scott with only a fifth of what he had expected. He fended off offers from Conner of naval guns and crews, but finally succumbed to the aggressiveness of Perry, who assumed command after the landing had been carried out. As the Navy's guns were moved ashore, Captain Robert E. Lee oversaw the construction of the Battery No. 5 position, which became the Naval Battery when manned by sailors.

While a wave of enthusiasm over the effects of the naval guns on the Mexican defenses led Scott to thank Perry and "our brothers of the Navy in the name of the Army for this day's work," there was no complementary offer of cooperation by Scott to the Navy in preparing surrender terms when San Juan de Ulloa capitulated on March 27. Nevertheless, Scott paid tribute[53] in a General Order to the Navy's "prompt, cheerful and able assistance" in his victory order,[54] and the forces he led inland to Mexico City included a contingent of about 300 Marines, whose storming of the heights of Chapultapec marked the climax of the campaign—hence the phrase, "from the Halls of Montezuma" in "The

Marines' Hymn.'' Vera Cruz became a benchmark in the history of American joint operations that would stand for almost a century.

The Crimean War

Seven years later, in the Crimean War, 1853–56, in the Anglo-French-Turkish landing in the Crimea, hesitancy on the part of defenders proved as much an aid to the invaders as did quality of organization and execution. The Allies landed on August 14th, rather closer to Sevastapol than the French thought wise, but without opposition. In spite of the especially poor organization of British forces, inter-Allied friction, long delays, confusion in landing control, and a major storm in the middle of it all, the expedition had four days to get ashore unmolested, and the Allies did not encounter Russian forces until the 19th. A 1,400-man British naval brigade served ashore, along with 64- and 32-pound guns.[55]

Allied military operations against the Russians, other than the major deployment in the Crimea, included campaigns in the Balkans and the Caucasus, and joint operations in the Baltic, where in August 1854, 10,000 French troops besieged a fortress in the Aland Islands with bombardment support from French and British warships.

The American Civil War

While glimpses of the technological revolution were seen in the Crimean War, a full view of the enormous effects of mass-produced steel, steam-powered warships, railways, telegraphy, and rifles came five years later in the American Civil War, the greatest conflict fought by a Western power in the nineteenth century and the first major industrial war. Many minor and several major joint operations marked the course of that struggle. The Federal Navy, although using ships that were primitive compared with those built even a decade later, was able to exercise its strategic mobility with little hindrance from the Confederates, in the Peninsula Campaign, at New Orleans in 1862, and at Mobile Bay in 1864, as well as supporting many assaults and sieges.

For the first year of the American Civil War, however, the main axis of operations lay in the Eastern theater.[56] As armies formed, weapons were amassed, and plans were framed, the Western Theater in western Kentucky and Tennessee remained relatively quiet. In the spring of 1862, however, growing awareness and capacity to act on both sides brought a quickening of operations in that region, where three major rivers converged to form a major strategic gateway between North and South. Farthest west ran the Mississippi, which, fed by the Ohio and Missouri, was the main artery of world trade for over a third of the nation, dominated by Confederate guns at various points all the way south to New Orleans. East of the northernmost Confederate bastion on the Mississippi was a fort at Columbus, Kentucky, which was linked to Jackson, Mississippi, and Corinth, Mississippi, by rail. Some sixty miles east of Columbus lay thinly garrisoned Fort Henry, its works weak and partly under water athwart the Tennessee, meandering to the southeast and then south. Close by to the east, on a high bluff above the Cumberland, which flowed east through Tennessee, stood an outwork of Nashville to the southeast, Fort Donelson, defended by a Confederate garrison of some 15,000.

For a generation, the heartbeat of agriculture and commerce in mid-America had been metered by the throbs, puffs, and whistles of steamboats and locomotives, and in 1862–63, the course of military operations in that region was shaped by those same vital forces. While neither side was at a high level of military practice, both were improving fitfully and confusedly. Ultimately, Union forces' naval superiority on the upper river proved crucial. In 1861, the Federals had stolen a march in technology. First, they bolstered steamboats with heavy timbers, then built a fleet of ironclad river gunboats and some rams as well. By the spring of 1862, the Western Flotilla under Flag Officer Andrew Foote, based on Cairo, Illinois, consisted of four ironclads and three timberclads. The reclaiming of the Mississippi basin by the Union hinged on the South's inability to catch up in that part of the naval race, and upon the mobility and tactical fusion of the Federal Army and Navy in their waging of riverine warfare.

In these operations, the importance of personal rapport between generals and admirals in joint operations, noted in earlier cases, was salient in the relationship of Major General Ulysses S. Grant and Foote. Their special relationship, however, stood on a solid organizational foundation, since the Navy's western flotillas had been placed under the command of the Army by Secretary of the Navy Gideon Welles. The Union's first major success in the West, the fall of Fort Henry on April 6, 1862, a product of joint operations, was essentially a Navy victory, since Foote had opened the bombardment that led to a capitulation before Grant's ground forces closed in. The next Union triumph came quickly but not quite so easily. Less than two weeks later, at Fort Donelson, the tactical equation was inverted. After four ironclads were damaged by the Confederate fire from fifty yards above the river and fell back, Grant's troops tightened their siege. His ''unconditional surrender'' demand became a household phrase when Donelson surrendered. Whatever success stemmed from his boldness and from Army-Navy fusion, it had been augmented by Confederate dispersion of forces and by fragmentation and dissonance in their higher command in the West.

General John Pope called for naval support for his move down the Mississippi, and the successful running of the gauntlet at Island No. 10 by two Union gunboats in early April allowed him to cross the river and force the island's garrison of some 6,000 to surrender. The event stood in sharp contrast with the performance of the Navy gunboats at the Battle of Malvern Hill in the Peninsula Campaign, whose supporting fire fell into the Union lines. Meanwhile, 120 miles to the southeast and sixty miles east of Memphis, the greatest battle in the West took place at Shiloh, on the Tennessee River just north of the Mississippi border. A

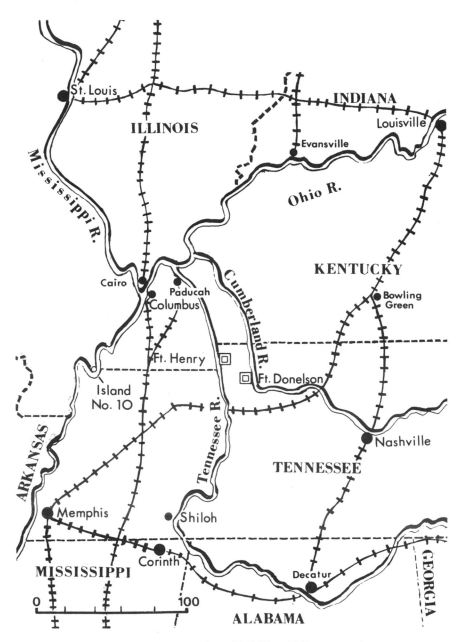

Western Theater of Operations, American Civil War, 1862

Confederate mass surprise attack yielded major success on the first day, as chaos and confusion swept the Union forces, many of whom were untrained. The clash became a "soldier's battle," and Confederate victory appeared certain to many on both sides at sundown, when jointness was brought to bear at a crucial moment. Two Union gunboats fired into ravines full of attacking Confederate troops, helping slow their pursuit. The next day, the massing of reserves reversed the tide of battle after another bloody day of close, hard fighting.

Unfortunately for the Union cause, General Henry Wager Halleck, the senior commander in the West, did not share Grant's and Foote's view of Army-Navy cooperation as the blades of a pair of scissors. As New Orleans fell to Admiral David Farragut's fleet in late April, Halleck's 110,000-man Army of the Tennessee crept forward against a Confederate force half its size retreating to northern Mississippi. The Western Flotilla was now commanded by Flag Officer Charles Davis, Foote having gone on leave to nurse a wound that ultimately proved fatal. After smashing the main Confederate gunboat fleet at Memphis on June 6, Davis moved south to Vicksburg and linked up with a squadron of Farragut's.

After Halleck declined the naval leaders' proposal for a joint effort against Vicksburg, they tried their own assault, and failed. General P.G.T. Beauregard bolstered Vicksburg while the river fell, forcing Farragut's withdrawal to New Orleans, and Davis' to Helena, Arkansas. With a "window of opportunity" closed, Federal strategic momentum in the West fell off for several months. Halleck went east to serve as general-in-chief in the summer, and Flag Officer David Dixon Porter replaced Davis in October. Grant, after regathering elements of the Army of the Tennessee that Halleck had dispersed, attempted to distract the main Confederate forces in Mississippi while Sherman, with some 30,000 men, went by steamer against Vicksburg in late December. After the attempted storming met sharp defeat, Grant wintered just north and across the Mississippi from Vicksburg, while Porter sought to crimp the Confederate supply flow across the south from Texas.

Naval skirmishing in early 1863 led to no clear result. An attempt by Farragut and Porter to link up at Port Hudson was confounded, as were attempts to move Union forces across the Mississippi north of Vicksburg. Grant rejected urgings from his lieutenants for a major thrust against Vicksburg by land through central Mississippi, and again chose a joint riverine strategy. After successful runs past Vicksburg's extensive defenses in April, Grant probed south for a crossing, while Sherman's and Porter's gunboats' feints against Vicksburg convinced the city's defenders that Grant's activity to the south was only a ploy covering Sherman's main effort. Grant, in an audacious gamble, cut loose from his river base and moved north toward Vicksburg by way of a long hook through Jackson, carrying rations in a ragtag assemblage of civilian vehicles and scrounging supplies. As Confederate forces groped to cut his nonexistent logistical "tail," Grant defeated Pemberton at Champion's Hill. After Sherman trapped the routed Confederate forces in Vicksburg and failed in two more attempts to storm the town with the gunboats' support, Grant began a slow, strangulating two-months'

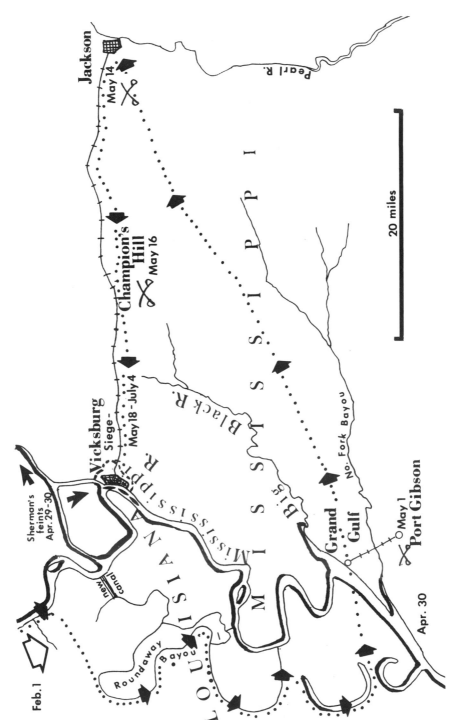

Approach to Vicksburg and Siege, American Civil War, 1863

siege. Much of the city was destroyed by naval and land bombardment, while famine throttled its populace and garrison, who huddled below ground. Another joint besieging force under General Nathaniel Banks, supported by Admiral Farragut's squadron, had Port Hudson in a tightening grip. The result of these efforts was a cluster of setbacks that dashed Confederate hopes in early July 1863. Vicksburg surrendered on the 4th, a day after Lee's defeat at Gettysburg, and Port Hudson fell on the 8th. Thus, as Lincoln proclaimed, "The Father of Waters" rolled "unvexed to the sea," the most effective extended American joint operations seen prior to World War II came to an end.

The Civil War, the first riverine war in the age of steam, set a basic pattern that was to be frequently repeated—in Burma in the 1880s, in various parts of West Africa in the late nineteenth and early twentieth centuries, on the Nile in 1896, in Mesopotamia 1915–17, in the Russian Civil War, on the Black Sea littoral and rivers of eastern Europe in World War I and II, in the first and second Indochinese Wars, and in South America. In spite of the special aura that persisted in the aftermath of those campaigns, the rapport between major commanders in the American West in 1862–63 was less than ideal. Admiral Porter's biographer, Richard West, deemed the collaboration of Grant and Porter as "professional and businesslike,"[57] but the latter advised the assistant secretary of the Navy that "we get along with them first rate. I get all out of them [the Army] I can, and give them nothing in return."[58]

Yet that fusion was far better than what was to be found in the Eastern theater, where, from the beginning of the war, Federal Army-Navy linkages had been acrimonious, early progress notwithstanding, when in 1862, a special amphibious division had been formed of fifteen regiments of volunteers from nautical regions of the country. Its commander, General Ambrose Burnside, worked closely with Flag Officer Louis Goldsborough, commander of the North Atlantic Blockading Squadron. The division embodied the spirit of joint operations that, although uneven in quality and effect, would steadily close down the South's blockade-running terminal ports, but the potential of the underlying concept was not fully developed, and questions of special tactics and methods were pushed into the background by concerns about supply, administration, and command-and-control. Its seizure of Roanoke in February 1862 without covering fire was as much due to thin Confederate defenses and sluggish reaction as to skill in landing speedily.[59]

Federal forces undertook many joint operations in the East, and later, in Louisiana and Texas. While the landing and withdrawal of McClellan's Army of the Potomac in the Peninsula campaign of 1862 was a classic display of strategic mobility provided by seapower, the effect was neutralized ashore by McClellan's cautious and plodding leadership, amid confusion, defeat, and retreat. The indiscipline of some Army units witnessed by naval officers generated bad feelings that endured long beyond the war, and Army-Navy friction also hampered thrusts aimed at plugging the conduits of contraband along the coast of the Confederacy. At Hatteras Inlet, in August 1861, Admiral Stringham and General Butler both ruffled their feathers in a territorial dance of interservice hostility. Nevertheless, in November of that year, Port Royal, South Carolina, was taken by a 12,000-man force commanded by General Thomas Sherman, mainly due to the effects of naval gunfire provided by a naval force under Captain Samuel Du Pont, who headed the South Atlantic Blockade Squadron.

The Navy's attempts at independent operations produced mixed results. One success was Goldsborough's attack on Roanoke in January 1862, with a follow-up occupation by the Army in early February. Viewed as "notorious for his bitter prejudice against the Army," Goldsborough later refused to shell York-town in support of ground forces on the peninsula due to his anxiety about the Confederate ironclad *Virginia/Merrimac* at Norfolk.[60] While Admiral Far-ragut had seized New Orleans in April without significant Army involvement until troops came ashore to assume garrison duties, Du Pont's failure at Charleston in April 1863 demonstrated that naval exclusivity in operations was not a universal formula for success. In Farragut's final major incursion on the gulf, at Mobile Bay in early August 1864, Army troops took no part in the assault, but cooperated closely with the Navy in taking forts in the area afterward.

Beyond a lack of clear doctrine and structure, jointness in the Civil War was also impaired by personal hostility between Secretary of the Navy Gideon Welles and Secretary of War Edwin Stanton, a discordancy echoed in the field in the Red River expedition of 1864, as a major strategic opportunity was lost by bickering between Navy and Army commanders. Rancor also marred the opening phase of the last major amphibious operation of the Civil War aimed at closing the major blockade-running terminus at Wilmington, North Carolina. The first attempt to take Fort Fisher in late December 1864 was marred by bickering, while the second, in mid-January 1865, which succeeded in spite of heavy losses, was marked by close and deliberate cooperation of Navy and Army commanders. In the first try, a shipload of explosives was detonated near the Confederate works a day before the landing. After a heavy naval bombardment, a 2,000-man force came ashore on Christmas, encountered Confederate defenses intact, and was withdrawn on the 27th. The uncooperative Army commander, Major-General Benjamin Butler, was sacked, and his successor, Major-General Alfred Terry, was ordered by General Sherman to work closely with Admiral Porter and to "defer to him as much as is consistent with your own responsibilities."[61]

In mid-January, some initial acrimony between Terry and Porter demonstrated how old habits were hard to break. After an onset of foul weather, 8,000 troops went ashore five miles north of the Confederate positions. Terry, checked by the well-sited but passive Confederate defenders, devised an attack plan with Porter relying on heavy naval gunfire to cover a general advance by 5,000 men, including naval and Marine elements. In the resulting melée, although some Federal Army and Marine units fled, the Confederates gave way and withdrew, and Fort Fisher's fall cut the last main artery of the logistically anemic Confederacy.

JOINTNESS IN THE LATE NINETEENTH CENTURY

While joint operations in the American Civil War far exceeded in scale anything seen until Gallipoli in 1915, most such undertakings in the late nineteenth and early twentieth centuries were small colonial-imperial military-naval incursions, port-forcings or punitive expeditions and demonstrations. Even though amphibious operations were viewed as risky at best in the military doctrine of that period, large undertakings always got ashore almost unscathed, even when landing close to major enemy forces. Examples include the 18,000-man Anglo-French landing at Pei-Tang in early August 1860 and follow-up attacks on the Taku forts; the U.S. Navy's amphibious landing near the Kanghwa forts in 1871; and the Japanese 2nd Army's landing of 40,000 troops and support elements north of Port Arthur in late October 1894 during the Sino-Japanese War.

Jointness in a broader sense was also altered by transoceanic cable systems in the late nineteenth century, which undercut diplomatic prerogatives and discretion of naval and military officers in distant places, their role as diplomats increasingly usurped by the civilian professional foreign service corps. As home governments closely monitored and directed events thousands of miles away, including the waging of war, cables also brought newspaper correspondents to a new level of power in the equation of war. The hunger of officers to be free of such scrutiny and restraint was to persist in the face of technological and political evolution thereafter.

The joint operations of several imperial powers roughly paralleled Anglo-American experiences. From the early nineteenth century on, the French Navy's Marine Infantry played a principal role in colonial warfare somewhat closer in essence to the U.S. Marine Corps' role in the "Banana Wars" of the twentieth century than to the Royal Marines. German marines played similar roles in the establishment of their short-lived overseas Empire, as did Dutch, Japanese, and Italian variants.[62] Functional jointness, with sailors serving ashore as "bluejackets" (that is, infantry and gunners ashore) alongside Marines and soldiers, was a regular mode of colonial warfare.[63] Such naval detachments sometimes operated far inland, as in the Indian Mutiny of 1857–58, in various campaigns in China, in the Sudan and Nile expeditions, and at Magdala in Ethiopia in 1867.

The extremely bloody War of the Triple Alliance, 1864–70, included extensive riverine operations. In 1865, Brazil, Argentina, and Uruguay formed a joint command under a Brazilian vice admiral, and the Allies' monitors and river flotillas coordinated closely with their land forces in the ensuing campaigns, culminating in the last pitched engagement, the Battle of Ypacarai in December 1867, which was followed by an extended guerrilla war. Several landing operations were carried out during the War of the Pacific, 1879–84, which Chile initiated in an attempt to end heavy Peruvian and Bolivian taxation of its nitrate industry. In November 1879, Chile, having gained naval supremacy, launched an invasion that gave it control of Bolivia's seacoast and of Peru's key nitrate-producing region. Two subsequent landings farther north set the stage for a series of Chilean victories that led to a peace settlement giving Chile control over key Peruvian territory and Bolivia's coastal province.

Naval brigades, usually including Royal Marine infantry and artillery, were present in the major landing at Tel-el-Kebir in 1882, which established British control over Egypt for the next three-quarters of a century; at Omdurman in 1896, where Kitchener avenged Gordon; and in the Boer War, 1899–1901.[64] Nor were such operations mere "walk-throughs." A Royal Navy officer, Lieutenant Wyatt Rawson, was killed at Tel-el-Kebir after navigating a night attack,[65] and half of the naval brigade was killed or wounded in a charge at the Battle of Granspaan in the Boer War.[66]

In the middle and late nineteenth century, as long-sequestered realms like Japan, Ethiopia, Indochina, and Korea were penetrated by the major industrial powers, changing patterns of settlement and trade, the technological advances, and the last surge of imperialist diplomacy set the stage for many combined or joint amphibious operations. As noted earlier, during the first three centuries of imperialist/colonial expansion, much of the extension of power radiated out from the sea and from river mouths, where most entrepôts, warehouses, forts, bases, and many plantations were located. The nineteenth century saw many advances from those coastal rinds and extension of direct and indirect rule and settlement, as incursions were launched into the "back country," with telegraphy, medical science, and railroads all augmenting the speed and scale of conquest. Repeating rapid-fire and automatic weapons and steam-powered transports and warships mounting heavier, more accurate cannon further altered the equation of military and naval power in favor of imperialism.

In the last quarter of the nineteenth century, railways and steamers loaded with troops, often with gunboats covering their movement, penetrated remote areas of Africa, Asia, and Latin America. Some landings and expeditions were symbolic, with little or no fighting involved, as "showing the flag" in itself deterred or ended "unrest." As the Nile, Irrawaddy, lower Niger, Mekong, and the Congo became conduits for Western dominance, functional cooperation of army and navy elements was common, much of it *ad hoc* and not carefully planned. Thus it was that by the eve of World War I, much of what was later labelled the Third World lay under the military political and economic sway of the longstanding imperial networks radiating from London, Lisbon, Madrid, Paris, Amsterdam, and Moscow, and newer versions extending from Brussels, Rome, Tokyo, Berlin, and Washington.

British Decline and the Fear of Invasion

The small-scale and incremental pattern of imperial expansion between the great dynastic wars accustomed Britain, the prime wielder of naval power from the Napoleonic Wars to World War I, to "muddling through" and improvisation. Although there were dozens of small joint undertakings, such operations were recognized in treatises on strategy and tactics but stood far from the mainstream of the imperial powers' armed services' doctrine. The relatively low priority assigned to jointness was reflected in the cursory treatment they received in the writings of Admiral Alfred Thayer Mahan, who shaped two generations of naval officers' world-view over much of the globe. Sometimes lyrical and often insightful, Mahan was vague in his treatment of "distant expeditions." He could not envision joint undertakings of great decisiveness, or carried out in the face of significant opposition, or under threat of enemy naval counterstrokes.[67] His focus on the great fleet battles of the age of sail denied him a fore-vision of Gallipoli, Saipan, Leyte, Okinawa, Sicily, Salerno, and Normandy. Whether he made the conceptual road to those events more winding is not easily answered, but joint operations were well off to the side of his world-view and not in sharp focus.[68] Mahan may also have been influenced by Jomini's conclusion, after extensive examination of the problems related to a wide range of descents over the previous four centuries, that it was "difficult to lay down rules."[69]

In spite of many nods toward jointness in professional writing, it was not a matter of central concern among U.S. military and naval professionals in the early twentieth century. In tracing joint operations on Samar in the Philippines from 1899 to 1906, Brian Linn noted the characteristic pattern of widespread coordination between relatively junior officers of the U.S. Army and Navy in the field, on an *ad hoc* basis and without clear underlying doctrine or consistent orchestration from above. Failure to pass on lessons learned or to establish joint administration structures, and "service rivalry and obstructionism was the rule rather than the exception among senior officers."[70]

The longstanding technical and economic edge of Britain was dulled in the late nineteenth and early twentieth centuries, and the advances of Germany and America were reflected in such crucial indices as steel production. As the British policy of maintaining a fleet as big as the next two maritime nations became increasingly burdensome, growing numbers of Britain's elites and masses felt less and less certain that the glories or profits offset the costs of empire and the butcher's bill of "little wars." When unexpected setbacks and losses in the Boer War, 1899–1901, and hostility from many nations added to that sense of futility, concern for defense of the homeland against naval attacks and sudden landings mounted. In the last quarter of the nineteenth century, the specter of jointness practiced by a potential foe now proffered a special menace, as the British, having used the sea to range, strike, and occupy a quarter of the world, feared that game might be played in reverse. I. F. Clarke, in *Voices Prophesying War,* traced the various popular scenarios of invasion that fed into public debate over conscription and militia reform and stimulated citizen marksmanship programs in Britain and in several other countries, including the United States.[71] In the early twentieth century, as British anxiety was stirred by Germany's major naval build-up, substantial credence was given to such dire scenarios as *The Battle of Dorking, The Invasion of 1910,* and *The Riddle of the Sands.* However extreme they may seem now, such concerns were not wholly irrational, given the cases and data at hand.

British and American naval successes against fortresses in China and Korea and the British victory at Tel-el-Kebir in 1882 drove home the fact that modern warships now stood a better-than-even chance against major fortifications and that Nelson's adage was *passe*. Beyond that, London's vulnerability to seaborne attack relative to other major European powers' capital cities had been recognized over many generations. When that dilemma was aggravated as the speed and gunpower of ships bounded forward after the Boer War, it was hoped that naval mines, stronger forts, and heavy artillery, railway guns, armored trains, and militia might contain a major incursion, while larger regular and reserve forces massed for a counterthrust.

The swelling tides of technology ran ahead of full recognition of the many implications. Although increasing concern about coordination and control was a regular focus of debate in Britain from the Crimean War onward, jointness was not dealt with in terms of structural realignment for the next half-century. The Royal Navy's roles as prime bulwark of the realm and as guardian of the tendrils of Empire was recognized in its title of "Senior Service." In spite of the many joint undertakings and the vast contingencies facing the political leaders of Britain throughout the late nineteenth century, there was little coherence in the shaping of strategy or in the conduct of operations. For example, in 1882, the Navy arrived off Alexandria a month and a half before the Army landing force.

Anxiety about far-flung commitments and concerns had led to the forming of the Colonial Defence Committee under the threat of the spreading of the Russo-Turkish War of 1878, but such issues as service blending, interoperability, and joint staff structure remained in abeyance. Throughout the late nineteenth century, however, pressure from the dominions for a rationalized imperial defense strategy and the last major scramble of western nations for colonies amid soaring technological development led to a sharpened focus on the complex problems of defending both the mother country and her scattered brood. Until the eve of World War I, the Navy received the main share of concern and resources, with a "maritime strategy" as the main axis of Britain's defense concerns.

Nevertheless, in 1890, with the achievements of the Prussian General Staff and anxiety about a "bolt out of the blue" surprise attack in view, a committee headed by Lord Hartington examined links between defense expenditures to strategy. In testimony to the committee, Field Marshal Sir Garnet Wolseley, the model for Gilbert and Sullivan's "model major general," called for a Ministry of Defence. That was to be a long time in coming, partly due to the fear of some that such a concentration of military power might subvert democracy, and the confidence of others that Britain needed no over-arching military policy. Beyond that, the Army and Navy were both anxious about their interests being taken out of their hands in any joint structure.

In the 1890s, a broad array of proposals for reform, including the structuring of a kind of high command, were set forth by various governments and individuals, even during a period of drift under Gladstone. It was, however, the

Anglo-Boer War of 1899–1901, in which the administrative chaos and tactical floundering of its Army embarrassed Britain and gave much cheer to its enemies, that gave major impetus to restructuring. Close scrutiny of defense organization by the Elgin (1902) and the Esher (1903) committees led to a proverbial maelstrom of controversy.

In essence, it was much like the intense struggle over centralization raging in the United States at the same time between Secretary of War Elihu Root and the Army's Adjutant General Frederick Ainsworth. In both Britain and America, creating new staff structures atop the services led to improved but relatively primitive interservice linkages. In Britain, although the idea of a Minister of Defence was once again shelved, an Esher Committee suggestion led to the forming of a Committee of Imperial Defence at the Cabinet level in 1904. Against a background of a series of crises stirred up by the ever-more bellicose Germany of Wilhelm II, British defense concerns were stretched between its traditional and long-dominant maritime strategy and the increasingly professionalized British Army officer corps' desire to build a large field army to bolster France against Germany. Meanwhile, under urgings from the dynamic and feisty First Sea Lord Admiral Sir John Fisher, the Royal Navy explored amphibious operations in Europe, which the War Office opposed. The Haldane reforms (1905–08) had led to creation of a modern and well-prepared British Expeditionary Force (BEF), reflecting the Army's preference for concentrating its forces. In 1911, General Sir Henry Wilson, Director of Military Operations, carried the day for the BEF in a debate with First Sea Lord Admiral Sir Arthur Wilson, after which First Lord of the Admiralty Winston Churchill joined Haldane in calling for a Naval War Staff as a counterpart with the recently formed Imperial General Staff. Although that initiative somewhat weakened the Committee of Imperial Defence (CID), the next year, young Royal Marine Captain Maurice Hankey became Secretary to the CID. A strong advocate of jointness, he played a key role in shaping British defense policy over the next quarter-century.[72]

Although plans had been shaped in British defense circles for a generation before World War I for amphibious operations from the Baltic to the Levant, substantial gaps between prognostication, theory, and practice remained that were ultimately thrown into relief during the Great War.[73] Military and naval professionals in several nations addressed joint operations, analyses ranging from considerations of supply, organization, and technology, to broader studies in the manner of Molyneux,[74] deriving technique from historical analysis.[75] After the Franco-Prussian War of 1870–71, however, theorists, commanders, and staffs increasingly focused on the problems of mobilizing and controlling ever-larger, faster-moving, and more destructive armies and navies in a major conflict in Europe.

American Jointness, 1898

Interservice relations in the United States at the end of the nineteenth century reflected the small size and relative insularity of the Army of the Great Republic.

When the Spanish-American War erupted in the spring of 1898, there were no joint plans, unified command structure, or much informal rapport at the top levels of the services. The U.S. Navy, as part of a drive toward modernization, had created a War College in the early 1880s that had prepared war plans, but the Army had none. Years of separate missions, geographic dispersion, inaction, and competition for scarce resources had produced a keen parochialism that became open hostility during operations in Cuba and continued into the Philippine Insurrection. On the other hand, the classic pattern of jointness increasing at the tactical level quickly emerged as the Army prepared to land at Daiquiri on the south coast of Cuba in June 1898. Secretary of the Navy John Long did not want sailors to help put Major General William Shafter's V Corps ashore. When the Army's plans went awry and much of its equipment was lost on the way, even though tensions were mounting between the senior naval commander, Admiral William Sampson, and General Shafter, the senior naval officers on the spot provided men and small craft, as well as a commander afloat and a beach-master ashore.[76]

The first point at issue between Sampson and Shafter was where the Army would land. After the Navy's attempt to block Santiago harbor failed, Sampson wanted the Army to storm the Morro forts so that his ships would not have to sweep mines under heavy fire. Shafter, however, chose to land well east of the main Spanish defenses and concentrations, and to slowly encroach on Santiago. Demands and counter-demands flowed between the two headquarters and up and down the respective army and navy chains of command from Washington. The squabbling in the field echoed back to Washington and allowed the eminent naval theorist Alfred Thayer Mahan to hold forth to the secretary of war on the special worth of capital ships versus the lives of troops. General-in-Chief Nelson Miles added fuel to the fire by suggesting that hay bales be piled on Army transports, which would then force the harbor.[77]

At this point, Shafter's forces were receiving indirect assistance on his right flank from the Navy. After he rejected the urging of Secretary of the Navy that the Army land farther to the east at Guantanamo Bay, a battalion of Marines was put ashore there. It was not an assault landing, and the force landed with bands playing. The only immediate casualties were caused by heat, although there was some scattered firing later. The light opposition from local enemy forces, which outnumbered it approximately ten to one, reflected the relatively unaggressive posture of the Spanish. But even their half-hearted and poorly sited defenses cost Shafter more than he expected, and it has been suggested that the Guantanamo lodgment, while aimed at gaining the Navy a shore installation, inadvertently kept Spanish forces off balance and made the campaign in Cuba far less protracted and costly than it might have been.[78] The Navy continued to oppose a storming of the harbor with Spanish mines uncleared and forts intact because that would put its expensive warships at risk. The Army hesitated to attack the key forts or press harder against the Spanish forces, whose outlying defenses and Mauser smokeless powder rifles had taken an unexpectedly heavy toll at El Caney, and at Kettle and San Juan Hills.

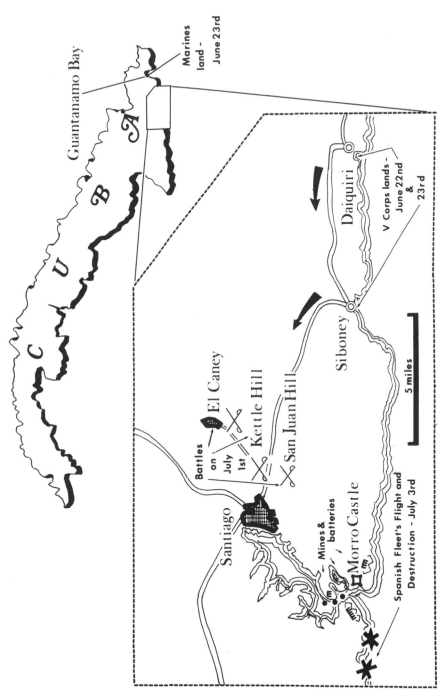

Guantanamo Bay

C U B A

Marines land - June 23rd

Daiquiri

V Corps lands - June 22nd & 23rd

Siboney

5 miles

El Caney

Kettle Hill

San Juan Hill

Battles on July 1st

Santiago

Mines & batteries

Morro Castle

Spanish Fleet's Flight and Destruction - July 3rd

U.S. Landings in Cuba, June 1898

In early July, Shafter called for naval assistance, having lost a tenth of his forces, and as Sampson went ashore to confer with him on July 3, the Spanish fleet sortied from the harbor mouth running west along the coast and was quickly destroyed. Army-Navy friction continued when Shafter, like Scott at Vera Cruz, excluded the Navy (and the Cuban rebels) from the surrender talks. Wrangling over the services' control of captured Spanish ships was finally resolved by President McKinley in favor of the Army. Following the Spanish surrender in Cuba on July 17, after Miles' proposal of a joint command under an Army general for the Puerto Rico landing was rejected, the Army's plan of advance was designed to avoid having to depend upon the Navy or allow it to share in the glory of conquest.[79]

The Imperial Aftermath

With the Spanish-American War having made America an imperial power, most U.S. colonial war joint operations over the next thirty years were carried out by Marines and bluejackets, since they were viewed as less threatening modes of intervention. It was, for example, on such grounds that President Wilson held the Army back in the first phase of the U.S. incursion at Vera Cruz in 1914, even though during the preceding decade, President Theodore Roosevelt and the U.S. Navy hierarchy had made a major attempt to truncate the U.S. Marine Corps.[80] From 1906 onward, the Corps moved aggressively to claim the special task of advanced base seizure and defense, a mission that fit into the growingly ornate "Orange" plan for war with Japan in the Central and Western Pacific. In spite of serving as legation and shipboard guards and colonial warfare constabulary, the Marine Corps nurtured the amphibious warfare role with slender resources over the next generation.

Another major result of the war against Spain sprang from the near-chaos of the Army's mounting an expeditionary force at Tampa and landing in Cuba. Further controversies arising from the Philippine Insurrection led to a series of reforms under the stewardship of Secretary of War Elihu Root. A new spirit of jointness appeared in stages, although muted, as the result of the Root Reforms, after the Army General Staff and the Navy's newly created General Board began to meet together from time to time as the Joint Board. As a not fully realized attempt to institutionalize the resolution of interservice jurisdictional boundaries, the Joint Board did not meet regularly or carry out joint contingency planning until 1919. Yet some substantial changes were made. In 1910, the principle of cooperation of commanders in joint operations à la Molyneux was altered to giving the Navy command afloat and up to the highwater mark. The Army was to command ashore, including Navy and Marine elements—the pattern applied in the 1914 Vera Cruz-Tampico incursions.

In spite of such attempts at coherence and rationalization, the United States lacked a true general staff, effective administrative continuity, and functional jointness on the eve of American entry into World War I. Although it was widely recognized that major extended operations could no longer be "single-service," especially in view of the rise of aviation, lack of appreciation of the implications of such trends among senior officers led the president of the Naval War College in 1916 to lament the lack of a linking mechanism and of coordination in management of the growth of the Army and Navy air services, as well as discontinuity between naval and military districts, which prevailed until 1942.

Whatever the imperfections of American policy and practice in respect to interservice relations at that point, while the great powers of Europe had worked out such problems to a somewhat greater degree of sophistication, their shortfalls were caught in the sharp and pitiless spotlight of war as they struggled with problems of jointness in World War I, 1914–18, while the United States lay a generation away from confronting its full glare in battle.

NOTES

1. For broad-gauge surveys, see John Van Duyn Southworth, *The Ancient Fleets: The Story of Naval Warfare Under Oars, 2600 B.C.–1597 A.D.* (New York: Twayne, 1968); Count Lefebvre des Noettes, *de la Marine Antique a la Marine Moderne* (Paris: Masson, 1935); William Ledyard Rodgers, *Greek and Roman Naval Warfare, 4th to 16th Centuries: A Study of Strategy, Tactics, and Ship Design* (Annapolis: U.S. Naval Institute, 1939); and Pierre Ducrey, *Warfare in Ancient Greece*, Chapter 6, "Warfare at Sea," translated by Janet Lloyd (New York: Shocken Books, 1985), pp. 179–96; also see Alfred Vagts, *Landing Operations: Strategy, Psychology, Tactics, Politics, from Antiquity to 1945* (Harrisburg: Military Service Publishing Co., 1952); and Bernard Brodie, *A Layman's Guide to Naval Strategy*, "Land-Sea Operations," Chapter 6 (Princeton: Princeton University Press, 1942), pp. 148–63.

2. For example, the ratio of rowers to marines in Athenian *pentekonters* was six to one, cf. Chester G. Starr, *Influence of Seapower on Ancient History* (New York: Oxford University Press, 1989), p. 22; in the Byzantine fleet, about three to one, cf., Rodgers, Greek and Roman Naval Warfare, p. 61.

3. For example, see Adcock, *The Greek and Macedonian Art of War* (Berkeley: University of California Press, 1957), pp. 38 and 40.

4. See Donald Kagan, *The Fall of the Athenian Empire* (Ithaca: Cornell University Press, 1987), pp. 37, 220–23.

5. Starr, *Influence of Seapower*, p. 14.

6. Hans Delbrück, *History of the Art of War in the Framework of Political History*, translated by Walter J. Rengroe (Westport, Conn.: Greenwood, 1975), p. 81.

7. Donald Kagan, *The Archidamian War* (Ithaca: Cornell University Press, 1974), p. 252.

8. See Southworth, *Ancient Fleets*, pp. 72–98; and for analysis, see J. B. Wilson, *Pylos 425 B.C.: A Historical and Topographical Study of Thucydides' Account of the Campaign* (Warminster, U.K.: Aris & Phillips, 1979).

9. Starr, *Influence of Sea Power*, p. 45.

10. Ibid., p. 57.

11. Cf. Graham Webster, *The Roman Imperial Army of the First and Second Centuries*, 3rd edn. (Totowa, N.J.: Barnes & Noble, 1985), p. 157.

12. Chester G. Starr, *The Roman Imperial Navy, 31 B.C.–A.D. 324* (New York: Barnes & Noble, 1960), pp. 58, 137, 167; for a description of the Roman effect on sea fighting tactics and technology, see W. W. Tarn, *Hellenistic Military and Naval Developments* (Chicago: Ares Publishing, 1984), pp. 145–52.

13. Starr, *Influence of Seapower*, pp. 68–75; and Michael Grant, *The Ancient Mediterranean* (New York: Scribner's, 1969), p. 300.

14. Yvon Garlan, *War in the Ancient World: A Social History* (London: Chatto & Windus, 1975), p. 130.

15. John Francis Guilmartin, Jr., *Gunpowder and Galleys: Changing Technology and Medieval Warfare at Sea* (Cambridge: Cambridge University Press, 1974), p. 70.

16. Rodgers, *Naval Warfare Under Oars*, pp. 10–15.

17. For example, see Helene Antoniadis-Bibicou, *Etudes d'Histoire Maritime de Byzance: a Propos du "Theme de Caravisiens"* (Paris: SEVPEN, 1966).

18. Steven Runciman, *Byzantine Civilization* (London: Edward Arnold, 1959), p. 155.

19. Ibid., p. 79.

20. For an analysis of the question of technology transfer, see Daniel Philip Waley, *Combined Operations in Sicily, A.D. 1060–1078* (London: British School at Rome, 1954). Papers, vol. 22, New Series, vol. 9, pp. 118–25.

21. Norman H. Baynes, *The Byzantine Empire* (London: Oxford University Press, 1962), pp. 141–43, 149.

22. See Romilly Jenkins, *Byzantium: The Imperial Centuries A.D. 601–1071* (London: Weidenfeld and Nicholson, 1966), pp. 188–261; and George Ostrogorsky, *History of the Byzantine State*, translated by John Hussey (New Brunswick, N.J.: Rutgers, 1969), pp. 116, 251, 357, 430, 483–525, 570, 853.

23. For the elite status of marines in the Venetian Republic's navy, see Frederic Lane, *Venetian Ships* (Westport, Conn.: Greenwood, 1975), pp. 10, 17, 24, 39, 184–85; and M. E. Mallett and J. R. Hale, *The Military Organization of a Renaissance State—Venice, 1400 to 1677* (Cambridge: Cambridge University Press, 1984), pp. 217, 454.

24. Rodgers, *Naval Warfare Under Oars*, p. 61; and David Talbot Rice, *The Byzantines* (London: Thames & Hudson, 1962), pp. 115–16, 121–22.

25. Lane, *Venetian Ships*; also see Alethea Wiel, *The Navy of Venice* (London: John Murray, 1910), p. 24.

26. Rodgers, *Naval Warfare Under Oars*, p. 121.

27. Guilmartin, *Gunpowder and Galleys*, p. 273.

28. See the contemporary battle map facing p. 144, in R. F. Foster, ed., *The Oxford Illustrated History of Ireland* (Oxford: Oxford University Press, 1989).

29. Winston Graham, *The Spanish Armadas* (New York: Doubleday, 1972); Colin Martin and Geoffrey Parker, *The Spanish Armada* (New York: W. W. Norton, 1988).

30. The most elegant dissection remains Garrett Mattingly, *The Armada* (Boston: Houghton Mifflin, 1959).

31. For a detailed description of a major Tudor combined operation, see W. Slingisbie, "The Voyage to Cadiz 1596," in Julian Corbett, ed., *The Naval Miscellany* (London: Naval Records Society, 1902), p. 37.

32. For overviews, see John Creswell, *Generals and Admirals: The Story of Amphibious Command* (London: Longmans Green, 1952); and Bernard Fergusson, *The Watery*

Maze: The Story of Combined Operations (New York: Harper & Row, 1961), pp. 17–23.

33. For example, see Michael Howard, ed., "The British Way in Warfare: A Reappraisal," in *The Causes of War* (London: Unwin Paperbacks, 1985), pp. 189–207.

34. Cf. Basil Williams, *The Life of William Pitt, Earl of Chatham* (London: Frank Case, 1966), p. 261.

35. Rex Whitworth, *Field Marshal Lord Ligonier: A Story of the British Army*, 1702–1770 (Oxford: Clarendon Press, 1958), pp. 396–439.

36. Quoted in Brodie, *Layman's Guide to Naval Strategy*, p. 150.

37. Whitworth, *Field Marshal Lord Ligonier*, Chap. 12, "Coastal Raids," pp. 250–68.

38. Thomas Molyneux, *Conjunct Expeditions or Expeditions that Have Been Carried on Jointly by the Fleet and Army with a Commentary on a Little War* (London: R. & J. Dodsley, 1759); for perspective on the strategic view from the highest echelon at that time, see Pitt's correspondence with Admiral Edward Boscawen, in Gertrude Selwyn Kimball, ed., *Correspondence of William Pitt, when Secretary of State, with Colonial Governors and Military and Naval Commissioners in America* (New York: Kraus Reprints, 1969), vol. i, p. 176; for a slightly earlier view of tactics, see Sir Herbert Richmond, *The Navy in the War of 1739–48* (Cambridge: Cambridge University Press, 1970), vol. iii, "Appendix on Tactics," pp. 253–67.

39. F. E. Whitton, *Wolfe and North America* (Boston: Little Brown, 1929), p. 198.

40. Molyneux, *Conjunct Expeditions*, p. 42.

41. Fergusson, *Watery Maze*, p. 20.

42. Creswell, *Generals and Admirals*, p. 99.

43. A. Temple Patterson, *The Other Armada: The Franco-Spanish Attempt to Invade Britain in 1779* (Manchester, England: Manchester University Press, 1960).

44. A succinct account is Michael Duffy's "A Particular Service: The British Government and the Dunkirk Expedition of 1793," *English Historical Review* 91:3 (July 1976): 529–54.

45. For a survey of amphibious operations in the Napoleonic era, see Brian Lavery, *Nelson's Navy: The Ships, Men and Organization, 1793–1815* (Annapolis: U.S. Naval Institute Press, 1989), pp. 310–16.

46. For a brief account, see J. Christopher Herold, *Bonaparte in Egypt* (New York: Harper & Row, 1962), pp. 376–77.

47. See J. Holland Rose, ed., "The Flemish Campaign," in *William Pitt and the Great War* (London: G. Bell & Sons, 1914), pp. 118–42; William James, *The Naval History of Great Britain from the Declaration of War by France in 1793 to the Accession of George IV*, vol. iv (London: Richard Bentley, 1859), pp. 423–43.

48. A detailed analysis is Wilbur S. Brown, *The Amphibious Campaign for West Florida and Louisiana, 1814–1815: A Critical Review of Strategy and Tactics at New Orleans* (University: University of Alabama, 1969), pp. 169ff.

49. K. Jack Bauer, *Surfboats and Horse Marines: U.S. Naval Operations in the Mexican War 1846–1848* (Annapolis: U.S. Naval Institute, 1969), pp. 63–66, 77.

50. Milo Milton Quaife, *The Diary of James K. Polk During His Presidency*, 4 vols. (Chicago: A. C. McClurg, 1910), vol. ii, p. 388.

51. John Polk Fleming, "Vera Cruz, 1847: A Lesson in Command," *Marine Corps Gazette* 63:9 (September 1979): 62–63.

52. Bauer, *Surfboats and Horse Marines*, p. 81.

53. Ibid., p. 97.

54. Ibid.

55. Byron Farwell, *Queen Victoria's Little Wars* (New York: W. W. Norton, 1973), pp. 72–73.

56. See Rowena Reed, *Combined Operations in the Civil War* (Annapolis: U.S. Naval Institute, 1978), esp. "Conclusions," pp. 304–88; and H. Allen Gosnell, *Guns on the Western Waters: The Story of River Gunboats in the Civil War* (Baton Rouge: Louisiana State University Press, 1949).

57. Richard S. West, *The Second Admiral: A Life of David Dixon Porter, 1813–1891* (New York: Coward-McCann, 1937), pp. 173.

58. Peter Karsten, *The Naval Aristocracy* (New York: Free Press, 1972), p. 254.

59. See Robert W. Daly, "Burnside's Amphibious Division, 1962," in Merrill L. Bartlett [Lt.-Col.-U.S.M.C.], *Assault from the Sea* (Annapolis: U.S. Naval Institute Press, 1983), pp. 88–93.

60. Laurence J. Legere, *Unification of the Armed Forces* (New York: Garland Publishing Co., 1988), p. 24.

61. Joseph E. King, "The Fort Fisher Campaigns, 1864–65," in Bartlett, *Assault from the Sea*, pp. 95–105.

62. For basic details on the history of the German imperial marines, see Egbert Thomer, *Sprung an die Küste* (Oldenburg & Hamburg: Gerhard Stalling Verlag), n.d. [1963], pp. 10–11.

63. For example, "The Sudan Campaign," in Daniel Hawthorne, *For Want of a Nail: The Influence of Logistics* (New York: Whittlesley House, 1948), pp. 200–37; and Philip Magnus, *Kitchener: Portrait of an Imperialist* (New York: E. P. Dutton, 1959), pp. 94–130. For a brief description of the role of Royal Navy gunboats in the 1896 Nile expedition, see Donald Featherstone, *Colonial Small Wars 1837–1901* (Newton Abbot: Newton & Charles, 1973), pp. 185–94.

64. For details, see William Laird Clowes et al., *The Royal Navy: A History*, vol. 7 (London: Sampson, Low Marston & Co., 1903), pp. 148–50, 345, 351–55, 379.

65. Peter C. Smith, *Victoria's Victories* (New York: Hippocrene Books, 1987), pp. 145, 157–58.

66. Byron Farwell, *Queen Victoria's Little Wars*, pp. 342–43.

67. For example, see Alfred Thayer Mahan, *Mahan on Naval Strategy: Selections from the Writings of Rear-Admiral Thayer Mahan*, ed. John B. Hattendorf (Annapolis: U.S. Naval Institute, 1991), pp. 187–280.

68. For a sharp critique, see Philip A. Crowl, "Alfred Thayer Mahan: The Naval Historian," in Peter Paret, ed. *Makers of Modern Strategy: From Machiavelli to the Nuclear Age* (Princeton: Princeton University Press, 1986), esp. pp. 460, 476.

69. Antoine Jomini, *The Art of War*, translated by G. H. Mendell and W. P. Craighill (Westport, Conn.: Greenwood, 1987, orig. publ. 1862), "Descents," pp. 226–29 and "Sketch of the Principal Maritime Expeditions," pp. 327–54. Jomini saw a need for: a deception plan regarding the landing site; a calm anchorage: simultaneous landing of all forces and as much artillery as possible; maximum aggressiveness; seizure of a strong point to protect the landing; and maintenance of the line of communication from sea to shore; see pp. 229–30.

70. Brian Linn, "The Struggle for Samar," in James Bradford, ed., *The Crucible of Empire*, U.S. Naval Institute Press, forthcoming.

71. The most sophisticated of this genre, Erskine Childers' *The Riddle of the Sands* (New York: Dodd, Mead, 1915), has been reprinted several times, most recently by the U.S. Naval Institute Press, and was made into a film.

72. For details of the evolution of British joint structures, 1856 to 1914, see Bill Jackson and Dwin Bramall, *The Chiefs: The Story of the United Kingdom Chiefs of Staff* (London: Brassey's, 1992), pp. 1–54.

73. See John Gooch, *The Plans of War: The General Staff and British Military Strategy, 1990–1916* (London: Routledge & Paul, 1974), on landing plans from the 1890s, pp. 18, 267.

74. For example, see A. Ludlow Case, *Landing Drill of Naval Brigade* (Washington, D.C.: U.S. Navy Bureau of Ordnance, 1875); Theodore B. M. Mason, *Organization of Landing Parties for Operations on Shore* (Washington, D.C.: U.S. Navy Bureau of Ordnance, 1875); and M. R. De Gouy, *Etude sur les Operations Combinées des Armées de Terre et de Mer: Attaque et Defense* (Paris: Berger-Levrault), 1882.

75. For example, Georges Armand Furse, *Military Expeditions Beyond the Seas* (London: William Clowes, 1897), vol. i, *Procedures,* and vol. ii, *Cases* (Paris: Berger-Levrault, 1882); and Sir George Ashton, *Sea, Land and Air Strategy: A Comparison* (London: John Murray, 1914).

76. Walter Millis, *The Martial Spirit* (New York: Literary Guild, 1931), p. 262.

77. Ibid., p. 323.

78. Bradley M. Reynolds, "The Impact of the Marine Assault on Guantanamo Bay and the Outcome of the Spanish-American War," in Frederick Harrod et al., *New Aspects of Naval History: Selected Papers from the 5th Naval History Symposium* (Baltimore: Nautical and Aviation Publishing Co., 1985), pp. 145–52.

79. Russell Alger, *The Spanish-American War* (New York: Harper & Brothers, 1907), p. 250. Some of the friction was readily visible in the commanders' exchange of messages, and some between the lines. For example, see n.a., Adjutant General's Office, U.S. Army, *Correspondence Relating to the War with Spain and Conditions Growing out of the Same and the Insurrection in the Philippine Islands and the China Relief Expedition Between the Adjutant General of the Army and the Military Commanders in the United States, Cuba, Puerto Rico, China and the Philippine Islands from April 15, 1898 to July 30, 1902* (Washington, D.C.: U.S. Government Printing Office, 1902); and Millis, *Martial Spirit*, p. 357.

80. James H. Alexander, "Route of Deployment—Vera Cruz, 1914," in Bartlett, *Assault from the Sea,* p. 137.

Chapter 2

Dark and Swift Narrows:
World War I

Before World War I, in spite of considerable evidence at hand, many military professionals, politicians, and intellectuals failed to sense how much evolving technologies had altered the nature of war. Some forevisions, like those of Ivan Bloch, a Polish banker, came closer to what was to occur than did the elaborate and confidently crafted war plans and doctrines. Military and naval leaders and their staffs concealed blind optimism and fervor beneath the pallid facades of rationalistic formats. Those who saw themselves as the masters of the new systems as the war began proved to be their servants, and ultimately their slaves and victims. Soon after hostilities broke out in mid-summer 1914, it was clear to many, through the gauze of censorship and beyond confident pronouncements and posturings, that grand schemes and hopes had been confounded. The Great War spawned political and social upheavals, as well as a host of revolutionary methods including jointness, which stood at the forefront of battle as the struggle began. In the opening campaigns in Western Europe in July and August 1914, aviation played a major role as unarmed reconnaissance aircraft provided ground commanders with a scope of view and speed in reporting never seen before.

THE WAR

The coming of war in 1914 confounded plans in many quarters. In Britain as elsewhere, a relatively quick decision was expected, and a mass lunge of key officers toward the fighting tore asunder the fabric of the upper-level staffs in Britain. The Committee of Imperial Defense was one casualty, as Prime Minister Asquith sought to grasp the reins of control through the Cabinet. After that proved unworkable, he created a War Council, where Captain Hankey joined Winston Churchill in setting forces in motion that led to the Dardanelles expedition. In 1915, the War Council was renamed the Dardanelles Committee, and by the war's end it had become the War Cabinet. It was a kind of joint structure, but far from the closely interleaved headquarters of a generation later.

Other variants of jointness soon appeared in campaigns in distant places. In early September 1914, a reinforced Japanese division landed unopposed near the German colony of Tsingtao in China, and was soon joined by other Japanese forces. Late in the month, a British battalion and a company of Sikhs from the Indian Army landed. Initially hampered by major storms, these Allied forces eventually besieged the colony, and overcame Tsingtao's relatively up-to-date defenses in early November after a sustained bombardment, with relatively few casualties on both sides.[1]

At the same time, the British mounted a joint expedition to seize German East Africa, under an elegant strategic plan designed to entrap an estimated 3,000 German-led *askaris*—African mercenary troops—in a double envelopment. The northern arm of the pincers, composed mainly of colonial volunteers and African troops, was to arc west and then south around Mount Kilimanjaro, while the south pincer, an 8,000-man Indian Army force commanded by Major-General Arthur Aitken, was to land and seize the port of Tanga, then move northwest to meet the northern force.[2] As a force of *askaris* led by Paul von Lettow-Vorbeck and several dozen German officers moved to Tanga, the advance of the northern British force was thwarted by its weak logistical system, harsh terrain, and drought.

Some aspects of the Tanga landing echoed American experiences in landing in Cuba in the Spanish-American War. Initial British naval probes were limited by a fear of mines, while the landing forces, mainly Indian Army troops raised for security and garrison duty, lacked physical conditioning, had no training in amphibious operations, and had not been out of the steamy confines of their troop ships since leaving Bombay. Aitken, whose arrogance matched a capacity for self-delusion, brushed aside the counsel of Africa-wise British officers and of the naval officers supporting the landing. He had also rejected both the offer of a battalion of King's African Rifles, closest to the Germans' *askaris* in field-craft, and of fire support from the heavy guns of the British cruiser, *Fox*. Poor intelligence, in-the-clear radio transmission, and descriptions in the British East African press of preparations and goals further tilted the scales against the British. Another parallel to Cuba 1898 was the failure to follow a combat-loading scheme. But there was also a critical difference. The enemy ashore put up a fight, when, after further floundering and delays, Aitken's forces landed after sundown on November 3. Initially thin and scattered fire from the Germans led him to conclude that he was unopposed, but he soon found that von Lettow-Vorbeck and his German officers had sited defenses skillfully. Snipers festooned the trees and range-marking flags actuated by trip-wires allowed the well-trained and eager *askaris* to mass firepower from a distance upon the areas of enemy movement that were revealed by them.

Although British forces overcame initial setbacks and pushed the German-led forces into Tanga on November 4, a sudden counterstroke by von Lettow-Vorbeck's *askaris* induced a panic that affected most of the Indian troops. Beyond their lack of training and field experience, and poor physical condition, the sense of shock and confusion was a product of the *askaris'* black-powder weapons. Initially seen as a disadvantage, the puffs of white smoke and whorls of dust churned up by the Germans' obsolete rifles and British light guns added to the turmoil. After many British officers had been cut down trying to rally them, Aitken's confidence in the Indian troops crumbled, and he called upon the Navy for help. Since there was no prior planning or teams ashore that could adjust naval gunfire, the several hundred 6-inch and 4.7-inch rounds fired in haste from HMS *Fox* inflicted a few friendly casualties and heavily damaged the port of Tanga, but left the Germans and *askaris* unaffected.

Von Lettow-Vorbeck expected his forces to fight a delaying action against superior British forces that would ultimately force him out of Tanga, and was amazed when he saw his focs withdrawing in as confused a manner as they had come ashore. Back in London, Field Marshal Lord Kitchener, secretary of state for war, was furious when he learned of Aitken's withdrawal and the loss of almost a fifth of his forces. Although "K" did not know the butcher's bill on the other side was fewer than seventy German officers and *askaris,* he did sense that Tanga was a major botch, and reduced Aitken to colonel. The lack of effective jointness at Tanga yielded very heavy costs, as the Allies pursued the Germans throughout East Africa over the next four years. Von Lettow-Vorbeck's small band, never more than 70,000, including many camp followers and bearers, lived off the land, using captured weapons and thin resources filtering through the blockade. Earnest efforts of over a quarter of a million Allied troops failed to bring him to bay, and he surrendered after the end of the war in Europe.

Mesopotamia

In 1915, joint operations developed on a grander scale in another exotic setting, in the riverine war in the Tigris-Euphrates Valley. The Mesopotamian campaign saw a fusion of land and naval forces that resembled both the Western campaigns of the Civil War and Kitchener's march up the Nile in 1896. In moving north from the Persian Gulf against the Turks, the British adapted about 500 local, light reed-hulled river craft called *bellum*—jokingly dubbed "war bellum" by the classically educated British (*bellum* means "war" in Latin). As these shallow-draft boats were poled across levees and field boundaries in the saturated to-pography of a region that was soon to be part of Iraq, they harassed the Turks like swarms of gadflies, swirling around the core of heavier rafts bearing machine guns or light mountain guns. These, in turn, screened the lightly armored Royal Navy craft limited to the deeper channels and main rivers, in some cases carrying Army heavy artillery to supplement their naval ordnance. Later in the campaign, after fighting became static during the Turkish siege of Kut-el-Amara, the British warships assumed the "role of a heavy battery in trench warfare." Jointness in "Mespot" also encompassed the new third dimension of warfare, as the Royal Flying Corps BE 2Cs dropped small sacks of food.[3] Some felt later that just one more squadron of such primitive airlift might have spared the British forces from the humiliating surrender of Kut in 1916.

The Cameroons: Getting It Right

Operations by Allied forces against the German Cameroons in Western Africa, 1914–16, stood in sharp contrast with the debacles elsewhere. There, the sharp differences in the climate cycle put a premium on riverine warfare inland during the May-October wet season, when the Royal Navy provided shore parties as well as a range of support from blockade and transport to direct combat support. An official historian saw the congenial relations among British and French commanders in this campaign and the complex variety of home, imperial and local forces as having produced to a "peculiar degree an object lesson in cooperation."[4]

The Dardanelles

The major instance of jointness in the "Great War" came in another peripheral theater, on the north side of the narrows of the Dardanelles linking the Black and Aegean seas. Those straits, dominated by the gaunt and desiccated Gallipoli peninsula jutting southwest from Constantinople and the Sea of Marmora, were a causeway for many bent on martial and naval enterprises since prehistoric times. Trojans, Achaeans, Hellenes, Romans, Byzantines, Venetians, Genoese, and Turks sailed past its desolate crags and valleys or dotted its edges with forts and towns.

Whether it has been the light, or the air, or the vivid clash of turquoise sky and "wine-dark sea" with arid browns and greys and tans, the region had conveyed an exaggerated sense of scale and drama to those who fought there, since the Trojan War inspired the *Iliad* and *Odyssey*. In World War I, such lyricism among combatants and witnesses was evident from the outset. Since the British elites had often flavored their imperial adventures with the classical images they absorbed in nursery and public school, many participants and observers in the Dardanelles expedition were affected, as the Crusaders had been, by Constantinople's exotic aura, and they struck classical heroic postures in letters, literature, history, art, and poetry. To many, the death from septicemia of Lieutenant Rupert Brooke of the Royal Naval Division on the eve of the amphibious assault proved a dark omen. Like Brutus, the ill-starred British ground force commander, Sir Ian Hamilton, was haunted by dark portents in his dreams, while Sir John Fisher, the First Sea Lord, railed shrilly, Cassandra-like, in high councils against the nemesis that he correctly sensed lay ahead in the Dardanelles. And a skillful Turkish commander, Mustapha Kemal, was to emerge as the greatest leader of his people of modern times. Although the mythic imagery that shaped lofty expectations faded quickly on Gallipoli's stark and pitiless haunches, the campaign engendered yet other myths, the smudgy traces of which persisted in military and naval circles for a generation, since Gallipoli came to be widely seen after World War I as a proof of the futility of major joint operations.

To take a slightly longer and less lurid view, in the domain of power politics, Britain, France, Turkey, Russia, and, finally, Germany had all pushed, feinted, scraped and sometimes collided in seeking control of the straits for generations before World War I. Various clashes and crises dotted the course of those tangled rivalries throughout the nineteenth century and three bloody Balkan wars, from 1908 to 1913, involving shifting coalitions of regional powers. As Bismarck and others foresaw, the unresolved frictions of the region plunged most of Europe into war.

The Gallipoli campaign of 1915 was a failure born of failure.[5] Early that year, after the Russians asked for help in distracting the Turks from the Caucasus front, First Lord of the Admiralty Winston Churchill had proposed a quick thrust into the Dardanelles to neutralize Turkish defenses, thus isolating the Germans from an ally and opening a major supply artery to Russia. When Kitchener refused to provide ground forces for a combined attack, Churchill assembled a contingent of obsolete British and French battleships under Vice Admiral Sackville Carden to assail the Straits on March 8. By March 17, the Allied fleet had neutralized the southernmost forts on the mainland and lower Gallipoli peninsula and advanced far enough up the Straits to gather their resources for a major effort toward Constantinople. Unfortunately for the British and French, the Turks and their German allies had been alerted by a British naval raid into the Straits in the autumn of 1914, and had bolstered their forts, doubled their land forces on the Gallipoli peninsula, and laid mine belts. After most mines were swept, Carden became critically ill and was succeeded by Rear Admiral John de Robeck, who, under orders to press on at all costs, moved his forces so deep into the Straits that the Turks, their forts low on ammunition, contemplated evacuating their capital. At that moment, six of the old capital ships struck mines in quick succession in areas that de Robeck thought had been swept. With two ships sunk and some 600 sailors dead, De Robeck withdrew, unaware of how close Nike (the Hellenic goddess of victory) was hovering. Over the next eight months, a quarter of a million soldiers on each side were killed or wounded as the Allies vainly pursued victory, and the theme of opportunities lost by hesitation, inertia, or bumbling so often seen in previous joint operations became the major theme of the shared ordeal of Gallipoli. Debates in the Allies' high councils during the war as to how close they had been to victory were not resolved until Turkish and German postwar accounts showed that they had been very close indeed—perhaps a matter of minutes at the outset. In the ensuing stalemates, the losses were all that much greater because the opposing forces were so closely matched.

As Allied goals and strategies shifted throughout the year-long campaign, interservice relations ranged from warm accord to acrimony. Kitchener held back ground forces in apparent deference to "Westerners" in the Army who felt that the western front was the decisive theater of war, and that was the opening *leitmotif* in a long, dissonant fugue. Ironically, just as naval operations had begun in the Dardanelles, Kitchener had relented, sending a first-class British division and General Sir Ian Hamilton as ground force commander.

After the naval attempt failed, the hunger in London for increased effort mounted. The War Council engaged in collective over-optimism as the French joined in, and, ignoring cautionary staff appraisals, sanctioned a major amphibious expedition, which mustered in Egypt in plain view of the Turks and Germans, with its forward base and staging area at Lemnos in the Greek isles. De Robeck retained naval command while Hamilton assembled his array of French, Australian, New Zealand, Indian Army, and British divisions. In a further bitter paradox, although the Straits offered Russia the only major access to Western supplies, the Tsarist regime could not abandon its long, keen interest in the Straits. Their concerns about the grinding down of their client, Serbia, warped their strategic view, and they blocked the use of three Greek divisions in Gallipoli.

Hamilton, a veteran of many imperial campaigns and a hero of the South African war, was articulate, energetic, cultivated, and charming. He grasped both the essence and the mechanics of jointness and was especially sensitive to the issue of the prerogatives of subordinate command—ultimately to a fault. As with many of his peers, Hamilton's long years of service and notable colonial war experience proved unreliable indicators of performance in major command.[6] But it is not easy to say who might have done better under the circumstances, since Hamilton and his newly assembled staff were forced to weave a vast and complex tapestry in great haste. Virtually "writing the book" on major modern amphibious operations, they worked hurriedly, without coherent staff work or guidance from higher echelons. Yet their haste offered little tactical value, for surprise had been lost, and the Turks and Germans had substantially strengthened defenses even further on the peninsula within a week of the failed naval attack.

British Army and Royal Navy planners, both separately and in constant interplay, dealt with daunting and unprecedented complexities, for the Gallipoli expedition saw the first major fusion of aircraft, large steam-powered armored warships, and vast ground forces requiring large amounts of supplies. It was also the first major assault landing against a position alerted and defended by sizeable forces of a major power equipped with modern automatic weapons and heavy artillery. In grappling with all this, Hamilton and his staff overcame many handicaps. Although provided with only sketchy background material and inaccurate maps, they drew up a landing site plan, which was then refined by Admiral de Robeck and his lieutenants and which blended land, sea and air elements.

The Navy arranged to gather boats, barges, auxiliary vessels, and warships, and to provide small craft pilotage, shore installation construction, naval gunfire target designation, lightering of transport and water, scheduling of all ship movements, coastal navigation, weather forecasting, minesweepings, aerial reconnaissance, command and control—as well as preparing procedures for the grim contingency of partial or complete withdrawal. As the special landing craft were being built and others modified, extensive loading and reloading of equipment was carried out in Egypt. Inter-Allied communications and logistics were dealt with, and a special deception scheme featuring dummy battleships was prepared. Yet amid all this work, done in barely a month, no full-dress planning exercises or rehearsals with troops and ships were carried out.

The expedition moved forward in mid-April to marshal in the Mudros harbor on Lemnos in the Aegean, amid a flurry of political and diplomatic byplay. In Britain, opposition mounted again to diverting troops from France and Flanders, where major offensives were also being prepared. The complex diplomatic dealings with Russia and Greece increased, as did British concerns for maintaining imperial prestige in "the East."

In late April, Nemesis hovered close over the Allied armada of seventy-seven ships bearing 75,000 troops. General Liman von Sanders' defending force of mainly Turkish troops, with a few German units, nearly equaled the Allied forces. The dry, rocky, tortuous, and steep topography and a vast jumble of natural obstacles favored the defenders, who virtually looked down the throats of the invaders. Since the expedition's preparations and obvious destination could not be concealed, especially after the move to Mudros, the plan hinged on the tactical surprise that would be caused by five simultaneous landings. The British 29th Division would land all at once on separate beaches around Cape Helles, the southern tip of the seventy-mile-long Gallipoli peninsula, while the Australian-New Zealand ANZAC Corps assaulted Gaba Tepe, fifteen miles up the western side. Two major feints were aimed at distracting the defenders, one by the French Corps, across the Southern Straits at Kum Kale, and one by the Royal Naval Division, with a heavy naval bombardment and elaborate fake embarkations, far up the west side of the peninsula, threatening its thin neck.

Optimism in the Allied camp was widespread but not universal. In 1906, British planners examining the landing of large forces in the Levant had considered Gallipoli and rejected it as a bad risk. Interservice relations remained strained at the top. There was strong personal animus between the aloof and crafty Lord Kitchener and the pugnacious First Sea Lord, Admiral Sir John Fisher, who, being a rung lower on the hierarchical ladder, chafed at having to defer to the magisterial "K," whom even Churchill deferred to in British War Council meetings and in respect to defense matters generally. The rapport between Churchill and Fisher, so strong while they modernized the Royal Navy before the war, now crumbled. The latter, like Achilles, sulked in his tent, but, unlike the Achaean hero, never came back on the field.

On April 25, the Gallipoli ordeal began. The assaults all fell far short of their objectives as confusion and lost chances abounded. Naval gunfire support, hampered by confusion and inadequate control, proved far less effective than hoped. Two battalions landing at undefended "Y" beach could have easily taken the commanding heights, but sat down to brew tea and sight-see, their colonels uncertain as to their mission or who was in command. As some detachments wandered far inland, Hamilton hesitated to override the commander in the zone, and rejected urgings of De Robeck's deputy, Commodore Roger Keyes, to commit his reserve on "Y" beach and cut across the peninsula, perhaps the foremost lost chance of success in the nine-month campaign. There were to be many of those on both sides, for the next morning, after the Turks deployed local reserves and inflicted 700 casualties on the British, and the landing force, stricken by panic, began to withdraw, the Turks lost nerve in the face of stiffening resistance and pulled back.

The forces landing on "S" and "X" beaches, like their comrades on "Y," met little opposition, but sat tight, awaiting orders that never came. In sharp and grim contrast, those landing at "W" and "V" met immediate and ferocious resistance. The latter became a slaughterhouse, as landing barges and the steamer *River Clyde* grounded unguided, all those aboard dead or wounded. As the sun rose, after airmen reported a broad crimson band of blood along the surf line off "V," the follow-up force was diverted to "W." Although the ANZACs had landed a mile away from their designated beach, they pressed inland, then collided with the Turkish 19th Division, rallied and deployed by the young General Mustapha Kemal. Although the ANZACs' commander, General Birdwood, wanted to pull out, Hamilton ordered him to stay and "dig, dig, dig"— purportedly the origin of the Australians' appellation of "Digger." By sunset on the 25th, the Turks, under massive naval bombardment and with half their forces lost in the landing zones, had held their foes on every beachhead far short of their objectives.

The Allied failure was later traced by the Dardanelles Commission to many causes, including the widespread lack of aggressiveness at all command levels and excessive secrecy on Hamilton's part. With strategic surprise lost in March and then tactical surprise in April, another stalemate developed—a microcosm of the state of affairs on the Western Front that the Gallipoli operation had been designed to remedy. As in the West, there were many harsh "lessons learned."[7] The inflated expectations regarding naval gunfire, based on the success of high-angle Krupp howitzers in Belgium in 1914, had been dashed and control systems were found wanting. The weak Turkish performance in the Balkan Wars of 1908–13 led to over-optimism. In the realm of jointness, the Allies failed to fully integrate higher-level staffs, to work out methods in detail, and to conduct exercises. Many recognized that problems remained unremedied. Although close and cordial relations between the services on the scene marked the rest of the campaign, they fell short of fully structured integration. Command facilities were not co-located; neither were staffs interleaved. As a lack of aggressiveness persisted at the upper levels, dissension within each service grew more intense as Gallipoli's poison worked its way into the Allied, and especially the British, political and military hierarchies.

Opinions and perspectives wavered and changed throughout the campaign.

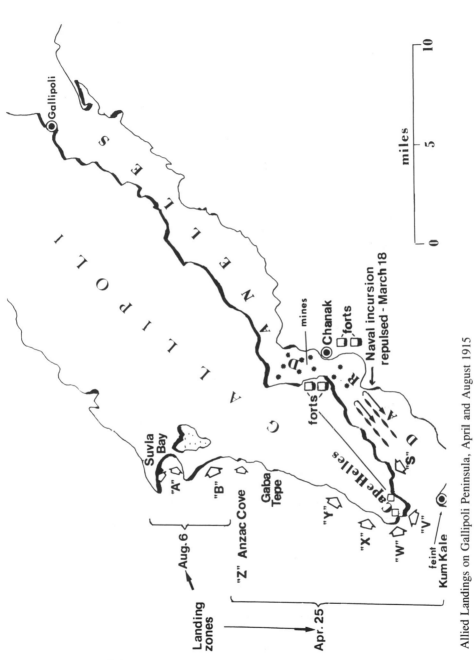

Allied Landings on Gallipoli Peninsula, April and August 1915

Admiral de Robeck, for example, had at first called for a landing, then for more ground forces after the failures on the 25th, then for another naval thrust. At the end of 1915, he blocked Keyes' proposal that the fleet assault the Straits. Nevertheless, De Robeck's men crowded the decks of the fleet to cheer Hamilton when he departed, proving jointness greater in the field than in the high seats of power.

As stagnation prevailed, the Allies anguished throughout the remainder of 1915 over whether to hang on, raise the ante, or quit. Political motives for staying on Gallipoli were much the same as those that had led to the expedition. In 1914, all the warring powers' governments and most of their military leaders expected the war to last only a few weeks. By the autumn of 1915, after two major British and two French attacks on the Western Front failed to break through, the quarter of a million Allied troops on Gallipoli were seen more and more as a relatively cheap way to divert German attention and tie up nearly half the strength of the Turkish Army, which might otherwise move against Russia or Egypt.

While discussion followed discussion, the campaign became a tactical quagmire for both sides. Both sides launched frontal attacks repeatedly, each facing unique but complementary problems. The Allies almost always had to advance up steep, twisting valleys, ridges, or hills, often without well-coordinated artillery support, or at times very little support at all, as the munitions shortage that erupted into a scandal in Britain led to a tight rationing of shells. The Turks' chronic problems, on the other hand, included being usually silhouetted against the skyline and frequent hammering from the big guns of the Allied fleet, whose volume and accuracy improved.

After a coalition government was formed in Britain in the spring, Churchill's star fell steadily. In May, De Robeck's call for another major naval stroke was derided in the War Council, soon to be renamed the Dardanelles Committee. Lord Fisher resigned, and Churchill's political fortunes seemed to be dashed forever. In November, he left Parliament and returned to what had been the career of his youth, taking command of a battalion in the trenches in France.

As the first major debate over unification of the armed services erupted in Britain with no ultimate resolution, the pitiless scorching summer on Gallipoli brought more casualties and truly hellish torment to both sides.[8] Thousands of bodies rotting between the lines raised a fierce stench, and clouds of flies beset all living creatures, gathering in buzzing clumps on food. Repellents had no effect, and netting and screening became rare treasures, while the swamped medical facilities approached the squalor of the Crimea. Lack of fresh food and water shortages added to the toll, and by early August, the fourteen Allied and sixteen Turkish divisions on Gallipoli were all wracked by various malaises that sapped both will and body.

In the last series of Allied attacks that began on August 6th, four British and two French divisions made slight gains at Cape Helles, and the ANZACs drew down Turkish reserves while three New Army divisions went ashore at Suvla

Bay. Once again, Nemesis stalked the beaches, as a chance to exploit weak local Turkish defenses was lost by the sluggish indecision of 9th Corps' commander, General Sir Frederick Stopford. Chosen as the most senior general available for a major command, Stopford had no such experience and had commanded no troops for many years. Whatever the effects of habits implanted in colonial warfare and the "old boy" system, Hamilton once again stood aloof as he had on April 25, deferring to a subordinate's authority as an opportunity was lost.

After Stopford and other commanders ignored chances to move forward at several points, the leisurely pace of their advance at Suvla, once it began, gave Mustapha Kemal another chance to plug gaps in the Turkish defenses, ruthlessly forcing his exhausted and confused troops in a counterattack that routed one of the "Kitchener Army" divisions. When Hamilton finally intervened and confronted Stopford and other commanders on the 8th, his orders layered onto theirs only further confused troops in motion under other directives. By August 10th, Kemal's 19th Division had routed a British brigade and the Turks held the key terrain around all the beachheads.

Once again, the Allies sensed a great opportunity lost, but, again, did not know how close success had been. In despair, the Turks almost abandoned the peninsula and only sharp prodding from von Sanders and Kemal drove them back to hold their positions. The gains won by major thrusts east of Anzac Cove by British, Indian, and ANZAC troops were wiped out in yet another counterattack led by Kemal, and the pattern was much the same at Cape Helles.

Major Allied attacks launched in mid- and late August also failed. On the 15th, Irish troops, poorly supplied with ammunition by the sluggish Stopford, nearly turned the Turkish flank, but were reduced to throwing rocks, and then were halted by tautly stretched Turkish defenses. The biggest Allied attack of the campaign came at Suvla on August 21, spearheaded by the 29th Division brought in from Cape Helles. After it failed in a bewildering haze of fog and local brushfires, Hamilton relieved Stopford and two other senior commanders. Amid all the hesitancy and floundering, Hamilton's relations with the Navy had remained cordial throughout, and aside from his brush with Keyes, and in spite of the lack of a joint structure, a high degree of cooperation prevailed at the operational level.

Autumn brought stagnation, and the winter more miseries. Fierce cold and blizzards were frequent, high winds and surf often assailed the exposed beaches, and during periods of calm, the plumes of smoke and steam aided Turkish gunners. Hamilton, in a deepening depression suffered by many in his command, begged in vain for more reinforcements and supplies. The Turks, too, were enervated, and minor fraternization became customary at various points along the perimeters. Another mirage of Allied victory appeared in the form of promises of major French reinforcement, which faded in September, however, after Bulgaria joined the Central Powers against Serbia. That shifted the Allies' attention to their base at Salonika, to which Hamilton was ordered to send two divisions.

After its pro-Allied government under Venizelos fell, Greece declared neutrality. In early October, with the Allied governments now debating between Salonika and the Dardanelles, Hamilton was asked by Kitchener to calculate probable evacuation losses, and his staff's extreme estimate of 40,000 was to hang like a sinister cabalistic talisman over the mounting gloom and resignation. After Hamilton became the scapegoat and was relieved, Kitchener visited the front in mid-November to judge Keyes' urgings to let the Navy off the leash for one last big try, in contrast to the proposal of General Sir Charles Monro, Hamilton's successor, to withdraw and use the forces elsewhere. After yet further indecision, Kitchener, resigned to major losses in the evacuation, gave orders at the beginning of December to end the prolonged agony.

The most brilliant phase of the Gallipoli affair now unfolded. While many shared Kitchener's fears of final carnage, the evacuation, like the Achaeans' first departure from Troy, was adroitly conceived and carried out with smooth stealth. Since the opposing trenches were only ten yards apart in some areas, and the Turks dominated the heights, the unavoidable sounds and sights of massing ships and troops led many to expect the Turks and Germans would concentrate fire and deploy reserves faster than Allied forces could leave. The direst visions had the Germans and Turks alerted at the very outset, and the evacuation disintegrating into panic and sheer butchery, with the fate of those aboard the *River Clyde* on the first day played out on a vast scale. Even relative optimists foresaw that after the first increments withdrew by appearing to be part of apparently routine traffic, and even some larger forces got away, the decline of activity and random fire would signal withdrawal to the foe, and some units would be overwhelmed.

Detailed evacuation planning was overseen by Lieutenant-Colonel Brudenell White, widely viewed as the most able Australian staff officer of the war, and Brigadier General Cecil Aspinall-Oglander. A shadow armada of small boats was gathered beyond the horizon in remote coves of the Greek isles. Vast hospitals were set up in the Nile Delta, and a fleet of medical vessels arrived, including converted Cunard-White Star liners. As the area was sealed off by naval forces and fake disease quarantines isolated the nearby Greek islanders, quite incredibly, the matter of evacuation was raised in the House of Lords, including details of General Monro's proposals. But the fates now smiled on the Allies, clouding the minds of the Turks and Germans, who judged the debate a British ploy.

Wounded and sick were already being routed out of the area instead of being treated locally, and more and more units were sent into "reserve." In mid-December, when the forces at Suvla and Anzac Cove were told of the plan, the news of failure caused no major slump in morale, and many volunteered to be the last off, ending planners' concerns about placing the leaders and best fighters in the last echelon to ensure discipline and fend off Turkish all-out attacks. A cycle of false replacements was set up, with men sneaking aboard vessels after sundown, then swaggering ashore at daybreak. Incremental reduction in artillery and small arms fire blended with a final smattering, as fewer and fewer guns fired more and more and were constantly shifted. Large arrays of dummy camp-fires were lighted each night.

Jointness reached its apogee amid these complex activities. Nocturnal boat traffic increased as supplies were prepared for destruction by fire or chemicals, while close air patrolling fended off German and Turkish reconnaissance. Improvised self-firing weapons were actuated as the exodus progressed. Over half of the troops were gone from Anzac by December 18th, and on the 20th—deemed ''Zed'' (Z) Day—the last 20,000 came out, beneath the intersecting trajectories of a major artillery duel. Animals were killed and supplies dumped *en masse* as the numbers in the trenches dwindled steadily. Before dawn on the 21st, after booby traps and barriers were set, the final vessel swung out from the shore as a huge mine dug beneath the Turkish trenches was detonated, triggering a vast winking arc of fire across the Turkish front. Only field hospital and medical personnel attending the very seriously wounded were left behind. At Suvla, there were no casualties. Those watching from the tail end of the armada at sunrise saw Turks swarming amidst the stacks of burning and abandoned stores. They salvaged much, but the evening after the withdrawal, the gods' wrath took the form of a heavy gale, drenching Suvla and Anzac Cove and tearing the piers asunder.

After Christmas, the British government approved Monro's request to withdraw the Cape Helles forces, and, in early January, the last sad chapter was written. As the French left, the battered 29th Division's remnants were put ashore to hold their zone. The weather worsened and rumors abounded as the Allied force shrank, their foes not believing that they would leave. Then, the long-feared nightmare came on January 7, as the Turks struck a massive blow. After hours of heavy shelling, masses of their infantry rose from the trenches, met a wall of fire, and reeled back. By nightfall, carpets of dead lay between the trenches, and all was as it had been before. Irony fell upon irony as the evacuation proceeded unhindered. Von Sanders saw the stiff defense as proof of British determination to stay, as for the first time, ''Johnny Turk'' began refusing to attack, in open defiance of his commanders. The final departure, as at Suvla and Anzac Cove, was punctuated by barrages and spells of quiet, against a faint counterpoint of thuds and crunching of boots on dirt, sand, gangplanks, piers, and decks. The fates frowned again after nightfall, as a storm interrupted the withdrawal several times, but the cooperation of seamen and soldiers overcame various hitches. Just before dawn, the last troops, including a divisional commander, were taken off against a backdrop of flickering crimson and gold blasts, fires from dumps, and shimmering Turkish flares, the pyre of a host of hopes and dreams.

The British official historian concluded that the central cause of operational failure at Gallipoli was Sir Ian Hamilton's excessive secrecy, which deprived his subordinate commanders of the sense of the general concept that might have caused them to seize initiatives at crucial points, and that stemmed in turn from entrusting the "chief command in the operation . . . to a general without the experience of high command in war." Beyond the suggestion of scape-goating, that line of argument would seem to doom any major joint operation commanded by a general lacking such experience to failure. Yet in many joint operations, some veteran commanders failed while some who were unseasoned triumphed. Alan Moorehead noted several other ironies. Although decorations were awarded to Monro and his deputy, no campaign medal was struck for the Dardanelles campaign. The cautious Monro was sent to command a field army in the BEF, while Admiral Wemyss, thirsting for glory, was ordered to the Far East. While it seemed that much was paid for naught, many techniques of modern jointness came out of the Gallipoli debacle, but the drawing of lessons was highly impressionistic and selective. Although various procedural checklists used by the British and U.S. navies over the next generation were derived from close studies of Gallipoli experience, many lessons were learned the hard way again and again in World War II, such as the need for: co-located naval and army gunnery control officers ashore; beachmasters and adequate beach parties; careful organization of supplies; diversions drawing enemy attention from main landing areas; special naval shells and fuses; gunfire control and targeting systems; and a headquarters ship dedicated only to command function.[9]

The broader historical impact of the Dardanelles is hard to appraise. It is still often referred to as a fiasco. A shrill and oft-quoted critique in American military and naval circles after World War I was Captain Puleston's caustic study that concluded with his doubt that "even Great Britain could survive another World War and another Churchill."[10] Others, like Churchill in *The World Crisis* and Lord Hankey in *The Supreme Command*, saw the Dardanelles as a lost oppor-tunity and assigned failure to "vacillation, delay and divided counsels."[11] Some suggested that Churchill, as prime minister in World War II, having suffered so much personally from the failure, shaped his strategic preferences and methods in its shadow.[12] More recent judgments have been cast in light of the relatively small resources committed and the huge rewards to be reaped if the expedition succeeded, or have focused on the inadequate command mechanisms at the highest levels and on the spot.[13] That it was grand tragedy in a special sense, in a war full of tragedies, there is no doubt from any quarter.

Oesel Island

The only other sizeable joint operation in World War I, much smaller than Gallipoli, was mounted by the Germans in the Baltic Sea against a less determined foe in a less hostile setting.[14] They sought to turn the Russian right flank by taking the islands of Oesel and Moon in the mouth of the Gulf of Riga. Operations were controlled by General von Hutier's 8th Army Headquarters at Libau, with the 42nd Division as the core assault unit, along with independent army battalions and a naval landing force. In the early fall of 1917, the German Navy had searched the Baltic ports for small craft, lighters, and barges to carry the landing force of 20,000 men. As several flotillas were massed for mine-marking and sweeping, thirty heavy units of the Baltic Fleet and dozens of smaller vessels escorted the transports, fended off surface attacks neutralized fortifications, made a major diversion into the gulf, and bid, an antisubmarine net. About seventy-five aircraft of various types, including six airships, were in support.

While Vice Admiral Schmidt's fleet trained the Army in landing methods in late September, the invasion fleet, including nineteen transports, moved rapidly eastward from Kiel to Libau. Aerial photo-reconnaissance, used cautiously to avoid alerting the Russians, helped in the choosing of landing sites in Tagga Bay. Much in the manner of most major amphibious operations throughout World War II, a lack of sufficient landing craft made it impossible to put all the assault units ashore simultaneously. In this case, an infantry regiment, a field artillery battery, and two waves were required.

On October 9, the force rapidly embarked from piers and anchored off Libau while advance naval landing forces went ashore on Oesel Island. After lightships took up stations on buoys placed by a U-boat, the main force left Libau from 6:30 A.M. to 12:25 P.M. on October 11, screened by over thirty torpedo boats. In a calculated risk, since minesweepers had not cleared the approach channel, Admiral Schmidt ordered the force to proceed, reaching Tagga without loss at 3:00 A.M. on October 12th. At 5:30 A.M., a special storm-troop company, in a battleship's motorboats towed ashore by a light cruiser, overwhelmed two Russian heavy batteries under the cover of destroyers' gunfire. Then, battleships' and battle cruisers' fire smothered the main shore batteries, while the transports, bearing the main force, screened by destroyers, entered Tagga Bay at 6:45 A.M.

As the sun rose, aircraft bombs and destroyer gunfire engulfed the Russian guns. At 9:00 A.M., the landing force began to board ships' boats lowered from the davits of transports whose captains risked grounding to minimize ship-to-shore transit. A battalion had been put ashore by 9:15 A.M., while Russian howitzer fire fell near the transports without result. Signal flags and large numbered placards placed by the naval parties accompanying the storm troops did not prevent some confusion, even though signal parties had preceded the main force. Indeed, several classic command-and-control problems were noted: poor Army-Navy radio net meshing; the lack of radio links to air elements; too much radio "chatter" and long, garbled messages; and the lack of a dedicated command ship.

In spite of spells of bad weather, landing operations continued for the next thirty-six hours, supplemented by modified harbor barges, rafts, and shallow-draft lighters. Eighty field guns, over 10,000 horses, 500 tons of ammunition, 2,200 vehicles and almost 600 tons of other supplies went ashore, as the landing force took all objectives, and captured 140 Russian guns and over 20,000 prisoners of war. At a cost of 396 German casualties, almost evenly divided between ground and naval forces, the landing set the stage for the German seizure of Riga, and presented the new Bolshevik regime with an immediate threat to Petrograd, its seat of power. While not perfect in execution, and carried out

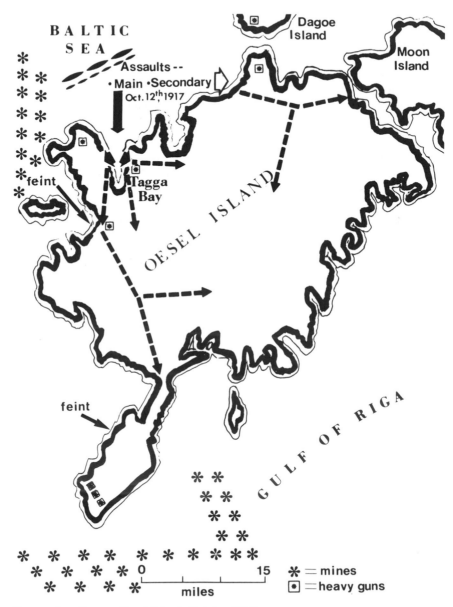

German Landings on Oesel Island, October 1917

against a foe whose morale and cohesion were crumbling, the Oesel expedition was the only successful opposed amphibious assault in World War I.

OTHER VARIANTS OF JOINTNESS

Beyond Tanga, Gallipoli, and Oesel Island, there were many instances of effective interservice meshing in the "Great War," including the German Navy's use of zeppelins for strategic bombing, and of sailors and marines in ground combat in China and East Africa; the deployment of American Marines and naval guns and French naval infantry in trench warfare in France; the key role played by Russian sailors as shock troops (and propagandists) in the Bolshevik Revolution; the Royal Naval Division's service in Belgium, on Gallipoli, and on the Western Front;[15] and the participation of the Royal Naval Air Service in the air defense of Britain, in which initial efforts at interservice cooperation were well short of ideal. The mounting German airship attacks against British cities cut across intense Army-Navy rivalry over aircraft production that resembled that of the Japanese armed services of World War II. Initial attempts to fuse the services in the air defense area saw the typical pattern of cooperation in the field being higher than at the top. As in other areas, the necessary diffusion of responsibility and decision in air defense stood in tension with the naval reflex to keep all reins short and tight, under the principle that the captain of a ship is held accountable for everything aboard his ship. Glimpsing a new order of things, a veteran of the air defense effort echoed Admiral Sir Percy Scott's call for "unity of control," suggesting that the "one and only method [with] . . . any prospect of success [was] . . . creation of a unified control of the national defense."[16]

The increasing diversity and complexity of jointness in World War I was a function of the surge in industrial technologies being applied to warfare, and of an increasing degree of division of labor and application of industrial methods in mass armies. For example, five U.S. Navy fourteen-inch railway guns in France fired 782 shots from early September to the end of the war. Since the largest Royal Navy ordnance ashore were twelve-inch guns, the American weapon served as the major counter-poise to the Germans' Langenboom guns, whose 24-mile reach allowed them to harass traffic off British ports directly across the English Channel.[17] The German Navy's specially designed "Paris Gun" (often misidentified as "Big Bertha"), perhaps the most elaborate special weapon of World War I, also involved complex jointness. Its siting and logistical networks meshed with Army supply and transport elements, and its firing schemes were intricately blended with Army artillery operations to mask its location.

Another glimpse of a new order of jointness came on St. George's Day, April 23, 1918, in the form of a Royal Navy-Royal Marine raid, which lasted about an hour, against German harbor installations at Zeebrugge on the Belgian coast. Although it failed to neutralize that submarine base, the operation received great public acclaim, more for the heroism of those engaged in steering blockships and troopships into position under close and heavy fire and for the audacity of storming parties cut down as they debarked on the quays than for its actual effect. A later enterprise of similar design at Ostend was somewhat more successful. Beyond its being seen as a heartening demonstration of boldness, Zeebrugge had a delayed effect on the history of joint operations. The commander of the operation, Vice Admiral Roger Keyes, won the Victoria Cross, and his reputation for being a fire-eater at Zeebrugge and at Gallipoli led Winston Churchill to name him Director of Combined Operations a generation later. By the end of the war, however, the British High Command structure was not a mutually supporting blend but two parallel structures that essentially dealt with two separate problem sets, without a mechanism for triservice planning and orchestration of operations. A Naval War Staff had been formed, but joint operations like the Zeebrugge raid were seen as unique, if not anomalous.[18]

CLOSE AIR SUPPORT IN WORLD WAR I

It is not generally appreciated that close air support evolved rapidly in several of the major combatants' air forces in World War I. The German Army air service, for example, developed a special class of durable ground attack aircraft, as they and the air services of other major nations grappled with such problems as artillery observation, liaison, aerial resupply, harassment of enemy rear areas, and closely coordinated and on-call attacks in the battle zone. As with other forms of jointness, close air support hinged on rapport between and among service command echelons and the complex interlacing of communications systems and doctrine. After World War I, it was seen very much as Saturday's child and far from preferred practice in most air forces, partly due to the fact that it harnessed air power to the immediate service of armies or navies, and was seen as both a waste of resources and a symbol of submission. To many U.S. airmen between the World Wars and in the early phases of World War II, close air support became a symbol of ground commanders tethering the air arm to serve as an artillery supplement of the ground forces.[19] Some saw it as a contaminant of the tactical purity of ground or naval combat.[20]

Nevertheless, close air support became well developed in World War I. In mid-May 1917, even as the Royal Flying Corps suffered heavy losses at the hands of the German Army's air service, the first steps were taken to provide direct air support to elements of British Third Army attacking astride the Scarpe River in the battle of Arras.[21] At the same time, on the other side, combat support squadrons (*Schlachtstaffeln*) were being formed to bolster the morale of German ground troops in Flanders and the coastal areas, and these successes led to an expanded program. Initially, reconnaissance aircraft were converted to the purpose, while, later, armored types were built to support attacking infantry and to neutralize enemy machine guns.[22] By the summer of 1918, as Allied air forces gained superiority over the Western Front, air support reached a high level of practice across a range of functions, including direct attack on targets in cooperation with ground troops, air contact to aid higher echelons in locating forces in motion, adjustment of artillery fire, and dropping messages and supplies.[23]

Ultimately, development of an air support system that would allow ground forces to use the capacity of aircraft to move quickly hinged upon effective radio systems. As in indirect artillery support, signalling devices other than radios and telephones such as panels, flares, lights, and klaxons, allowed some linking of ground units with aircraft. Errors in perception and confusion persisted, and such devices allowed no conversation or rapid exchange of complex data. Although transportable radios went into service in the last months of World War I, they used code transmission. Rapid response and fine-tuning was out of reach in World War I. "Robust" airborne radio-telephone systems were a generation away, and widespread use of flexible voice transmission systems would be needed to provide the seedbed from which rapid, precise close air support systems would evolve. Beyond that, over the next generation, many believed artillery a cheaper and more accurate way to support ground forces.

Close air support also raised a range of thorny questions about command process. One of those was elementally structural. In the near-chaos of modern battle, close air support offered a way to overcome the errors and complexities of the vast information networks that flowed from headquarters to forward units. Even in the ponderous infantry-artillery battles along the great trench lines in 1914–17, the utility of information degraded rapidly as a function of time and distance from the battle zone. Beyond the demonstrated utility lay a series of interlocking paradoxes. Many airmen opposed having their forces controlled by ground commanders, while they, along with tank advocates and submariners, were widely seen as a threat to the military-naval status quo. Like the artillerymen and engineers of the seventeenth and eighteenth centuries, as bourgeois technicians and proletarian artisans, both advocates and masters of the mechanization and rationalization (and hence de-romanticization of war) undercut the dominance of aristocratic officer corps. Like the light infantry tactics of the Napoleonic age, the "new ways of war" raised perhaps the most vital structural—and political—question, which is still being debated at the end of the twentieth century: At what level in the chain of command should the flow of combat information lead to decision and action?

The premium on speed of thought in mechanized warfare on the ground and in the air, and on what Russian psychologist Boris Teplov deemed "operational thinking," as compared to more deliberate analysis and reflection, also implied a need for moving the control of battle down the chain of command, at least until communications technology allowed central orchestration at a higher level of effectiveness than had been seen during the Great War. While an obvious corollary was a need for younger commanders, such implications were not widely accepted by those at the highest levels of power, military or civilian, in most nations after World War I. Neither were the new forms of mechanization all that popular at lower levels in the armed forces. For example, in spite of being proven marginal, horse cavalry remained a key element in British and American tactical doctrine. More importantly, to the extent that jointness in its various forms was seen to lie beyond the "tribal" boundaries of the main military-naval-air structures, and to be linked to a threatening military-technical, and by derivation, social revolution, it shared the orphan's plight of the array of "new ways" being shunted off to the far margin of concerns between the world wars.

Air support was not wholly abandoned, however. After the war, as various air forces and armies continued to address the problem with varying degrees of enthusiasm, "lessons" were no more easily preserved and passed along in the realm of close air support than those learned in other types of joint operations. The American Army's Air Service had observed British and French methods extensively, but much was still left to be learned the hard way, especially in structuring air-ground communications techniques and channels,[24] even though the British had first worked out such procedures by 1915.[25]

PERCEPTIONS OF MARGINALITY: JOINTNESS, 1914–18

Since World War I ended just as close air support was hitting its stride, techniques and equipment were lost in the often chaotic dismantling of forces. Beyond that, the focus of many airmen was set on other roles for air power, most essentially, the mounting of massed heavy bomber attacks. By the time the next major war in Europe came a generation later, most ground commanders were dubious, airmen were loath to engage in such practices, and the experiences of World War I, as those of China and Spain, were discounted.[26]

Beyond that, in spite of many advances, joint operations were seen to be well off to the side of the turbulent mainstream of war that major commanders and staffs, governments, and industrialists struggled to navigate in World War I. At the war's beginning, the basic forms of military operations were not far in essence from those seen at the end of the American Civil War, in Prussia's wars of expansion, and in the Russo-Japanese and the Balkan Wars. Mass armies were mainly made up of riflemen, supported by horse cavalry, light, mobile artillery, and a sprinkling of machine guns. They were deployed from railways, and their movement and logistics, coordinated mainly by telegraphy, were dependent on horsedrawn transport. Those themes were amplified on the great fixed fronts— the Eastern, Western, the Italian, and Salonika—on which the strategic balance of World War I hinged. Slightly modified by aviation, mechanization, wireless telegraphy, and poison gas until late 1918, the basic tactical pattern remained the grinding battles of infantry and artillery.

Orchestrating the complex tangles produced by surging technological innovation and mass forces exceeded the capacity of military staffs and governments for much of the war. The sense of fatalism seen in the Dardanelles campaign sprang from deeper wellsprings of general frustration, and a growing sense among the armies and navies and their parent societies that, in Emersonian terms, things were, indeed, in the saddle and riding them. Perhaps due to the sense of futility of trying to grapple with those grim torrents, or as a reaction to the vast horror, many military professionals ignored or rejected the implications of the "new ways of war." Beyond introducing bewildering technical complexities to the intricate matrices of combat, new types of jointness—both parallel to and linked directly in some instances with tanks, aircraft, submarines, and chemical warfare—eroded old forms and traditions of warfare, and increased the engineers', scientists', and artisans', that is, the bourgeoisie's control over warfare.

In any event, such variants of jointness as amphibious warfare, close air support, and special operations, viewed as sideshows during the war, were shunted offstage as the guns grew cold in late 1918. With most of the vast armies and navies quickly shrinking, many at high levels in the armed forces of the victorious powers felt it was time to get back to business or "soldiering" as usual, which often meant scrapping the various technical systems that had appeared during the war, or putting them well off to the side. It was also widely believed that many such exotic activities had been momentary novelties and would have little significance in future wars, whose outcome, if indeed they came at all, would hinge, not on crackpot diversions, but on nations' ability to deploy battleship fleets and masses of infantry and artillery. Relatively few voices were raised in opposition to such prevailing wisdom, which included the widely shared conclusion that the Dardanelles campaign had demonstrated the futility of amphibious assaults against fixed defenses and that airplanes, aside from limited reconnaissance and ground attack roles, were marginal in the larger equation of warfare.

It was Nelson's "a ship cannot fight a fort" in modern dress.

NOTES

1. Charles B. Burdick, *The Japanese Siege of Tsingtao: World War I in Asia* (Hamden, CT: Archon, 1976), pp. 80–86.

2. For various perspectives of the Tanga landing and withdrawal, see Charles Miller, *Battle for the Bundu: The First World War in East Africa* (New York: Macmillan, 1981); Paul von Lettow-Vorbeck, *East African Campaigns* (New York: Robert Speller, 1957); Heinrich Schee, *Deutsch-Östafrika im Weltkriege* (Berlin: Deutsche Verlag, 1935); and L. H. Gann and Peter Duignan, *The Rulers of German Africa* (Stanford: Stanford University, 1977); and for a brief survey of the Tanga landing, Gallipoli, and the Gulf of Riga, see James B. Agnew, "From Where Did Our Amphibious Doctrine Come?" *Marine Corps Gazette* 63:8 (August 1979): 52–59.

3. A. J. Barker, *The Bastard War: The Mesopotamian Campaign of 1914–1918* (New York: Dial Press, 1967), pp. 65–67, 310, 418.

4. Sir Charles Lucas, ed., *The Empire at War*, Vol. iv (Humphrey Milford, U.K.: Oxford University Press, 1924), p. 116.

5. For detailed accounts, see the British and Australian official histories; Winston Churchill, *The World Crisis* (New York: Scribner's, 1927); Alan Moorehead, *Gallipoli* (New York: Harper & Row, 1956); and for a British political-diplomatic perspective, see

Llewellyn Woodward, *Great Britain and the War of 1914–1918* (London: Methuen, 1967).

6. See James L. Stokesbury, *British Concepts and Practices of Amphibious Warfare, 1867–1916* (doctoral dissertation, Duke University, 1968).

7. For a list of lessons, see *The Final Report of the Dardanelles Commission*, Part 2, *Conduct of Operations, etc.*, Cmd. 371 (London: His Majesty's Stationery Office, 1919), pp. 6–26.

8. John Gooch, *The Plans of War: The General Staff and British Military Strategy, 1900–1916* (London: Routledge and Kegan Paul, 1974), p. 322.

9. Maurice Hankey, *The Supreme Command 1914–1918* (George Allen and Unwin, 1961), pp. 382, 391, 401; and Beda von Berchem, "The German Oesel Expedition," *U.S. Naval Institute Proceedings* 59:12 (July and December 1933).

10. W. D. Puleston, *The Dardanelles Expedition: A Condensed Study* (Annapolis: U.S. Naval Institute, 1927), p. 168; also see William S. Wood, "The Dardanelles Disaster," in *Colossal Blunders of the War* (New York: Macmillan, 1932), pp. 138–55.

11. Hankey, *The Supreme Command*, Vol. 2, pp. 456–63.

12. See Trumbull Higgins, *Winston Churchill and the Second Front* (New York: Oxford University Press, 1957).

13. For example, Paul Guin, *British Strategy and Politics, 1914 to 1918* (Oxford: Oxford University Press, 1968), p. 116; Moorehead, *Gallipoli*, p. 323; and Woodward, *Great Britain and the War of 1914–1918*, p. 77.

14. Erich von Tschischwitz, *Blaujacken und der Feldgraue Gegen Oesel* (Mylau, Germany: Carl Krueger, 1934); and n.a., *The Army and Navy During the Conquest of the Baltic Islands in October 1917*, translated by Henry Hossfeld (Fort Leavenworth: Command and General Staff School Press, 1933).

15. An amalgam of various Royal Navy reserve components, as well as Royal Marine and recalled retired Guards Officers, the division resisted several energetic attempts of the army hierarchy to break down its nautical customs and traditions; cf. Douglas Jerrold, *Royal Naval Division* (London: Hutchinson, n.d. [1927]).

16. A. Rawlinson, *The Defence of London, 1915–1918* (London: Andrew Melrose, 1924), pp. vi, 256–57.

17. N.a., *The United States Naval Railway Batteries in France* (Washington: Naval Historical Center, 1988).

18. For details of the British High Command in World War I, see Bill Jackson and Dwin Bramall, *The Chiefs: The Story of the United Kingdom Chiefs of Staff* (London: Brassey's, 1992), pp. 53–108.

19. For example, James A. Warden III, *The Air Campaign: Planning for Combat* (Washington, D.C.: National Defense University, 1988), p. 103.

20. For example, see Trevor N. Dupuy, *A Genius for War* (London: MacDonald and Jane's, 1977).

21. H. A. Jones, *The War in the Air*, Vol. iii (Oxford: Clarendon Press, 1931), pp. 378–79.

22. Paul Deichmann, Noel Parrish, and Albert F. Simpson, *German Air Force Operations in Support of the Army*, ed. Little B. Atkins (New York: Arno, 1962), pp. 5–6.

23. For extensive details on methods, see H. A. Jones, *The War in the Air*, Vol. vi (Oxford: Clarendon Press, 1937), pp. 416ff.

24. For example, see William Mitchell, *Memoirs of World War I* (New York: Random House, 1969), p. 261.

25. Claude Graham-White and Harry Harper, ''Advent of Airplane Control,'' in *Aircraft in the Great War: A Record and Study* (London: T. Fisher Unwin, 1915), pp. 266–77.

26. Lee Kennett, ''Development to 1939,'' in B. Frank Cooling, *Case Studies in Close Air Support* (Washington, D.C.: Office of Air Force History, 1990), pp. 57–58.

_____ Chapter 3 _____

Backwaters and Rivulets:
Jointness Between the World Wars

U.S. ARMY-NAVY RELATIONS, 1918–40

While they were quickly receding, the tides that had run toward increased interservice meshing during World War I were recognized in the National Defense Act of 1920. The conflicting priorities and turmoil of mobilization were still clear in the memories of those who framed that legislation. Although it lacked the funding needed to give substance to its underlying philosophy of ending the "expansible Army," the act created, on paper, a large, active-reserve, multi-tiered force-in-being, which was to be led mainly by officers trained in an expanded ROTC program and overseen by a strengthened general staff. The dimension of jointness was recognized in the creation of an Assistant Secretary of War to plan for and monitor mobilization. While the Navy was not brought within the full scope of that new office, the Joint Board, with representation from the Army's new War Plans Division and the Navy's Chief of Naval Operations' staff, would meet regularly between the World Wars and address strategic questions to a degree not seen before, although that arrangement fell well short of true structural jointness.

Some in the Congress had wanted to go further. The first of a series of bills that appeared over the next quarter-century calling for service unity and a "super general staff" was submitted to the U.S. Congress a few months after World War I. In 1920, the first bill proposing a Department of National Defense was introduced into Congress by Reed Smoot, based on a concept of W. F. Willoughby, director of what later became the Brookings Institution.[1] Although none of the series would be passed into law, the executive branch dealt with some salient organizational problems by creating joint planning committees and service boards to coordinate such activities as munitions and aviation. The Joint Munitions Board was formed in response to the crucial need for a standing coordinative entity that had been recognized during World War I. Beyond that, operational coordination was addressed squarely by the services themselves in 1920, in the first version of a publication known over the years as *Joint Actions of the Army and Navy* (JAAN) and the meetings of the Joint Board now were regularized and increasingly substantive.

Initially, JAAN focused on allocating coast defense responsibilities, since large-scale amphibious operations were widely judged as unlikely or impossible after Gallipoli. The 1927 JAAN, for example, included detailed definitions and service missions; coordination of Army and Navy operations, with unity of command dealt with on a basis of mutual cooperation; nuances and questions of protocol; such wartime joint operations as overseas movement, assault landings, and coastal defense; communications, including codes; and coordinating agencies.[2] The lack of guidelines from high civilian authorities was left unaddressed. Although the State Department worked closely with the Navy and Marine Corps in such areas as Latin America and China, not until 1935 did the State Department participate in Joint Board activities regularly.

The Army and Navy did agree in the mid–1920s to allocate regional primacy of command, the principle of "paramount interest" now prevailing over "unity of command," in the establishment of the "executive agent" concept that prevailed from World War II until the late 1950s. Under JAAN ground rules, the Navy stood preeminent in the Pacific and the Army in Panama and Alaska, a division of interest that was visible in the Army's dominant role in Operation Just Cause in Panama in 1989–90.

Between the World Wars, the essence of jointness was continually being affected by advances in aviation technology. In 1931, for example, Army Chief of Staff General Douglas MacArthur and Chief of Naval Operations Admiral William Veazie Pratt concurred that coastal defense beyond 200 miles was the Navy's responsibility, while the Army Air Corps and Coast Artillery were responsible inside that limit. In the late summer of 1938, however, after the Army Air Corps staged a major media event by intercepting the Italian liner *Rex* 800 miles out at sea, the Navy moved to amend *Joint Operations of the Army and Navy* to reduce Army seaward flights to a hundred miles, while Navy land-based aircraft were unlimited in their excursions.[3] The functional collapse of the MacArthur-Pratt agreement in the late 1930s reflected that technological developments over the decade were outpaced by monitoring and the adaptation of organizational architecture, relationships, doctrine, and procedures. With many ambiguities and anomalies remaining unaddressed or unresolved by interservice "diplomacy," it became increasingly apparent that wartime operational necessity in the spirit of the Prussian concept of the "law of the situation" would prevail over concerns for precise jurisdiction so carefully addressed in war plans. Since the President, Secretary of the Navy, Secretary of War and/or the Army's and Navy's commanders had to determine when the practical demands of "unity of command" prevailed over the territorially based principle of "mutual cooperation," much ultimately fell between the figurative cracks.

Unification and Air Power

As the Great Depression intensified between 1930 and 1933, the Democrat-controlled Congress had not concurred with President Herbert Hoover's attempts to reorganize the executive branch, but also resisted Roosevelt's restructuring of Federal executive branches. The armed services were viewed as lying outside the burgeoning cluster of New Deal agencies when the search for stringent economies led to fresh demands in Congress in the early 1930s for a Joint General Staff and administrative consolidation. The Army's relatively favorable reaction and the Navy's reluctance set the polarity of a debate that would continue intermittently for the next decade. In the late 1930s, as another wave of proposalsg to create a Department of National Defense rose, the Navy hierarchy argued that since America was isolated from zones of imminent world conflict, ground-based air forces would only be able to operate if they were carried across the oceans, which seemed a fanciful prospect in that age of isolationism. In much the same spirit, Congress opposed funding development of an intercontinental bomber until 1938.

Neither was Army support of unification wholly enthusiastic, for its doctrine tethered aviation to the ground forces' needs, as did that of Japan, France, and Germany in the mid–1930s, and of the Soviet Union after Stalin's purges. As organization and doctrine lagged behind the changes being wrought by the surge in speed, range, and durability of aircraft in the 1930s, U.S. Army airmen continued to call for an independent air service, to no avail. In 1925, the Morrow Board had placed the Air Corps under close ground forces' control and, a decade later, constraints were only somewhat eased by the Drum and Baker boards' deliberations, which led to a strategic bombing force under a separate headquarters, as well as an air staff and an Assistant Secretary of War for Air.

In 1938, the prominent military journalist, George Fielding Eliot, set forth the basic line of argument that the Navy followed after 1943, attacking unified command and Department of National Defense concepts by citing several negative historical cases, including Trafalgar,[4] and opposing the creation of a separate air force.[5] In accepting the need for combined planning and suggesting a Committee of National Defense, much like the existing Joint Board,[6] Eliot correctly sensed the political realities. Another decade of lobbying, debate, and World War II stood between the air power enthusiasts and their hope for a separate Air Force, while functional fusion at the top lay half a century away.

The U.S. Marine Corps Between the Wars

Amid the bitter interservice squabbling of the late 1940s, the claim was often made that the U.S. Marine Corps had developed amphibious warfare to a high level of doctrine and practice between the World Wars. While that path was not as smooth, straight, or well-paved as suggested,[7] one key point was 1921, the year that the eccentric, ill-starred, and brilliant Marine Corps planner, Earl Hancock Ellis, completed his monograph, *Advanced Base Operations in Micronesia*, a major baseline in the U.S. Navy's war plans for fighting Japan over the next two decades. Between the wars, studies and war games at the Naval War College at Newport and at Marine Corps Staff College at Quantico were intertwined with Fleet Landing Exercises (FLEXes) conducted at various locations in the Caribbean, in Panama, and in Hawaii. These generated lessons that were ignored and relearned, some of them again and again. Such problems as a scarcity of landing craft, snarled beach activities, and problems with combat loading were carefully noted, only to reappear in subsequent exercises and in World War II operations. Although studies at the U.S. Naval War College led to the drawing of landing craft designs in 1929, there was no supply of drop-front landing craft on hand when war came, and many of the types used in World War II were derived from British designs.[8]

A significant change in organization and terminology was wrought in 1923, when the USMC Advanced Base Force became the Marine Corps Expeditionary Force, reflecting the fact that throughout the 1920s and the early 1930s, the Marines' main activity was the waging of "banana wars," that is, serving as constabulary or fighting "small wars" in the Caribbean and Central America. As the Great Depression deepened, President Hoover, moving toward a less heavy-handed American policy toward Latin America, left the Army and Navy relatively intact as he reduced the Marine Corps budget and withdrew it from Latin America. Although the Marine Corps was aligned toward amphibious warfare after 1933, its lack of funds prevented establishing permanent joint elements and continuity. Nevertheless, some gains were made. In 1935, the *Tentative Landing Operations Manual* was published, the basis for the U.S. Navy's Fleet Training Publication 167—*Landing Operations Doctrine*—of 1938.

Although ever-larger amphibious exercises up to U.S. entry into World War II enfolded Army, Navy, contract transports, and Marine elements, the quality of performance remained uneven, and administration, coordination, and institutional memory remained weak without joint staffs. The shortage of landing craft noted repeatedly would remain a chronic problem until late in World War II. And the classic view persisted that operational success depended on "the personality of the two commanders, in their ability to sink their own desire for preeminence toward the successful accompaniment of a joint task." As will be seen, that left much to fate.[9]

When, in the spring of 1941, under War Plan "Gray," a major task force was formed to land in the Azores, it was, not surprisingly, hampered by a shortage of transports as well as landing craft. Transient fusion appeared when the Army's 1st Infantry Division and the 1st Marine Division were placed under the First Joint Training Force commanded by Marine Corps Major-General Holland M. Smith. Intended for service in the Atlantic initially, Smith, the First's headquarters elements, and the 1st Marine Division were sent west in 1942 to become the core of the Marine Corps amphibious forces in the Pacific War.

After the United States' entry into World War II in December 1941, joint exercises continued on both coasts until just before Operation Torch, the invasion of North Africa in November 1942. In spite of all the efforts over two decades, the United States had no amphibious force per se, or doctrine allowing either a firm base for quick mobilization or for quick deployment at a high level of effectiveness. A year into the war, training exercises fell well short of an acceptable level of performance, and the Army had begun to build its own major amphibious command. Even though the Joint Chiefs of Staff had assigned the Navy overall control of amphibious operations in early September 1942, it was only the following spring that Army Chief of Staff General George Marshall and Chief of Naval Operations/Commander-in-Chief of the U.S. Fleet Admiral Ernest King resolved differences on that issue. The amphibious aspect of jointness, however, was only one of its facets.

CLOSE AIR SUPPORT ON THE EVE OF WORLD WAR II

By 1939, as World War II began in Europe, the design and control of air forces was subject to several conflicting polarities, including a sharp widening in speed between fighters and bombers. Seemingly clear-cut choices about apportionment of air power had been made in those countries that had formed independent air services: Italy in 1912, Britain in 1918, France in 1932, and Germany in 1935. Yet such structural independence did not mean that air services were freed from support of armies and fleets, and dedicated to strategic bombing.

Throughout the 1920s and most of the 1930s, low levels of funding in all the major western nations (apart from Germany, which had no air forces at all until the mid–1930s) had curtailed missions, warped expectations, and reinforced insularity and hostility. In Britain, decisions about which eggs to put in the proverbial baskets led to an increasing priority assigned to strategic bombing and fighter defenses in the late 1930s at the expense of cooperation with the Army. In the United States, as strategic air power advocacy rose among Army Air Corps officers wrapped in the chains of doctrine that subordinated them to the ground forces, most of their technical, intellectual, and political effort was expended on the concept of a strategic bomber force.

The most ardent strategic air advocates in the United States, like Billy Mitchell and later, Alexander de Seversky, hoped to make field armies and great fleets irrelevant by striking at the heart and key nerve centers of an enemy nation to win a quick victory. When war came, U.S. Army airmen, in spite of official doctrine, rated providing support to ground forces in close combat with enemy ground forces as a distant third priority. Their prime goal was winning air superiority and attacking deep into enemy territory, thus drying up the flow of supplies and reserves to the battlefield. By 1939, the concept of "attack aviation," that is, low-altitude strafing and light bombing by special types of heavily armored aircraft, had been abandoned in favor of "light bombardment," but without a clear doctrinal vision of how air power would support ground forces.[10]

In the late 1930s, even in air forces where close support was more readily accepted, difficulties in communication netting, and discontinuities in organization prevented quick response. In maneuvers, request-to-response time ranged from about two hours in the Soviet Union to eight hours in the French air forces.[11] All the major air forces were struggling to envision contingencies of combat and the form of the air weapon that would prove most effective in the unforeseeable context of future wars and battles. Would a scalpel be needed? A rapier? A bludgeon? An axe? Lack of certainty did not prevent many airmen from making strong assumptions and claims. This was evident in the many strong assertions regarding the pioneering and development of close air support by the U.S. Marine Corps between the World Wars, and later. Proposals for immediate support of ground combat forces were set forth in 1919 in the *Marine Corps Gazette* by the Corps' first rated pilot, Alfred A. Cunningham, and the first experiments with dive bombing were carried out in Haiti that year. Marine close-air support broke Sandino's siege at Ocotal in 1927 and was refined in subsequent operations in Nicaragua in the late 1920s and early 1930s. Although a close-air support role for Marine Corps air elements was defined in Navy and Marine Corps doctrine as it related to the Fleet Marine Force, attempts to procure an attack aircraft in the late 1930s were unsuccessful. An official history saw Marine Corps aviation on the eve of American entry into World War II with "major operational problems still unsolved and the concept of close air support itself as yet ill-defined,"[12] conforming to the Army's exclusion of those targets in the battle zone that could be brought under artillery fire.[13]

Purportedly, the U.S. Marines' tactical air and glide-bombing efforts in Nicaragua in the late 1920s and early 1930s impressed Ernst Udet, later production chief of the Luftwaffe and a top World War I ace.[14] While working as a stunt flyer in the United States in the 1920s to step around the ban on military flying in Weimar Germany that had been imposed by the Versailles Treaty, Udet purchased two Curtiss Hawk fighters in 1927 and sent them to Germany, where it has been suggested that analysis of them and subsequent bombing experiments in the early 1930s led the Luftwaffe to fixate on dive bombers. (This account is not accepted by all aviation historians.) In any event, a doctrine, later deemed "Stukamania," was developed. Based on the bombing accuracy of the Stuka JU–87 dive-bomber, it stunted Nazi long-range heavy bomber development, and retarded the Luftwaffe's development of jet fighters.[15] In the short run, however, German air tactics, although primitive by later standards, had developed far enough in exercises in Russia, 1925–35 and in Spain, 1936–39, to stun the Third Reich's foes in the early blitzkrieg campaigns of World War II.

Between the World Wars, the British fell far back from the high level of practice they had attained in close-air support by 1918. Beyond tight budgets and the higher priority assigned to air defense and bombers, the visions of the mechanized warfare advocates like J.F.C. Fuller and B. H. Liddell Hart, in which aircraft closely supported wholly mechanized armies, were unpopular in many quarters. One infantry commander formally complained that an RAF pilot in an exercise flew so "excessively low" that the "morale of the troops especially the infantry was being badly shaken by his head scraping and air-splitting dives."[16] No implication seems to have been drawn from that, although some sophisticated experimentation was carried out during British operations on the northwest frontier of India in the mid–1930s.[17]

JOINTNESS AND U.S.-BRITISH RELATIONS, 1939–41

In the late 1930s, like great planets emerging from deep space and disturbing the course of smaller worlds circling a sun, European military structures, methods, and experiences induced gravitational effects on the American defense establishment. After the Munich agreement of 1938 presaged war, a major influx of British and French capital boosted American military production, especially in the aircraft industry. After the war in Europe began in September 1939, the U.S. Neutrality Acts, passed in 1936 and 1937 to seal America off from foreign wars, were modified to allow the Allies access to the products of their investment under a "cash-and-carry" provision.

In the summer of 1939, President Roosevelt had indicated in an executive order that he as commander-in-chief would henceforth establish joint structures. After France fell in June 1940, Anglo-American military interaction, overt and covert, increased dramatically. Landmarks in Anglo-American cooperation in 1940 included the "Destroyer Deal" in September and the Tizard scientific liaison mission in October, and in March 1941, the Lend-Lease Act, and increasingly naval cooperation in the quasi-war in the Atlantic in the summer and fall. Less visible were the secret ABC–1 Agreement in January 1941, in which the United States agreed to fight Hitler first if war came, close linking of British intelligence with the U.S. Office of Strategic Services, and the combining of U.S., Canadian and British efforts in the Manhattan Project in late 1941. By August of that year, when President Roosevelt and Prime Minister Churchill met off the coast of Newfoundland to frame the Atlantic Charter, extensive collaboration had made the U.S. armed services increasingly aware of British combined operations and the Royal Air Force's evolving air support systems.

Propinquity did not lead to full emulation or to unqualified admiration. When Admiral Mountbatten, then head of Combined Operations, visited American installations on Hawaii in the late summer of 1941, he was amazed at the separation of the U.S. Army and Navy commands, a view that paralleled Lawrence Legere's observation that "the Joint Board and other joint agencies failed to accomplish satisfactory inter-service coordination between the two World Wars."[18] The Japanese attacks on Oahu on December 7 threw that lack of jointness into harsh relief.

JOINTNESS IN THE BRITISH ARMED FORCES, 1918–40

Between 1918 and 1939, the British armed forces kept jointness closer to the center of their doctrinal concern than did the Americans. Although much reduced in strength and scarred by the memory of Gallipoli, the British services continually addressed "combined operations," both amphibious warfare and other joint undertakings, in war plans and in exercises. Although full-scale service unification was not much more popular than in the United States, the British developed a rather more sophisticated counterpart to JAAN. When Ian Hamilton proposed a "United Services General Staff under a defense ministry" and a "United Service Staff College," deploring the lack of a manual on triservice coordination in 1921, the deficiency was being remedied.[19] The next year, a new chapter, No. 13, was added to British *Field Service Regulations* that addressed the problem of interservice command and set forth a doctrine based on the principle of joint responsibility, with separate staffs and commanders. Many labored over the next two decades on the complex questions of jointness as they tried to shape war plans that would not be, as Lord Hankey described those of 1914, a "toy aeroplane."[20]

The Royal Marines in Imperial Defense

As in the United States, Britain's Marines had long been an institutional form of jointness. Although their respective functions were quite different within their parent navies, both managed to survive threats of truncation between the World Wars. For the Royal Marines, the challenge came in 1923, due to the many duties they had performed during World War I, much like the U.S. Marines' tangle of roles in the early twentieth century. The next year, the Madden Report reaffirmed the spectrum of missions, including supplementing naval gun crews, raising independent Royal Marine units to seize and defend outlying bases and conduct raids under naval control, and serving as a connecting link between the Army and the Navy. The report noted that while the Royal Marines were not colonial infantry like U.S. and French marine units, that was expected to change, since Britain was the major interventionist power between the World Wars. Across the reaches of empire, the proverbial "natives" were restless, as were potential rivals, especially the Japanese and Italians. In 1927, the Royal Marines, by then recognized as the linchpin of British joint planning, doctrine, and operations, played a rapid response role in the crisis at Shanghai, as 1,000 were landed. In 1935, 1,600 Marines bolstered the major imperial naval base at Alexandria during the crisis over Mussolini's invasion of Ethiopia.

From 1918 to 1939, the British Army-Royal Navy annual combined exercises led to some refinements in doctrine and practice, but no well-equipped or sizeable standing force. The same cycle of weak institutional memory and continuity of practice seen in U.S. exercises was visible in the British 1931 and 1938 manuals. Both noted that major problems confronted in exercises had also been encountered at Gallipoli, such as the need for a clear objective in designing an operation, data on the area of activity, and secrecy and deception. The tactical and technical problems—special loading methods, beachmaster duties and the need for headquarters ships, and command and control problems—were all encountered, again and again, when war came.

The haunting after-image of Gallipoli and the relative aggressiveness of naval as compared to Army commanders in that campaign was reflected in both the Royal and U.S. navies' dominance over amphibious operations. That also sprang from the fact that naval vessels would carry an expedition, provide gunfire support, and carry supplies, and that naval commanders would decide whether or not to land or withdraw, and had to protect a landing or lodgement or carry out a withdrawal against hostile naval attack. The capital investment in equipment at risk and the need for heavy gunfire support also tipped matters in the naval direction.

British joint exercises between the World Wars were held in home waters, India and the Far East, with the defense of Singapore against seaborne invasion as a major contingency. As with American exercises, these very small operations lacked many mechanical devices and procedures that were recognized as vital, but that would not be available until the last half of World War II.[21] Ongoing exercises and the work in 1938 of subcommittees had generated a sequence of landing craft designs. Efforts along that line quickened after the Committee of Imperial Defence established, at Captain Bertram Wilson's suggestion, an Inter-Services Training and Development Center (ISTDC) near Portsmouth, under the Deputy Chiefs of Staff. The efforts of the ISTDC's small staff, commanded by Captain L.E.H. Maund, had substantial influence on British and American landing craft design and production in World War II.[22]

High-Level Interservice Relations in Britain Between the World Wars

In the United States and Britain after World War I, the powerful effect of air power upon all services, doctrine, and practice was recognized in naval circles before Billy Mitchell's bombing tests against anchored warships off the Virginia coast in 1921. Admiral William Sims, who headed U.S. naval forces in Europe during the war, urged the conservative U.S. Navy hierarchy in the early 1920s to accept the full implications of air power, while in Britain, Admiral Sir Reginald Custance envisioned land and sea battles as "one great whole" based on "mutual dependence." Foreseeing that wholly independent action by any service would be very rare henceforth, he coined the term "Aery" to represent the air service plus any combination of traditional forces.[23]

By World War I's end, the Royal Air Force (RAF) had already intruded into the traditional services' preserve, especially the Army's. When Air Marshal Sir Hugh Trenchard became Chief of the Air Staff, he gained support from Winston Churchill, now back in the government, and from T. E. Lawrence and eager young RAF officers in carving out a role for the RAF as both a rapid response element and a deterrent force in imperial policing. Both the Army and Navy opposed it, however economical it might be.[24]

Over the two decades between the wars, various political, social and economic forces impinged on British preparations for war. Many politicians and military professionals suffered from the traumas of a war whose enormous destruction and horror created a widespread sense that anything was better than another one. In Britain, massive reductions in air, ground, and naval forces, paralleled by the shift of priorities toward imperial defense, were followed by further naval cutbacks after the Washington Naval Conference of 1921–22. A ''Ten-Year-Rule''—postulating year after year that no major war would occur during the next decade—underlay the British defense budget from 1919 until the early 1930s. It undercut research and development, modernization, readiness, and the relations of the services with industry, as well as the strength and quality of active forces. The anti-militarism of the Labour Party, powerful pacifist sentiment and lobbies, the Great Depression, and appeasement all served to render the substance of British power a faint pastel behind a ruddy mask of posturing and symbolism.

Although there was no opportunity for building substantive underpinnings, let alone a solid superstructure of joint operations, some steps toward jointness at the top were taken. Some were of marginal utility. A Coordinating Committee, formed in 1923 to deal with Staff Duties in Combined Operations, generated a flow of memoranda on such subjects as landing craft, which it was recognized should be quiet and roomy, and elemental considerations of bombardment and air cooperation. For a year, much concern was devoted to interservice semantic differences, especially the RAF's mandatory ''is to'' versus the Navy's ''will.'' The committee did not sit from 1925 to 1934, when it was finally concluded that assigning officers to it was a waste of time.[25] A more solid footing was established when a Joint Planning Committee to the Chiefs of Staff was formed in 1923, and a Committee of the Chiefs of Staff, charged with formally advising the chairman of the Committee of Imperial Defense, was created.

During the war, many saw a need for a triservice structure, like Lord Haldane, who in 1917 had called for a revitalized Committee of Imperial Defence (CID). Although others urged formation of a Ministry of Defense, the Mond-Weir Committee, examining ways to further government economy, had considered how duplication in service administration might yield savings. Nevertheless, things went back to functional separateness at the top after the armistice of 1918. After the CID was blended with the Cabinet Secretariat, Maurice Hankey, as secretary of both, became a kind of shadow chief of general staff. In 1922, when the prospect of war with Turkey loomed in the Chanak crisis, dysphasia in planning and coordination between the services led Prime Minister David Lloyd George to consider the creation of a triservice structure. At the recommendation of the Salisbury Committee, a CID subcommittee of the Chiefs of Staff Committee was formed. A major step forward toward jointness, it persists in essence today in both the American and British command structures.

The Chiefs of Staff Committee did not bring service rivalry to a halt, or even reduce it, since it provided a forum for identifying, clarifying, and debating

differences. The strictures of the Ten-Year Rule and widespread pacifist sentiment were major factors in shaping the Chiefs of Staff's annual reviews. They
reflected the old polarities of a maritime imperial defense strategy versus the
Army's imperial garrisoning, as well as its concern about Soviet threats to India
and the Middle East. After 1925, the Army and RAF faced the new contingency
of sending forces to Europe to fight a Locarno War, if the guaranteed boundaries
of France, Belgium, or Germany were violated. The main cross-element that
had led to the forming of the Chiefs of Staff Committee was the air dimension.
Concern for air defense against France had risen sharply in 1922, at the same
time that the RAF was arguing vigorously that using air power in imperial defense
and "policing" dissidents was far cheaper than troops. The Navy remained
concerned about America as well as Japan, and focused much attention on
Singapore, which Trenchard, as Chief of the Air Staff, suggested could be better
defended by torpedo planes than long-range guns. Navy-RAF wrangling over
the control of aircraft carriers resulted in the ultimately baneful compromise that
the RAF would control carrier pilots and carrier-borne aircraft, an arrangement
that prevailed until 1939 and retarded British naval aviation for the next generation, and well into World War II. Yet the Chiefs of Staff Committee was a
major step toward improved lateral communication and jointness.

The rising sense of impending war in the mid–1930s led to increased funding,
both of which served to reduce interservice friction somewhat. Hankey, in his
twilight years, with the assistance of its chairman, Admiral Sir Ernle Chatfield,
had been able to bring the Chiefs of Staff Committee to a high level of cooperation
and lucidity as the source of strategic appreciations. Keeping interservice balance
was especially difficult inasmuch as the principal Conservative politicians of the
era, Stanley Baldwin and Neville Chamberlain, pitched funding priorities toward
air defense. On the other side of the Parliamentary aisle, the Labour Party had
also taken a shine to the RAF, partly due to Trenchard's aggressive courting of
it in the 1920s, but also because of its image of modernity, technology, and
relative freedom from social class bias relative to the older services, and the
promise of waging war with minimal costs and casualties. At the same time,
the debate between advocates of a peripheral, heavily maritime strategy, who
included the military theorist B. H. Liddell Hart and some Army principals,
sought to keep the Army out of a continental war and aligned toward imperial
defense.

Other major steps toward jointness came when the Imperial Defense College
was established in 1927 and in 1935, when Sir Thomas Inskip was named
Minister for Coordination of Defense.[26] Although his authority was little more
than symbolic, Inskip's rise marked the beginning of a decline in the influence
of Hankey, who flavored the defense policy process with a mix of continuity,
insight, deviousness, and aversion to systematic administration.[27] Most importantly, Inskip's appointment was an increase in degree of formal recognition of
the principle of jointness.

Yet those adjustments were incremental responses to major proposals for reform. For example, Liddell Hart, in a series of articles in the *Times* in 1935–36, proposed a Ministry of Defense under a nonpolitical civilian minister appointed for a set term. He could have been speaking of other hierarchies in other times in his critique of the pernicious effects of "give and take," a process that had led to smoothing over and avoiding principal issues and critical disjunctures.[28] Such calls for reform went unheeded, and the changes noted provided little more than a skimpy blueprint and mock-up of the structure of jointness that would be erected in the heat of battle. As Ronald Wingate observed on the eve of war, "Only the officers of the services assigned to the Committee of Imperial Defense . . . were able to see the whole picture outside the strait-jacket of their individual services."[29]

The costs of lacking a more broadly shared view did not all come due immediately when war came. The bills for a lack of long-range aircraft for escorting convoys, of a close-air support system, and of resources to carry out amphibious operations were not tendered for months or years.[30] Some of the shortfalls accruing from a lack of intelligence fusion and orchestration did not become fully visible until after the war.[31] Yet the pitch of the playing field of interservice politics and the polarity of informal alliances between the services did shift substantially in the 1930s. Army-RAF relations had strengthened as service chiefs and other principals who played major roles in World War I and engaged in turf battles, like Admiral Beatty and Air Marshal Trenchard, passed off the scene. Although an Army-Navy alliance was formed against the RAF in the early 1920s, as the Navy deferred to the Army's playing the main expeditionary force role, the conditions under which it had been framed were altered during the 1930s. The League of Nations faltered and failed as German, Italian, and Japanese intimidation and expansion mounted, and as great advances were made in aviation technology. By the mid–1930s, senior Army officers had come to see their primary roles as guardians of imperial defense and providing a force for a Locarno War, with the RAF as the main expeditionary element. At the same time, the ascendancy of air power in tactical and strategic equations reduced the airmen's anxiety while weakening the skepticism and antipathy of many soldiers and sailors, if not their anxiety about that change.[32] Nevertheless, RAF-Navy relations remained cool during much of the 1930s, and the RAF's control over air crews aboard ship until 1937 seriously retarded the modernization of the Fleet Air Arm relative to the United States and Japan.

As the resultant divergent views of each of the armed services prevented a steady alignment, rising public anxiety regarding air defense after Hitler's coming to power in 1933 was heightened by grim scenes from Ethiopia, Spain, and China, as well as popular culture visions of aerial holocaust, from Shaw's play *Heartbreak House*, to the film version of H. G. Wells' *Things to Come*. As a result, the prime concerns of the air defense of Britain, modernization of bomber command, and imperial defense put RAF support of army operations on the margin of concerns, and development of common air support doctrine and techniques in abeyance.[33]

JOINTNESS IN COLONIAL WARS

With some exceptions, a spirit of chilly distance prevailed between the British Army and Royal Air Force in colonial warfare between the World Wars. From 1918 onward, the RAF had maintained air and armored car squadrons to augment "air policing" and "air control" of "restive tribes" along imperial frontiers in the Middle East and along India's northwest frontier. At the same time, the French Army held air power on a closer rein in Morocco and Syria, where joint air-ground tactics took the form of *combinaison de colonnes*, as two or more columns of armored cars and light tanks rapidly penetrated dissident areas, preceded and covered by aircraft.

Alhucemas

It was in a colonial war, in September 1925, that France and Spain carried out the largest amphibious operation from Gallipoli to Shanghai, 1937. In 1921, the massacre of a Spanish column of 20,000 men by Rif tribesmen led by Abd el Krim had generated major political reaction in Spain, and General Primo de Rivera became virtual dictator in 1923. As the Rif insurgency spread to French Morocco, embarrassment for the Páinlève government in France mounted as the Communists opposed government policy and the costs soared. The French tried to collaborate with Spain without directly entering the war, but when an alarming counterstroke by Abd el Krim's forces threatened Tangier, and Britain organized a small force to protect the Neutral Zone, already taut Anglo French relations were strained further. (The public's romanticizing of the Rif rebels in Britain and the United States was reflected in Sigmund Romberg's musical comedy, *The Desert Song*.)[34]

In discussions between Primo de Rivera and French Marshal Henri Petain and their staffs, it was recognized that although Krim's headquarters in rough terrain at Ajdir presented overland attackers with complex defenses, it lay relatively open to the sea. Spanish staffs had studied a landing in the area since 1911, and among those involved in planning was young Colonel Francisco Franco, the Spanish Foreign Legion's co-founder.[35] On January 30, 1925, at Alcazar Soreir, twenty Spanish ships had landed 6,000 men from fifteen armored lighters.[36] The experience led to the construction or modification of some 100 special vessels, as well as the purchase from the British of twenty-six "K" lighters used at Gallipoli. The Franco-Spanish Alhucemas expedition of September 1925 was, with its 18,514 men and ninety-six aircraft, close in scale to the Oesel landing.[37] On September 8th, they landed a brigade group at Ceuta, its ultimate goal the Rifian capital of Ajdir. The 6,000-man Spanish Army combined arms task force included mountain artillery, light tank and engineer detachments, three regular infantry battalions, and two Spanish Foreign Legion *banderas*. Its overall commander was General Sanjurjo, and the assault force was under Colonel Franco. The Rifs were distracted by major French and Spanish columns driving on their bastions east and west of Tetuan and Fez, and then by a three-battalion feint at Melilla on September 2nd. After Rifian forces were diverted by another assault landing feint on September 6th, strong currents and winds drove the convoy to the west, causing a day's delay.

In the main landing on September 8th, at 6:00 A.M., the big ships of the almost 100-ship Franco-Spanish armada, including three battleships, six cruisers, and ten destroyers, blanketed the Alhucemas area with fire. In keeping with a hard-won lesson of the Dardanelles, they concentrated on the beach, while two battleships stood by for counter-battery fire. After the "softening up," tugs and gunboats towed the British-built and Spanish-modified "K" lighters to within a kilometer of the beaches. As at Tarawa eighteen years later, partly due to poor reconnaissance, several lighters grounded on an outer sand bar. Fortunately for the Spanish, the Rifs' underwater remote-controlled mines on the bar were not detonated.

Urged on by Colonel Franco, the main landing force suffered about fifty casualties while wading ashore, some up to their necks, while others landed west of Alhucemas at Cebadilla. After seizing key terrain and digging in, the troops and then the ships came under scattered fire from about forty Rif 75 mm and 105 mm guns, reportedly commanded by a Soviet colonel.[38] First-day casualties were 117 killed and wounded. Accounts of the effect of the light tanks vary. Some suggested their seizure of the commanding road was crucial, and that along with pre-invasion warning leaflets, they panicked the Rif tribesmen who were defending the beach. However, others judged that the shock effect of the big ships' guns slowed the Rifian response, or that the diversions were crucial. Haphazard sea-land communication and artillery control techniques hampered accurate, effective shooting. Control grids were hand-drawn and asymmetrical, and the army artillery officers spotting for ships' guns stayed with their batteries, contrary to practice at Gallipoli, where sending naval officers ashore had improved gun-spotting. In any case, the bores of most of the ships' guns were worn smooth by the campaign's end.[39]

The landing force lay vulnerable to a major Rif counterstroke for several days, when heavy weather on September 14th stopped the flow of troops and supplies ashore. Rif attacks were fended off while troops subsisted on sardines, hardtack, and closely rationed water. By the end of the second week, the lodgement was solidly established under an umbrella of 190 naval and 32 land-based heavy guns, supplemented by occasional air attacks. By September 20th, 20,000 men plus mortars, horses, and mules were ashore, and on the 21st, Spanish forces pressed forward over a parched, rock-strewn moonscape, against ever higher and steeper hills. As they moved beyond the range of naval guns against thickening Rif resistance, casualties soared. Close-in scrambles for high ground, fragmented skirmishes, and battles amid filth and dust held Spanish gains to an average of 600 meters a day. The Legion served as shock troops and in "fire brigade" roles when colonial troops lagged, or encountered mine fields and

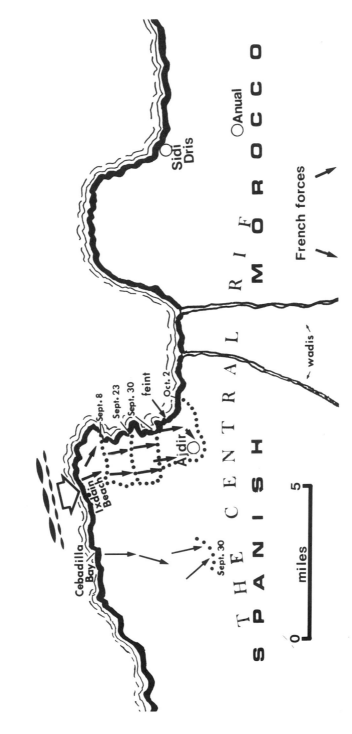

Mediterranean Sea

Franco-Spanish Assault Against Rif Rebels' Headquarters (Alhucemas, Morocco), September 1925

bolted. In late September, after their capital at Ajdir was captured and looted, the Rifs fell back.

During the advance, although the beachheads had been improved by a long "T" pier, the digging of wells, and fortification of the perimeter, beach organization and supply remained somewhat sloppy and confused. Nevertheless, the thrust at the heart of the Rifs' domain was mortal. Ajdir's fall and other setbacks undercut Abd el Krim's prestige with the tribes. After a quiet winter and complex negotiations in the spring, the Rif leader surrendered unconditionally at the end of May 1926, and was sent into exile.

JOINTNESS IN FRANCE BETWEEN THE WORLD WARS

In the French armed services between the World Wars, jointness was a matter secondary to the contingency of fighting a Locarno War against Germany. Support of the Army in sustained ground warfare dominated allocation of resources and organization, as French planners assumed, as in World War I, that Britain would be an ally and play the principal role at sea. Thus, the Navy received no clear planning basis in the form of budget guidelines, and frequent shifts in the government undercut the framing of strategic assumptions. Not only did the fleet suffer, like the U.S. and British navies, from the effects of the Washington and London naval arms limitation treaties, but also from the status of a more junior service. Although the Army received just over half the defense budget, and the Air Force just over a quarter, the French Navy was able to gain control over shipboard aircraft in 1932, after much acrimonious bickering, at the moment when the Herriot government took a strong stand in favor of abolishing national air forces and airlines and of establishing an international air force under League of Nations control. Throughout the 1930s, the changes in government were interthreaded with a series of arguments over creating a National Defense Ministry and/or an overall commander of the French armed forces. While interservice compacts and arrangements patched over some service differences, such jury-rigging fell well short of being a clear unified doctrine. The overall driving logic remained the vision of grinding battles with Germany along the northeast frontier, in which the French Navy's combat aircraft would supplement the *Armée de l'Air*.[40]

The two most prominent Air Ministers between the World Wars, Pierre Cot and Guy la Chambre, each grappled with problems of interservice friction and lack of doctrinal coherence and coordinative structure. The unsettling effect of air power on interservice politics, which increased with the creation of an Air Ministry in 1928, was reflected in the early 1930s in the anxiety in the traditional services over "defection" of naval aviators to the *Armée de l'Air*.[41] Although Cot's and la Chambre's differences over strategic air power and close-air support became a major point of concern in postmortems of the fall of France in 1940, each had tried to foster coordination in many respects as, for example, in Cot's decree of August 22, 1936, ordaining a formal structuring of interservice liaison, as well as such overlapping functions as research and development, procurement, and training, and la Chambre's support for the creation of a National Defense Committee.[42]

In the aftermath of Munich, with the coming of war widely accepted, a host of deficiencies within the services impaired attempts to develop a working close-air support system, including rigidity, parochialism, and excessive seniority among air officers, and weak Army-Air coordination, practice, and structure. In the Navy, a generation of economy and compartmentalization had led to shortages in anti-aircraft weapons and modern aircraft, supplies of which would be in transit from foreign sources at the time of France's fall.[43]

Jointness existed in fragments and far more on paper than in substance. When war came, France's senior military commander, General Maurice Gamelin, was formally Chief of Staff of National Defense with a triservice staff but mainly concerned with direction of the Army in a major ground campaign against Germany. Looking at a commander of the *Armée de l'Air* long past his prime, and air-ground cooperation not much beyond the circulation of a manual, A. D. Harvey observed that the French Air Force in 1940 had "no mind to match its body."[44]

JOINTNESS ON THE EVE OF WORLD WAR II

In 1939, the Russian armed services, like the United States', remained under the control of an Army-dominated general staff, without the French or German facades of triservice unified commands. Although the British and Italian service linkages fell well short of functional unity, the Japanese Army and Navy stood in virtual opposition, like the shogunates of old. Nevertheless, a deal had been cut, apportioning naval air power to support the Army in China while the Army's air elements faced the Soviets in the north. The China invasion of 1937 did not reveal to the very much impressed Western observers the Japanese Army and Navy's lack of coherent doctrine, training, and procurement in respect to amphibious operations. Yet in 1939, of all the major powers, only Japan could mount even a modest amphibious operation.

As World War II came, jointness could be found in the format if not the essence or substance of the *Wehrmacht* or the French high command, and in many nodes of inter- and intra-service meshing and ad hoc teamwork in various armed forces. Developments in signal and aviation technology and in mechanization had generated scattered, uneven, and informal accommodation and fusion. But in spite of extensive training, thought, and development in several countries between the World Wars, jointness remained a peripheral concern in the shaping of military doctrine and practice. The peculiar German-Russian fusion from 1925 to 1935 led each to generate a variant of close-air support that transcended American, British, and French systems of air-ground cooperation. U.S. Army Air Corps' observation and attack doctrine and equipment fell well short of that visible in Ethiopia, Spain, and China. Although there were many seedlings of jointness in the wind and linking tendrils, many of which grew quickly when fed by the stimuli and nutrients of war, much confusion, mischance, and floundering would be seen in joint operations throughout much of World War II.

NOTES

1. Demetrios Caraley, *The Politics of Military Unification: A Study of Conflict and the Policy Process* (New York: Columbia University Press, 1966), p. 7.

2. Joint Board, *Joint Action of the Army and the Navy* (Washington, D.C.: U.S. Government Printing Office, 1927).

3. Robert F. Futrell, *Ideas, Concepts, Decisions: A History of Basic Thinking in the United States Air Force, 1907–1964* (Maxwell Air Force Base: Air University, 1974), p. 46.

4. George Fielding Eliot, *The Ramparts We Watch: A Study of the Problem of American National Defense* (New York: Reynal and Hitchcock, 1938), pp. 332–36.

5. Ibid., p. 328.

6. Ibid., p. 332.

7. For various perspectives, see William F. Atwater, *United States Development of Joint Landing Operations, 1898–1942* (Durham, N.C.: Duke University, 1986); Kenneth J. Clifford, *Amphibious Warfare Development in Britain and America from 1920 to 1940* (Laurens, Pa.: Edgewood, 1983); and Jeter A. Isley and Philip A. Crowl, *The U.S. Marines and Amphibious War: Its Theory and Practice in the Pacific* (Princeton: Princeton University Press, 1951).

8. Michael Vlahos, *The Blue Sword: The Naval War College and the American Mission 1919–1941* (Annapolis, Md.: Naval War College Press, 1980), pp. 145–49; and Isley and Crowl, *U.S. Marines and Amphibious War*, pp. 3–5.

9. Atwater, *Development of Joint Landing Operations*, p. 65.

10. Lee Kennett, "Development to 1939," in B. Franklin Cooling, ed., *Case Studies in the Development of Close Air Support* (Washington, D.C.: U.S. Government Printing Office, 1990), p. 52.

11. Ibid., pp. 30–31.

12. Edward C. Johnson, *Marine Corps Aviation: The Early Years, 1912–1940* (Washington, D.C.: Headquarters, U.S. Marine Corps, 1977), esp. pp. 27, 53–56, 61–65 and 79.

13. See Chief of the Air Corps, *Employment of Aviation of the Army* (Washington, D.C.: U.S. Government Printing Office, 1940), p. 22.

14. For a brief account, see E. B. Potter and Chester Nimitz, *Sea Power: A Naval History* (Englewood Cliffs, N.J.: Prentice Hall, 1960), p. 637.

15. See Edward L. Homze, "The Luftwaffe's Failure to Develop a Heavy Bomber Before World War II," *Aerospace Historian* (March 1977): 20–26; and Cajus Bekker, *The Luftwaffe War Diaries*, trans. and ed. Frank Ziegler (Garden City, N.Y.: Doubleday, 1968), pp. 31, 38, 40–42, 165, 253.

16. David Divine, *The Broken Wing: A Study in the British Exercise of Air Power* (London: Hutchinson, 1966), p. 207.

17. John Slessor, *The Central Blue: Recollections and Reflections* (London: Cassell, 1956), pp. 124–30.

18. Laurence J. Legere, *Unification of the Armed Forces* (New York: Garland, 1988), p. 185.

19. Ian Hamilton, *The Soul and Body of an Army* (New York: Doran, 1921), pp. 245, 247, 254.

20. Lord Hankey, *The Supreme Command, 1914–1918* (London: George Allen & Unwin, 1961), p. 162.

21. Stephen Roskill, *Naval Policy Between the Wars*, vol. 1, *The Revival of Anglo-American Antagonism, 1919–1929* (New York: Walker & Co., 1968), pp. 539–40.

22. J. D. Ladd, *Assault from the Sea, 1939–1945: The Craft, the Landings, the Men* (Newton Abbot, U.K.: David Charles, 1976), p. 16.

23. Reginald Custance, *A Study of War* (Boston: Houghton Mifflin, n.d. [c. 1920], pp. 86–91.

24. For varying perspectives, see Edmund Ironside, *High Road to Command: The Diaries of Major-General Sir Edmund Ironside, 1920–1922* (London: Leo Cooper, 1972), pp. 183–92; W. S. Chalmers, *The Life and Letters of David, Earl Beatty* (London: Hodder & Stoughton, 1951), pp. 379–81; and Andrew Boyle, *Trenchard* (New York: Norton & Co., 1962), pp. 365–76.

25. *Public Record Office* file, *AIR* 2/1061/S22870.

26. For an overview of these developments, see E. J. Kingston-McCloughry, *Defense Policy and Strategy* (New York: Praeger, 1960), pp. 108–16.

27. For a critical perspective, see Brian Bond, *Chief of Staff: The Diaries of Lieutenant-General Sir Henry Pownall* (London: Leo Cooper, 1972), pp. 8, 18–19.

28. B. H. Liddell Hart, *Europe in Arms* (London: Faber & Faber, 1937), pp. 185–211.

29. Ronald Wingate, *Lord Ismay* (London: Hutchinson, 1970), p. 38.

30. Arthur J. Marder, *From the Dardanelles to Oran* (London: Oxford University Press, 1976), pp. 45, 52, 57.

31. See F. H. Hinsley et al., *British Intelligence in the Second World War: Its Influence on Strategy and Operations*, vol. i (New York: Cambridge University Press, 1979), esp. pp. 42–43, 84–85, 125.

32. See *PRO AIR* 2/1288, "Address by Chief of the Air Staff to Imperial Defense College, 1930"; in 1933, General Pownall saw the RAF as more disposed to interservice cooperation than the army, cf. Bond, ed., *Chief of Staff*, p. 8.

33. For a detailed analysis, see Brian Bond, *British Military Policy Between the Two World Wars* (Oxford: Clarendon Press, 1980), esp. pp. 212–13 and 339; for a discussion of service images, especially the army's, see Paul Kennedy, *Strategy and Diplomacy, 1870–1945* (London: George Allen & Unwin, 1983), p. 204.

34. Some Americans joined the French in the struggle. The *Escadrille Chirifiènne*, a squadron composed of five U.S. and five French pilots that flew over 600 hours supporting French forces, was disbanded in November 1925 due to public uproar and diplomatic complications after Chaouen was bombed after being declared an open city, and use of poison gas by the French was alleged; cf., David S. Woolman, *Rebels in the Rif: Abd el Krim and the Rif Rebellion* (Stanford: Stanford University Press, 1968), p. 202.

35. For various perspectives on the formulation of the plan, see Joaquin Arrara, *Francisco Franco: The Times and the Man*, trans. J. Manuel Espinosa (Milwaukee: Bruce Publishing, 1938), p. 79; and George Hills, *Franco: The Man and His Nation* (New York: Macmillan, 1967), pp. 133–40. C. V. Usborne, *The Conquest of Morocco* (London: Stanley Paul, 1936), p. 287, suggested that Marshal Lyautey proposed the landing to the French government. Primo is given credit by Cesar Gonzales Ruano, *El General*

Primo de Rivera (Madrid: Ediciones de Movimento, 1954), pp. 85–87, while a Franco biographer traced the concept to Jose Sanchez Guerra, Spanish minister of war in 1922; cf. Brian Crozier, *Franco* (Boston: Little Brown, 1967), p. 60.

36. Walter Harris, *France, Spain and the Rif* (London: Edward Arnold, 1927), p. 156.

37. For details of organization and strengths, see Francisco Gomez-Jordana Souza, *La Tramoya de Nuestra Actuacion en Maruecos* (Madrid: Editora Nacional, 1976), pp. 123–49; and for brief accounts, Ricardo de la Cierva, *Franco* (Barcelona: Editorial Planeta, 1986), pp. 87–89; Hills, *Franco*, pp. 138–40; and Harris, *France, Spain and the Rif*, pp. 155–70.

38. Hills, *Franco*, p. 135.

39. For details, see G. H. Smith, "Military Operations in Spanish Morocco and a Comparison with the Dardanelles Campaign," *Naval Review* 22:2 (February 1934): 83–85.

40. Gabraiel Auphan and Jacques Mordal, *The French Navy in World War II*, trans. A.C.J. Sabalot (Annapolis: U.S. Naval Institute, 1959), pp. 11–18.

41. Ronald Chalmers Hood III, *Royal Republicans: The French Naval Dynasties Between the World Wars* (Baton Rouge: Louisiana State University Press, 1988), pp. 90–92.

42. Dominique Boussard, *Un Probleme de Defense Nationale: l'Aeronautique Militaire au Parlement, 1928–1940* (Vincennes: Service Historique de l'Armée de l'Air, 1983), pp. 98, 127.

43. For contemporary and partisan perspectives, see Pierre Cot, *Armée de l'Air, 1936–1939* (Paris: Editions Bernard Grasset, 1939), and "Pertinax," *The Gravediggers of France: Gamelin, Daladier, Reynaud, Petain and Laval, Military Defeat, Armistice, Counterrevolution* (Garden City, N.Y.: Doubleday, Doran, 1944). For a recent analysis, see Robert Frankenstein, *La Prix de Rearmament Francais 1935–1939* (Paris: Sorbonne, 1982).

44. A. D. Harvey, "The French Armée de l'Air in May-June 1940: A Failure of Conception," *Journal of Contemporary History* 225:4 (1990): 477–565.

Chapter 4

The Cresting Torrent: Jointness in World War II

COMBINED OPERATIONS

Although still the greatest naval power in the world, in September 1939, the British entered World War II ill-prepared for joint warfare, with only a few landing craft on hand, and viewing an amphibious assault of any size against a defended shore as an unlikely prospect. In spite of Admiral Lord Chatfield's efforts as Minister for Coordination Defense in 1939–40 to keep the services in harness, the surge in pressures induced by going to war saw little of the smooth meshing that had matched the twilight of Hankey carry over into military, naval, and air operations. Prime Minister Neville Chamberlain's caution and hesitance in peacetime marked the desultory performance of British forces from the beginning of the war in September 1939, in spite of Churchill's attempts as the First Lord of the Admiralty once again to infuse aggressiveness and coherence into Britain's waging war.

The first glimmering of a very harsh dawn did not come until April 1940, in the form of the hastily improvised Nazi invasion of Norway. Seeking the prizes of a strategic bastion on the northern seas and control of coastal traffic from Swedish and Norwegian iron mines, the Germans improvised a functionally unified command. Weaving air forces and parachute and mountain troops deftly, they held back larger but more poorly integrated British, French, and Norwegian forces for a month in the north at Narvik. Although they were finally forced to withdraw there, German successes further south forced an Anglo-French evacuation.

The frustrations of Norway began a long series of efforts that eventually brought British and then Anglo-American operations to the highest scale and quality of joint warfare ever seen. The immediate implications of Narvik were the need for many more landing craft, for special ships to oversee, control, and support joint operations, and for more careful planning and coordination between multinational forces, as well as among the various arms and services. Yet all this had been learned before, in war and peacetime exercises, and good intentions yielded no immediate benefits. Delay, frustration, and failure dogged the course of British Combined Operations for the next two and a half years. Especially disturbing at the outset was the way in which Allied failure in Norway seemed to confirm the fears of many that Gallipoli proved the impossibility of major joint undertakings in modern war—even though the Germans had done it. While some saw Churchill as the architect of yet another fiasco, others saw the German victory as a product of air power over sea power.

Norway also appeared to be a triumph of a German unified command over a fragmented Allied command structure, since the Nazis assigned authority on the basis of function. Each locality and level was under a specified armed forces commander. Neither did the Germans share British and American reverence for the high-tide mark as a fixed boundary between sea and ground combat. Ironically, their appointment of an army general as theater commander set the pattern of future Allied combined operations in the Mediterranean, France, and southwest Pacific in World War II, and in most subsequent wars as well.

British concern over joint operations was momentarily eclipsed by further German victories. From May 10th to mid-June, the Nazis overran the Low Countries and conquered France, and the British Army was driven back across the Channel, losing most of its equipment and any prospect of returning for a long time. In the massive evacuation of some 350,000 troops at Dunkirk, as in Norway, the lack of landing craft and special ships to carry tanks, vehicles, guns, or troops from the beaches reinforced a resolve to strengthen British jointness that came from the top. When Churchill became prime minister on May 10th, amid converging calamities, he moved vigorously to take control of war-making, naming himself Minister of Defence (MOD), but without an actual ministerial bureaucracy. MOD administration was placed under the Cabinet Office, and the military Coordinating Committee that had been headed by Inskip and Chatfield was made into a Defence Committee, whose main axes of concern were operations and logistics.

More importantly, Churchill infused the machinery of war with a vigor based on long experience and knowledge. The new structures, and his close links to the War Cabinet and Chiefs of Staff Committee and dual role as Minister of Defence and Prime Minister gave him a controlling view down every conduit of authority. The clarity of service boundaries faded in stages under the glare of Churchill's restless and eager involvement in each facet of administration and operations, although it was often the source of much frustration and despair on the part of many subordinates.[1]

One of his first initiatives was his directive to begin planning, training, and development of equipment for a return to the continent. With Britain under siege and facing likely invasion, special groups formed from the Territorial Army grew into the Special Services Force—the Commandos—and other elite units overseen by Combined Operations headquarters, which became a field laboratory for testing joint methods, doctrine and equipment. Their insignia was a tommy-gun superimposed on an anchor and wings, and their first commander was Admiral of the Fleet Sir Roger Keyes. As noted earlier, he was a Victoria Cross winner in World War I and a "fire-eater" at Gallipoli and at Zeebrugge. As head of Combined Operations, however, Keyes fell short of the mark, partly due to his hard-charging style, but also due to conflicting priorities and interests in the British war effort, as many came to see Combined Operations as a drain on the armed forces.

Combined Operations eventually carried out dozens of major and minor attacks, including raids on Väagso and the Loföten Islands in Norway, the Bruneval raid, the fiasco at Dakar in French West Africa (depicted with such acidity by Evelyn Waugh, a Commando veteran, in his *Sword of Honour* trilogy), and the bloody failure at Dieppe in August 1942. Beyond all the setbacks, losses, and successes, the dashing image of the Commandos transcended any resources the Nazis were forced to allocate to defense or damage done; for example, one German soldier was killed during the raid on the Lofötens in late December 1941. Nevertheless, from 1940 to 1942, the Commandos served as a symbol of Britain aggressively carrying out military operations in Europe.

Jointness in British operations was not exclusively a product of Combined Operations' efforts. In the spring of 1941, as the Nazis overran Yugoslavia and Greece, the British blocked a seizure of power by pro-German elements that threatened British lines of communications and major oil pipelines. As Nazi advisers and aircraft arrived in growing numbers, Churchill urged a response by the very thin British forces in the region. In mid-April, Air Vice Marshal H. G. Smart, the commander on the spot, arranged to airlift a British infantry battalion from Karachi into southeastern Iraq, to serve as advance guard for 10th Indian Division units arriving by sea. A series of quick-bounding motor columns, orchestrated with air landing thrusts from eastern Jordan ripping northward across Iraq, dislocated the German-Iraqi build-up at Mosul in the north.[2]

From mid–1940 to the spring of 1942, however, jointness suffered from uneven operational skill and experience, from the skepticism of many commanders, staff officers, and civil servants, from delays, setbacks, and runs of bad luck. Although the Commandos fell well short of the original goal of being the school and model of aggressiveness for the large forces pinned down in Britain, much was achieved by Combined Operations as the feisty Keyes oversaw the building of a sturdy superstructure foundation laid down by Maund and the ISTDC. His star plummeted in late 1941 after he suspended major operations after Dakar to engage in further training, thus heightening frustration and tension among the Special Service forces and displaying a heedlessness to Combined Operations as a propaganda tool. Keyes was downgraded to Director of Combined Operations in late 1941, and given the passive mission of overseeing development, advising and aiding forces, and preparing joint operations.

In late 1941, the mounting U-boat war and setbacks in the Royal Air Force's strategic bombing offensive stood as grim counterpoints to Rommel's African triumphs and the Red Army's reeling retreat, while in the Far East, the Japanese, now the third Axis partner, assumed a challenging posture. Those calamities had drawn attention, resources, and support away from Combined Operations, and the likelihood of major British amphibious operations in Europe faded— although since mid-July the Soviets had demanded a "Second Front," a landing in Western Europe.

After Keyes left in early 1942, fortune smiled more warmly on his successor, the young Rear Admiral Lord Louis Mountbatten, who took charge during the darkest days of the war in mid-March 1942. American entry into the war was radically reshaping Allied strategy, but U.S. forces had not taken the offensive anywhere. The Russians had held on through the bitter winter but faced a renewed Nazi onslaught in the spring, while pressure mounted in the United States and Britain for a Second Front, a major invasion of northwest Europe to take pressure off the Soviets. Such an operation conformed to the secret ABC–1 agreement made by the United States, Britain, and Canada in early 1941, that if America came into the war, they would focus efforts in Europe against Germany and Italy. As American zeal mounted in early 1942, a product of anger, impatience, inexperience, and naivete, some, especially on the Republican right wing and in the U.S. Navy, sought to shift American efforts to the Pacific. Fury over the Japanese attack at Pearl Harbor and the plight of MacArthur's forces trapped in the Philippines increased pressure on American leaders to send forces to the Pacific. From January to August, most U.S. forces going overseas went westward, a flow that U.S. military leaders threatened to continue if no major landing in Europe was made in 1942.

At that point, Mountbatten's influence increased as he was made a lieutenant general and air marshal—and a member of the British Chiefs of Staff. In May, Anglo-American debate over the Second Front mounted, a small team of U.S. staff officers joined the Combined Operations staff, just as the first successful joint and combined operation of the war took place—the seizure by Anglo-Free French forces of the port of Diego Suarez on Madagascar, a triservice force amphibious assault in the face of determined opposition. In mid-September, two more major landings secured the island. Although Diego Suarez fell short of perfection—command liaison was lacking, there was no dedicated command ship or air plan, gunfire direction was weak, and the ships were not tactically loaded—it succeeded.[3]

Dieppe

The last major Combined Operations "show," a large raid against the northern French coastal resort town of Dieppe on August 19, 1942, was a major failure. Eighty percent of the mainly Canadian assault force was captured or torn to bits by the solid defenses. Nearly 4,000 of the 5,000 who went ashore were lost, as were 106 planes and 29 tanks, while German losses were less than 600 men and about 50 aircraft. While failure had been foreseen in some quarters, and Bernard Montgomery, then a lieutenant-general and head of Southeast Area Command, tried to stop it, many believed—and still do—that Dieppe was pressed from high levels of the British government to show the Americans and Russians the high costs of a Second Front. Any conspiracy theory must be viewed against the setbacks and mischances in joint operations throughout history. An operation of the scale, complexity, and unbalanced design of Dieppe would have suffered substantial losses in any case.

What good came out of the affair? Since 1940, in spite of the fact that what Combined Operations planners and practitioners learned was often not applied in subsequent doctrine or operations, the state of the art of major assault landings had been advancing overall. Many of the techniques and lessons bought with blood along the way were applied over the next two and a half years in North Africa, the Mediterranean, and in northwest and southern France. Most importantly, Dieppe showed frontal assault of a defended port was impossible. Since ordinary naval ships and craft could not provide adequate close-in fire, major modifications were made to existing landing craft and new types were produced to bolster landing forces with close-in firepower, such as mass rocket-firing craft using radar ranging, and a new type, the landing craft gun. Snarls on the beach led to upgrading of the training and the status of shore parties, to clearer marking of beaches, and the creation of special pilotage teams. As at Dakar earlier and in Operation Torch two months later, the need for separate headquarters and fighter direction ships was driven home. A standing, cohesive unit of landing craft—Force "J"—was formed to serve as a rapidly responsive reserve. Other lessons included the identification of a need for: more durable and speedier landing craft for the support elements; "Ducks" (DUKWs), or buoyant-hulled trucks; landing ship tanks (LSTs), which ultimately proved the key element in all major amphibious operations; better "water gap" bridging devices; hydrological surveys; bigger shore-party labor increments; tighter anti-aircraft discipline; and closer cooperation in planning and command and control at high air and naval command levels.[4]

THE WIDENING SPECTRUM

After Dieppe, the scale and tempo of joint operations increased dramatically. Even a minimally detailed chronology of joint operations from November 1942 to the end of World War II would exceed the limits of a single volume, especially in view of the fact that jointness had grown to encompass far more than amphibious operations. For example, an unresolved problem of jointness in the campaign in northwest Europe stemmed from the fact that anti-aircraft elements protecting tactical airfields were under Army ground forces' control. Since they were sometimes assigned to support units in the midst of the campaign, "friendly fire" and lack of coordination often resulted.[5] The most dramatic major joint operations, however, were amphibious—Tarawa, Normandy, and Anzio, for example—some of which remained well known in the United States, Britain and Western Europe after World War II as the result of films, popular books, and television series. Many others faded away or were never widely visible, like the major Australian efforts in Indonesia, a wide spectrum of covert and special operations, British activities in the eastern Mediterranean and Aegean, and the extensive Soviet operations along the Black Sea littoral and up the Danube. Throughout the war, joint operations proved far more varied and exacting than anticipated even by early 1942. Those who, at the onset, had envisioned such undertakings in terms of bold color dashed off in the manner of Turner or Van Gogh found them more akin to the Flemish masters, or indeed to watchmaking. Even such basic problems as working out common terminology and apportioning jurisdiction and tasks proved exceedingly complex and demanding of time and thought.[6]

The first major Allied amphibious operations took place in the Mediterranean and European theaters, where the British and American armies and navies and then the Canadians executed several major assaults before the first large U.S. Marines Corps assault landing in the Pacific. The first of these was Operation Torch, a three-pronged effort against North Africa on November 8, 1942, by an Anglo-American force of just over 100,000 within and outside the Straits of Gibraltar. The second, Operation Husky, on July 9–10, 1943, was a two-pronged descent on the southern and southeastern coast of Sicily by British and American forces of over 150,000. Although outnumbered three-to-one by Axis ground forces, the Allies, with air superiority in a nearly reverse ratio, lost just over 16,000, while German and Italian casualties were almost ten times as great when they withdrew some 100,000 men to the mainland in mid-August. The third, Operation Avalanche, a major Anglo-American landing at Salerno on the west coast of the lower boot of Italy, came on September 9, a week after the British Eighth Army crossed the Straits of Messina, and in tandem with an unopposed British landing at Taranto.

Each landing in the sequence sharpened Allied skills in joint operations in several dimensions, each teaching a new set of bitter lessons, as earlier failures had. Increasing scale and frequency generated complexities in coordinating loading and unloading, and some lessons were not easily assimilated. In Torch, for example, as at Gallipoli and Dakar, having the landing force commander's headquarters aboard the naval task force commander's flagship proved a mistake, as the landing force commander afloat was whisked away as the ship dealt with naval priorities. Naval gunfire and air support was thin and poorly coordinated at many points, and there were too few and poorly organized shore parties, which led to logistical snarls. Many landing craft were lost in the pounding Atlantic surf and, later, due to lack of repair and reassembly resources.

The poor meshing of parachute and glider troops with the Air Forces' drop and tow elements that caused dozens of gliders to be dropped out at sea in the Sicily landing had appeared on a smaller scale in North Africa and remained

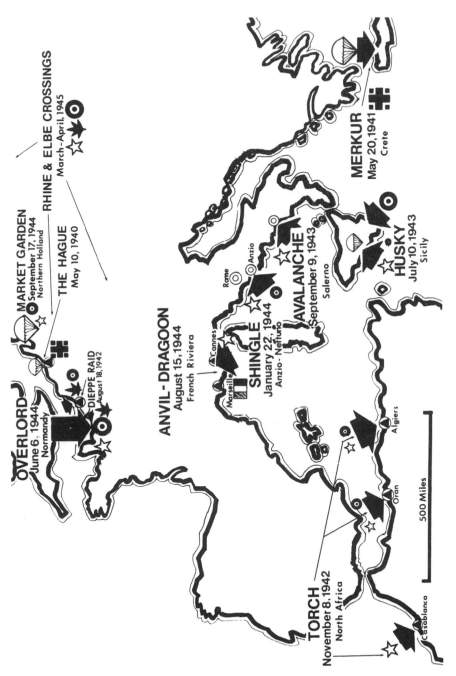

Major Allied Joint Operations in Western Europe and the Mediterranean, 1940–45

chronic throughout the war. Weak links between air and naval elements led to mass anti-aircraft barrages shooting down several planeloads of U.S. airborne troops being flown to battle over the invasion armada in Gela harbor. Yet improvements were being made across a broad front, and at Salerno, advances in naval gunfire control proved crucial, both in the landing phase and in the repelling of a major German counterattack on September 13.[7] Other lines of refinement included improvements in landing craft control, navigation, and coordination, the use of dedicated command ships, the supplementation of naval gunfire with gun- and rocket-bearing landing craft, and beach reconnaissance. A symbolic maturing of jointness came in the assemblage of seventy-two admirals and generals on June 28, 1943, known as the "Field of the Cloth of Gold," to work out the complex jurisdictions and protocols in Operation Husky.

On the other side, the Germans, although generally weak in jointness after Norway, aside from tactical air operations, launched a combined amphibious-airborne on the Greek island of Leros in mid-November 1943, overwhelming the British-Greek-Italian garrison of 9,000 men after four days' intense fighting. It was an exception to an overall pattern of interservice relations that was poor, in spite of the apparent unity suggested by the structure and semantics of the *Wehrmacht*, and command of German forces in North Africa and Italy by Air Marshal Albert Kesselring.

On January 22, 1944, the Allies attempted to exploit their growing skill in amphibious operations by outflanking the German *Gustav* Line and landed nearly 50,000 British and American troops at Anzio-Nettuno on the southern outskirts of Rome.[8] Of all major World War II amphibious operations, it most resembled Gallipoli. The assault went ashore without opposition and gained all goals in a solid lodgment, but sluggishness and hesitancy on the part of VI Corps commander, Major General John P. Lucas, and 5th Army Commander Mark W. Clark allowed the Germans time to mount a counterattack and contain the beachhead. The Anzio undertaking was also constrained by shortages of landing craft and theater reserves being diverted to the forthcoming landings in France and in the Pacific. Neither was it coordinated with the grinding battles in southern Italy. As the Germans assailed the beachhead's defenders throughout the spring of 1944, Lucas was replaced by Major General Lucian Truscott. Anzio finally fell when the Allies' major offensives astride the Apennines, supported by a heavy air offensive, led to the fall of Rome two days before the Normandy invasion.

The Western Allies' joint and combined planning and operations peaked in Operation Overlord, D Day, June 5–6, 1944, when three airborne, one armored and six infantry divisions descended upon Normandy. Thousands of air attacks had been made over several months to isolate potential invasion zones and confuse the Germans, reaching a crescendo on D Day, when a massive naval gunfire bombardment arched over the vast swarms of landing craft and ships that crowded the Channel. In spite of major difficulties encountered by the U.S. forces on Omaha Beach, which put the issue there in doubt for a time, a lodgment was gained on all five beaches by the end of June 6, at a cost in lives of roughly just over a third of those lost in taking Iwo Jima, in what Churchill deemed ''the most difficult and complicated operation that has ever taken place.''[9]

The next major joint-combined operation in Europe, Anvil-Dragoon, on the French Riviera, on August 16, 1944, was the product of intense British-American controversy. The former preferred a thrust into the Balkans, the latter, a diversion of German forces in France from Overlord. The assault, later dubbed the ''Champagne Campaign,'' because enemy resistance was light and casualties minimal, experienced losses of some 250 out of slightly less than 100,000, the lightest of any large-scale World War II amphibious assault.

The last major triservice undertaking in the European theater came in late March 1945, in the Rhine crossing by Patton's Third Army in southern Germany on the 22nd, and by British and American forces of Montgomery's 21st Army Group farther north the next day. In both cases, naval landing craft and crews were transported overland, and, as in Overlord, the web of jointness encompassed close-air and tactical air support. In the north, the scale was much larger and preparation was more elaborate, including the dropping of a British and an American airborne division.

Aside from the extensive riverine operations on the eastern front from 1941 to 1945, Soviet forces in the Baltic and Black Sea carried out over 100 landing operations, involving a third of a million troops. These did not reflect fusion *inter pares*, since the Red Army dominated in planning and control, and most were hasty, involving small units, often naval infantry and light artillery teams under a battalion in size. The biggest were the landing of three brigades in the Kerch area in February 1943, and of a 1500-man task force with light artillery on Hoglund Island in the Baltic in September 1944. Two peaks in intensity came, one in 1941, as the Nazis advanced into the Ukraine, and in 1944, as they were driven back out.[10]

ANOTHER KIND OF JOINTNESS: AIRBORNE OPERATIONS

Airborne operations loomed much larger in the equation of jointness in northwest Europe than in other theaters of war. Like amphibious operations, they were constantly affected by a scarcity of transport. The Germans had first employed airborne forces in the spring of 1940 in Norway, then in Holland and Belgium. Their seizure of Crete in Operation Merkur in May 1941, in the face of a British monopoly in sea power, led both Western Allies to form airborne forces. The British first used theirs in small special operations, then in company- and battalion-sized drops in Torch, ascending to division and corps scale, along with glider-borne forces, in Sicily, in the Normandy invasion, and finally, in northern Holland in late 1944. All the major drops in North Africa and Europe involved both British and American airborne forces, the most ambitious and controversial of these being Operation Market Garden, an airborne-ground assault in September 1944. Launched as Allied armies literally ran out of gas while pursuing German survivors of the Normandy battles, Market Garden aimed first at overrunning German V-weapons sites in Holland and second at outflanking what were believed to be thin German defenses. Airborne forces were dropped on bridges across the three northern tributaries of the Rhine so that advancing British ground forces could cross the north German plain. It led to the decimation of the British 1st Airborne Division, two-thirds of which fell into German hands, and a tenth of which fell in combat. Montgomery later deemed it his greatest mistake, and many agreed.

Just before Market Garden, longstanding problems of poor linkage between air transport and airborne troops and the frequent idleness of airborne units had led to a heated exchange of telex messages among General Henry H. Arnold, chief of the Army Air Forces, General Eisenhower, Allied supreme commander, and General George C. Marshall, U.S. Army chief of staff. The question of jurisdiction had first emerged when airborne forces were formed in 1940–41. Arnold then argued that the Army Air Forces should control them, pointing to the fact that most German paratroops were commanded by the Luftwaffe. In early 1944, he proposed dropping five Allied airborne divisions on Paris just before D Day, and continued to prod Marshall and Eisenhower on their employment afterward.

In any event, links between the Army Air Force's troop carrier command and the airborne troops were neither close nor warm. As in the RAF and Luftwaffe, U.S. airmen disliked dropping paratroops and towing gliders. In airborne operations, unarmed transports had to fly slow and low, holding steady formations under heavy enemy and sometimes friendly fire, before dropping their loads. Training time for airborne operations was minimal, and playing the role of jumpmaster and working with airlift crews during the drop were not favorite tasks of airborne troops. Some major commanders, including Mark Clark and Omar Bradley, saw airborne operations as a waste of high-quality troops and scarce transport planes. Beyond that, most airborne operations in World War II were marked by major error, confusion, and a high accident rate, with disabling injuries averaging about 10 percent and drops rarely within the designated zones and often miles away. While some were tragic, like the drops into the sea off Sicily and planes shot down over Gela, the confusion sometimes bemused the enemy, in what James Gavin called "SAFUs"—self-adjusting foul-ups.

To symbolically link airlift and parachute and glider forces, the First Allied Airborne Army was formed in late summer 1944, headed by Army Air Forces Lieutenant General Lewis H. Brereton and a staff of seasoned airborne and air officers. Bradley had ordered his forces to overrun scheduled airborne drop areas, hoping to use the idle transport planes to supply his forward elements. Several operations before Market Garden were canceled, as airborne divisions sat waiting for a mission, including a possible mass jump into Berlin. One major airborne operation followed that disaster, as U.S. and British airborne divisions were dropped within Allied artillery range across the Rhine in late March 1945.

Although no mass airborne assaults deep into well-defended enemy territory were made after World War II, dozens of small operations were carried out by the French paras in Indo-China, 1948–54, and somewhat larger drops were made by the British and French at Suez in 1956, the Belgians in the Congo in 1962, the Israelis in the Sinai in 1948, 1956, and 1967, and by the United States in Korea in 1951, on Grenada in 1983, and in Panama in 1989. Success and failure aside, airborne became a kind of military cult, with complex aspects of jointness in airborne operations and utility often overshadowed by the image of individual heroism prevailing in the face of depersonalizing technology.

JAPANESE JOINT OPERATIONS IN THE PACIFIC

In the opening months of the Pacific War, the Japanese Army and Navy carried out a series of airborne and amphibious operations, from the north Pacific through the Philippines and Malaya down to the Indonesian archipelago. Far more improvised than they appeared at the time, these successes were as stunning to the Japanese as to their foes, although much had been made in Western naval intelligence circles of the special ship the Japanese used in invading China in 1937, which dispensed landing craft through doors in the stern. It was not known that there were only two such ships and that Army-Navy rapport was extremely weak. They also employed many dozens of shallow draft, drop-door landing craft of a type that neither the Royal nor U.S. navies had in service at the time, or in large numbers until well into the war.

On December 8, the day after Pearl Harbor, three amphibious assaults by a 100,000-man force, including armored forces and guns, spearheaded the Japanese conquest of Malaya. Guam fell on December 10, and, after initially being repulsed, the Japanese made a successful amphibious assault on Wake Island on December 23. A series of minor lodgments on Luzon and other Philippine islands further south preceded the main invasions at Lingayen Gulf and Limon Bay, followed by the skillful withdrawal by General Jonathan Wainwright of his forces into the Bataan peninsula, where they held out until April. Hong Kong fell on Christmas Day to joint air-naval-ground attacks and an amphibious landing.

In January and February, the Dutch East Indies were overrun in a series of amphibious operations on Tarakan, in the Celebes, and Sumatra. In early May, a major Japanese assault captured the island fortress of Corregidor, leading to the surrender of most American forces in the Philippines. The success of those collaborations was all the more remarkable given the deep hostility between the Japanese armed services. Meshing of forces in the Pacific War's opening campaigns was more uneven and less orchestrated than appreciated at the time. Most landing craft had been developed by the Army, but the Navy had produced some of its own, and practice, doctrine, and equipment also varied. Naval ground elements landed on Wake Island, Guam, and at Amboina in the Dutch East Indies, while the Army assaulted Luzon, in Malaya, and at Hong Kong. Coordination also suffered as the samurai spirit blunted the inclination to use radios, and after those early successes, momentum fell off sharply.[11] Their Aleutian landings in June 1942 were unopposed, although major assaults against well-prepared defenses would have followed Japanese victory in the Coral Sea or Midway naval battles.

The sharp division between the Japanese Army and Navy arose partly from the residue of feudalism. Each served as a rallying point for different clans when the samurai were disarmed in the mid–1870s in the course of the Meiji Restoration. The dichotomy also arose from each of the services' technology and style being shaped by different foreign influences, the Navy primarily by Britain and the Army by Germany. Further divisive effects were wrought by the effects of the great combines, the *zaibatsu*, which arose from Japanese industrialization. That tension was reflected in the formal statement of imperial defense policy of 1907, a product of an intense debate between the Japanese Navy and the Army, in which Navy strategists sought to defend Japan with far-flung naval operations that were aimed at keeping enemies, primarily the United States, at a distance, and then wearing them down as they approached, to allow a final battle on more or less equal terms. Under that scheme, Japanese diplomacy was to be aimed at using China to counter-balance Russian strength, and direct involvement in Asia was to be avoided, just as Britain had given up holding possessions in Europe in the modern era. The Army, however, wanted to develop an Asian land empire and ultimately drive out the Western nations. In stages, the latter outlook prevailed, aside from the opening months of World War II. Even then, the elaborate fugue of amphibious and airborne campaigns had been hastily improvised and was split regionally between the services.

As World War II progressed, Japan's military capacity proved to be far less balanced and amphibious than many observers expected. Although Premier Tojo, an Army general, and the War Ministry attempted to strengthen Army-Navy rapport late in the war, old habits and attitudes persisted at many points.[12] For example, the Japanese Army had to build its own transporter submarines to supply garrisons bypassed by American "island hopping" in 1943–45. Lack of jointness also hampered procurement, as the Japanese Army and Navy, like the German armed services, competed for industrial output until late in the war. Consequently, the Japanese aviation industry was wracked by waste and poor coordination.[13]

U.S. JOINT OPERATIONS IN THE PACIFIC WAR

In spite of the lack of a formal joint structure before America's entry into World War II, common concern had led to some limited fusion in Hawaii. In January 1941, for example, the air chiefs of each service there co-wrote a report on deficiencies in long-range air patrol coverage, but it led to no significant improvement. While joint radar exercises were carried out from June 1941 onward, and one actually detected the Japanese attack's first wave, overall fusion was weak.[14] After Pearl Harbor, however, tides ran strongly toward jointness when Prime Minister Churchill came to Washington with a large staff to meet with President Roosevelt in the Arcadia Conference, in late December 1941 to mid-January 1942. The Joint Chiefs of Staff was formed ipso facto as the U.S. service chiefs conferred with British counterparts in the Combined Chiefs of Staff. At the same time, the first major joint and combined inter-Allied head-quarters American-British-Dutch-Australian Command (ABDACOM) was es-tablished as a massive strategic debacle was unfolding in Southeast Asia.

ABDACOM's newly appointed supreme commander in chief, the first so designated in the war, Field Marshal Sir Archibald Wavell, was an able and thoughtful commander who had presided over the British victory in Egypt in 1940, then suffered defeats in North Africa and Greece in 1941 while enduring scorn and interference from Prime Minister Churchill. After his forces recaptured Italian East Africa in 1941, Wavell went into the proverbial wilderness as com-mander in chief in India. Exhausted, Wavell found himself at the helm of another sinking ship on January 15 as he assumed command of ABDACOM. Hong Kong, Guam, and Wake Island had fallen, the Japanese had pierced the ''Malay Barrier'' at several points, seized Thailand, and were overrunning Malaya. By late February, after Singapore fell and Allied naval forces north of Australia were whittled away, ABDACOM was dismantled, and new lines of theater command responsibility were drawn. Thus amid defeat and confusion, a prec-edent was set, and supreme commanders would be appointed in Europe, the Mediterranean and southwest Pacific, central Pacific and Pacific Ocean area, and later in southeast Asia. Although China was dealt with through a modified and less satisfactory arrangement, by the end of the war, all supreme commands were joint and combined (i.e., inter-Allied) to varying degrees, and in the Med-iterranean, Europe, southwest Pacific and southeast Asia, Allied staffs and de-puties were heavily interleaved.

Looking back at the evolution of joint organization in the Pacific, an American scholar observed that ''the United States had not perfected an adequate doctrine for amphibious operations by the outbreak of World War II'' and that progress between the wars had ''derived as much from Army and Navy contributions as from any original development by the Marine Corps.''[15] Both services were found wanting in the Pearl Harbor hearings, and the lack of joint command structures, practice, and contingency plans and methods was visible for many months afterward, as doctrine, resources, and sometimes, inclination were lack-ing.

As the tide of Japanese conquests crested and Americans strove to reverse it, there was little enthusiasm at high echelons initially for waging amphibious warfare. Nevertheless, while ground warfare and Army commanders dominated the strategy and operations in the Mediterranean, Europe, southeast Asia, and the southwest Pacific, the oceanic geography of the Pacific theater highlighted the naval dimension, which appealed to many Americans as a way to wage war using technology and space rather than expending life in heavy, sustained ground fighting. Beyond that, the view of Pearl Harbor as a sneak attack and a deeply

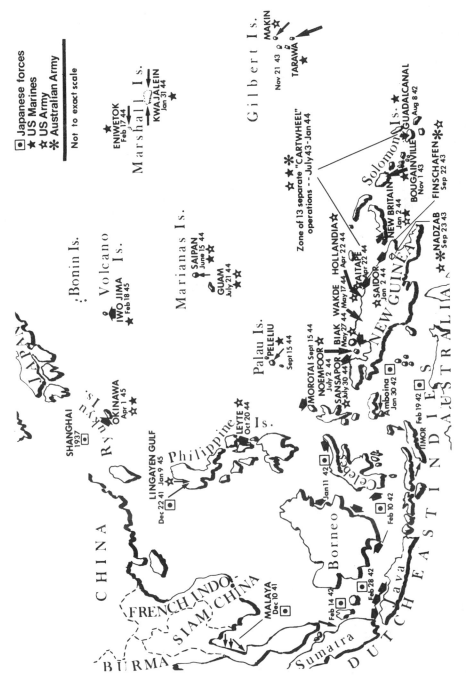

Major Allied Joint Operations in Asia and the Pacific, 1937–45

racist fury flavored much of the American public's view of the war against Japan. Admiral King, striving to divert strategic attention and resources from Europe, found a sturdy fulcrum for his lever in the fact that over 90 percent of Allied landing craft and, most crucially, the large Landing Ship Tanks (LSTs) were built in the United States. While he exercised the right of eminent domain to the point that some, like Chester Wilmot, saw him as a dog in the manger,[16] Sir Charles Snow later argued that a shift in production priorities from heavy bombers to landing craft might have ended the war in 1943.[17]

As noted earlier, the major units preparing for joint operations in the Atlantic had been dispersed in the months after Pearl Harbor, with 1st Amphibious Task Force Commander Major General Holland M. Smith and the 1st Marine Division going to the Pacific. Smith, nicknamed "Howlin' Mad," presided over the shaping of the Marine Corps' V Amphibious Force, working in harness from mid–1943 onward with Vice Admiral Richmond Kelly "Terrible" Turner. In spite of all the preparations of the 1930s and early 1940s, the first American landing in the Pacific War did not come until early August 1942, in the Solomon Islands. The assault landings against opposition on Gavutu and Tonambogo led to near-disaster, and in the latter, to withdrawal of the first landing force. Both were marked by the same error and confusion seen in the interwar FLEXes. Supplies lay jammed and disorganized on the beach, as they would three months later in Operation Torch, the invasion of North Africa, and again at Tarawa.[18] On the second night, the carriers withdrew to leave the troops on Guadalcanal momentarily to the mercy of the Japanese Navy, which won a major night battle off Savo Island.

By the summer of 1943, however, the meshing of air, naval, Army and Marine forces and of New Zealand and Australian units had progressed substantially. A main Japanese base on New Georgia was taken in late August, and in September, Australian and American forces carried out airborne, air-landing, and amphibious feints and assaults at Lae-Salamaua and Nadzab on the north coast of New Guinea. Vella Lavella and Bougainville fell in October and December 1943, respectively, as Rear Admiral Daniel Barbey's Seventh Amphibious Force began the series of bounds that landed American or Australian forces at points across the "back" of New Guinea, into New Britain, and ultimately at Leyte and Lingayen in the Philippines in the fall and winter of 1944.

Tarawa

The first full-scale Navy-Marine Corps assault landing against a strong fortified Japanese position came just over half-way through the Pacific War, at Tarawa in the Gilbert Islands. The proof test of the Marine Corps' doctrine of advance base seizure through assault landings against solid defenses, closely supported by the fleet, it was a bloodbath, and it almost failed, due to equal shares of chance, weak intelligence, and erroneous doctrine and practice. Although a number of difficulties encountered in exercises over the previous decade had not

COLORADO COLLEGE LIBRARY
COLORADO SPRINGS
COLORADO

been remedied, Julian Smith, Second Marine Division commander in the assault, later described Tarawa as a "battle of firsts."[19] Several of the lessons learned that he cited—poor control of follow-up echelon craft, the need for a ship dedicated only to command and control, and a shortage of firepower on craft close to the beach—had been noted in analyses of Gallipoli, in postmortems of Navy-Marine Corps FLEXes, in the evolution of Combined Operations doctrine in Britain, and in the after-action analyses of Dakar, Dieppe, and Operations Torch and Husky.[20]

Beyond any question of causes or precedents neglected, by sundown on the first day, with a third of the U.S. landing force on Tarawa dead or wounded and communications between commanders afloat and troops ashore faltering, withdrawal was considered, then rejected. After the equivalent of another battalion was lost after the reserve was committed, Tarawa was taken, by sheer courage, will, and fire power. The bloody tariff of the first serious assault landing sent waves of anguish rolling back to the United States, while the Navy and Marines urgently revised their amphibious warfare techniques.[21] Yet even though harsh experience proved a stern tutor in the Pacific, in Europe, and the Mediterranean, as the war progressed, efforts to pass on dearly bought lessons and intertheater liaison seem to have been uneven, perhaps due to the semi-autonomy of the various theater commands.

As joint operations increased, quality of practice improved proportional to the expanding flow of materiel, manpower, and experience—and in a "direct ratio to the distance from Washington."[22] To the extent that service parochialism seemed to veer from the goal of victory, it risked becoming the focus of journalists' attention, for example, in spite of censorship and self-censorship, the Pearl Harbor hearings and the "Battle of the Smiths" on Saipan the summer of 1944. In the latter instance, after Holland M. Smith relieved the commander of the Army's 27th Infantry Division, Major-General Ralph Smith, a journalistic furor and the subsequent condemnation of the former's action by a review panel aggravated interservice feuding that continued after the war.

Cartwheel

The Marines' bloody ascent of the central Pacific ladder and major landings in the Mediterranean overshadowed the evolution of jointness to a very high level of practice in the southwest Pacific theater of war in Operation Cartwheel and the Bismarck Archipelago campaign. The use of such terms as "island hopping" and "bypass strategy" in reference to MacArthur's system tended to blur the sophistication of the underlying concept, with the arrows swirling and sweeping on World War II battle maps tending to a graphic reductionism that obscured the flexibility in fusion and creative pragmatism. In Cartwheel, air forces, strategic and tactical, land forces fighting ashore, and in amphibious landings and raids, and naval forces were constantly fine-tuned and "packaged" under a strategic plan that hinged on a high level of interservice cooperation.

Elkton III, the plan drawn up in 1943 for the reduction of the Japanese stronghold at Rabaul, northeast of New Guinea and northwest of the Solomons, was a product of MacArthur's close rapport with his air chief, George Kenney, and Admiral William "Bull" Halsey, and their staffs. Based on a strategic double-envelopment scheme, it envisioned advancing the "bomber line" toward Rabaul, a concept based on extension and overlapping of the operational radii of air forces (and not just bombers), operating from an advancing wave-front of bases, striking Japanese airfields, shipping, and naval forces, and providing umbrellas of support for advancing naval and ground operations. The resultant "air, land and sea action" was in essence a flexible, fluid, and continuous orchestration of multiservice elements in continuous operations, as opposed to the landing-and-advance inland pattern in North Africa and Europe or the one-island-at-a-time pattern of Marine-Navy assaults. Ultimately, the operational radius of fighter aircraft proved the vital factor in setting goals in time and space.[23]

JOINT LOGISTICS IN WORLD WAR II

Molyneux and all analysts since have recognized that logistics in joint operations required special attention and organization. The use of "combat loading" at Vera Cruz in 1847 and the lack of it at Daiquiri in 1898 have already been noted. Yet tiering supplies aboard ship to meet the demands of operations—combat loading—was a technique mastered and forgotten again and again over the next two centuries, perhaps because normal loading of ships for port-to-port transport calls for filling all spaces, placing heavy items lowest, and balancing the ship. In combat loading, however, spacing is needed to allow quick access to items needed most in battle, usually ammunition, guns, medical supplies, and combat rations. What and how much is needed is often uncertain until battle is joined. Beyond the obvious different effects on weight and density, stowing supplies in open arrays for easy identification and quick unloading reduces the amount each ship can carry.

In World War I, the Allied logistical system was reshaped throughout the relatively brief Gallipoli campaign, and many special problems had been identified in interwar exercises held in the United States and Britain. Congestion in loading and unloading, phasing of supplies, providing medical support, and the complexities of controlling water and land traffic and labor on the beaches and inland intruded repeatedly in peacetime exercises and maneuvers, in wartime rehearsals, and in operations throughout World War II.

Foremost among the logistical differences between the European and Pacific arenas was the much greater distance from home ports and bases to operational areas in the latter. Not only was the construction of major bases from the ground up often required in the Pacific, but the dearth of amenities and sparse local purchase options required carrying more of what *might* rather than what *would* be needed. As the primitive sense of logistics of many U.S. Navy line and Supply Corps officers was rapidly altered by war, the vastness and sparseness of facilities in the Pacific were reflected in the increasingly complex organization and division of responsibility, and in the establishment of independent operational commands with special staffs headed by a commander from one service.[24] In most cases, friction stemming from turbulent, ongoing change and the shifting of boundaries and discontinuities was smoothed out by men of good will.[25] The triumph of pragmatism over formality and turf concerns was symbolized in naval officers' wearing Army khaki uniforms, and the Navy's supplying U.S. Army Air Force strategic bombers with bombs, and providing medical care to Army troops between ports of embarkation in the United States and the high water mark on the beach.[26]

Although many accepted such blurring of boundaries and functions, all did not go smoothly and evenly.[27] For example, Combined Operations staffs bent on rationalizing doctrinal development and planning found that ''more than once . . . equipment . . . produced as a rush job at one Service establishment existed already at another, stacked in heaps.''[28] A steady state and total coherence could never be reached, and the many agencies' continual refinement of techniques in the wake of operations was not in phase. Because logistical requirements in joint operations so often diverged from expectation, uncertainty was accepted and institutionalized. From early 1944 onward, ''blockships'' began to operate, that is, transports loaded with a range of items under a system of ''blocks'' or ''consists,'' made up of increments of supplies spaced and organized, often in pallet form, to allow quick access and unloading in combat areas without having to move other items. Blockships sailed directly from U.S. ports to rendezvous with invasion forces, both before and after landings, thus bypassing the break-of-bulk sequence in the routine logistical flow, and the regular requisition system, which was brought into play several weeks after operations. Ultimately, thirteen types of blockships and 125 blocks were deployed.

Although the resultant reduction in carrying capacity, duplication, and the non-use of some items seemed wasteful to some, the system saved much time by reducing rehandling. Beyond that, new supplies and equipment went into combat zones that had been loaded under safe and modern conditions in U.S. ports, and the speed of access in battle was assured.[29] In another logistic ''short-circuit'' in the Pacific War, Admiral Chester W. Nimitz, the Pacific fleet commander, sent agents to the United States to speed the flow of materiel through direct contact with the Navy bureaucracy and industry.[30]

The complexity of joint organization grew as the war progressed, as in all theaters of war, joint administrative and command subloops grew out of other loops. Proliferating friezes of authority, communications systems, and task specialization were denoted by acronyms like JASCO, UDT, and ESB (Joint Assault Signal Companies, Underwater Demolition Teams, Engineer Special Brigades). By 1943, the basic doctrinal guidelines and coordination loops developed by British Combined Operations for amphibious force commanders encompassed fifty-one major organizations.[31] Like the production systems that flowed into it, most of the mechanism of jointness was not involved in battle. Many who worked within its toils were consigned to anonymous drudgery of the kind described aboard the AK 601 in Thomas Heggen's *Mister Roberts*, which sailed from Tedium to Apathy and back again. At the cutting edge, advances in the Allies' state of the art were offset in 1944 by Japanese tenacity and changed tactics. The first glimpse of that was seen southeast of the Philippines on Peleliu in the summer of 1944, where a shift from waterline defense to deep tunneling in steep terrain negated much of the effect of preparatory bombardment. Planned as a mere walk-through flank-clearing exercise, Peleliu turned into a costly and lengthy nightmare, adding to the animus of many Marines toward its proponent, General Douglas MacArthur. On the "other side of the hill" on Peleliu, lack of Japanese Army-Navy jointness was reflected in the completely separate fortification and shelter systems that each service constructed.[32]

In that summer of 1944, the principal U.S. Marine and Army amphibious efforts were further north, in the Marianas Islands. Although listed as a strategic goal early in the war, Admiral King's proposals to assail them were long relegated to the margins, by both the U.S. Joint Chiefs and the Anglo-American Combined Chiefs of Staff, and brought forward only slightly in priority in the Quebec Conference in the summer of 1943, then moved to the head of the queue at the Cairo Conference, where King received a sharp boost from Arnold who, as head of the Army Air Forces, was now properly concerned that B–29 Superfortress bases being built in southwest China might soon be overrun.[33]

Beyond the "Battle of the Smiths" noted earlier, substantial friction between field artillery and supporting naval aviation appeared in operations on Saipan and Tinian, arising mainly from heavy concentrations of fire directed from the former island against the latter.[34] With an elaborate chain of communication that required eight points of message-handling up and down the net in processing air strike requests,[35] the cumbersome and sluggish system produced a minimum half-hour lag between request and delivery, again, a sharp contrast to the pragmatic fusion of Army and Marine Corps field medical systems.[36] Once again, lessons learned or relearned included a call for more radio frequencies and better orchestration through combining or co-locating field artillery, air and naval gunfire control centers.[37]

A major shock came in Operation Detachment, the landing in February-March 1945 on Iwo Jima, a volcanic ash heap defended by some 22,000 Japanese Army and Navy troops, which the Army Air Forces sought as an auxiliary landing site. The operation, which planners expected would last a week, lasted over a month, with one quarter of the landing force, almost 7,000 men, killed or wounded. That made the impending invasion of the Japanese homeland appear an even gloomier prospect. The difficulties on Iwo Jima sprang from both the unexpected depth and complexity of Japanese fortifications and shelters, and a slump in Navy-Marine Corps jointness. A tension had long been implicit in joint operations between landing forces' fire support needs and naval concerns for the threat from enemy sea and air elements. After both the Salerno and Tarawa landings in the fall of 1943 dramatized the problem,[38] Admiral King recognized a need for accurate on-call fires and for a massive increase in the scale of preparatory area bombardment and insisted on supplementing Neptune, the naval portion of Overlord, with twenty-nine heavy U.S. Navy warships.

As the scale and pace of joint and combined operations mounted, the menu of refinements in technique lengthened, some items deriving from British practice.[39] Training in fire support intensified, linkages between command, gunfire, and air control elements were improved, and new aiming techniques were worked out.[40] The overall result, however, was not as dazzling as some newsreels and postwar television documentaries suggested. Colonel Heinl, in paying tribute to Admiral R. L. "Close-in" Connolly, rated naval gunfire support at Tarawa, Saipan, and Peleliu all as "poor" as he traced the scaling down of the bombardment program for Iwo Jima to the Navy's shift of resources toward raids against Japan's coast. With the original support program for Iwo Jima cut from ten to three days and the heavy ships reduced from sixteen to eight, over three-quarters of the original target list was left untouched.[41]

Jointness in the Pacific War reached its highest scale of practice in the Okinawa campaign. Over a half million men were involved from April to July 1945 in the main prelude to a two-stage Anglo-American-Australian invasion of Japan slated for late 1945 and 1946. Twelve thousand American soldiers, Marines, and sailors and over 100,000 of 105,000 Japanese defenders died on that bastion of the Island Empire. The bloody attrition of the major ground battle was augmented by waves of kamikaze suicide aircraft attacks that sank thirty-three and damaged over 300 Allied ships, and killed over 4,000 sailors. Although discontinuities between the services' structures "caused many delays in . . . deployment of equipment and supplies," cooperation on Okinawa reached the highest level seen in modern military-naval history until Operation Desert Storm.[42] Thus Marine Corps official historians deemed it the "culmination of amphibious development in the Pacific War," in which "interservice cooperation was the keystone of success." Army and Marine Corps artillery, armor, and air support control loops were cross-linked with field artillery, air and naval gunfire support from battalion level up.[43]

The scale of jointness by the end of the war was reflected in the fact that 40 percent of U.S. Navy ships were dedicated to amphibious roles. Admiral Daniel Barbey's 7th Amphibious Force, for example, supporting MacArthur's Southwest Pacific Theater, carried out forty-eight major amphibious operations. Procedures and organizations had been developed to balance naval fears of enemy naval and/or air incursion with Army concerns regarding interdiction of supplies, counter-attacks by enemy land force, and the ability to exploit opportunities.[44] Neither were the anxieties of the former based on vague presentiments. In the Makin landing in late November 1943, paralleling the Tarawa assault, the Army lost just over 200 men, while Navy support forces lost 752. The heavy naval casualties off Okinawa in 1945 also underscored that dilemma.[45]

The pattern of amphibious operations varied from theater to theater. Those in the southwest Pacific faced less resistance on the beaches than did most Mediterranean, European, and central Pacific assault landings. The North African and Sicilian landings had encountered moderate to severe resistance, while at Tarawa, Salerno, and Omaha Beach, the stiffness of defenses had put the issue in doubt, and at Anzio, led to stalemate. The main Guadalcanal landing was unopposed, and the British incursion into southeastern Italy, the landing phase at Anzio, and the southern France operations were all relatively easy. Even though the central Pacific saw the highest frequency of determined resistance, and thirteen of the sixteen U.S. Marine Corps assault landings met determined and well-sited opposition,[46] U.S. Navy and Marine casualties in all their Pacific campaigns were less than those of the U.S. Fifth Army in Italy.[47]

CLOSE-AIR SUPPORT IN WORLD WAR II: QUALITATIVE ASPECTS

As was the case of other forms of technology bent to the service of war, the adapting of aircraft to military and naval purposes was not always well thought out or universally appreciated. Air power was often misapplied, its potential ignored or denied, partly due to the exaggeration and optimism of advocates and the skepticism of some military and naval professionals. Objective appraisal was not made easier between the World Wars, due to the light of media glamorization and the inflated claims of enthusiasts throughout the industrialized world. The sometimes wild assertions and poses of exuberant modernity struck by early military and naval aviators obscured the extent to which the new arm was a direct offshoot of armies and navies, and the fact that the air services, as extensions of national armed power, could not avoid many of the dilemmas facing armies and navies in an age of rapid technological evolution. That was partly due to the fact that, from the late nineteenth century onward, it was recognized that air operations constituted a change in dimensionality. When armies and fleets were arrayed forces in rough opposing lines as in "conventional" land and sea combat; they might maintain effort from a minimum of several minutes in raids and skirmishes, to hours in battles, months in campaigns, and even years in the case of blockade and siege. Air power, however, was applied in a transient and momentary way, aerial combat and bombing attacks being measured more in seconds than minutes. Outside the realm of science fiction, there was not much expectation that air forces would be locked in sustained battle. In World War I, air power, tactical and strategic, was usually applied against an extended system at multiple points rather than at a point of concentration, and moments of contact were very brief. By the end of that conflict, the vision of air power enthusiasts, like the proponents of infiltration and tank tactics, was an attack against the nerves and arteries, not the outer skin or sinews of enemy forces, aimed at quickly destroying the enemy's capacity to wage war with minimal casualties.

As an antidote to the romanticization of aviation, Field Marshal Lord Slim of Burma suggested a concept of "air-mindedness," based on a view of aircraft not as "a weapon (in itself vs. a carrier of weapons), a sporting adjunct, or a bag of tricks, but as a platform."[48] Yet Slim's relentless common sense over-looked the way in which, from World War I onward, the diffuseness and rapidity of air combat tended to blur its non-physical effects, both immediate and residual. Like artillery fire and tank attacks, air power often had a psychological impact beyond the immediate damage done by bombs, bullets, or shells. In late July 1944, soon after Field Marshal von Kluge assumed command in northwestern France from Rommel, who had been wounded by a British fighter-bomber, he advised Hitler:

There is no way . . . (given) the enemy air forces' complete command of the air, we can . . . counter-balance its annihilating effect unless we withdraw from the battlefield. Whole armored formations . . . caught beneath bomb-carpets of the greatest intensity . . . are more or less annihilated.[49]

The sound of aircraft often caused attention, action, and resources to be diverted by the threat. Even light, unarmed planes posed a menace since they might direct the fall of bombs or artillery, or take photographs. Thus, air attack often not only yielded residual physical effects, such as downed bridges and buildings or smashed equipment, but psychological ones as well. Those subjected to the presence of hostile aircraft were forced to react in some way by fleeing, cowering, or employing camouflage, maneuver, or anti-aircraft fire. Although the Stuka Ju 87 dive bomber caused one-twentieth of American casualties in the Mediter-ranean and Europe in World War II, a fifth of American combat troops rated them as most frightening among the nine main German weapons in World War II.[50]

Thus, the complex physical processes of air war have posed a special problem for enthusiasts, critics, analysts, and historians alike in attempting to depict their often blinding and stunning speed. Since it has often been very difficult to draw a clear line between physical and psychological effects of weapons in warfare, the psychic aspect is a dimension of both jointness and combined arms often lost sight of or vaguely implicit in doctrine, in mechanistic fire-exchange mod-eling, and in the command-staff process. Beyond the specific effectiveness of air power measured in numerical terms, in World War II, many involved in ground combat felt it was good to have somebody helping out when things were going tough, while others carried grudges about not being helped out. Since the movement of armies and fleets was easier to portray and visualize than the fluidity of air war, both patterns and effects of air power—at the time and in military history—were often blurred. In histories and "after-action" reports, the impact of air support was often described by vague allusion, statistics, or anecdotes.

Tactical Air Power in the Opening Campaign of World War II in Europe

Doctrine varied widely among the major powers as to how closely air elements should support ground forces. As the war began in September 1939, most of the Luftwaffe stood at the service of the army. In Manchuria, Japanese Army air elements covered the Kwantung Army while the Japanese Navy supported army operations in China. The Italian Regia Aeronautica, uneven in quality, was pitched somewhat more toward naval support and strategic missions, while the substantial strategic bomber component of the Soviet Air Force had been put in some disarray by Stalin's purges. After the Finnish campaign of 1939–40, in which it attacked towns and cities extensively, the Voyenno-Vozdushnoye Sily (VVS) became mainly a tactical air force. The French Armée de l'Air's general staff virtually ignored directives from the Ministry of Aviation to prepare to carry out a major close-air support role, and in the great battles of 1940, French aircraft of varying quality were dribbled away in piecemeal, out-of-phase attacks, many shot down by friendly fire.[51]

The Royal Air Force entered the war with some elements dedicated to ''Army cooperation'' but was unable to deliver ordnance on the front line at the request of ground units. Fighters were allocated an interceptor role, while the durable but sluggish Westland Lysander high-wing monoplanes were assigned to reconnaissance and spotting functions. The closest thing to a battlefield support aircraft was the underpowered Fairey Battle, a ''day bomber'' resembling a giant monoplane fighter, but which was far more ponderous. In the spring of 1940, Battle squadrons supporting the British Expeditionary Force attacked targets well beyond the front line, such as key bridges. Most were decimated in the first few days by German anti-aircraft fire and Luftwaffe fighters, and the few survivors quickly withdrawn. In spite of that experience, Royal Air Force tactical doctrine continued to be based on the premise that the best way to neutralize enemy air activity was not by fighting defensive battles over the front line, as the Germans had tried to do in World War I, but by attacking deep into the enemy rear, thus killing the metaphorical tree of the enemy's air power and ground forces by cutting their roots. Nevertheless, by the end of 1940, experiments in the RAF in Britain led to the issuance of a directive on ''close support bombing,'' and the establishment of control net ''tentacles'' at Army and Corps headquarters.[52] These reflected lessons learned in the early blitzkrieg campaigns, when the Allied ground forces' lack of air elements that could quickly be brought to bear against enemy ground forces proved an especially serious deficiency in fast-moving, fluid battles in which artillery was often out of touch with or far behind infantry and armored units.

Contrary to the popular view of the Luftwaffe's surgical application of air power to aid rapidly advancing ground forces, the *Wehrmacht's* close-air support system did not function at a high level of execution in the opening campaign of World War II in Poland in September 1939. Neither were many problems identified there—target-marking and signaling deficiencies, attacks on friendly troops due to reliance on bomb-lines in fluid situations, failure to co-locate ground and air headquarters, and lack of meshing radio frequencies—wholly remedied when the Battle of France began in May 1940, even though dedicated attempts had been made to fold experience into improved tactics.[53]

In view of the dominance of the ground forces over the other services, and of artillery in the tradition and doctrine of Russian-Soviet ground forces, close-air support in the Red Army[54] in World War II did not constitute jointness in the same sense that it did in Western forces, where the thickness and height of interservice boundaries had led to memoranda of agreements, semi-formal pacts, and the like. Ironically, Soviet close-air support came closer to the "attack aviation" concept of the U.S. Army between the World Wars than to what the Americans later developed in the press of battle. As the Red Army and VVS recovered from the great rending of the opening phase of the war on the eastern front in 1941, the healing and reconstitution of the Soviet military system led to a progressive metamorphosis of control and practice at least somewhat similar in essence to the American and British experiences. By the time of the Battle of Kursk in mid–1943, co-location of air and ground headquarters had led to an establishment of a separate ground-control net.[55]

However, the Western Allies had no direct counterpart to the Soviets' premier ground attack aircraft, the Ilyushin–2 Shturmovik. Much along the lines of the Americans' concept of a well-armored, low-altitude attack plane, it was an extension of the type that the Germans had developed in World War I and let languish, and perhaps a byproduct of the German-Soviet collaborative training from 1925 to 1935. After the war, a German analyst judged the Shturmovik "the decisive instrument of air warfare from the time the Russian command assumed the offensive,"[56] seeing its primary effect as "of a psychological rather than a material nature."[57] The Soviets also diverted many of the cannon-firing P–39 Airacobras provided by the United States under Lend-Lease to ground attack, even though the U.S. Army Air Force (USAAF) did not use P–39s extensively in such a role.[58]

Neither of the Western Allies' air forces succumbed to pressures to develop a massive dive-bomber force had that mounted in the wake of the Nazi blitzkrieg victories and the vivid image of the Stuka in newsreels. Although the U.S. Army's chief of staff, General George Marshall, pushed hard for developing such a force, and several squadrons of land versions of Navy dive bomber types were sent to north Africa and the southwest Pacific, they saw only limited operations.[59] Most USAAF leaders were opposed to a tactical system that harnessed air power so tightly to ground units.[60] Thus, the main line of genealogy of successful Western Allied close air support in World War II flowed from Marine Corps/Navy efforts in the Pacific and from the Royal Air Force's Desert Air Force.

Metamorphosis in North Africa and Italy, 1941–43

The RAF, like the British Army, was hard pressed in the opening campaigns of World War II and the overall pattern of setback and frustration was only broken from time to time, by the Battle of Britain in the autumn of 1940, by successes against the Italians in north Africa late that year, in the reconquest of Ethiopia and the thwarting of Axis plans in Iraq in 1941. By mid–1942, many in Britain, America, and elsewhere felt that the long roster of Allied defeats portended Axis victory. In that roiling cauldron of anxiety, strange mixtures were concocted, as the bureaucratic boundaries between and within the armed services began to blur. Turf-maintaining reflexes were not wholly numbed by the sense of urgency, but they were sharply reduced in many instances. The rapid evolution of Allied tactical air power sprang from a close rapport between RAF and Army leaders in the north African desert. In late 1940, the Italians, who joined the Nazis in the war in June, entered Egypt, threatening the Suez Canal and Middle East oil. Although vastly outnumbering British Empire forces there, Mussolini's armies were hurled back in disarray, and great swarms of them became prisoners of war. The Italians gained some breathing space in the spring of 1941, when Churchill ordered a major portion of Field Marshal Wavell's forces to Greece, depleting British strength in Egypt just as Major-General Erwin Rommel and Panzerarmee Afrika arrived. After Greece and Crete fell to the Nazis, the British lost initiative in north Africa for most of the next year and a half.

As Rommel's forces began operations, using the basic elements of earlier blitzkrieg campaigns—tanks, motorized support elements, and the JU 57 Stuka dive bomber—the latter proved increasingly vulnerable. Heavy Stuka losses over the English Channel in 1940–41 foreshadowed those in the desert, where British, Commonwealth, and French forces came to realize its bark was worse than its bite. By mid–1942, the Desert Air Force had wrested control of the air from the Luftwaffe and Regia Aeronautica, paving the way to the shift in the tactical balance on the ground. During the same period on the eastern front, Luftwaffe air operations had become increasingly linked to supporting the Army. From 1943 onward, shortages of artillery and anti-tank weapons, aggravated by the Allies' strategic bombing offense, increased the German Army's dependence on air support. The air control network was decentralized, and pairing higher-level ground and air headquarters was replaced by assigning dual-service radio teams to the division level. The Luftwaffe's use of bomb-lines gave way to light signals, rockets, panels, and so on, and in a manner similar to the Allied forces in northwest Europe, air control signal vehicles accompanied Panzer forces.[61] By 1944, over three-quarters of Luftwaffe combat operations were in support of ground forces, adding further to the slowing of jet development, and to their being built as light bombers rather than fighters.[62]

The Royal Air Force leaders, driven to ruthless pragmatism by frustration and defeat, were willing to make major alterations in its equipment and doctrine, but, like the American airmen, they also rejected a major dive-bomber program. (The lack of British shore-based dive-bombers led to some embarrassment in the "Channel Dash" of German naval forces from France to Norway in 1942, which revealed some seams in the fabric of British jointness.) Nevertheless, air-ground cooperation increased in the Desert War, producing what John Terraine deemed "intimate relations between the two services at key points," from top echelons to forward elements, just as artillery observation and fire control led to functional blending of infantry, artillery, and air elements in World War I.[63] As air power was moved away from close control by ground commanders in stages, the new systems developed by the Royal Air Force and the British Army began to "click" in north Africa in late 1942. What was gained on the one hand was lost on the other. Although the medium bombers and fighters were let off the leash to ravage enemy installations deep behind the front, close-air support led to a closer yoking of air power to ground forces than some advocates of "pure" air power could accept. Debates over that balance went on throughout the war, amid the clangor and din of battle, and well beyond.[64]

The goads of imminent and actual disaster, experience, trial and error, as well as mounting Allied industrial production, research, and development all helped to close and then reverse and widen the gap between British and German operational art. From early 1941 onward, a new type, the fighter-bomber, appeared. Initially, the durable Hawker Hurricane fighter type was assigned a tactical strafing role. An early modification, the "Hurribomber," was fitted with bomb-racks, but tactics soon shifted from light bombing to strafing. While fighters of all combatants' air forces often attacked targets of opportunity, what had often been random practice was now orchestrated by Army-RAF radio links, and tactical power was increasingly concentrated closer to the fighting front.

In north Africa, the Desert Air Force's tactical air support had initially consisted of sweeps deep behind Axis lines to attack airfields, transport, and anti-aircraft guns. As communications improved, mobile Air Support Control teams of RAF and Army officers began to operate in the forward battle zone and developed common terminology. Eventually, linking of these elements' signal nets extended to all levels, and mobile control teams in vehicles kept closer touch in fluid situations. The lag between a call for close air support and delivery shrank from hours in late 1941 to fractions of an hour by early 1943. New versions of the Hurricane festooned with cannon and air-to-ground rockets, along with other fighter types and light bombers, reflected the pattern of rapid evolution.

As the British and American Tactical Air Forces were formed in Tunisia in early 1943, a schism in air power doctrine and practice was being resolved. In the Desert War, before the El Alamein victory in October-November 1942, a close working relationship had developed between General Bernard Montgomery, commander of the British 8th Army, and Air Marshal Sir Arthur Coningham, chief of the Desert Air Force, and their staffs.[65] In early 1943, however, estrangement developed as the Allied armies and air forces converged on the German-Italian bastion of Tunisia. Montgomery, the first victorious Western Allied major commander in the war, had become a media superstar and much less prone to share glory. Coningham and other air officers, sensing they had given too much away, now insisted that the main role of tactical air was to strike deep behind the front lines, and "dry up" the enemy with operations under the command of airmen.

The dilemma was depicted in the film "Patton," in a scene set in north Africa in the spring of 1943. In that dramatization, drawn from U.S. General Omar Bradley's memoirs, Patton complained about lack of overhead air support to Coningham, then Allied Tactical Air Forces Commander. As Coningham began explaining the logic of drying up enemy air power at the roots, Luftwaffe bombers strafed the building. At this point, as in other instances, American and British airmen formed a common front in framing a doctrine that maximized their independence from the other services. Yet air-naval links were far weaker than those that had developed between air and ground forces.[66] Soon afterward, the new U.S. Army Field Manual 100–20 placed tactical air elements under the centralized control of the theater air commander, not the local ground commander, and set the limit of aerial engagement beyond the range of friendly artillery "except in emergencies."[67]

Increasing Allied aircraft production and refined communications eroded that doctrine, however. The Western Allies' near-total air superiority in north Africa in the spring of 1943 set a pattern that generally prevailed during the rest of the war in the ground campaigns. At the same time, round-the-clock bombing of Germany had begun in earnest, as the Allies gained the upper hand in the Battle of the Atlantic. In July, the Red Army gutted the *Wehrmacht* in the giant tank battles around Kursk. Although major reforms would soon be carried out by Hitler's production minister, Albert Speer, the Luftwaffe was being overwhelmed by the Allies in all categories of aerial warfare, except in defending Germany against daylight raids. That bastion would also crumble in the spring of 1944.

Although the example of the Luftwaffe's early success was in view as U.S. Army and Army Forces joined battle with the *Wehrmacht* in north Africa in November 1942, and operations increased in the southwest Pacific at the same time, there was no clear reference to the use of dive bombers or fighter bombers in their doctrine.[68] Quality and quantity of American close-air support lagged behind the British until well into the Italian campaign. Alan Wilt identified several factors beyond the differential in combat experience that contributed to that gap, including weaker training and less effective communications loops and procedures, as well as the reluctance of many U.S. senior airmen to play a role subordinate to ground commanders.[69]

By the end of the north African campaign in May 1943, as the air-ground cooperation techniques of the Royal Air Force had progressed substantially, the Americans picked up speed, partly due to organizational osmosis. After Allied air superiority had been gained, the North African Tactical Air Force aimed at interdiction, attacking targets well in the rear of enemy forces. By the time of Operation Husky, the invasion of Sicily in July 1943, a new doctrine had been set forth by the U.S. Army Air Forces. It reflected the strong influence of Air Marshal Coningham over U.S. airmen's thinking in North Africa, and echoed the British Middle East Commander, Field Marshal Sir Harold Alexander, whose view of co-equivalence of air and ground command in turn reflected the rapport between Montgomery and Coningham. The immediate effect of the new doctrine, however, was that on-call air support was not used in the Sicilian campaign.[70]

In spite of the official doctrine of deep penetration, or what later became known as "interdiction," British and American close-air support systems grew in size and sophistication. Although the Sicilian campaign was fought without close air support, soon afterward, in Italy, Wing Commander David Hayson developed the "Rover David" and "Paddy" control teams that led to American "Rover Frank" and "Joe" variants, that is, advanced motorized signal teams. The Americans began to pick up the pace of innovation and introduced "Horse-flies"—Forward Air Control light planes—in Italy, a technique applied in France soon after the Normandy invasion, making daylight movement by Nazi vehicles extremely dangerous.[71] A mobile operation post at brigade headquarters and a special air photo designation grid aided target identification. The "cab rank" system was also introduced, in which fighter bombers on the way to designated targets loitered for a few minutes in a control zone near the front before carrying out their mission, ready to respond immediately if an urgent target was identified by "Rover David" controllers operating from armored cars.[72] Thus, the inter-service control and approval loop that presented a problem in other settings, including Vietnam, was shortened substantially.

In the invasion of northwest Europe in June 1944, tactical air was meshed with field artillery and naval networks as well as the signal communications networks that connected heavily mechanized forces.[73] Ground forces advancing from the Normandy beachhead received naval gunfire support for a month and a half after the landing.[74] As the cab ranks of fighter-bombers orbiting near the front grew in numbers and their speed of response increased, rockets increased their capacity to "bust" armored vehicles and trains. By the end of the Normandy campaign, the average lag between request and response was down to less than five minutes. The arrival of the RAF's Typhoon heavy fighter added to the effect, as they shattered over 150 Nazi tanks in a single battle. When the Germans tried to move mechanized forces of any size in daylight, the result was columns of their vehicles abandoned, shattered, or burned out, with vast carpets of human and equine corpses surrounding them, forevisions of the "Highway of Death" of the Gulf War.

In late summer 1944, Allied leaders, concerned that closing the gigantic pincers around the German 7th Army after the Normandy breakout completely might lead to combat between the converging Allies, decided to leave the jaws open and let Tactical Air Forces do the job. In what Richard Hallion deemed the "classic example of combined arms, mechanized, air-land, coalition warfare," the so-called Falaise Gap became a vast charnel house, as for a brief moment, the *Wehrmacht* had no major forces between the vast killing ground and the heart of Germany.[75]

Throughout the rest of the war in northwest Europe, in Italy, and on the eastern front, the Allied armies came to take air superiority and close-air support for granted, except when bad weather broke the magic link from time to time, as in the Battle of the Bulge. When the sun broke through after two overcast weeks, and thousands of Allied planes took off, it was taken for granted that the Nazis had been beaten. In the campaign in northwest Europe, employment of tactical air power, as one practitioner saw it, had become a product of "opportunism [and] flexibility in planning and control" with a premium on "initiative and ingenuity." Each armored division had about a dozen air officers in tanks controlling air strikes along the front and flanks with VHF radios. In addition to attacking targets on request, supporting aircraft carried out armed reconnaissance deep behind German lines and provided cover for advancing columns. The planned strikes central to tactical air doctrine in 1943 had been virtually abandoned,[76] and "pure" infantry-to-infantry and armor-to-armor combat became increasingly rare.[77] In combined arms tactics, fusion of infantry, artillery, tanks, and aircraft through such functional cross-links as radio frequency overlaps and assignments of artillery and observers to ground units was matched at higher levels by ever-closer meshing of air and ground staffs, artillery, and air control centers. Again and again, the high fighting quality of German infantry and armor was offset by the blending of Allied air support, artillery, armor, and ground forces, as each side's decisions regarding force balance and production priorities made early in the war yielded increasingly different results in battle.

Enthusiasm about the flowering of close-air support (CAS) was not universal, for some airmen were concerned that the old leash of ground commanders' control over air power had been strengthened and shortened. Others felt that the capital cost of aircraft and trained air crews was too high for results that it yielded. However, in late 1944, British operational researchers calculated that the loss of approximately three pilots and five aircraft in CAS missions was offset by the "saving" of a battalion of ground troops.[78]

CAS in the Pacific

In the Pacific and Far East, varying command methods and locales produced different patterns of effects. A relatively close approximation to the European theater's state of the art was to be found in Burma, where such key figures as Slim, Cochran, Alison, and Mountbatten were functionally minded. Colonel Philip Cochran had been involved in close-air support operations in north Africa before going to Burma, and there, along with John Alison, oversaw the forming of the 1st Air Commandos. The application of air power in Burma followed Slim's view of it as basically a utilitarian platform. Air Commandos and other American air units in the area provided a wide range of services in the harsh and complex environment of Southeast Asia, from mass glider-borne operations and the support of long-range penetration forces and clandestine operations, to aerial resupply and reinforcement, medical evacuation, interdiction, and close-air support. The Air Commandos' special "package" of aircraft, including light liaison aircraft, transports, medium bombers, gliders, and several fighter types and its variegated mission profile were later judged too expensive and exotic to become an integral part of the American air force structure. The units' experiences served as a mainly symbolic precedent the U.S. Air Force's special operations unit created in the early 1960s.

Farther to the east, the refinement of U.S. Marine Corps dive-bombing and tactical air support in the Guadalcanal and central Pacific campaigns ran counter to a shrivelling away of U.S. Army Air Force close-air support and the end of the use of land-based dive bombers in the southwest Pacific in 1942–43. While at first glance it might seem that the widespread joint operations and close-in fighting with well-sited Japanese defenders would have put a special premium on the development of CAS in the Pacific, many major assault landings were carried out in New Guinea and the islands north of it in 1943–44 without it.[79] Nevertheless, constant refinements were made in providing air power more immediately in support of ground operations during the campaigns in New Guinea and the Admiralties, and by December 1943, air control parties were assigned down to regimental level. Targets hit by the U.S. Army Air Forces were usually at least 500 yards beyond the fighting front, usually against such key points as artillery and airstrips, and request-to-response time was several hours. The Australians, however, developed their own forward air control system more like that evolving in the Mediterranean campaigns, employing Vultee Vengeance dive bombers and light fighters for close-in work.[80] Whatever the causes of regional differences in practice, it was not due to a lack of innovative capacity. MacArthur's air chief, George Kenney, showed great tactical creativity in other respects, but when Army forces in the Philippines were offered Marine and naval close-air support in late 1944, they were unenthusiastic due to unpleasant experiences. Some Army units had a standing rule that no tactical air targets were to be designated at less than 1,000 years from forward positions. Their reluctance soon vanished after Marine Corps air strikes hit point targets only dozens of yards from forward positions, and a special citation presented to the Marines by the Sixth Army commander, General Walter Krueger, reflected a widespread change of view throughout his command.[81]

As the war progressed, moreover, Marine Corps tactical air support was undercut by being denied access to escort carriers, and by organizational resistance within the Navy and Marine Corps. Ironically, they proved their effectiveness to skeptical Army commanders in early 1945, while the main burden of air support for the wholly Marine Corps assault on Iwo Jima in February fell upon Navy and Army fighters, leading Robert Moskin to observe that "Marine close air support for Marines had not yet come into its own."[82] In spite of the widely held belief that Marine Corps experiments with close-air support in Nicaragua in the 1920s carried through directly in doctrine and practice to World War II campaigns in the Central Pacific, Marine airmen did not receive special training in such operations or carry out such missions until 1943. CAS missions were not flown on Guadalcanal, although some were carried out against nearby islands, in experiments with CAS that were byproducts of accidents of war and adaptation, not of a deliberate shaping of doctrine and technology. When P–39 Bell Airacobras and Curtiss P–400s were diverted to CAS duties after they proved unable to stand up against first-line Japanese fighters, the existing communications nets were found inadequate for such operations.[83]

The rising curves of subsequent refinements blended in late 1944 and 1945, when on-call strikes and control of attacking aircraft by ground controllers increased in the Philippines campaigns, and Army-Army Air Force air support teams augmented by Marine Corps JASCOs directed almost 50,000 sorties. Navy fighter bombers operating from carriers and Marine shore-based dive and fighter bombers as well as a wide array of Army aircraft, including heavy bombers and Royal Australian Air Force elements, supported ground and naval operations in the Philippines and southwest Pacific in the final phase of the war.[84] While the high level of effectiveness generated praise and enthusiasm in some cases, it led to inflated expectations and frustration in others. Even on Okinawa, where practice reached its pinnacle in the Pacific War, most CAS missions were predesignated, the request-strike lag averaged fifty-five minutes, and errors caused dozens of casualties, as many friendly targets were hit or subjected to close calls—including General Roy Geiger, the senior Marine commander.[85]

By the end of the war, tactical air support frequently blurred across the line into what had previously been seen as the realm of strategic air power, that is, massed heavy bombers. On Okinawa, from April to July 1945, while close-air support was being applied across service boundaries on a broad scale, large formations of strategic bombers were used frequently against targets, a practice that had begun in Europe early in World War II, when the Soviets concentrated strategic bombers at the front in the Finnish campaign in 1939–40. The Luftwaffe had picked up that theme occasionally during the early blitzkrieg campaigns, most notably at Rotterdam in May 1940. In the summer of 1942, the Soviets used some 800 bombers to break up a German armored thrust toward the Caucasus oil fields,[86] and carpet-bombing by massed medium bomber formations was also often seen in the Desert War. In Italy, in the controversial bombing of the Monte Cassino Abbey in the spring of 1944, almost 10,000 tons of bombs were dropped along the fronts of the 5th U.S. and 8th British armies.

In northwest Europe, massed heavy bombers were used in a tactical mode on D Day, and during the Normandy campaign in the battle for Caen. In Operation Goodwood, July 18th, 1944, 1,676 heavy and 343 fighter bombers delivered 7,700 tons along the British and Canadian front in support of a major attack. Soon afterward, in August, over 10,000 tons were dropped in Operation Cobra, a two-phase attack involving almost 3,300 aircraft, as preparation for the American breakout at St. Lô. Whole German units were shattered, disoriented, and deranged, but the moon-like landscape of craters also impeded advancing forces. Bombing errors' infliction of substantial losses on friendly troops included the death of the chief of U.S. Army Ground Forces, General Lesley J. McNair. Caen and Cobra were flavored with controversy, J.F.C. Fuller later deriding them as "colossal cracking."

The single largest tactical use of strategic bombers in World War II was Operation Queen, October 16, 1944, when some 4,500 Allied aircraft, about half of them U.S. and British heavy bombers, dropped just over 10,000 tons on towns in the rear of the German front facing the U.S. First Army. The depth of the raid was designed to prevent the friendly casualties suffered in Cobra. While it did substantial damage to key German communication and transport centers and smashed some units, the distance from the battle zone allowed the Germans to recover, and the raids did not noticeably affect operations.[87] It was the last such practice in Europe, except in the set-piece combined operation across the Rhine in late March 1945, so carefully planned by Montgomery and his staff.[88]

Employment of heavy bombers in a tactical role by U.S. air forces continued after World War II. In Korea, mass B–29 raids were directed against North Korean forces around the Pusan perimeter in the late summer of 1950, and against troop concentrations later. The practice reappeared in the Arclight strikes against known and suspected mass targets in South Vietnam by B–52 Strato-fortress bombers, and most decisively, against the North Vietnamese siege of the U.S. Marines at Khe Sanh 1968, and in the B–52 raids against Iraq's Republican Guard Forces in Operation Desert Storm in 1991. The question of the tactical value of "colossal cracking" was not fully resolved by the passing of time.

Land-Based Long-Range Aircraft in Sea Warfare

In submarine and carrier warfare in World War II, the fusion of air and naval elements proved crucial. In the summer of 1940, very long-range aircraft (VLRs) began to loom large in the Battle of the Atlantic, as the Germans used Focke Wulf 200 Condor four-engined civil transport planes to spot targets for U-boats, and, sometimes, to attack merchant ships. Although they were not designed for rough weather, prolonged fighting with heavy loads, or strenuous maneuvering, and few in number, Condors cut deep into the Atlantic jugular. Fortunately for the Allies, divi.ions in the Nazi command structure led to a failure to capitalize on those initial successes. Lack of cooperation in procurement and poor operational coordination between the Luftwaffe and Kriegsmarine, especially in monitoring convoys and in assisting U-boat "wolf packs," threw away their early lead.[89] Later, the "lack of uncertainty of support of naval operations" by the Luftwaffe also blunted German attempts to slash at passing Russia-bound Allied convoys from their Norwegian bastion.[90]

Soviet Admiral Gorshkov later saw the Nazi U-boat's failure as a product of submarines not receiving support from other forces, essentially from long-range aviation,[91] echoing the view of Admiral Karl Dönitz, chief of the German submarine forces, that "Germany was waging war at sea without an air arm . . . a feature as much out of line with contemporary conditions as it was decisive in its effect."[92] Yet Dönitz overstated the case, for there had been some fusion. Up to June 1941, when withdrawn from service in the Atlantic, the Condors of Kämpfgeschwader 40 had sunk 750,000 tons of Allied shipping ranging far out over the Atlantic, even west of Iceland, during flights between bases in Norway and France.[93] As stiffening Allied defenses inflicted heavy losses, the Condors assumed a reconnaissance role, but their shadowing of Allied convoys was a key element in the wolf-pack tactics of 1942–43. They were not as maneuverable or well-armed as Allied VLR aircraft, especially the B–24 Liberators, which they met in increasing numbers in ponderous dog-fights. Six to eight flights per day by its twenty-five planes put a heavy strain on KG 40, while attempts to develop a better plane failed. Luftwaffe VLR development, like its heavy bomber and jet projects, was hampered by the fixation on dive-bombing capacity. Although Condor–U-boat linkage was later seen as the zenith of Luftwaffe and Kriegsmarine coordination,[94] even that was judged a "hodgepodge and not streamlined homogeneous command at all" with deleterious effects on development and procurement,[95] a consequence of Göring's dictum that "everything that flies belongs to me."[96] On the other side of the ledger, the Navy failed to call off air reconnaissance missions when no U-boats were available to exploit sightings.[97]

German defeat in the Atlantic came gradually and in increments. In late 1942 and early 1943, the Nazi U-boats suffered a defeat when they mounted heavier anti-aircraft weapons and tried to fight it out on the surface with Allied VLR aircraft. On June 6, 1944, KG 40, now equipped with Ju 88C, long-range fighter-dive bombers, was decimated when committed against the Allied invasion of Normandy. While many in the Luftwaffe and Kriegsmarine sensed their advantage sliding away, prospects on the Allied side seemed no brighter until late in the war.[98] Slow to learn, the Royal Air Force's Coastal Command and Royal Navy anti-submarine elements finally recognized the importance of VLRs in negating their Luftwaffe counterparts, as well as in suppressing and directly attacking U-boats. Unlike the Nazis, they eventually learned to "play ball," the Royal Navy's diversion of naval equipment to Coastal Command being described by John Terraine as "inter-service cooperation at its best."[99]

Nevertheless, the efforts of all three major combatant nations in the Battle of the Atlantic were hampered by parochialism. Even when the growing importance of air power in anti-submarine warfare was being driven home in the grim statistics of sinkings in 1942–43, the U.S. Navy and the Army Air Force bickering over control of VLRs, especially B–24 Liberators, was not resolved until September 1943. Only then, after the crisis of the Battle of Atlantic had passed, did General Arnold agree that USAAF aircraft could be flown by Navy airmen from shore bases. The Navy's official historian of World War II, Samuel Eliot Morison, saw the services' dickering as due to "conflicting personalities and service ambitions" and discrediting to both sides.[100]

The actual effect of various systems in the Battle of the Atlantic was measured imperfectly in "kill" credits and distorted by subjective impression. Wartime newsreels, postwar films, novels, and television documentaries tended to convey an impression that most submarine killing was done by convoy escort vessels. As with close-air support, the effect of air power in anti-submarine warfare (ASW) was remote, diffuse, and hard to appraise. Yet there were some indicators.

No convoy escorted by a blimp lost a ship, and those with carrier escorts or constant air cover fared far better than others both in respect to losses suffered and in the killing of submarines. A similar pattern was visible in the Pacific, where, although Japan's anti-submarine warfare efforts were poorly structured, their long-range flying boats gained great respect from the Allies.

Assigning credit for performance in attacks on submarines was imperfect, often angering combatants whose memories did not jibe with data gathered at the time or when enemy data became available later. Ambiguity also arose from the difficulty of apportioning the exact effect of each element in air-naval attacks. Neither was it possible to measure the indirect, suppressive effects of aircraft reconnaissance, when the sound or sight of aircraft thwarted or discouraged U-boat activities. The imprecision in measurement was reflected in the fact that while about a quarter of U-boat kills were by aircraft, almost the same number were due to cooperative undetermined effects.[101] A peculiar tribute to the importance of VLRs in anti-submarine warfare was paid in the form of the bureaucratic fighting over their control between the U.S. Navy and Army Air Force that resumed after World War II.

THE BURGEONING OF SPECIAL OPERATIONS

Concepts of special operations and *kleine kriege*—small wars—were recognized in military theory in the eighteenth century, and evolved both in theory and practice in the nineteenth century. In stages, from the mid-nineteenth century onward, repeating rifles, high explosives, automatic weapons, radios, motor vehicles, and aircraft altered the nature of special operations, sometimes yielding advantage to terrorists/freedom fighters, sometimes to light military units, and usually fleetingly. In World War I, new forms of specialized warfare appeared, such as the motorboat and human torpedo units of the Italian fleet, mountain troops, the *nettoyers* of the French army, T. E. Lawrence's harassing of the Turks, von Lettow-Vorbeck's East African campaigns, the *Sturmtruppen* and the infiltration tactics of the German Army, and the *arditi* of the Italian Army.

World War II saw a far greater mushrooming of light forces, for example, Corps Franc, Commandos, Rangers, Brandenburgers, and so on, which relied on individual courage, skill, and special training to achieve highly focused effects, psychological as well as physical. Most "mobs for jobs" were formed within the boundaries of particular services and often used for tasks other than what they were originally created for, like the U.S.-Canadian First Special Service Force.[102] "Special ops" generated new forms of jointness, as they crossed service and agency boundaries in planning and execution. Military and intelligence operatives bent on forming local guerrilla forces, sabotage, assassination, or raids on enemy rear areas were often carried and/or supplied by aircraft, ship, or submarine or a mix thereof. After France fell, the Royal Air Force, though sometimes reluctantly, committed substantial resources to support clandestine activities, as did the Soviet and U.S. Army Air Forces, and the Italian, British, U.S., and Japanese navies as well.

In other instances, "conventional" forces carried out special missions, several instances of which during World War II are well known. On April 18, 1942, the "Doolittle Raid" on Japan was carried out by U.S. Army Air Force B–25 Mitchell medium bombers flying from a U.S. Navy aircraft carrier.[103] In mid-August 1942, the 2nd Marine Raider Battalion raided Makin atoll in the Gilbert Islands, conveyed by two large mine-laying submarines.[104] Especially controversial was the improvised joint "special" operation, using a conventional unit of the Army Air Forces to perform a mission conceived by the Navy—the Yamamoto mission.

After U.S. Navy signal decryption experts intercepted a detailed itinerary of Japanese Admiral Isoroku Yamamoto, Army Air Forces P–38 Lightning long-range fighters were sent to intercept his command aircraft on April 18, 1943. Yamamoto was killed, but debates over who actually shot down his aircraft and whether the action was within the laws of warfare continued long afterward.[105] Such stridency of claims reflected the gap between conventional warfare, in which great deeds and individual heroism are marked and praised, and "special ops," in which anonymity, unsung achievements, and teamwork are central values.

JOINT OPERATIONS: DESCENT FROM THE ZENITH

In 1945–46, the vast apparatus of joint and combined operations so carefully and painfully crafted crumbled rapidly, the smooth click and hum of operational competency sometimes fading away in a matter of minutes, as peace came. Although demobilization plans had been carefully honed and put into action from 1943 onward, the euphoria of victory, homesickness, and visions of permanent peace, augmented by the founding of the United Nations and nuclear weapons as a nemesis of further warfare, all added to the speed and scale of demobilization. Yet some joint operations continued, as amphibious, naval, and air forces transported millions of returning prisoners of war, refugees, and Allied forces in 1945–46. In Southeast Asia and Indonesia, small skirmishes and then major colonial wars erupted. In China, as withdrawal of U.S. forces came in stages, the mounting civil war slowed the erosion of proficiency and keenness. The return to peacetime routine in other occupied areas and at home was paced by the massive "mothballing" of the U.S. Navy, and reduction of the U.S. Marine Corps to one-sixth and the army to one-tenth of their respective strengths at the end of the war. The capacity to carry out anti-submarine, amphibious, and carrier warfare, airborne operations, and close-air support was almost gone by mid–1946. Although operational fusion was nearly moribund, the next half decade would be marked by the fiercest battles over jointness in American military history.

NOTES

1. For details of the early wartime mechanism, see Bill Jackson and Dwin Bramall, *The Chiefs: The Story of the United Kingdom Chiefs of Staff* (London: Brassey's, 1991), pp. 117–216.

2. For a terse description, see Albert Merglen, *Surprise Warfare: Subversive, Airborne and Amphibious Operations*, trans. Kenneth Morgan (London: George Allen & Unwin, 1968), pp. 50–54; for personal perspectives, see John Masters, *Bugles and a Tiger* (New York: Harper & Brothers, 1955); and William Slim, *Unofficial History* (New York: David McKay, 1959).

3. Fergusson, *Watery Maze*, p. 166.

4. For a list of lessons learned at Dieppe, see PRO DEF 2/1773, *After-action Report on Dieppe Raid*, pp. 88–89; for a detailed operational account, see Charles P. Stacey, *Official History of the Canadian Army in the Second World War*, vol. 6 (Ottawa: Clautier, 1955), pp. 375ff.

5. N.a., *Condensed Analysis of the Ninth Air Force in the European Theater of Operations* (Washington, D.C.: Office of Air Force History, 1984) [orig. publ. 1946], p. 25.

6. For example, see PRO ADM 1 13187-MO 11217/1943, *Bridging the Gap Between Landing Craft and Shore in Combined Operations: Army and Navy Responsibility*; for perspective on praxis late in the war, see A. V. Arnold, "Preparation for a Division Amphibious Operation," *Military Review* 45:2 (May 1945): 3–11; also see PRO ADM 1–13099/MO 52438/1943, *Combined Operations: Report and Recommendations in the Light of Experience*; ADM 1/15678, *Amphibious Combined Operations: History of Development and Technique*, Parts I and II.

7. N.a., *Salerno: American Operations from the Beaches to the Volturno, September 9–October 6, 1943* (Washington, D.C.: Center of Military History, 1990), pp. 27–30.

8. The standard work is Martin Blumenson, *Anzio: The Gamble that Failed* (Philadelphia: J. B. Lippincott, 1963); for a basic account, see N.a., *Anzio Beachhead 22 January–25 May 1944* (Washington, D.C.: Center of Military History, 1990).

9. For a discussion of the difficulties of exact casualty estimation for Overlord, see Chester Wilmot, *The Struggle for Europe* (New York: Harper & Brothers, 1952), p. 293.

10. W. L. Atschkassow, "Landing Operations of the Soviet Naval Fleet During World War II," in Merrill L. [Lt. Col. U.S.M.C.] Bartlett, *Assault from the Sea: Essays on the History of Amphibious Warfare* (Annapolis: U.S. Naval Institute Press, 1983), pp. 299–308.

11. For parallel perspectives, see Hans G. V. Lehmann, "Japanese Landing Operations in World War Two," pp. 105–201, and R. A. Stewart, "The Japanese Assault on Timor, 1942," pp. 203–9, both in Bartlett, *Assault from the Sea.*

12. Background on Japanese interservice tension rivalry can be traced in Saburo Hayashi and Alvin Coox, *Kogun: The Japanese Army in the Pacific War* (Quantico, Va.: Marine Corps Association, 1959); also see Mark R. Peattie and David C. Evans, "Sato Tetsutaro and Japanese Strategy," *Naval History* 4:4 (Fall 1990): 38.

13. Rene J. Francillon, *Japanese Aircraft of the Pacific War* (London: Putnam, 1979); and D. Clayton James, "American and Japanese Strategies in the Pacific War," in Peter Paret et al., eds., *Makers of Modern Strategy from Machiavelli to the Nuclear Age* (Princeton: Princeton University Press, 1986), pp. 718–19.

14. Homer N. Wallin, *Pearl Harbor: Why, How, Fleet Salvage and Final Appraisal* (Washington, D.C.: Naval Historical Division, 1968), pp. 43–49.

15. William Felix Atwater, *United States Army and Navy Development of Joint Landing Operations, 1898–1942* (doctoral dissertation, Duke University, 1986), pp. iii–iv.

16. L. F. Ellis, *Victory in the West*, vol. i (London: Her Majesty's Stationery Office, 1962), pp. 513–14; also see J.M.A. Gwyer, *Grand Strategy*, vol. iii, Part 1 (London: Her Majesty's Stationery Office, 1964), p. 515.

17. A.J.P. Taylor, *Beaverbrook* (New York: Simon and Schuster, 1972), p. 526.

18. Atwater, *U.S. Army and Navy Development*, pp. 170–74.

19. Julian C. Smith, "Tarawa," *United States Naval Institute Proceedings* 79:11 (November 1953): 1163.

20. For a detailed description of the evolution and function of headquarters ships, see J. D. Ladd, *Assault from the Sea 1939–45: The Craft, The Landings, The Men* (Newton Abbot: David and Charles, 1976), Chapter 7, pp. 119–32.

21. Robert Sherrod's *Tarawa: The Story of a Battle* (New York: Pocket Books, 1944) gave a frank account of the battle and its aftermath to the wartime public.

22. Laurence J. Legere, *Unification of the Armed Forces* (New York: Garland Publishing Co., 1988), p. 284.

23. For details, including the Cartwheel warning order, see John Miller, Jr., *U.S. Army in World War II: The War in the Pacific: Cartwheel: The Reduction of Rabaul* (Washington, D.C.: Office of the Chief of Military History, 1959), esp. pp. 12–26 and 381–83.

24. See Atwater, *U.S. Army and Navy Development*, pp. 157 and 174.

25. Harland D. Bynell, "Joint Logistics at an Advanced Base in the Pacific," *Military Review* 26:5 (August 1946): 23–28.

26. Mary Ellen Condon, "Medical Aspects of Amphibious Operations Involving U.S. Army Forces in the War Against Japan," pp. 276–90, in Daniel M. Masterson et al., eds., *Naval History: The Sixth Symposium of the U.S. Naval Academy* (Wilmington, Del.: Scholarly Resources, 1987); also see John W. Jamison, "Medical Service in Amphibious Operations," *United States Naval Institute Proceedings* 78:1 (January 1952): 22–30.

27. For a post-Torch perspective, see PRO ADM I–13167/MO 296/1943, *Supplies for Invasion Forces Landing on Enemy Beaches*.

28. Fergusson, *Watery Maze*, p. 92.

29. F. W. Greene, "Supply of Amphibious Forces," *Military Review* 26:9 (December 1946): 39–57.

30. PRO ADM I 16330, *U.S. Naval Organizational and Logistical Problems in the Central and South Pacific/U.S. Navy Commands and Staff Organization*, pp. 12–13.

31. PRO DEFE 2/1773, *History of Combined Operations Organization, 1940–1945* (London: Amphibious Warfare HQ, 1956); for details on British joint and combined organizational structures "at the creation," that is, 1940, see J. R. Butler, *Grand Strategy*, vol. ii (London: Her Majesty's Stationery Office, 1957), pp. 259–60; for the state of networks in 1944–45, see John Ehrman, *Grand Strategy*, vol. vi (London: Her Majesty's Stationery Office, 1956); for details of the elaborate combined and joint structures, see Forrest Pogue's *The Supreme Command: U.S. Army in World War II—The European Theater of Operations* (Washington, D.C.: Office of the Chief of Military History, 1954), pp. 90, 99–101, 127, 269, 324, 590; for an overview of the orchestration of complex

elements, see William H. Billings, Jr., "Task Force Planning," *Military Review* 26:4 (1946): 75–78.

32. Frank O. Hough, *The Assault on Peleliu* (Washington, D.C.: U.S. Government Printing Office, 1950), p. 201.

33. Carl W. Hoffman, *The Seizure of Tinian* (Washington, D.C.: U.S. Government Printing Office, 1951), p. 16.

34. Ibid., p. 127.

35. Carl W. Hoffman, *Saipan: The Beginning of the End* (Washington, D.C.: U.S. Government Printing Office, 1950), p. 251.

36. Ibid., p. 125.

37. Hoffman, *Seizure of Tinian*, p. 127.

38. For example, see John Gordon IV, "Joint Fire Support: The Salerno Experience," *Military Review* 69:3 (March 1989): 38–62.

39. See PRO ADM 1/12929-MO 53085/1943, *Requirements for Naval Supporting Fire During Combined Operations Obtaining Necessary Inshore Artillery Fire*; and ADM 1/16040-MO 7475/1944, *Need for a Common Procedure for Naval Bombardment: Discussion with U.S. and Allied Navies—Report by Admiralty Committee*.

40. Harold A. Bivins, *An Annotated Bibliography of Naval Gunfire Support* (Washington, D.C.: Historical Division, Headquarters, U.S. Marine Corps, 1971); Fergusson, *The Watery Maze*, pp. 321–23; Donald W. Weller, "Salvo-Splash! The Development of Naval Gunfire Support in World War II," Part 1, *U.S. Naval Institute Proceedings* 80:8 (August 1954): 839–46, and Part ii 80:9 (September 1954): 1011–21; for a perspective on the orchestration of ground artillery, naval gunfire, and air support at the end of World War II, see Charles L. Thomas, "Development of a Fire Support Plan for an Amphibious Operation," *Military Review* 25:12 (March 1946): 28–33; for the Vietnam era, James D. Hessman, "Resurgence of Naval Guns in the Age of Missiles," *Navy* 12:6 (June 1969): 32–34; and for a recent view, see n.a., *Field Manual 6–20, Fire Support in Combined Arms Operations* (Washington, D.C.: Headquarters, Department of the Army, 1984).

41. Robert D. Heinl, "Target: Iwo," *U.S. Naval Institute Proceedings* 89:7 (July 1963): 77–82; also see Whitman S. Bartley, *Iwo Jima: Amphibious Epic* (Washington, D.C.: Historical Branch, Headquarters, U.S. Marine Corps, 1954), pp. 19–50.

42. Charles S. Nichols and Henry I. Shaw, *Okinawa: Victory in the Pacific* (Washington, D.C.: Historical Branch, Headquarters, U.S. Marine Corps, 1955), pp. 29, 288.

43. Ibid., pp. 17–19, 269–71.

44. N.a., *Seventh Amphibious Force Command History—10 January 1943–23 December 1945* (Shanghai: 7th Amphibious Force, 1945), p. ii–28; for the evolution of shore parties, see pp. ii, 36, 41.

45. N.a., *The Capture of Makin: 20–24 November 1943* (Washington, D.C.: Center for Military History, 1990), p. 56.

46. Frank Hough, *The Island War: The United States Marine Corps in the Pacific* (Philadelphia: Lippincott, 1947), p. 11.

47. From testimony of Fleet Admiral William Halsey, p. 240, U.S. Congress, House Committee on Armed Services, 81st Congress, 1st session, *The National Defense Program: Unification and Strategy* (Washington, D.C.: U.S. Government Printing Office, 1949).

48. William Slim, *Defeat into Victory* (London: Cassell, 1956), p. 165.

49. Hilary St. George Saunders, *Royal Air Force, 1939–1945: The Fight is Won* (London: Her Majesty's Stationery Office, 1974), p. 130.

50. Samuel A. Stouffer et al., *The American Soldier: Combat and Its Aftermath* (Princeton: Princeton University Press, 1949), p. 232.

51. Faris R. Kirkland, "The French Air Force in 1940: Was it Defeated by the Luftwaffe or by Politics?" *Air University Review* 36:3 (September-October 1985): 101–17.

52. Lee Kennett, "Development to 1939," in B. Franklin Cooling, ed., *Close Air Support* (Washington, D.C.: Office of Air Force History, 1990), p. 53.

53. See Williamson Murray, "The Luftwaffe Experience, 1939–1941," in Cooling, *Close Air Support*, pp. 85–98.

54. Kenneth R. Whiting, "Soviet Air-Ground Coordination, 1941–45," in Cooling, *Close Air Support*, p. 148.

55. Ibid., p. 133.

56. Walter Schwabedissin, *The Russian Air Force in the Eyes of German Commanders* (New York: Arno Press, 1960), p. 214.

57. Ibid., p. 334.

58. For an overview of the development of U.S. air support doctrine, see Gary L. Bounds et al., *Larger Units: Theater Army-Army Group-Field Army* (Fort Leavenworth, Kan.: Combat Studies Institute, 1985), pp. A–17, A–20, A–26, A–28.

59. The main types were the A–24 and A–25, variants of the SBD Dauntless and SB2C Curtiss Helldiver, respectively.

60. David Brazleton suggested that their demise was more a consequence of "Air Force policy than . . . performance deficiencies"; cf. "SDB Dauntless," in *Aircraft in Profile*, ed. Charles W. Cain (New York: Doubleday, 1971), p. 185.

61. Williamson Murray, "The Luftwaffe Experience, 1939–41," in Cooling, *Close Air Support*, pp. 98–99.

62. For details on organization, see Paul Diechmann, Noel F. Parrish, and Albert F. Simpson, *German Air Force Operations in Support of the Army*, Littleton B. Atkins, ed. (New York: Arno Press, 1962), pp. 124–39, 153, 163–67.

63. John Terraine, *A Time for Courage: The Royal Air Force in the European War, 1939–1945* (New York: Macmillan, 1985), p. 346.

64. For example, Alexander P. De Seversky's critique of tactical air power and brief for long-range heavy bombers, *Victory Through Air Power* (Garden City, N.Y.: Garden City Publishing Co., 1943), esp. pp. 112–13; for a refutation, see F. O. Miksche, *Is Bombing Decisive? A Study in the Organization and Tactical Employment of Modern Air Fleets* (London: George Allen & Unwin, 1943), Ch. 4.

65. For details, see Francis de Guingand, *Operation Victory* (New York: Scribner's, 1947), p. 192.

66. Alan F. Wilt, "Allied Cooperation in Sicily and Italy," in Cooling, *Close Air Support*, p. 226.

67. For an overview of the evolution of air-ground operations in major U.S. Army structures, 1930 to 1973, see Gary L. Bounds et al., *Larger Units: Theater Army-Army Group-Field Army* (Fort Leavenworth, Kan.: Combat Studies Institute, 1985), pp. A17–20, A16–28; for the state of affairs in 1943, see n.a., *Field Service Regulations: Command and Employment of Air Power* (Washington: U.S. Government Printing Office, 1943); and Wilfrid H. Hardy, "Aviation in Support of Ground Troops," *Military Review* 23:6 (June 1943): 5–10; and "The Air Support Command," *Military Review* 23: 7 (July 1943): 13–17.

68. David Syrett, "The Tunisian Campaign, 1942–43," in Cooling, *Close Air Support*, p. 156.

69. Alan F. Wilt, "Allied Cooperation in Sicily and Italy," in Cooling, *Close Air Support*, pp. 199–200.

70. Syrett, "The Tunisian Campaign, 1942–43," in Cooling, *Close Air Support*, pp. 157, 183.

71. Wilt, "Allied Cooperation in Sicily and Italy," in Cooling, *Close Air Support*, p. 218.

72. For details of the evolution of the Royal Air Force system, see Denis Richards and Hilary St. George Saunders, *Royal Air Force, 1939–1945* (London: Her Majesty's Stationery Office, 1975), vol. i, p. 2, 161–62, 351–52; Hilary St. George Saunders, *Royal Air Force, 1939–1945* (London: Her Majesty's Stationery Office, 1975), vol. iii, pp. 119, 122, 129–32, 284–86; and Richard P. Hallion, *Strike from the Sky: The History of Battlefield Air Attack, 1911–1945* (Washington, D.C.: Smithsonian Institution Press, 1989), pp. 181–83.

73. For a brief description of activities in a Forward Air Control Center in northwest Europe in 1944, see Mark Murphy, "Fighter Control: Nerve Center of Battle," *Air Force* 27:10 (October 1944): 61 and 63; for a detailed account of the evolution of air control and close air support in the Normandy landing, lodgment, and breakout, see W. A. Jacobs, "The Battle for France, 1944," in Cooling, *Close Air Support*, pp. 237–343.

74. Clifford, *Amphibious Warfare Development*, p. 233.

75. Hallion, *Strike from the Sky*, pp. 222–27.

76. Walter A. Smith, "You're Covered!" *Military Review* 27:4 (April 1947): pp. 48–54.

77. For contrasting views on that state of affairs, see Asher Lee, ed., "Supporting the Army," pp. 115–29, in *Air Power* (New York: Praeger, 1955), as compared with Trevor N. DuPuy's view in *A Genius for War* (Englewood Cliffs, N.J.: Prentice Hall, 1977), p. 3.

78. Wilt, "Allied Cooperation in Sicily and Italy," in Cooling, *Close Air Support*, p. 220.

79. For example, see Joe Gray Taylor, "American Experiences in the Southwest Pacific," in Cooling, *Close Air Support*, pp. 302, 305. For a succinct description of optimum praxis in the Pacific in World War II, see Miles Browning, "Carrier Air Support of Assault Landings," *Military Review* 24:11 (November 1944): 17–20.

80. Ibid., pp. 310–13.

81. S. E. Smith, ed., *The United States Marine Corps in World War II* (New York: Random House, 1969), pp. 694–708.

82. J. Robert Moskin, *The U.S. Marine Corps Story* (New York: McGraw Hill, 1982), pp. 353–57.

83. See Taylor, "American Experiences in the Southwest Pacific," in Cooling, *Close Air Support*, pp. 298–301.

84. Ibid., pp. 327–32.

85. Robert Sherrod, *History of Marine Corps Aviation in World War II* (San Rafael, Calif.: Presidio Press, 1980), pp. 320–21, 408–12.

86. B. H. Liddell Hart, *The Other Side of the Hill* (London: Cassell, 1951), p. 303.

87. Charles B. MacDonald, *The Siegfried Line Campaign* (Washington, D.C.: Center for Military History, 1984), pp. 404–5.

88. For operational details of such operations, see J. W. Perkins, "Use of Heavy Bombers on Tactical Missions," *Military Review* 26:5 (May 1946): 18–21.

89. See Anthony Martiennssen, *Hitler and His Admirals* (New York: E. P. Dutton, 1949).

90. A. E. Sokol, "German Attacks on the Murmansk Run," *U.S. Naval Institute Proceedings* 78:6 (December 1952): 1341.

91. S. G. Gorshkov, "Navies in War and Peace," *U.S. Naval Institute Proceedings* 100:4 (September 1974): 61.

92. Karl Dönitz, *Memoirs: A Documentary of the Nazi Twilight* (New York: Belmont Books, 1959), p. 93.

93. For operational organizational details, see Cajus Bekker, ed., *Luftwaffe War Diaries*, trans. Frank Ziegler (Garden City, N.Y.: Doubleday, 1968), pp. 256–58.

94. W. H. Tantum and E. J. Hofschmidt, *The Rise and Fall of the German Air Force* (Old Greenwich, Conn.: WE Inc., 1969), p. 44.

95. Karl Bartz, *Swastika in the Air* (London: William Kimber, 1956), pp. 38–40.

96. Dönitz, *Memoirs*, p. 30.

97. Tantum and Hofschmidt, *Rise and Fall*, p. 107.

98. For example, Friedrich Ruge, *Der Seekrieg: The German Navy's Story, 1939–45* (Annapolis: U.S. Naval Institute, 1965), pp. 159–61.

99. John Terraine, *A Time for Courage: The Royal Air Force in the European War, 1939–1945* (New York: Macmillan, 1988), pp. 242–44.

100. Samuel Eliot Morison, *History of United States Naval Operations in World War II*, vol. i (Boston: Little Brown, 1947), pp. 246–47.

101. For a discussion of the problems of anti-submarine warfare in the Battle of the Atlantic and of the estimation of effects, see Marc Milner, "The Dawn of Modern Anti-Submarine Warfare: Allied Responses to the U-Boats, 1944–45," *Royal United Services Institute Journal* 134:2 (Spring 1989): 61–68.

102. For an overview of special operations in World War II, see Roger Beaumont, ed., *Special Operations and Elite Units: A Research Guide* (Westport, Conn.: Greenwood, 1988).

103. Edward Jablonski, *Airwar*, vol. 2 (Garden City, N.Y.: Doubleday, 1971), Part 2, Ch. 3, pp. 49–72.

104. Moskin, *Marine Corps Story*, Ch. 5, pp. 254–56.

105. For example, see Burke Davis, *Get Yamamoto* (private publication, n.d., c. 1987); for a brief and dispassionate account, see Jablonski, *Airwar*, Part 2, pp. 105–8.

Chapter 5

Fitful Ebb and Flow: Jointness from 1943 to 1991

SQUARING OFF: 1943–45

Although interorganizational meshing within the Anglo-American alliance and its close affiliates reached the highest level yet seen in warfare in World War II, it fell well short of perfection. One student of the process observed that the U.S. Navy and the Army Air Forces each suspected "that the other was using the war . . . to put the other out of existence."[1] However aloof the Navy—or navies—have tended to be, even casual observers found the diatribes of some air power advocates unsettling, most especially those of Alexander De Seversky, who in 1943 called for disbandment of ground and naval forces. It was recognized within the Army Air Forces that any value gained by such publicity was offset by its stridency and rashness.[2]

As anxiety in the Allied camp over the war's outcome eased from mid–1943 on, the U.S. military and naval bureaucracy focused once again on unification.[3] Tension between the Army and Navy mounted when the Special Planning Division of the Army General Staff devised a U.S. General Staff (Joint) Plan[4]— the "Tompkins Plan"—and forwarded it to the Select Committee on Postwar Military Policy of the House of Representatives. Although a committee headed by Admiral F. O. Richardson produced a milder version of earlier unification plans, the dilution was not enough to prevent the chairman from formally dissenting. More fuel was added to the fire in 1944, when, in hearings in late April and early May, Army Deputy Chief of Staff General Joseph T. McNarney, an airman, offered his plan for a Department of the Armed Forces and a Director of Common Supply.[5]

During World War II, benefits of fusion and coordination and the artificiality of service boundaries had stood forth in many operational settings, for example, the close cooperation between General Bradley and Admiral Kirk and their staffs during the planning for Operation Overlord-Neptune. Traditional service structures had come under assault from many quarters, including dissident retired Admirals Ramsey Logan and Thomas Hart (former commander of the Asiatic fleet), who proposed what senior naval officers later deemed virtual heresy, a concept of "aero-amphibious war" that would lead to a more generalist approach to the art of war in the modern era.[6] Many others supported unification in the spirit of Eisenhower's dictum that there was "no such thing as separate land, sea or air war."[7] The examples of Allied defeats stemming from poor interservice linking still lay at hand, such as Norway, Dakar, the fall of Crete, Southeast Asia, and the German Navy's dash up the Channel, supported by the Luftwaffe. Further revelations about Pearl Harbor were about to be made,[8] and Axis failures in jointness were coming into view.

In the spring of 1945, the two foremost champions of jointness died: President Roosevelt in April and Frank Knox, Secretary of the Navy, a month later. The president, although a major Navy advocate in his first two terms, had increasingly turned a favorable eye toward Army and air interests from 1938 onward, even though he had named Admiral William Leahy his personal chief of staff in 1942. Secretary Knox had tended to compromise with the Army on the question of joint structure, but his successor, James Forrestal, did not. The Select Committee's final report in mid-June correctly observed that the time for change was "inopportune," and Admirals Halsey and Nimitz, who had spoken out for service unity earlier, were brought back in line. Later in the year, amid chaotic demobilization and the first phases of the Cold War, military journalist George Fielding Eliot laid out a middle way, proposing a design for a military nexus born of wartime perspective that called for flexibility and autonomy of the services, relying on coordination to maintain "constant balance between military and foreign policy, between power and objectives." That model eventually prevailed, but only in a very broad if not crude sense, and only after a half-decade of bitter infighting between the services, and with the ideals of functional operational balance, orchestration, and coherence in war subordinated to fiscal and territorial forces.[9]

No single clear voice rose above the clash of proposals, concepts, and claims in the late 1940s as the parochialism that had characterized Army-Navy relationships historically re-erupted, moderated only temporarily by the pressures of war. Nuclear weapons added a new dimension to the strife as the Air Force was created as an independent service. As the Truman administration's attempts to grapple with the Cold War and keep defense spending under tight limits widened the gap between service missions and funding, the mounting struggle generated an expanding torrent of reports, hearings, books, and articles.[10]

THE BATTLE OF THE POTOMAC

Just as the relatively mundane matter of a Danish freighter venting steam drew the British and German fleets into their great battle at Jutland, a catalyst arising from bureaucratic process—competing postwar manpower estimates[11]—triggered the "Battle of the Potomac." The wellsprings of the "battle," however, lay much deeper. When, in early 1945, Assistant Secretary of War Robert Patterson, and Generals of the Army Eisenhower, MacArthur, and Arnold called for unification to reduce federal defense expenditures and to end the insularity that had contributed to Pearl Harbor, Fleet Admirals Leahy and King counterattacked, the latter deeming the proposal "revolutionary, dangerous and unnecessary." Leahy argued that an overall service chief would usurp the presidential constitutional authority,[12] while King asserted that "the most definite and most important lesson is that to attempt unity of command in Washington is ill-advised in concept and would be impracticable of realization."[13] He had seen early in World War II that ground-air-naval structure would end the Navy's ability to protect its interests if an argument came to a formal vote. Although King managed to block the functioning of a triservice operation, over a dozen joint boards and committees had been formed at the upper reaches of the American defense hierarchy by 1945.[14]

After Eisenhower stepped down as supreme commander in western Europe to become Army Chief of Staff, he bluntly echoed the view of many other senior commanders in proclaiming that warfare had become joint for all practical purposes, and that unification would reduce the services' superstructure by 25 percent.[15] At the end of July, setting forth his views on unification in more detail, he called for: universal military service; unification of upper command and staff structure, including a single chief of staff; an independent Air Force; maximum interservice assignment of officers, from initial training onward; clear definition of service functions; and common procurement and research and development systems.[16]

On the other hand, Marine Corps Commandant Arthur W. Vandegrift, although not always favorably disposed toward creative diversity within his service, followed King's lead in expressing fear that a single decision point atop the national command structure would stifle development. Meanwhile, Secretary of the Navy James V. Forrestal asked Ferdinand Eberstadt, a colleague in business and an experienced defense bureaucrat, to undertake a study that ultimately proposed a model based on the principle of coordination as opposed to formal joint structure.[17]

That approach did not sit well with Roosevelt's successor, President Harry S. Truman, a former senator from Missouri who had been an Army National Guard artillery officer in France in World War I and whose populist, anti-elitist sentiments were matched by a strong will. He called a White Conference on unification in May 1945 in an attempt to mandate interservice cooperation. That fell well short of his hopes and led to another phase of debate and maneuver. As the bitterest infighting between the U.S. armed services in their history began in earnest, and arguments and models flowed from every quarter, to many, the Eberstadt Report sounded like sweet reason amid the mounting din of claims and counterclaims regarding strategic bombing and naval aviation. More importantly, the report undercut Truman's call in December 1945 for a centralized Department of National Defense. That had echoed Eisenhower's proposal, including a single secretary, a chief of staff, and integrated strategic planning, budgeting, research and development, and procurement. Several meetings and exchanges of letters with the Secretaries of War and of Navy only clarified the main points of contention: The Navy opposed a single Department of National Defense and a separate Air Force; all the services disagreed on the control and apportionment of aviation; and the Army and Air Forces wanted the Marine Corps reduced to a token constabulary force.[18]

In his memoirs, Truman traced his grappling with squabbling services to his days in Congress. During the war, he had chaired the Senate's Special Committee Investigating the National Defense Program, widely known as the Truman Committee, confronting much "duplication of time, material and manpower." As a senator, he saw service parochialism reflected by congressmen who represented service interests, most notably Carl Vinson, a Georgia Democratic congressman and the staunchest navalist of them all. Like many others, Vinson saw service rivalry as a variant of constitutional separation of powers.[19] Truman, on the other hand, had written a magazine article in 1944 proposing postwar consolidation of supply and a joint general staff, basing his conclusions on postmortems of the Pearl Harbor attack.[20] All through the struggle, he gave little weight to the powerful effect that the tension between retrenchment and expanding missions was having in fueling the debate.

Paradoxically, the Navy hierarchy discounted the animosity between air power advocates and ground commanders between the wars, assuming the close tactical air-ground rapport in wartime portended a common front against the Navy afterward. Beyond losing a chance to build a political alliance, the Navy was vulnerable in other respects. Although the Army had also been caught flat-footed in Hawaii and the Philippines, the newsreels of Pearl Harbor released in the middle of the war showed mainly burning warships. The aloofness and insularity of the "silent service" also cost much, and public opinion polls at the war's end ranked the Navy's leaders far below the Army and Army Air Force commanders. In 1946–47, cordial relations between General of the Army Eisenhower and his air commander, General of the Army Carl Spaatz, soon to be the first chief of staff of the independent Air Force, also fueled anxiety. In any event, the Navy missed an opportunity at this point, and the Army-Air Force estrangement over tactical air power that followed those luminaries' retirement failed to blunt Army-Air Force joint attacks on the Navy and Marine Corps in the late 1940s.

Beyond that, many World War II Army and Army Air Force veterans and civilians saw naval officers as privilege-conscious and foppish elitists, and some World War I veterans still saw the Navy as a slacker service. As noted, Navy casualty rates, aside from naval aviation, submarine force, and Marine Corps losses, were lower than the Army's and the AAF's. More importantly, nuclear weapons seemed to threaten navies with obsolescence. The atomic bomb tests, Operation Crossroads, conducted at Bikini Atoll in the Pacific in 1946, were interpreted by observers much according to their predispositions. While the Navy pointed to the survival of many ships, although tethered and closely bunched, air power enthusiasts stressed the prodigious damage done by one bomb, which many viewed as having made naval task forces and amphibious operations obsolete. In Cold War planning and popular analyses alike, by the late 1940s, a primary assumption was that a major war would be fought quickly by nuclear bombers, while submarines, convoy escorts, and carriers would be vulnerable to the point of irrelevancy.

As part of his energetic defensive infighting, Forrestal formed the Naval Industrial Association which, like the Navy League created in the 1870s, linked industrial and naval elites to gain support in budget battles.[21] The U.S. Naval Institute, a product of that earlier era of political scrapping, provided a scholarly format for navalist arguments. Army and Air Force civilian auxiliary structures with substantial lobbying power were in the field, for example, the Reserve Officers Association, the National Guard Bureau, various branch associations, the Civil Air Patrol, the Air Force Association, and the Association of the United States Army soon joined their ranks.

Clio, the muse of history, was now fettered to the grindstones of various factions as the debate mounted. U.S. Marine Corps advocates claimed corps preeminence if not monopoly in developing amphibious warfare theory and praxis between the World Wars, with British and Franco-Spanish developments, Combined Operations, and the six major assault landings in the Mediterranean and European theaters out of view.[22] On the other side, an Air Force advocate invoked a *Wehrmacht* general's argument that the war might have been won "through strategic bombing alone," but a desire to win quickly led to the reliance on "combined operations."[23]

As the chaotic demobilization of 1945–47 had progressed, the confident—and sometimes strident—tone of such air power advocates as De Seversky was not much dampened by the U.S. Strategic Bombing Survey's mixed findings, and their assaults on seapower were assisted from other quarters. In 1946, in *The Case Against the Admirals*, William Bradford Huie, a wartime naval officer, assailed the Navy from many compass points, citing an unfair share of five-star flag ranks during World War II,[24] wasteful plush facilities, duplication, elitism and racism,[25] and the revulsion of those at the "fighting fronts" toward "the old foul-ups" and Washington as a "hive of petty intrigue."[26] As Truman's and, later, Forrestal's frustrations in trying to ease service feuding were stymied by service lobbying, the Navy's influence was maintained by Admiral Leahy, who remained as presidential chief of staff until 1949.

The National Security Act of 1947

A White House meeting, in May 1946, modified much of Truman's proposal and his "twelve points," and sent the revision forward to Congress in June. Those efforts, further reshaped by the congressional process, finally led to the

National Security Act of 1947, which based jointness once again on a strong assumption of interservice goodwill, a commodity that soon proved to be in very short supply. The organizational design in that law drew very heavily on British wartime defense structure, in spite of the fact that, all the high resolve born of defeat during the war and much careful thinking out of the complex combined operations problems notwithstanding, the British armed forces had quickly retreated into their separate organizational bastions when the war ended and abandoned the high level of joint practice. The National Security Council, for example, was a variant of the Committee of Imperial Defense, which had caught Forrestal's fancy to the point that he invited some key CID members to Washington.[27] The 1947 act followed Eberstadt's report in providing for a weak Secretary of Defense, a separate Air Force, a Central Intelligence Agency, a joint staff with a rotating chairmanship, a National Security Council, and a vaguely defined central structure called the National Military Establishment, renamed the Department of Defense in 1949.[28]

Although strident in opposing unification and jointness in many instances, the Navy did not fight a battle at every crossroads. Thus, the first postwar "specified" command, that is, a command formed within one armed service to perform a function for all the others, was created in 1946, the Military Air Transport Service (MATS), under the Army Air Forces. In October 1946, the first regional commands were created, in which a commander of the service with primary interests in the area commanded subelements of other services, following old lines of jurisdiction from the JAAN. That pattern was reflected in the Navy's Commander in Chief Pacific Fleet/Pacific Ocean Area (CINCPAC/POA) having overall command in the Vietnam War, and in the preponderance of U.S. Army elements in the Panama invasion of December 1989, in an Army unified command area,[29] and in the Gulf War.

The Navy's position in resisting jointness had been undercut to some extent as the final series of Pearl Harbor hearings revealed the weak interservice structural links in that debacle. The memories of stinging setbacks on Oahu and the Philippines in the first hours of World War II faded slowly, affecting structure and doctrine over the next generation. Beyond that, fragments of language and doctrine of World War II jointness lived on.[30] The ghost of Pearl Harbor could be glimpsed on the battlements in the American nuclear war battle–management system, in which all major command substructures were closely dominated by a single service—the Air Force. Neither did the vast intertwining of services and Allies in World War II in North Africa, Italy, Europe, Southeast Asia and the Southwest Pacific fade wholly from organizational practice and memory. Small tidal pools of expertise, preserved here and there in doctrine and records of praxis, filled back up in the United States in the Korean War, and in Britain at Suez and the Falklands War, although much reduced in scale and sophistication in both cases, while some service and Allied linkages of SHAEF—Supreme Headquarters, Allied Expeditionary Force—were retained in NATO.

The complex implications of the mounting threat of nuclear war were not fully grasped by advocates of centralization. The danger of channeling communications to a single apex and the value of multiple "loops" were not considered by former President Herbert Hoover, who, at Truman's behest, conducted a major study of the federal bureaucracy that had grown up over the course of the New Deal and World War II. Seeking to efficiently restructure the national security organization, Hoover lamented "disharmony and lack of unified planning . . . interservice rivalries . . . [and] divided responsibility and allegiances"[31] and military security dependent on "the creation of a genuinely unified military arm."[32] Beyond overlooking the creative diversity argument and dismissing the check-and-balance dimension that many in Congress approved, Hoover and many others could not foresee that the American peacetime defense apparatus would be maintained for the next two generations at levels far higher than those of his youth and tenure as president.

The final phase of the interservice feuding of the late 1940s and some of the sharpest exchanges arose over control of the United States nuclear arsenal and its delivery and command-and-control systems, fast becoming the major elements in the U.S. defense nexus—and magnets for appropriations for supporting conventional systems as well. The Army Air Forces stood well ahead in this struggle even before the war ended. Air power advocates had gained much advantage from the Air Corps' and Air Forces' image of modernity. Even though strategic bombing did not bring victory over Germany by itself, the USAAF, aided by the media and Hollywood, had cultivated a youthful image as the service of the future, and at the end of the war, stood ready to serve as the main U.S. component in the United Nations' standing forces. Although quickly forgotten as the Cold War intensified, and the U.S. Air Force became the mainstay of American nuclear deterrence, that role was, for a passing moment, more than a vague vision. Specific provisions had been made for a UN military element, with support from Churchill and from Stalin in the Dumbarton Oaks Conference. A Military Staff Committee had been created when the United Nations was formed in early 1945. That contingency remained active after the U.S. Air Force was created in 1947 and, as late as mid–1949, a Secretary of the Air Force declared the intent of the United States to provide air power as a means to maintain world peace, deeming such cooperation with other nations "real unification."[33]

Not only had the Army Air Forces' leaders developed strong publicity skills during their lean years and sharpened them during the war, they had also overseen the destruction of dozens of German, Italian, Japanese, and Balkan cities, in raids whose effects were close in scale to that of the nuclear weapons dropped on Hiroshima and Nagasaki. Thus, as the Cold War intensified and the practice of "nuclear diplomacy" began in the Iran crisis in 1946, and the build-up of Strategic Air Command began, the brand new U.S. Air Force became the senior service in strategic and budgetary terms.

The Demise of Forrestal

After the 1947 National Security Act was passed, the interservice squabbling continued at a lower level until 1949 when Forrestal, now the Secretary of Defense, strove vainly to end it. Against the background of interservice squabbling that included formal meetings at Key West and Newport in 1948, and solemn pseudo-diplomatic agreements among the Joint Chiefs that were soon broken, the officer corps of all three services became widely infected by a virtual hysteria. As zeal and emotion transcended specific issues, General Eisenhower returned to active duty in January 1949 to assist Forrestal in closing the wounds, but to no avail, since the National Security Act of 1947 had given the Secretary of Defense little authority to match his grave responsibilities. Worn down by a decade of exhausting service, he resigned at the end of March 1949, fell into deep depression and committed suicide at the end of May.

A main polarity of conflict that paralleled the squabble between the Army-plus-Air Force and the Navy was the re-eruption of the old argument between the airmen and ground forces over close-air support.

Carl Spaatz, when chief of the Army Air Forces, had promised Eisenhower that tactical air forces would stay as a majority priority in the independent Air Force.[34] After he retired after serving briefly as the first U.S. Air Force chief of staff in April 1948, General Hoyt Vandenberg, his successor, downgraded the Tactical Air Command (TAC) to a second-tier priority, as the Cold War shunted priorities toward long-range bombers and nuclear weapons. Thus, "victory through air power" became baseline doctrine, as many assumed long range-strategic bombing would play the key role in an all-too-likely general war.

This allowed the determined Vandenberg to steal several marches in the night in the course of the bitter infighting. As the first of the new fleets of intercontinental B–36 bombers were delivered in 1949, the Air Force's principal military control of nuclear weapons was further strengthened as it gained control over their development. A series of major developments that further bolstered its position included a Communist coup in Czechoslovakia in the spring, Mao's conquest of mainland China in early 1949, the first test of a Soviet atomic bomb late that year, and airpower's symbolic victory in the Berlin airlift of 1948–49.

At this point, the Navy called into question Air Force claims of being able to wage decisive aerial warfare against the Soviet Union, as other critics attacked the concept of strategic bombing, the new superbombers' mechanical reliability, and pointed to the nearly fatal shortage of escort fighters in World War II. Air power advocates in turn questioned Navy plans to play a major strategic nuclear war-fighting role by launching medium bombers from aircraft carriers around the "rimlands" of Eurasia, carrier task groups' ability to defend against submarines, mines, and air attack, and the effectiveness of the small nuclear bombs that carrier-based aircraft carried. While rising, the tensions between the Army and Air Force over close-air support remained a minor issue at this point. Yet the Army took the Navy's side when Eisenhower collided with General Vandenberg, who wanted the Navy restricted to escort carriers of about 20,000 tons, while Eisenhower correctly foresaw the utility of at least a half-dozen fleet carriers in even a small, limited war.[35]

The Revolt of the Admirals

The final, furious skirmish flared up just after Forrestal resigned, when the new Secretary of Defense Louis Johnson, a strong Air Force partisan, quickly applied major defense economies, even though the gap between service missions and money had widened sharply as the Truman administration's containment policy increased tasks while holding defense funding to a third of the federal budget. Bolstering the Strategic Air Command's B–36 bomber fleet, Johnson cut other service programs, including much of the Air Force's non-strategic aircraft procurement. A crisis erupted after he canceled construction on April 23, 1949, of a major carrier, the *United States*. Its keel had just been laid, since it had been guaranteed funding to completion as part of the Key West Agreement of mid-March 1948. After Secretary of the Navy John L. Sullivan resigned on April 26, part of the Navy's officer corps and civilian bureaucrats entered into what General Bradley, chairman of the Joint Chiefs of Staff, later deemed "open rebellion." With the "silent service" no longer silent, trumped-up charges of graft on Johnson's and Secretary of the Air Force Stuart Symington's part were made, then withdrawn. In September, a senior naval aviator released confidential data to the press questioning the B–36's tactical utility and mechanical reliability, and charging that an Army-Air Force cabal sought to dismantle the Navy's aviation program.

As the "Revolt of the Admirals" became a public spectacle in the fall of 1949 in the House Armed Services Committee hearings, the squabbling grew shrill and primitive. Admiral Arthur Radford deemed the B–36 a "billion dollar blunder," while General Bradley labeled the Navy officer corps "Fancy Dans" who refused to "hit the line" unless "they can call the signals."[36] With forced composure, Eisenhower testified, describing the quarreling as pointless, declaring the defense budget too small to meet missions, and urging Congress to get into the budget cycle sooner and not wait to sort out the armed services' and the administration's finished budgets. He also expressed concern that public debate provided valuable information, aid, and comfort to the United States' enemies.

While there was no real evidence of Prussianism[37] or incipient Praetorianism, the interservice bickering affected the public view of military authority and professionalism. The sand-box fight had done much damage by the time Eisenhower testified toward the end of the hearings. During World War II, many veterans and civilians had chafed under the military caste system and witnessed waste, ineptitude, silliness, and corruption of the kind portrayed in such postwar novels, plays, and films as *Mister Roberts*, *The Naked and the Dead*, *Command Decision*, *Twelve O'Clock High* and *From Here to Eternity*. In the vast melée of adversary journalism swirling around the debate, books with sensational titles like *Disaster through Air Power* and *Air Power: Key to Survival*, and a torrent of opinion pieces and magazine articles carried the fray to millions of Americans in the twilight of the golden age of American mass circulation periodicals, when print journalism was still a main source of information.

The hearings did not, as the Navy hoped, serve as what Paul Hammond called "a kind of court of appeal" in which they could win their case against unification. Ultimately, many shared the view of Eisenhower, incorporated in the House Committee on the Armed Services final report, that "rigidly held professional opinions in all services, and Navy fear of a minority position in council stood in the way of achieving that degree of unification and resultant economies that the President and Congress so fervently anticipated when the law of 1947 was enacted."[38] In the end, the committee's conclusion favored no party to the debate, while the administration learned what its economies had cost politically, in a foretaste of the price soon to be paid in the currency of blood and near-defeat in Korea. Congress came to realize that its committees could not favor any service, but that it could blunt the Secretary of Defense's initiatives. And the public learned that neither organizational reforms nor the bitter lessons of war had ended interservice rivalry. All the services lost more than what they realized was at risk, as their parochial squabbling undercut both public reverence for the architects of victory and for the mystique of military professionalism,[39] and sharpened a sense among some critics of what David Bolton deemed "specialization by economic default."[40]

At the same time, the limited public view of the hearings in that pre-television age and collateral arguments in the media produced a distortion as adversaries sought to win arguments and gain resources rather than strike a balanced view, and in maneuvering around security classification with some deftness, pioneered the tactic of the media leak. In perhaps the most rash prediction made during the debate, General Bradley, chairman of the Joint Chiefs of Staff, deemed major amphibious operations obsolete—a year before the Inchon landing.[41] Since the flights over the Soviet Union by B–36 reconnaissance planes could not be made public to offset Navy claims of their vulnerability to Soviet air defenses, Bradley obliquely pointed out that the Navy's carrier-based medium bombers would face the same air defenses as the Air Force's long-range strategic bombers.[42]

The battle had casualties other than Forrestal. The case of Hugh Knerr threw human costs of the "Battle of the Potomac" into sharp relief. Knerr, a Naval Academy graduate who served in the Air Corps, had become a major advocate of a separate air force in the popular press before and during the early part of World War II. After stories circulated that he was levered out of the aircraft industry by Navy pressure, he returned to active duty as a logistician and was promoted to brigadier general during the war, but was blocked from promotion and removed from active duty after the war, apparently due to pressure from the Navy hierarchy. In the heated atmosphere of 1949, it was more important that many believed such allegations than whether they were true.[43]

After Forrestal's suicide generated a sense of remorse and conciliation in the Congress, amendments to the 1947 act strengthened the secretary of defense's powers and reduced the service secretaries' role, while in the extended hearings over the B–36 bomber in the House, the tone of discussion became muted and technical. The new Chief of Naval Operations, Admiral Forrest P. Sherman, proved more adroit than the strident navalists who opened the battle. A special Navy weapons study group report published in early 1950 cast some doubt on certain aspects of the Air Force's strategic capacity, but it also accepted the likelihood of much damage being done, reflecting the Navy's shift from questioning Air Force capacity to deliver nuclear weapons effectively to seeking a major share in wielding them.

As the 1950s began, other events and forces further altered the tenor of interservice rivalry. Nuclear-powered submarines were moving beyond the drawing board stage, and it became clear that nuclear-powered super-carriers were more than fanciful visions. The creation of NATO in 1949 and the stronger U.S. naval and Air Force presence in the Mediterranean were changing the strategic landscape as the development of a hydrogen bomb began. The super-weapon, far more destructive than atomic bombs, reduced the need for a high degree of accuracy and thus offered the Navy the role of "oceanic deterrent," a major, wholly naval element based on nuclear-powered and nuclear missile-bearing submarines, albeit under SAC control.

THE KOREAN WAR

The three-year struggle in Korea began when the North Korean People's Army (NKPA) attacked across the 38th Parallel on June 25, 1950, and quickly shattered and routed the South Korean Constabulary. As American units were hurriedly deployed from Japan, the Truman administration grappled with a contingency for which there had been no serious preparation. As Vincent Davis noted, Korea broke the fixation in U.S. defense planning on a major nuclear strategic war in Europe and ended the expectation that future wars involving a superpower would only be fought with nuclear weapons.[44] The inability of the armed forces to perform missions resulting from the Truman administration's conflicting policies of containment and stringent economies was also revealed. In 1950, many still held high hopes for the United Nations, which had played a strong role in halting "limited" wars in Palestine and Kashmir, and the UN flag flew over the headquarters of the U.S. Armed Forces Far East during the Korean War.

The Korean War was fought under the direction of the Joint Chiefs of Staff as structured by the National Security Act of 1947 and the amendments of 1949, although the latter provided the chairman with an office and joint staff. Not a voting member of the Joint Chiefs until 1986, the chairman would play the role of conciliator and conduit to the Secretary of Defense and President, conveying to them the sense of the chiefs, and not his own judgment, when they failed to concur on major issues of policy and doctrine. The Korean War was paralleled by a major increase in defense spending and a build-up of forces in Western Europe, which increased the sense of common threat and reduced competition for resources. While that was reflected in the relatively few "splits" in opinion that the chairman of the JCS had to convey up the chain of command, the onset of an era of relative good feeling masked the fact that the JCS was in essence a council of war of the kind that had been such a brake on initiative, especially in joint operations, over the centuries.[45]

The utility of amphibious warfare, of sealift, both logistical and evacuatory, of naval and Marine Corps close-air support, and of naval gunfire were all placed in a fresh perspective. When the Korean war began, the Marine Corps' Fleet Marine Force had declined to less than the size of a single World War II Marine division, and the Navy's array of 600 amphibious ships of August 1945 had shrunk to less than 100. The last major U.S. Navy amphibious operations had been carried out in the Chinese Civil War in the late summer of 1947, when the U.S. 7th Amphibious Force put a Nationalist division ashore at Shikiuso, south of Tsingtao, on August 27th. On September 30th of that year, although a landing attempt at Weihaiwei was repulsed, the Nationalists took an island close by, which the Communists had regained by November.[46]

After the U.S. withdrawal from China in 1946–47, the 7th dwindled to a shadow of its once formidable size and quality. Such forces were not seen as a desirable assignment by most career naval officers. Admiral Daniel Barbey, commander of the 7th in MacArthur's Southwest Pacific Theater and in China after the war, pointed out that assignment to such duties during the war was not "career enhancing," and that 90 percent of his staff of 100 officers were serving "for the duration."[47]

In early July, 1950, in spite of the enfeebled state of jointness, MacArthur proposed a major amphibious landing in northwest South Korea at Inchon to sever North Korean lines of communication and thus paralyze and confuse its commanders. With the remnants of the South Korean constabulary and U.S. forces sent from Japan hard-pressed in the southeast corner of Korea around Pusan, evacuation seemed likely. The Inchon proposal seemed all the more astounding, since, beyond the vast shrinkage of U.S. Navy amphibious forces, the ephemeral but vital meshing of people and skills had also been torn asunder. The high degree of disarray was visible in the opening days of the Korean War as the Marine Corps scraped together a 5,000-man Provisional Brigade, which sailed from San Diego on 14 July. Structurally, the Marine Corps was a Navy sub-element, and its commandant was denied a full seat on the Joint Chiefs of Staff. The growth of the Marines in World War II to a field army of nearly half-a-million with sizeable tactical air elements had generated substantial bitterness. In the late 1940s, the Army and the Air Force, with substantial support from the Johnson and Truman administrations, had tried to have the Marine Corps legally limited to 50,000, peace or war, its air units reassigned to the Army and Air Force, and its role as a major amphibious element in the U.S. defense establishment ended. Yet Marine Corps advocates in the Congress successfully waged a skillful rear guard action against the converging ring of foes, including President Truman, who had derided the USMC as a mere "police force."

As the Cold War intensified, 1946–50, conflicts had increased in frequency and intensity along the Eurasian "rimlands," as predicted by geopolitician Nicholas Spykman in 1943. In the confrontation along that political fault line between the Communist "land animal" and the Anglo-American "sea animal," naval power had played a mainly passive and usually symbolic role, and amphibious operations came to be seen in defense circles as a thing of the past. In spite of the fact that covert operations increased, also requiring close coordination of the armed services, jointness was engaged in grudgingly, on an ad hoc basis. Some rejuvenation of amphibious capacity began in 1949, however, when General MacArthur, as commander in chief of the Far East forces, became concerned over possible Soviet threats to northern Japan. He had used Marines to train Army forces during World War II and immediately afterward, and in early 1950, he requested Marine training support, which had just begun when the Korean War began.

On 4 July, MacArthur met with his chief of staff, Major General Edward Almond, and two senior Marine officers to discuss the concept of landing at Inchon, which evolved into Operation Chromite. As initial concerns about adequate training and sea-lift were overcome in the course of hurried planning, forces and supplies were gathered and put into the pipeline all the way from the United States to the Mediterranean.[48] The North Korean People's Army further pressed the battered South Korean and U.S. forces in the shrinking enclave around Pusan, where, against odds of five-to-one, Lieutenant General Walton Walker conducted a skillful defense, based on a mobile reserve and support from a variety of Air Force, Navy, and Marine air elements.

Marine Corps amphibious experts helped prepare an unopposed landing by the 1st Cavalry Division to bolster Pusan, while General MacArthur conferred with Marine Lieutenant General Lemuel Shepherd, then commander of the Fleet Marine Force in the Pacific. Chromite plans initially called for the Inchon landing, not yet approved by Washington, to be made by two Army divisions and a Marine regimental combat team. After MacArthur mused nostalgically about the high quality of performance of the 1st Marine Division in the New Britain campaign in World War II, Shepherd promised a somewhat leaner 1st Division for the operation.

It is not clear how much MacArthur was exercising his sense of irony in reaching out to the Marine Corps and the Navy. While he knew many Marines had been hostile toward him in World War II, he also recognized that the Marine Corps had kept the flickering flames of jointness alive in the realms of close-air support and amphibious operations. In any case, he was clasping hands over the bloody chasm of interservice rivalry that had only just begun to close as the Korean War had begun.

Tactical Air Power

As Marine training elements scrambled to prepare the 1st Cavalry for its landing at Pohang-dong on July 18, 1950, the degradation of jointness since World War II had also become apparent in the province of close-air support. As the North Koreans closed in around Pusan, B–29 heavy bombers had hammered targets in North Korea and along NKPA lines of communication, while U.S. Air Force F–80 Shooting Star jet fighters out of Japan flew close-air support missions. In the summer of 1950, individual pilots' heroism in close-air support and forward-air control missions and improvisation filled in the gap until a functioning tactical mechanism could be put in place. Hampered by inadequate local control procedures and poor maps, U.S. fighter bombers could remain in the battle zone only a few minutes, and some saw such thin performance as a by-product of Vandenberg's breaking of Spaatz's pledge to Eisenhower that "tac air" would be a major USAF priority. Service politics seemed to be at work as Navy and Marine pilots were sent by Air Force controllers against strategic targets deep into North Korea, although they were trained, equipped, and ready to provide close-air support, and ground commanders, as in World War II, were calling out for it.

As the volume of air support increased steadily and provided crucial aid to the UN forces in the perimeter, Vandenberg protested against mounting press criticism that close-air support structure and doctrine had been weakened by the downgrading of tactical air in the Air Force's organizational hierarchy, and in early 1951, the exit of General Elwood "Pete" Quesada, maestro of U.S. tactical airpower in northwest Europe, 1944–45.[49] Indictments of Air Force doctrine and practice in the popular press,[50] and fulsome praise for the Navy-Marine CAS led to further Air Force rejoinders, including a defense of jets over propeller planes in ground support, one stage in a debate that has persisted down to the present time.[51] In a further irony, even as the Air Force controllers of the air war sent carrier-based fighters against strategic targets, B–29s played a tactical role on the Pusan perimeter even to the point of low-attitude strafing—with no clear result. The anomaly was the result of MacArthur's staff urging the Air Force to hearten UN troops with some heavy air activity, in hopes that massive strikes would also intimidate the enemy. By summer's end, after the list of strategic targets was exhausted, the Far East Air Force commander, General George Stratemeyer, was able to modify and end some of those practices. Many Korean cities and towns lay in ruins, and the military effects of that vast devastation were uncertain. Over the next three years, as in the Pacific campaigns of World War II and in Vietnam, Navy-Marine close-air support and, along the coastline, naval gunfire were much sought-after by ground forces. As jointness in several areas was revivified, the Air Force did a great deal of refurbishing of tactical aviation, however reluctantly. The struggle of U.S. Marine ground commanders for close links with the Marine air elements controlled by Air Force commanders remained an ongoing theme.[52]

Inchon

Strategic bombing had eased off as preparations for Inchon increased. At the beginning of August 1950, the 1st Provisional Marine Brigade arrived in Korea and, a week later, joined a portion of the Army's 25th Infantry Division in the Pusan Perimeter, to carry out the first formally planned UN offensive operations of the war. At this point, the concern of the Joint Chiefs of Staff and others experienced in amphibious operations mounted to the point that the JCS dispatched the Army chief of staff, General J. Lawton Collins, and Admiral Forrest P. Sherman, the Chief of Naval Operations, to Japan in mid-August to scrutinize MacArthur's Chromite plan, since it would functionally commit the flow of forces available for some time to come, against very long odds. After MacArthur defended his concept with special eloquence, drawing a strong parallel to Wolfe's surprise of Montcalm at Quebec, Collins and Sherman, the latter still somewhat dubious, returned to Washington and, depending on the sources, the Joint Chiefs or Secretary of Defense Louis Johnson gave the necessary approval.[33] After assent was given, the increasing pace of preparations for Chromite began to strain the Marines' logistical and administrative networks. Jointness in the manner of World War II reappeared, as Air Force and Army supply sources were blended to provide common stock items in the logistical flow, but all of the organization pieces could not be assembled before the actual landing. Part of the 1st Marine Division's staff was in Korea with the Provisional Brigade; other members were flown to Japan in late August as the division left by sea, and would not be gathered in one work place until after Inchon. Nevertheless, the Marine-Navy-Army staff in Tokyo began to develop the interservice rapport seen in World War II. Since most senior Inchon planners had previous operational experience, jointness was not just a mere term or a bureaucratic goal to them but a system of planning, procedures and habits of mind based on combat-tested practices.

Their goal, Inchon, the port city of Seoul, lay half-way up the western side of the Korean peninsula, close to the NKPA's lines of communication. Serious risk balanced great opportunity. Unlike Gallipoli, haste and surprise offered special premiums in Operation Chromite. Even though a rehearsal was not possible, the Inchon planners, unlike Hamilton and de Robeck and their staffs before the Dardanelles, did not have to build a joint structure, doctrine, and practice from the ground up. Since Inchon had an extremely high tidal range, only three feasible dates for a landing were left in 1950. When less hazardous alternate sites further south and dates beyond the September 15th "window of opportunity" were suggested, MacArthur held out, bent on maximizing surprise.

In Japan, aboard the headquarters ship USS *Mount McKinley* at Kobe, the 1st Marine Division planning staff was immersed in detailed planning and gathering widely scattered and unevenly trained and equipped units from various crannies. Six battalions came by sea from the Mediterranean, while some reservists undergoing training on the West Coast had been civilians on the 4th of

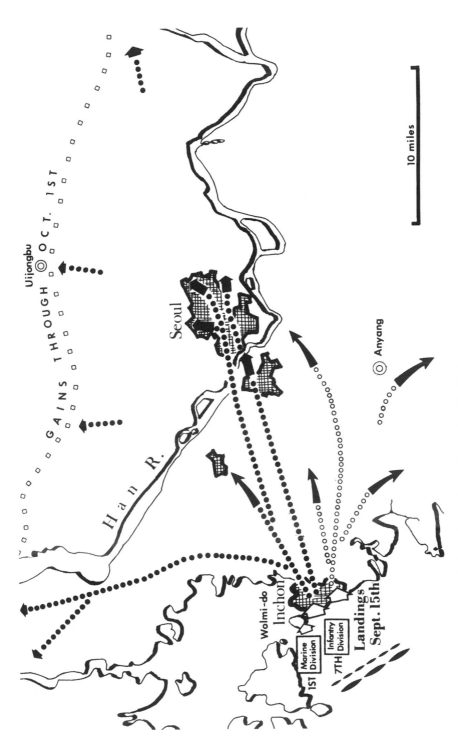

UN Forces Assault Landing at Inchon, South Korea, September 15, 1950

July. Marine air units and the 5th Marines in combat at Pusan also had to be folded into the ensemble. As the NKPA closed in on Pusan, much of the perimeter in southeast Korea came under artillery fire. Even though Walker's forces were being bolstered, the enclave was becoming too crowded for easy maneuver and dispersal.

Preparations addressed a range of complex details well known to World War II joint planners: calculating aircraft flight paths to avoid the peak trajectory of naval gunfire; air, ground, sea, and inter-Allied liaison; and orchestration of such joint task elements as the ANGLICO teams—the Air-Naval Gunfire Liaison Companies, the restructured U.S. Army 7th Infantry Division that included 8,000 Koreans, and the 1st Korean Marine Corps Regiment, which landed on the Marines' left flank. Diversions were staged while long scaling ladders were being built. How far the lush administrative facilities of World War II lay in the past was reflected in the staffs' sharing of plan copies by circulation, due to lack of duplicating facilities.

As shipping was gathered, the U.S. Army's X Corps headquarters was formed. Its energetic commander, Major General Edward Almond, was dissuaded by Marine planners from approving last-minute schemes involving special operations and light armored task forces. As complex elements folded together with relative smoothness, another major gamble was made, when the main task force steered through the edge of a major typhoon, a risk keenly appreciated by those who remembered the disaster of 1945. The main elements were assembled—nineteen attack transports and supporting ships, four cruisers, seven destroyers, and three large LSMR—landing ship medium (rocket)—vessels, as well as minesweepers and LSTs, including several manned by Japanese crews. After a five-day preparatory bombardment, paralleled by the shelling of other sites, on D Day, September 15th, commanders and staffs held their breath as two 1st Marine Division battalions seized Wolmi-do Island. It had seemed especially ominous when the North Koreans had begun to fortify the port in earnest just before the assault. Knowing a breach in security could yield mass slaughter on the scale of the Dardanelles and Dieppe made many anxious, including MacArthur, who became nauseated from nervous strain while watching the bombardment. Anxieties faded quickly, and within hours it was clear that Inchon was a major strategic victory. It was, however, less than dazzling technically. While some errors were "givens" and others accidents of war, some stemmed from the loss of once highly honed skills. Many units involved were untrained and strange to each other, damage and smoke made visibility poor much of the time, and maps were inaccurate. A shortage of compasses and radios and strong currents led to several landings in the wrong zones. Snarls of troops, vehicles, and supplies on the beaches led to jamming and bewilderment, as supporting fire from the first LSTs that landed inflicted two dozen casualties on "friendlies."

In spite of all the hitches and confusion, momentum was maintained by conforming to the World War II practice of advancing when in doubt. By 17 September, the 2nd Engineer Special Brigade, in the manner of such Army units during World War II, imposed some coherence on the flow of supplies to forces now well inland. Five days after the landing, the Marines, moving to the north and west, had crossed the Han River, while the U.S. Army's 7th Division, driving east and south, linked up with 1st Cavalry Division advance elements driving north from Pusan. Two days later, Seoul, the battered capital of South Korea, was retaken as the Marines prepared for withdrawal in early October. President Truman did not let the opportunity pass to express his views on jointness in his message to MacArthur after Inchon: "I am particularly impressed by the splendid cooperation of our Army, Navy and Air Force. . . . The unification of our arms established by you and by them has set a shining example."[54]

Inchon and the Pusan breakout had, as MacArthur hoped, formed the jaws of a pincers movement that led to the rout and substantial disintegration of the NKPA. Inchon was also the last major amphibious landing made by any armed force against firm resistance to the time of this writing. Suez faced weak opposition, and the Falklands/Malvinas landing was much smaller and unopposed. At the same time, although jointness had become a great deal more than amphibious operations, the spirit or substance of it was not pervasive in the Korean War. Robert Futrell, the U.S. Air Force historian of that conflict, noted "an absence of any vestige of unification principles" at its outbreak.[55] MacArthur's ignoring of Joint Chiefs of Staff directives and aversion to the CIA may have been a matter of habit and style,[56] given the hostility of his staff to the Office of Strategic Services during World War II, or it may have been a reaction to the attempt of the first chairman of the Joint Chiefs, General of the Army Omar Bradley, to play the role of "honest broker."[57]

While General George Stratemeyer, commander of Far East Air Forces (FEAF), was unhappy with MacArthur's staff's "micromanagement" of air operations, FEAF's meshing with Admiral C. Turner Joy, the naval commander in the Far East, was not at all smooth.[58] Neither did fate smile on the joint structure in Washington or the stability of the chain of command closer at hand. Vandenberg, the Air Force chief of staff, stricken with cancer, retired in May 1951, and Sherman, the Chief of Naval Operations, died in July. While Army generals Bradley, the JCS chairman, and J. Lawton Collins, Army chief of staff, were still in harness when the war ended in July 1953, the Secretaries of Defense also changed frequently during the Korean War. General George Marshall succeeded Johnson in late 1950, was replaced a year later by Robert Lovett, and the war ended with Charles E. Wilson in that role, while MacArthur had three successors as Far East commander. While official historians later saw the Korean War Joint Chiefs as "closer to that of World War II than to the one that evolved after . . . Eisenhower's [1958] reorganization," many sensed that the JCS had lost stature through its indecision in the fall of 1950 regarding the Inchon landing, and in a more general inclination to consensus and detachment from the role of strategic orchestration and direction.[59]

EISENHOWER'S "NEW LOOK"

When Eisenhower became president in 1953, many expected him to move toward unification in keeping with the sentiments he expressed at the end of World War II, but he did not do so until halfway through his second term, and even then sought incremental rather than revolutionary change. Perhaps that was due to all that he learned about the intractability of large organizations to control, reform, or restructure as commander of the Allied Expeditionary Force in northwest Europe, 1944–45, and as Army chief of staff, president of Columbia University, Forrestal's military adviser, and Supreme Commander, Allied Powers in Europe.

The Korean War ended six months after Eisenhower's inauguration. His program of defense realignments and reductions, labeled the "New Look," shifted the balance of resources sharply toward the Air Force and reliance on both strategic and tactical nuclear weapons, and away from ground forces. Much to the consternation of many of Eisenhower's former Army associates, Strategic Air Command (SAC) grew in power and prestige, while the Army was cut to half its Korean War strength. Throughout the 1950s, SAC's bomber force comprised the mainstay of the policy of "massive retaliation" promulgated by Eisenhower's Secretary of State, John Foster Dulles, and derided as "brinkmanship" by his opponents. Discouraged by those trends, many career Army officers resigned or retired early, most notably Chief of Staff General Maxwell Taylor, and research and development chief, Lieutenant General James Gavin.

Soon after Eisenhower took office, a flow of proposals for restructuring the Joint Chiefs came in waves until the mid–1980s. The first came from the Rockefeller Committee, which included retiring Army Chief of Staff J. Lawton Collins' suggestion that the JCS be taken out of the chain of command and function without a military staff. After several other studies appeared, in his second term, Eisenhower asked Congress for a revision of the National Security Act of 1947, reiterating the view he had expressed at the end of World War II that "separate ground, sea and air warfare is gone forever."[60] The result was the Department of Defense Reorganization Act of 1958, which aimed at unification, not a merger or "a single chief of staff over the armed forces nor an overall general staff," but a "closely integrated . . . efficient team of land, air and naval forces."[61]

How far the armed forces remained from that goal was reflected in American intervention in Lebanon that year, where, despite disparities in supplies and methods between the Army and Marines, the latter was heavily dependent on the former.[62] As army official historian Roger Spiller noted: "The pressure of Joint Operations was most acute—or at least more immediate—within the Specified Command itself. None of the service elements had much trouble in conducting its own affairs; it was when the Army, Navy, Air Force and Marine operations coalesced that procedures were put to the test."[63] Cases of poor meshing included the lack of common radio frequency, of signal links between Army artillery and naval gunfire control networks, and of standard signal panel codes and maps.[64]

From Korea to Vietnam, somewhat stronger U.S. Army-Air Force links were forged in the realm of close-air support, both in equipment development and training exercises, although they fell well short of Army desires.[65] By 1957, under the logic of "massive retaliation," the rubric, "airpower and the modern army," meant that the Army manned the anti-aircraft missile sites ringing major U.S. cities, while the Air Force provided the Army with reconnaissance and limited transport and airlift. Close-air support lay far from the strategic long-range concerns of war planners in that period.[66] Jointness, where it counted, was seen to lie in the strategic realm, where the Air Force functionally commanded Army and Navy forces under the aegis of the Strategic Air and North American Air Defense Commands. Overall, the services remained functionally unto themselves under command structures and turf agreements shaped by the interservice wrangling of the late 1940s.

The problem did not go unnoted. Halfway through the Eisenhower years (1953–1961), after lengthy hearings on air power, a Senate subcommittee observed there was "too much form and too little substance" in interservice functions.[67] Even though the issue of close-air support had become less divisive, Army-Air Force antagonism mounted on the issue of the development and control in combat of guided missiles, the Air Force insisting that Army weapons' range should not exceed 200 miles, the same distance that dominated Army-Navy fights over coastal defense roles in the 1920s and 1930s. Tension surged dramatically after the Soviets successfully tested an intercontinental missile in September 1957. Amid public furor following the orbiting of Sputnik in early October, Air Force attempts to launch an American satellite were dogged by accident and failure. Ultimately, an Army rocket, developed to well exceed the 200-mile limit, put the first U.S. satellite into orbit.

McNamara and the Joint Chiefs

In 1961, Eisenhower's 1958 restructuring put a significantly enhanced control system in the hands of John F. Kennedy's secretary of defense, Robert S. McNamara. An Army Air Forces systems analyst in World War II and former Ford Motor Company president, McNamara become the most powerful political overseer of the military in Washington since Edwin M. Stanton, Lincoln's secretary of war.[68] What many saw as the further weakening of the Joint Chiefs of Staff authority in the 1960s was only one facet of McNamara's dominance. Yet that does not seem to have been his intention. The planning-programming-budgeting system (PPBS) he introduced in the early 1960s was a lever that he worked on the fulcrum provided by Eisenhower's 1958 reforms. As William Kaufmann noted in the middle of that process: "It integrate[d] both the complementary and competitive functions of the services, . . . [providing] a substitute for unification and establishment of a single Chief of Staff."[69]

Until the late 1950s, the Joint Chiefs of Staff had operated within the bounds of a major paradox. With no direct involvement in the budget process, its guidance of defense doctrine and structure was by general directive rather than firm control. As a result, although the JCS's primary strategic concern was the unified commands, it had no mechanism to match intention with purpose, since the money flowed through the Department of Defense to the CINCs—Commanders-in-Chiefs—the "sinks." A major change came in 1958, when Secretary of Defense Neil McElroy asked the JCS to comment on the budget, and McNamara formally forged links between strategy and resources by bringing the JCS into budget-shaping at the very earliest stages of the cycle.

Pressing such reforms upon the Department of Defense as creation of the Defense Intelligence Agency, Strike Command and the Defense Supply Agency, McNamara was thwarted when he tried to force a common fighter on the Navy and Air Force, insisting on "minimum divergence from a common design" to meet both services' needs. Many saw that as a case of putting good ahead of best, and prolonged infighting erupted. Two very different aircraft types—the swing-wing F–111 and the F–14—resulted, and McNamara failed to impose jointness by employing an economic model of choice against military-naval resistance.[70]

Overall, McNamara did little to strengthen jointness at the operational level. In the early 1960s, the perceived low quality of officers assigned to the Joint Staff and the Navy's marked disdain for such duty led the Chief of Naval Operations, Admiral Arleigh Burke, to observe, "The Navy is being eaten alive."[71] During the 1960s, pressures on the Joint Chiefs to reach interservice accord smothered dissidence and turned the JCS into a consensus-seeking bureaucracy. Ill-prepared to shape war-fighting doctrine and with lessened authority and capacity to provide military professional advice and direct war, the JCS was far from being the ferocious watchdog that might snap its leash, which opponents of a supra-service general staff had feared since the late nineteenth century.[72]

Tacit collective support for policies and methods often overlay individual members' or services' differences. It has been suggested and denied that frustration and anguish expressed in private by members over "going along to get along" came to a crescendo in 1967 over the bombing of North Vietnam, which the JCS reportedly saw as futile, but which many senior administration officials saw as a valid strategy. During the Vietnam War and long afterward, the apparent failure of major military leaders to stand openly against policies that they opposed, by resigning or speaking out to their civilian overseers, was much discussed within the services and fed into the Weinberger Doctrine and Joint Chiefs of Staff reform debates of the early and mid–1980s.[73]

THE ROAD TO VIETNAM

In the early 1960s, major expansion of U.S. and Soviet ICBM (inter-continental ballistic missile) and nuclear submarine forces vastly complicated the already tangled problems of doctrine and command and control, which bomber fleets had engendered. Herman Kahn, in his disturbing tracts on nuclear war dynamics, dramatized the danger of accident or provocation sparking a nuclear holocaust. Issues of jointness seemed marginal if not irrelevant in that dramatic and preoccupying context, and the Air Force held sway over nuclear war battle management, even after the Navy deployed its Polaris submarine force.

Neither did Maxwell Taylor's reforming impulses have much influence on that state of affairs structurally. Early in the Kennedy administration, many feared and others hoped that bringing him into the administration portended major reform. Taylor, an airborne division commander in World War II and Far East commander at the end of the Korean War, had been Army Chief of Staff while much of Eisenhower's "New Look" was imposed—mainly at the expense of the Army. After he retired in protest in 1958, in a best-selling book, *Uncertain Trumpet*, he proposed backing away from the Eisenhower-Dulles doctrine of "massive retaliation" by strengthening American defense capabilities across the "spectrum of response." Taylor also urged dissolving the Joint Chiefs and appointing a single defense chief of staff, advised by a Supreme Military Council of generals and admirals retired or on their last tour, who would advise the President, Secretary of Defense, and Congress.[74]

As the Kennedy administration shifted defense resources toward the Army and bolstered special operations, Taylor had served as military adviser to Kennedy and then as a very powerful chairman of the Joint Chiefs of Staff before going to Saigon as ambassador at Lyndon Johnson's behest in July 1964. In spite of Taylor's urgings, Kennedy had followed Eisenhower's caution regarding making major structural reforms in defense too early. In spite of some consolidation and smoothing in the early 1960s, the services remained secure in their fiefdoms, and the resultant disynchronicity that marked interservice dynamics in the Vietnam War was visible in the Cuban Missile Crisis of 1962, as disbandment of a joint task force and assumption of direct command of planning and preparation by the commander of the Atlantic Fleet added another dimension of complexity to a process viewed as chaotic. As a freshly constituted staff grappled with mounting complexities, snarls developed in respect to communications, air support, fire support, airspace allocation, logistics, and liaison, leading to reliance on informal communications amid substantial confusion.[75]

Vietnam: A Dearth of Jointness

The Vietnam War was fought with far less jointness than World War II or even Korea. That was true of "combined-ness" as well, since adherence to the principle of war of "unity of command" was lacking at the highest levels.[76] From early 1962 to the departure of the last U.S. tactical forces in 1973, Military Assistance Command Vietnam (MACV or "Mack-vee") was the principal U.S. headquarters "in-country," that is, in South Vietnam. General William Westmoreland served as MACV commander from 1965 to 1968, and General Creighton Abrams from 1968 to 1973. Designated a "subordinate unified command," and originally formed to link the Republic of Vietnam government with U.S. Military Advisory and Assistance Group personnel, MACV reported to the Navy CINCPAC (Commander-in-Chief Pacific Fleet) in Hawaii. Without a functional theater structure of the kind seen in World War II and the Korean War, MACV commanders lacked command authority over sea and air activities beyond South Vietnam's borders. Neither did they have formal jurisdiction over South Vietnamese and Allied forces, or the many U.S. bureaucracies exercising salient influence over the war, such as the Agency for International Development (AID), the Central Intelligence Agency (CIA) and Civil Operations and Rural Development (CORDS).

Such concepts as a Combined U.S.-Vietnamese Command and "encadrement," the formation of Vietnamese units around U.S. leaders and units, although favored by McNamara, were opposed by those who felt that South Vietnamese morale would be weakened by a structure that Americans clearly dominated, while others feared the image of neo-colonialism.[77] Although General Bruce Palmer observed that "undivided responsibility and unified direction of the war were conspicuously absent,"[78] as in earlier wars, jointness did appear spontaneously, in the form of an ad hoc resolution of overlapping function and structure, or as the result of carefully designed doctrine laid down at various points. Sealift, airlift, and air-sea rescue organizations and the riverine force were examples of the first, and the Defense Intelligence Agency, of the second.

Overall, however, there was "no unified conflict management" within the American command structure, between the Vietnamese and the Americans, or among the various Allies. As Robert Komer, Earl Ravenal, and others observed, each armed service and major civilian sub-bureaucracy "played out their institutional repertoire."[79] The air war against North Vietnam, for example, was waged through the separate Air Force and Navy chains of command, with substantial detailed planning and oversight by the Offices of the President and Secretary of Defense, as well as other elements of what constituted, however inchoate, the "High Command" in Washington.[80] As noted earlier, Generals Westmoreland and Abrams, as commanders of Military Assistance Command Vietnam, 1965–68 and 1968–72, respectively, were not theater commanders à la World War II, but under the Navy's Commander in Chief of the Pacific Fleet and Pacific Ocean Area, Admiral U.S. Grant Sharp, headquartered in Hawaii. Neither did most American military and naval professionals want a joint command.[81]

That crazy-quilt command structure has been ascribed to many causes. One was the widespread sense throughout the Vietnam War that the end was imminent, and that a major overhaul *in media res* would waste time. Others saw the tangle in Vietnam as a reflection of the jumbled national security nexus in Washington, long deemed a "puzzle palace," any serious reform of which was unlikely. Since the hierarchy and fragmented defense bureaucracy offered no coherent leadership, orchestration, or military judgment, that flavored all below it. Yet another complicating factor was the interplay of personalities, a "fuzzy" but quite real swirl of forces that stood far away from any rationalistic model of organizational mechanics. Beyond that, neither Johnson nor McNamara were seen as encouraging flexibility or creativity among subordinates.[82] Beyond such factors lay other subtle shaping forces. The promotion dynamics of the armed services tended to select for drive, enthusiasm, obedience, and physical stamina. As American military professionals applied high technology and heavy firepower, a spirit of "can do" and "piling on" was noted by foreign observers. Some tried vainly to swim against the tide of applying ordained but ill-suited methods, for example, David Hackworth's view in cool reflection of his beloved airborne and the Marines being "too eager, too motivated, too aggressive."[83] The resultant intense provincialism led to a lack of sensitivity and sophistication regarding Vietnamese culture and language among American elites, civil and military, and consequent widespread misperception and "mirror-imaging." Both the Kafkaesque nature of bureaucracy per se and perversities and anomalies that seemed to abound in Vietnam were also noted. Beyond that lay the amorphous pattern of operations: the absence of clear-cut fighting front and rear areas much of the time, the flickering pattern of brief engagements and skirmishes, and the even more murky and diffuse realms of special operations, psychological warfare, and intelligence.

Special Operations

The dysphasic interaction of services and agencies reached its richest complexity in the realm of special operations, details of which emerged slowly during the war and after the fall of South Vietnam in 1975.[84] There was some joint structuring with South Vietnamese headquarters, for example, the Joint Operations Center, which handled tactical air support,[85] but South Vietnamese insistence on air support and artillery requests being processed through a long bureaucratic chain blunted the operational edge substantially, and led to various back-channel techniques, such as Special Forces' use of the CIA direct loop to Saigon to request air strikes.[86] A sharp jurisdictional contest between the services erupted early in the Vietnam War as Air Force Chief of Staff Curtis LeMay, after a tense confrontation with MACV commander William Westmoreland, harangued Major General Joseph H. Moore, then senior Air Force officer in South Vietnam, for abandoning USAF interests to the Army.[87] Although counterinsurgency (COIN) doctrine and warfare lay far from the Air Force's prime focus of interest in the early 1960s (that is, a major, short nuclear war), a rising interest in COIN in the Kennedy administration led Air Force officers to use their relatively small "Farm Gate" operations to offset an increasing Army dominance which the Air Force Director of Plans then saw as a graver long-term threat than momentary Viet Cong successes.[88]

While the use of back-channels, which left no trace in official or private records, blurred and erased the historical trail to an indeterminate extent, some disynchronous links between the services in special operations were mapped by Benjamin Schemmer in his autopsy of the abortive Son Tay Raid, including tensions between the Central Intelligence Agency and Defense Intelligence Agency,[89] and various failures in interservice communications and computer links.[90] The entwining of the special operations community with intelligence agencies, as well as the State Department and the Agency for International Development as "quasi-services," further complicated the matrix of jointness. However, this was not as peculiar to Vietnam as many believed, since a growing influence of non-martial nodes in war-making networks was visible well back in the modern era, from the Renaissance onward, in, for example, the Jesuits and Sir Francis Walsingham's intelligence service.

Close-Air Support

A blurred pattern was also visible in the close-air support arena. Although the Air Force upgraded "Tac Air" after Korea, Army-Air Force infighting rumbled on throughout the 1950s. It peaked just before the major commitment of U.S. forces to Vietnam, in a debate at the Joint Chiefs level over the Army's expanding use of helicopters and employment of the twin-engined *Mohawk* as gunships. While the former was approved and "air mobile" divisions were formed, the latter was denied. Generally silent in the Korean War during the Air Force-Marine Corps tussle, the Army had stolen some counter-marches in the night, increasing its light-air elements in the late 1950s and aligning more and more of them to "aerial fire support." A series of boards and reports generated by Secretary of Defense Robert McNamara's call for clarification of issues in 1962 had not resolved basic differences. After a squabble with the Air Force in 1962 over jurisdiction over the *Caribou* close-air support aircraft and Air Operations Centers, the Army "lost direct control of its aviation units."[91] The thicket of control networks and sluggish response times visible in the opening phase of major U.S. involvement in Vietnam was sorted out to some extent over time, but a lack of unified effort and operational orchestration persisted. Some differences were smoothed over after a series of maneuver tests led to the signing of an interservice compact in the spring of 1965,[92] but the general state of affairs was expressed in a comment on the "Concept for Improved Joint Air-Ground Coordination" by an Air Force colonel: "We had to learn the hard way—all over again."[93] Extra stages and loops in the communications pyramid resulted from a doctrine that maintained Air Force hegemony over an activity that lay far from its primary interest.

Nevertheless, substantial improvements were made in tactical air techniques through increased cooperation between the U.S. Air Force and Army between the Korean and Vietnam wars. Communications links increased, Army helicopter and fixed-wing aircraft strength rose, and the Air Force bought F4-D fighter bombers based on a Navy design. As more deft interaction of ground and air power was focused on major maneuvers in the early 1960s, the Navy began to phase out its large-gun warships, and the Marines were allowed to retain their CAS components.

The tension between the desire of most commanders to "pile on" as opposed to the "light touch" in COIN/LIC—low-intensity conflict—doctrine and practice was not brought into balance in Vietnam or subsequently.[94] A special dilemma in "unconventional warfare" sprang from the tactical unit commanders' desire to minimize casualties and beat the enemy in their immediate zone of action by using weapons that sometimes caused "collateral damage." However rare such instances were, one photograph of a napalmed child could offset the "purely military" successes gained in many local fights, for in Vietnam, very little, until the final phase, was "purely military." Nevertheless, service doctrine and momentum usually prevailed over concern for the psychological aspect of war, which had once been seen as a major element in both the exercise of air power and in special operations. When the Air Force's defoliation program, Operation Ranch Hand, generated negative effects in the realm of psychological warfare, it took a very long time to rein it in.

Although U.S. advisers and aircraft had flown on-call strike missions during the "advisory" period of the early 1960s, close-air support operations in Vietnam began in earnest during the late winter of 1965–66.[95] In April of that year, CINCPAC Admiral Sharp had defined close-air support as the top priority in air operations in Southeast Asia.[96] Attempts to "Vietnamize" air operations in the South were deferred, as A–1 Skyraiders were retrieved from the South Vietnamese and re-marked with U.S. insignia, and Vietnamese airmen were no longer required to fly along with Americans. French installations were improved and new bases built to receive the expanding flow of Air Force and Marine tactical air squadrons, while Navy and Marine carrier planes began to operate from "Dixie Station," the carrier force off South Vietnam, "blooding" airmen to Vietnam conditions prior to moving to "Yankee Station" in the Gulf of Tonkin and conducting air operations against the North.

The growing archipelago of bases and forces was connected by a complex communications network. As the war escalated sharply in 1965–66, command-and-control "loops" ran from operations over Laos and North Vietnam back to Pacific Fleet Command in Hawaii, while those in South Vietnam were under General William Westmoreland's Military Assistance Command Vietnam. The latter's air deputy, Major General Joseph Moore, commanded air operations—except for Army aviation elements, and the Marine Corps air wings in the northern part of South Vietnam. There was little of the intermeshing of policy and political elements or unity of command seen among the Allies in World War II.

Problems arising from a not wholly rationalized structure and lack of coherent strategy were compounded by turf-guarding regional commanders who often impeded the shunting of air units assigned to them to other critical zones. There was also a lag between forward units, the Direct Air Support Center in each corps area, and the Tactical Air Control Center at MACV. At the cutting edge, however, the delay within the loops was shortened by Forward Air Controllers (FACs) in light liaison planes, who orchestrated air strikes in combat, using and modifying techniques developed in northwest Europe in 1944–45 and refined in Korea. One development widely hailed in the field was the arming of FACs with light machine guns and rockets to provide immediate response.

The overall state of affairs in the domain of close-air support reflected some decline in flexibility. Two-thirds of tactical air strikes were planned in advance, and various obstacles in the complex communication nets usually hampered quick reaction. In some areas, South Vietnamese government approval was required to employ artillery or air support, and reluctance was often viewed by Americans as a sign of fear, subversion, or corruption. However often that was the case, many Americans were insensitive to the predicament of the South Vietnamese fighting their own people, to the psychological and political effects of some weapons and tactics, and to U.S. forces being seen as technological bullies. Such disinclination to decouple method from concern about effects was reflected in the establishment of "Free-fire Zones," later renamed "Specified Strike Zones," where rules of engagement were much relaxed.

As after many wars, drawing lessons from Vietnam proved well short of a science, including conclusions regarding close-air support. While CAS improved enough to satisfy General Abrams, problems had emerged again and again. The massive reappraisal that came at the end of McNamara's tenure in 1968 continued under his successor, Secretary of Defense Clark Clifford, when it was found that air-ground force ratios, fixed early in the war by interservice turf agreements, had not been adjusted to operational realities over time.[97] Absence of enemy air power and a high density of tactical anti-aircraft weapons in the field in South Vietnam through most of the war, the American hunger for closure with an evasive foe, and equating of the shock and sound of weapons' impact with absolute effect all led to a strong reliance and, some believed, over-reliance on CAS, psychologically and physically. It was, after all, difficult to argue with those saved from desperate plight by armed helicopters, FACs, or the roar of mini-guns that CAS was not a positive element in the tactical equation.[98] Yet in spite of all that, Vietnam may have been the apogee of CAS practice in a prolonged war.

Sideshows and Aftershocks

Amphibious operations, a prime form of jointness in World War II, were a faint theme in Vietnam. Early in the war, U.S. Marines mounted some small-scale amphibious landings that were unopposed, and a major invasion of North Vietnam was discussed publicly from time to time. Given the state of jointness in the U.S. forces at that point, it would have required more good fortune than has been the norm in the history of joint operations, let alone in the Vietnam War.

Riverine warfare paralleled the French experience in the 1st Indochina War,[99] and led to extensive and prolonged Army-Navy cooperation.[100] Once again, effectiveness hinged on principals getting along, leading one observer to reflect a decade later that since "dedication, mutual respect and willing cooperation" cannot always be presumed, poorly defined command and control opens the "potential for disaster."[101]

The service insularity evident in Vietnam contributed to confusion and tragedy in an after-span of that war. The flounderings attendant to the Cambodian seizure of the U.S. freighter SS *Mayaguez* in 1975 were widely seen as due to sophisticated command-and-control technology allowing high echelons to interfere. After Khmer Rouge patrol boats seized the ship on May 12, 1975, 60 Marines were dispatched aboard Air Force helicopters to the ship. Due to communications snarls and weak intelligence, it was not known that the crew had been removed and released. After the rescue force received heavy fire, over a battalion of Marines was committed in a counter-stroke against Kom Tang Island. Fifty U.S. servicemen were killed, forty were wounded, and three were missing, while four U.S. helicopters were lost and nine heavily damaged. Some observers saw the affair as a "microcosm of the [Vietnam] war," that is, goals were unclear, levels of response did not match the situation, losses were unexpectedly high, and lack of jointness was evident.[102] Here, a postmortem suggested, "members of each service were absorbed in their own responsibilities, . . . and had not worked together before, [and] the chain-of-command was dispersed."[103]

Indeed, in the last phase of the Vietnam War, the Joint Chiefs' organizational marginality was reflected in reports of a Navy enlisted man passing National Security Council information to the chairman of the Joint Chiefs. Even before the war ended, the *Pentagon Papers* and later memoirs and histories presented large fragments of a picture of the JCS's anguish, of the soul-searching of various members and General Earl Wheeler's managing of "splits." By the end of the conflict, it was clear enough that the United States' high command fell far short of the hopes of Truman and Eisenhower, let alone such elegant models as Wilkinson's or Shaposhnikov's "brain of an army," or the classic general staffs of European variety.[104] A generation later, Dean Rusk, secretary of state from 1961 to 1968, observed: "One mistake we made was not having a unified command. Our military always talked about unity of command, but we never achieved it," while noting that the interpositioning of CINCPAC in the hierarchy of command "fuelled bickering over priorities and resources."[105]

The scrambling for helicopters, air support, and Marines and lack of functional jointness in the *Mayaguez* affair was an echo of another incident in which weak fusion in the U.S. armed force nexus had also been thrown into relief as U.S. involvement in Indochina reached its peak. Just before noon, on January 23, 1968, all major U.S. headquarters in the Pacific and in Washington received the message that the USS *Pueblo*, an intelligence vessel, was being threatened by North Korean naval vessels. *Pueblo* was promised that "some Air Force birds are winging your way," but 5th Air Force did not place aircraft on alert until two and a half hours later—a few minutes before the *Pueblo* was boarded.[106] In spite of the vast resources of the U.S. forces in the Pacific and many complex communication nets, none could be brought to bear to prevent *Pueblo* and its crew from being seized by the North Koreans and held for over a year. There were no fast-response air elements under the immediate control of the U.S. 8th Army, the major command in whose immediate zone of control the *Pueblo* was being towed into port by the North Koreans. Neither did the Joint Chiefs of Staff, the Secretary of Defense, or the White House situation room constitute functional operational headquarters that could monitor and orchestrate resources across service boundaries.[107] Thus, the *Pueblo* and *Mayaguez* incidents, a full generation after Pearl Harbor and the United States' emergence as a superpower, reflected the extent to which the American apparatus of command was complex and ill-coordinated, to a great extent due to a lack of functional jointness.

JOINTNESS IN THE TWILIGHT OF EMPIRE

As noted earlier, in Britain, as in the United States, structures and attitudes of jointness faded away quickly after World War II, despite many solemn resolutions made in the immediate wake of disasters and victories. As in the United States, the day-to-day bureaucratic processes of peacetime service life reduced interservice contact, while competition for limited resources added to friction. Lack of a clear and steady vision of Britain's role in the postwar world also clouded clarity of concept and organization. As Franklyn Johnson noted, "Restructuring of defense was made more difficult by Cabinet inability to decide what long-term policies the services should carry out."[108] The practice of muddling through, established in better times, persisted after 1945, as the empire shrank. Britain, physically, financially, and psychically battered in the World Wars, slid out of great power status, as contrasting Conservative and Labour views toward maintenance of empire were resolved by scarce resources. Britain had been nearly bankrupt on the eve of receiving Lend-Lease from the U.S. in the spring of 1941, and the war had worn out and damaged much of its industrial and commercial base and exhausted its financial reserves. Dilemmas deferred by wartime stringencies and American aid reappeared as the war ended, blighting the laurels of the last imperial triumph. Over the lean decade, 1945–1955, Britain lived on short rations, buoyed up by American loans and then by Marshall Plan aid.

Although the war remained sharp in British memories for the next two generations, many of the images of combined and joint operations faded quickly. As in America in the immediate postwar period, some major commanders waxed enthusiastic about jointness. Montgomery, like Eisenhower, pushed for unified defense policy and balanced forces in the late 1940s. Nevertheless, immediately after the war, the British Labour government under Clement Attlee reconstituted the split between prime minister and Minister of Defence, and downgraded the latter to the near-cloutless coordinating structure along the lines of the prewar Minister of Coordination of Defence. Several of the old joint committees were retained: Intelligence, Planning, and the Chiefs of Staff. The result was a retreat of the services back into their fiefdoms, a process accelerated by the membership of the latter, Field Marshal Montgomery, Admiral of the Fleet Andrew Cunningham, and Air Marshal Arthur Tedder, powerful personalities all. The creation of a chief above the service level, permitting independent judgment, did not come about in Britain until 1957, and in the United States, until 1986.

In Britain, as in the United States for almost four decades, the issue of centralization and coordination of the services was constantly discussed and debated but unresolved. Britain's strategic roles oscillated across a shifting field, from a prime focus on a major war in Europe and upon nuclear war, to the "real world" of many low-intensity conflicts amid the shrinkage and residue of empire. Neither the NATO environment nor even Suez and the Falklands meshed with the plans for elaborate joint institutions and practices drawn at the end of World War II, which had included a research and development establishment, a school, multiple training sites, and extensive cross-service training.[109]

As resources and inclinations dwindled, incoherence in defense structure, compromise, and incremental change[110] bolstered a predisposition to short focus.[111] After World War II, the role of the British Minister of Defence had been expanded from the adjunct title created by Churchill during the war to a separate Cabinet portfolio. In practice, however, the minister became a coordinator rather than a true director. In operations, the services went their own ways bureaucratically, with ad hoc committees much like eighteenth-century councils of war overseeing affairs in remote areas. Nevertheless, the principle of local command unity held up generally, meshing the Colonial and Foreign Office, Special Branch, military, and local security elements in the many wars of imperial retrenchment. Until the early 1980s, British attempts to centralize command fell as far short of a rationalized unified command structure as did NATO and the American defense system, in spite of how dramatically the Suez expedition of 1956 had demonstrated the loss of proficiency in joint operations.[112]

Suez

The Suez crisis of 1956 was a major switchpoint in modern British—and French—history as well as in the history of the postwar Western alliance.[113] An Anglo-French consortium had built the Suez Canal in the late 1860s and controlled it throughout the British occupations of Egypt, 1881–1952. The canal was seized in July 1956 by Colonel Gamel Abdel Nasser, leader of the colonels' junta that ruled Egypt. In championing militant pan-Arabism, Nasser had launched commando raids against Israel's southern frontier and supported the Algerian rebellion against France in the mid–1950s. Although Egypt's strengthened links with the Soviet Union as Premier Khrushchev called for "wars of national liberation" raised concerns in the West, there was no clear unity among NATO's three major powers in their reaction to the seizure of the canal. As with Gallipoli, the goals of the Suez expedition were vague at the outset and shifted throughout. No clear statements of strategic purpose flowed from a central source, and to make matters worse, two chief actors, British Prime Minister Anthony Eden and American Secretary of State John Foster Dulles, were seriously ill, while Eisenhower, the U.S. president, was in uneven health. Eden resigned just after Suez to recuperate, and Dulles died the next year.

Many in Britain felt Dulles' withdrawal of U.S. aid to Egypt in the summer of 1956 had led Nasser to seize the canal and seek Soviet solace. In any case, American attitudes toward Britain and France ranged from faint support to hostility as the crisis mounted. In late July, for example, while strongly condemning forceful recapture of the canal, the United States provided U–2 spy aircraft photos and special equipment to its main NATO allies, gestures that the British and French viewed as a wink of assent.

The French were the most avid throughout, committing two divisions and their Mediterranean fleet at the outset, while Walter Monckton, Eden's Defence Minister, was cautious at the outset, due to widespread fears of stirring up anger in the Third World toward neo-imperialism. Beyond that, many in defense circles, and politicians and the public as well, were amazed to find how little of the joint apparatus of World War II remained. There were, for example, no amphibious staff officers or RAF pilots with experience in major airborne drops. Recent British military experiences had been in small counter-insurgency campaigns in Cyprus, Kenya, and Malaya, and in static, linear ground warfare in Korea, while the French, grappling with the mounting Algerian revolt, had left much of their joint experience and equipment behind in Indochina.

When the British Chiefs of Staff estimated that it would take at least six weeks to mount an airborne-amphibious attack against Egypt, Monckton opposed the undertaking. The Chiefs were split in regard to the feasibility of the undertaking. Mountbatten, with a solid feel for the resentments of former colonies, came close to resigning in protest, and violated precedent in writing to the prime minister urging him to pull back. Air Marshal Sir William Dickson, the chairman of the Chiefs of Staff, was ill and often absent from meetings. Field Marshal Lord Templer, Chief of the General Staff, favored pressing on, while Chief of the Air Staff Sir Dermot Boyle was neutral and compliant to orders. Political tides raced toward action in the late summer, however, as public outrage toward Nasser mounted in Britain and France, and even Labour Party leader Hugh Gaitskell compared Colonel Nasser to Hitler and Mussolini. In early August, the first major steps toward forming a joint expedition were taken as a war of nerves began. Allied troops and aircraft carriers moved openly toward the eastern Mediterranean, and propaganda radio broadcasts urged Nasser's overthrow. French and British staffs met secretly to plan Operation Musketeer. General Sir Charles Keightley, as supreme commander, with a French admiral as his deputy, and General Sir Hugh Stockwell, as ground force commander, with General Andre Beaufre, a well-known military intellectual, as his deputy.

Musketeer was much larger than the Falklands expedition. The British provided 50,000 men and 100 naval vessels, including three aircraft carriers, and the French supplied 30,000 men and thirty naval vessels, including two carriers. As eighty transport vessels and some 20,000 vehicles were assembled in staging areas in Britain, Algiers, Malta, and Cyprus, planners coped with both a shortage and obsolescence of landing craft and trucks, a dearth of transport aircraft, and widespread mis-meshing of British and French systems ranging from menus to metric English standards. NATO was only seven years old, and little progress had been made toward interoperability. Grappling with the widening range of unforeseen problems and possibilities, commanders and planners became frustrated at their inability to get clear statements from political authorities on goals and rules of engagement.

Nevertheless, the first phase of planning was quickly finished and, on August 10, 1956, Eden gave his approval to proceed, just as political support began to ebb and diplomatic wrangles began. Commonwealth countries and the United States expressed concern, as the Conservatives suffered setbacks in public opinion polls. Behind the scenes, the French discussed a diversionary operation with the Israelis, concerned that the Egyptians might be able to use their array of Soviet equipment effectively. The main zone of Allied attack was shifted eastward from Alexandria to Port Said, as the French planned to fill in for Israeli forces moving west through Sinai.

Portents worsened as the summer waned. The Soviets increased both the flow of arms to Egypt and threats against Western neo-colonial adventurism, as Dulles set the tone for subsequent American diplomacy in the affair by echoing Soviet concerns. In mid-October, UN resolutions condemned the use of force in the canal crisis. Three weeks before the American presidential elections and D Day of Musketeer, the Israelis began diversionary attacks against Jordan. After the Iraqis dispatched forces, King Hussein called for British help. At that point, with a secret Israeli representative now on their staff, the French urged a change in plans, proposing a thrust to recapture the canal. Contingencies of overthrowing Nasser and the collapse of Egyptian military resistance were included, as French airborne forces moved to Cyprus. On October 18th, Monckton resigned and was succeeded by Anthony Head.

During the last week in October, the Arab states formed a united command, while the British conducted a major training exercise, Operation Boathook. The Anglo-French combined headquarters was aboard ship and on the way, as were parts of the armada, when the Israeli government formally sanctioned the start of its part of the operations. In the late afternoon of 29 October, with Israeli paratroops descending on Mitla Pass in the Sinai, British and Israeli aircraft moving into Egyptian airspace in various zones, and French planes covering Israeli cities, crisis now became epidemic. Anti-Communist risings erupted in Poland and Hungary, a coup attempt failed in Syria, and, in a shrill UN debate, the British and French, for the first time, vetoed hostile resolutions. Musketeer was presented on the basis that since Israeli-Egyptian battles threatened the canal, the British and French must secure the vital waterway and force the combatants to withdraw, a translucent if not transparent fiction, since many observers knew how long it took to mount major inter-Allied joint operations. As international opposition increased, the Suez expedition triggered a spasm of nationalistic fervor in France and in Britain, anger in Washington, Moscow, and in many parts of the world recently or still under colonial rule. A great cleft had opened in the Western alliance as the British Parliament approved government action by a 52-vote margin, and the French Chamber of Deputies by 186 votes, while in the United Nations, Britain vetoed an American condemnatory resolution.

On October 31st, General Keightley was ordered to seize the main ports on the canal and stop the fighting. Loading convoys had begun the day before, as Israeli tanks stormed Mitla Pass and British propaganda assailed Egypt with leaflets and broadcasts. At sunset, over 200 British and French planes struck a dozen Egyptian airfields. Nasser demanded withdrawal and may have threatened resignation to gain support in his own camp, while the Egyptians dispersed the remnants of their Air Force southward and scuttled a fleet of concrete-filled blockships in the Suez Canal. As opinion polls in Britain surged in favor of the Eden government's actions, oil pipelines crossing Syria were cut.

By the time that D Day approached, the Musketeer plan had undergone several revisions. The long psychological-warfare campaign included in the first version had been trimmed as events unfolded rapidly. After the Israelis took Sharm-el-Sheikh and proposed a cease-fire, the U.N. General Assembly called for a peacekeeping force. Gaitskell now did a volte-face, as a Conservative protest movement mounted, and rowdy debates led to the first suspension of the British Parliament due to disorder since 1924.

The sequence of ironies continued relentlessly. Eden, like the Kaiser in 1914, became increasingly anxious as he sensed the enormity of the forces in motion. On 4 November, rising acrimony from the Americans, the French, the Soviets, and the splintering of his own party led him to hold back a tank division scheduled for Musketeer. As forces went into motion in the final phase, Eden attempted to alter landing beaches and delay an airborne drop. The invasion began at dawn on November 5th, a thousand British and French paratroops descending on Port Said, commanded by a French airborne control aircraft, and a second wave went in during the early afternoon. While a Soviet diplomat was helping hand out weapons to the Egyptian populace, the Soviet Union presented Israel with the prospect of annihilation and, soon afterward, threatened to attack London and Paris with nuclear rockets. Then, on a less strident note, it suggested joint intervention to the United States.

On November 6th, in the predawn half-light, Royal Marine Commandos spearheaded the tank force landing, and, at daybreak, French forces at Port Fuad carried out the first helicopter-borne assault. By nightfall, Port Said had surrendered, and British and French patrols were advancing inland. Securing of the

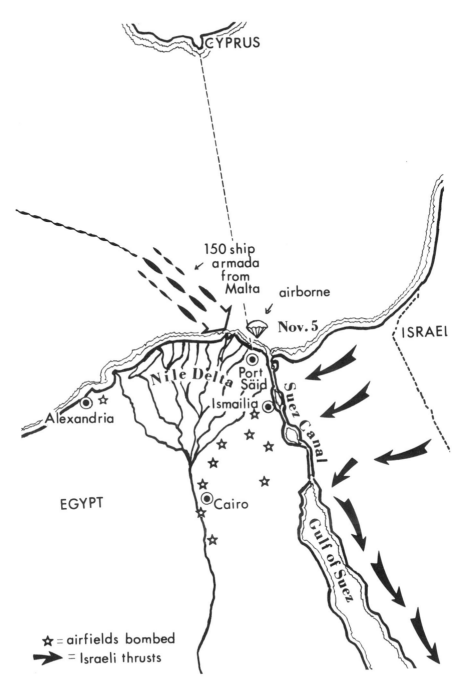

CYPRUS

150 ship
armada
from
Malta

airborne

Nov. 5

ISRAEL

Port
Säid

Nile Delta

Ismailia

Suez Canal

Alexandria

EGYPT

Cairo

Gulf of Suez

☆ = airfields bombed
➤ = Israeli thrusts

Anglo-French-Israeli Attacks on Egypt, October–November 1956

canal was expected in less than a week, and clearance in less than a month. Although matters were well in hand militarily, the Eisenhower administration, with the election imminent, now went beyond voting with the Soviets against the British, French, and Israelis in the United Nations. When a sterling crisis erupted, the United States blocked a British International Monetary Fund withdrawal that would have shored up the pound. As the British moved to halt military operations, the French chafed at their being blocked from independent action by being enmeshed in the toils of joint command.

Political vagueness and turmoil were not the only parallels with Gallipoli. While the financial crisis heightened, and the British were thwarted in seeking other ways to strengthen their currency, the weather in the Mediterranean worsened, as so often in the history of joint operations, and thwarted an attack on the Canal scheduled for the 7th. Fuel rationing, presaging a three-week gasoline drought later in the autumn, began in Britain, as economic pressure and diplomacy dashed the palm of their military victory from the hands of the British, French, and Israelis.

THE AFTERMATH OF SUEZ

What lessons were gained from the Suez expedition? Once again, much was relearned—the need for ready force, for trained planners, for modern landing craft in sufficient numbers, for trained airlift crews, and for adequate communications.[114] In keeping with the pattern of World War II, complex political-diplomatic and military-naval-air elements intertwined, and the political consequences of joint operations proved much greater than anticipated, a product of poorly defined goals and purposes at the outset. The issues at stake proved to be well beyond Eden's impulse toward "knocking Nasser off his perch." The Egyptian dictator emerged from defeat politically strengthened, while the Western alliance had fallen out over the issue of "out-of-area" operations, and NATO's influence on the world scene was substantially weakened. The sick Eden and sicker Dulles, the enigmatic Eisenhower, the guileful Nasser, the artfully irate Soviets, and widespread hostility toward fading imperialism all combined to decouple NATO unity in Europe from a Western international strategic accord. That unresolved discontinuity, so visible in the Vietnam era, was offset in stages a generation later by the Thatcher-Reagan rapport during the Falklands in 1982 and in the Libyan raid of 1987, and in the forming of the coalition against Iraq in 1990–91.

Beyond that, Defence Minister Duncan Sandys and many others in British defense circles saw how cumbersome the National Service, that is, conscript forces, were in a rapidly developing crisis. He soon opted for phasing out conscription, thus freeing many regular troops for unit assignment, as well as funds for research and development, rapid response aircraft, and amphibious elements. That shift in philosophy yielded rewards over the next generation in several cases, including the blocking of an Iraqi takeover of Kuwait in 1961.

Another result of Suez was a renewed assault on the Royal Navy's aircraft carrier force in spite of an effective tactical performance in operations. From the late 1940s onward, attacks on the utility of surface naval power, including aircraft carriers, in British strategy had been launched by both Conservative and Labour Ministers of Defence. In the wake of Suez, Sandys saw both cruisers and carriers as redundant, while a decade later, Denis Healey would renew the assault, with an eye to focusing British naval forces on NATO commitments. Reflecting substantial bi-partisanship in defense policy, the last fleet carriers departed on the eve of the Falklands War.

Other proverbial chickens roosted quickly. De Gaulle soon came to power and took France off to the margin of NATO, while giving the Americans a bitter taste of *revanche*. The Israelis looked more ardently to their own devices, as did the British, who in their next budget slashed their conventional forces and began to dismantle their network of overseas commitments, many of which served U.S. interests. In the Vietnam War, both the French and British stood well back in the wings, the former with acrimony, the latter with very faint encouragement, while America waded into its own futile out-of-area excursion. Meanwhile, each of the Suez allies proceeded to build its own independent strategic nuclear forces.

In Britain, after Suez, a wide variety of strategic and tactical contingencies and actual operations continued to splay doctrine and procurement. As the British defense budget was trimmed, Soviet naval expansion and build-up of forces in Europe, small conflicts from Belize and Brunei, to the alleys of Ulster and *wadis* of the south rim of Arabia, created diverse polarities. In the 1960s and 1970s, growing reliance on systems analysis and computers seemed to do little but aid in diagnosing the syndromal patterns of the "British disease" and measure the decline of British military power under both political practices, which continued into the early Thatcher years.[115] Throughout the 1970s, small wars lay farther and farther from the primary foci of strategic Central Europe and the Atlantic approaches, and the decline of interest in amphibious and related forces and in much else in the defense realm was manifest in the 1981 Defence White Paper, "The Way Forward."[116]

The Falklands

Whether that document encouraged the Argentine junta to move on the Falkland Islands remains a provocative question. The underlying assumptions of it were almost immediately tested during the scrambling to launch an expedition to the Falklands in the autumn of 1982. The dearth of certain types of weapons, especially aircraft carriers, and of various supplies crimped both logistics and operations, but a joint command structure had been created, rekindling the essence of the supreme-commander model of World War II. The expedition was closer in scale and format to World War II combined operations than any joint effort mounted by British forces since Suez, or by the United States since Korea. While the invasion force confronted no fixed shore defenses, it might have. In any event, once again, many lessons were relearned: the premium on flexibility and improvisation; the need for rapid modification and assembly of merchant ships; and the unexpected importance of ''minor'' details in meshing the services' doctrine, command and control, and logistics. Beyond those lay the old familiar problems with landing craft and air support, and the navy's and army's respective divergent tactical concerns regarding safety of the covering fleet as opposed to land battles to be fought at the end of an 8,000-mile-long logistical conduit, in a manner faintly evocative of the Okinawa campaign. And in a final parallel with earlier instances, changes in British defense policy after the Falklands war were made in the same spirit of firm resolve following previous joint operations, especially the retention and bolstering of amphibious forces scheduled for oblivion,[117] and the further strengthening of jointness at the highest command levels in the form of a ''fully unified Defence Policy and Operational Staff.''[118] The latter marked the end of a long struggle.

Throughout the 1950s, Admiral Mountbatten, as First Sea Lord and then as chief of the Defence Staff, had labored mightily for service unification, a cause that he had championed since his immersion in the triservice ambience of Combined Operations in 1941–43 and during his tour as Southeast Asia Theater commander, 1943–45. The long-range effects were greater in form than substance, and any shrinkage in the service chiefs' clout over the next three decades was more a function of economic and political problems and the steady shrinkage of British military power and commitments than of those reforms.

During that time, the services were able to gather back some degree of relative autonomy. When the Thatcher government eliminated the Service Secretariats, it was as much to end their functioning as a source of parochialism and a fulcrum for political levering as a search for economy. Although major defense retrenchments had been made on the eve of the Falklands War, fiscal stringency was eased somewhat afterward. ''Fortress Falklands'' was established, followed by the thawing of the Cold War. Experiences in the South Atlantic, especially close calls in respect to some of the weapons systems involved, created a new sense of the value of jointness, rapid-deployment forces, and naval power relative to nuclear deterrence and NATO. The reforms of Defence Minister Michael Heseltine, however, seemed to some as just more vigorous chops of an ax that had been swung for over a generation. His reliance on computer-based analysis was much in the spirit of Denis Healey, and his move to reduce the service chiefs' authority seemed contradictory to the special chemistry of Mrs. Thatcher's interaction with the chiefs during the Falklands War, and the marginal role played by the chief of the Defence Staff. The positive chemistry and her keen sense of structure and authority seemed to prove the adage in British defense circles that people were more important than structure. Not surprisingly, the chiefs fought back to gain assurance of continued access to the prime minister.

In the Gulf crisis and war of 1990–91, however, in parallel with the

U.S. Chairman of the Joint Chiefs, a sea change in authority ran in favor of the Chief of the Defence Staff, who directed operations without close consultation and left the service chiefs the role of trainers and suppliers. No one had ever challenged the flow of authority from the prime minister and Cabinet to the forces, but the route had now become more direct, although Mrs. Thatcher, after setting guidelines, had left the business of fighting to the commander on the scene.

AFTER VIETNAM: CLOSE-AIR SUPPORT

In Vietnam, the manifold elements in the spectrum of air power had rarely been orchestrated. The siege of the Marine enclave at Khe Sanh in 1968 had led to major wrangling at the highest U.S. command levels over control of air elements. Although a central Air Force air operations controller was appointed for the duration of the operation only, praxis fell well short of intent. In Vietnam, although jointness was scarce, there was little immediate sense, aside from Komer's critique, that success in World War II or frustration and failure in Vietnam were related to jointness and coherence of strategic policy, doctrine, and operations. Concern about jointness and fusion mounted in the late 1970s as the United States and its Western allies focused more closely on NATO theater war scenarios, the Soviet naval and Warsaw Pact build-up generated visions of imminent warfare in the North Atlantic and in Central Germany.

The arguments regarding close-air support in the resultant doctrinal exegesis were not far in essence from those made between the World Wars. Should CAS aircraft be modifications of standard high-performance planes, which, like the fighter-bombers of World War II, could hold their own in regular air-to-air combat, or at least get away quickly? Should CAS be carried out by attack helicopters, by short and vertical take-off and landing aircraft like Harriers or Ospreys? Or was it best provided by special types, like the A–10, designed to stay aloft for long periods, slow but heavily armored and maneuverable, deployed immediately over the FPOT (forward position own troops) while deep air thrusts by high performance aircraft shattered Eastern Bloc supporting echelons? Could a single major type with fighter characteristics cover the full range of conflicts and roles that might emerge? Here the dilemma of moving aircraft long distances quickly versus advantages in operations of sturdy and easily maintainable low-and-slow workhorses like the old Skyraider and A–10 intruded itself. In the Gulf War, the latter stood forth, despite many gloomy prognostications. As in World War II, the debates of the 1970s and 1980s reflected the tension and confusion between interdiction—sealing off the battlefield from supporting elements—and the providing of on-call support quickly to ground units in combat. Sorting out Army and Air Force "roles and missions" and related aircraft purchases lay at the heart of "Air-Land Battle" doctrine formulation.

On the other hand, creation of a U.S. Army aviation branch in the 1980s reflected the fact that major evolutions of technology and growing enthusiasm for jointness had not put old territorial impulses and reflexes to rest, or altered air commanders' vision of battlefield air interdiction as akin to the "attack aviation" of the 1930s. It also reflected a more general hostility to centralized direction of combat, in a kind of Luddite reaction to advances in command-and-control systems.[119]

Limited War and Jointness

Soon after Hiroshima, some observers, such as Liddell Hart and F. O. Miksche, saw that warfare would be reshaped by compression effects arising from the fear that limited war might lead to a nuclear exchange. Most of the wars waged by the superpowers and their clients yielded relatively low casualties. Exceptions were Korea, and the Iran-Iraq war, both resembling World War I, with trenches, bunkers, and mass artillery barrages, and some phases of the Indochina Wars, that is, Dien Bien Phu and Khe Sanh. The Cambodian holocaust echoed the methods of Attila, Genghis Khan, Stalin, and Hitler. Close-air support seemed to have little utility in small conflicts of the Cold War, since terrorists, insurgents, and guerrillas strove to avoid presenting fixed large or clear targets. As noted in the case of Vietnam, in such settings, the physical and psychological side-effects caused by strategic and tactical air power sometimes offset its utility, since, as in World War II, it was difficult to determine what its impact had been.

American military professionals, vendors, and analysts often viewed CAS problems in terms of statistics and specifications that bore little direct relationship to the fluid and chaotic complexities of combat.[120] Neither did lessons selected from one "real world" always apply in another. For example, on the eve of the 1973 Ramadan/Yom Kippur/October War, the Israelis deployed behind fixed defenses and relied on tactical air support and tanks as their tactical mainstays. When the Syrians and Egyptians breached their lines on the Golan Heights and in Sinai, respectively, Israeli counterstrokes were decimated by hand-held anti-aircraft and anti-tank missiles in forward areas, and by mechanized radar-equipped anti-aircraft guns protecting their foes' artillery and key points. Reportedly, half of their close-air support sorties were lost in the first day's fighting, and their initial tank assaults were shattered. After the war, the Israelis and others reconsidered the balance of forces, especially the utility of combined arms and the relative costs of close-air support versus field artillery, in consideration of a grim ratio of missions flown to planes lost.

The air campaign in Operation Desert Storm, vast and dramatic, reflected some of those same difficulties encountered in earlier wars, including the image of technological bullying, difficulty in selecting and finding targets and measuring results. The political nature of civil wars, limited wars, and insurgencies often precluded or limited the use of weapons designed for conventional warfare. The problem with napalm and defoliation in Vietnam has already been noted. In the late 1940s, some Greek pilots refused to use napalm against their countrymen,[121] while in South Vietnam, Skyraider aircraft provided by the United States to the RVN Air Force for close-air support were held in reserve by the government to use as symbols and direct instruments of coercion in a civil context.

Jointness in low-intensity conflict (LIC), where the use of military forces is highly focused and restrained, often relies more on police, propaganda, and intelligence and military support elements than on military combat units. The special premium on subtleties like political sensitivity, deviousness, and creativity in LIC was recognized in the Malayan Emergency in placing troops under Special Branch, as Lieutenant General Sir Harold Briggs and Sir Robert Thompson brought what Noel Barber saw as "joint thinking" into planning by forming war councils composed of administrators, soldiers, airmen, and policemen. In their daily deliberations, deemed "morning prayers," they wove threads of operational fusion into a "rope of coordination."[122]

JOINTNESS OF A KIND: FROM VIETNAM TO DESERT STORM

From the early 1970s to the late 1980s, frustrations and setbacks led U.S. military professionals and others to question many of their basic doctrines, structures, and premises. The American military system came under heavy criticism after the Vietnam War for a series of failures in the realm of "operational art," a term derived from Soviet doctrine referring to the level of conducting war between strategy and tactics. An Israeli air attack on the U.S. intelligence ship *Liberty* in 1967 in the Six Day War had revealed malfunctioning of U.S. strategic communications in essence similar to the *Pueblo* affair described earlier. The failure of the well-planned and executed commando raid on the North Vietnamese prison-of-war camp at Son Tay in 1972 and the confusion and error marking the rescue operations in the *Mayaguez* incident in 1974 have also been noted. Widespread confusion arising from a major test of U.S. command-and-control systems in Operation Nifty Nugget in the fall of 1978,[123] and a false alert of the strategic command-and-control system a year later led to increased funding and reforms over the next decade. At the same time, some advocates of reform were proposing a new tactical emphasis on maneuver warfare tactics and light forces, with minimal dependence on command-and-control links to higher echelons and less reliance on mass firepower. These basic precepts seemed attractive to those lacking faith in command, control and communications systems' effectiveness or resenting over-supervision by their superiors. Somewhat paradoxically, reformers also sought to strengthen the role of the chairman of the Joint Chiefs of Staff, and the regional "sinks"—commanders in chief—to offset perceived micromanaging of operations from the White House, Pentagon, and higher headquarters in the field that characterized the Vietnam War.

The drive for reform was also shaped by other technical developments. Although Vietnam and dozens of other conflicts, including the Soviets' replication of U.S. limited-war frustrations in Afghanistan, involving superpowers or their surrogates did not catalyze nuclear exchanges, the appearance of ever-more sophisticated conventional weapons, such as "smart weapons," fuel-air explosives, and such derivatives of Strategic Defense Initiative research as rail and light-gas guns, began to blur the nuclear threshold. Many programs that burgeoned in the defense build-up of the Reagan administration had been started earlier, such as the "Electronic Battlefield," initiated in the Nixon years by General William Westmoreland, and, in the Carter administration, the Strategic Defense Initiative—Star Wars (SDI), Harold Brown's articulation of the doctrine of "horizontal escalation," and the cruise missile. As various lobbying groups promoted a defense expansion in response to the Soviet build-up in Eastern Europe in the 1970s, the weakness of the Joint Chiefs of Staff came under close scrutiny By the end of that decade, a critic deemed the Joint Chiefs "a product of history, not of logic," and the air, submarine, and surface elements of the Navy were called "semi-feudal."[124]

Amphibious warfare, the linch-pin of jointness in World War II, was off to the side in these exegeses, as Marine Corps amphibious elements shrank after the Vietnam War as part of a general retrenchment, in spite of slowly rising concern among some "reformers." The Navy's amphibious force had dropped to sixty-five ships by the late 1970s, holding steady at 15 percent of U.S. active naval forces over the next decade, providing sea-lift for approximately two and a half divisions of Marines, a level maintained since Korea. The 2.3 percent increase in amphibious elements from 1980 to 1989 contrasted sharply with the Navy's 26 percent growth over the decade.[125]

EAGLE CLAW AND AFTER

Problems with special operations during the Vietnam War, especially the Phoenix program and the Green Beret murder case, led some military professionals and analysts to judge such "black" activities beyond the capacity of the American military and the tolerance of the political system. Others, however, felt such missions could be carried out properly if adjustments were made. In spite of their doctrinal and structural separation from general forces, covert operations and elite forces were often cited in the debate over reform, and the litany of failure that usually included the Son Tay Raid, the *Pueblo*, the *Mayaguez* affair, and Operation Eagle Claw in April 1980. The latter failed because its special units from each of the armed services were hastily combined to free U.S. hostages held in Teheran. The failure of Eagle Claw, the first deliberate U.S. military operation since Vietnam, was seen as yet further proof of chronic incapacity. However effective such analyses were, the Holloway Committee and other studies traced a concatenation of maladroitness worthy of Gilbert and Sullivan, but far less comedic. Any question of culpability and accident aside, Eagle Claw threw service insularity into public view more vividly than at any time since the "Revolt of the Admirals." Some critics argued that snarls in organization, training, and execution in the raid stemmed from over-preoccupation with jointness and various services seeking a "piece of the action."[126]

Whatever the specifics of that very complex case, it set the tone of criticism as the pattern of setbacks persisted in the Reagan administration, in spite of major increases in defense spending. In Beirut, in the fall of 1983, a truckload of high explosives detonated at the U.S. Embassy killed 243 Marines, while Operation Urgent Fury, a joint operation against Grenada conducted at the same time, succeeded at odds of twenty to one, but also quickly came under critical scrutiny. The former was clearly due to slipshod local security. In the latter, the tension between the chipper official descriptions of nearly flawless execution as opposed to less enthusiastic versions in the defense professional press and in military circles led to speculation about what might have happened if the expedition, close in scale to the British Falklands foray, had encountered serious resistance. Beyond several unpleasant turns of fate of the kind that led Clausewitz to describe war as the "province of chance," critics noted a lack of effective multiservice planning, of joint control structures and procedures.[127] Such revelations led to mounting concerns about coordination, and, in stages, to formal interservice diplomacy aimed at increasing fusion.

In the late 1970s, the Navy and Air Force developed joint policies for war at sea, including the use of B–52 bombers in maritime roles. In 1984, the "31 initiatives" were "signed off" on by the Army and Air Force chiefs of staff, which formalized coordination in such areas of jointness as air defense, special operations, and command and control.[128] Rather than a political ploy to offset the Navy's surge in status in the Reagan administration, the initiatives, expanded later, were mainly products of Air-land Battle doctrine.[129] However successful they were in that context, the initiatives failed to prevent an opening of the old debate between the Army and the Air Force late in the decade over the question of which service should buy and control close-air support aircraft.

The waves of reform did not all move synchronously. Enthusiasm in American military circles for "maneuver warfare" in the post-Vietnam period stood in tension with some contingencies and certain aspects of jointness. Many, even in the Marine Corps, came to see giving subordinate commanders wide latitude for free maneuver in battle as a universal good, although it was well out of phase with the close planning, firm structure, and the tight phasing and orchestration of firepower of amphibious operations.[130]

The Maritime Strategy: Against the Quickening Current

At the same time, the Navy had designed another logic for maintaining autonomy, the Maritime Strategy. The first version of it appeared in the 1950s, based on a vision of low-intensity conflicts raging along the rimlands of Eurasia, but falling well short of the assumption of all-out nuclear war that pitched defense budgets in favor of the Air Force. "Victory is out," suggested one proponent, and "real peace . . . [is] a remote possibility."[131] A similar uncertainty was visible in other variants. One invoked the British naval squeeze on Napoleon after Trafalgar as a model, because it had "no constricting rigidity of plan nor any premature commitment" and took "timely advantage of opportunity."[132] Like the Maritime Strategy and maneuver warfare of the 1980s, the 1950s model was not linked to other services' general theater war plans but to generic principles of "dispersion, flexibility and mobility,"[133] since the pattern of future war was uncertain.[134]

Both the origins and purposes of the Maritime Strategy of the 1980s have been debated at length.[135] Although its chief promulgator was the dynamic and feisty Secretary of the Navy, John Lehman, its component themes and phrases can be found in the works of various nineteenth- and early twentieth-century American and British naval pundits,[136] as well as in those of more recent writers on naval affairs.[137] Often deemed a "procurement strategy" aimed at persuading Congress to fund a 600-ship Navy, the Maritime Strategy was also a step back from jointness, steering against the strongest tides toward centralization in U.S. defense structure seen since the late 1950s. Its basis was the U.S. Navy's launching of a major assault on the Soviet Navy, primarily against its main bastion, the North Cape and northern seas that sheltered Russian nuclear missile submarines. Thus, much of the fleet's anti-submarine forces, Atlantic Marine Corps elements, carrier task forces and submarines were vectored well away from support of the main U.S. Army and Air Force and NATO theater/general war operations, and from the great battle on the central German plain, that lay at the heart of NATO war plans. Onerous missions like convoy protection, major amphibious operations and mine/anti-mine warfare were placed off to the side in a scenario in which the expanded Navy conducted global warfare against Soviet sea power, far in concept and essence from the grand-strategic meshing of Allied armed services in World War II.[138]

Contingencies of global naval war-waging were, at least at the level of public visibility, much murkier in the Maritime Strategy than the salient operations aimed at the North Cape. For example, the fleet's functions in "broken-backed [sic] war" or post-nuclear war scenarios were not addressed. Some doubted that the Navy would be able to grapple quickly with the Soviet fleet in the event of war, or that the Soviets would choose to engage according to the Navy's expectations at any point. Whatever the underlying intent, it was a model for employing U.S. Navy-controlled sea, air, and land power separate from the other services. Collaborative in only a general sense, the Maritime Strategy countered the argument that "modern technology offers the opportunity to dominate the oceans without necessarily building vast fleets of surface ships."[139] Motives and purposes aside, in the post-Cold War era, its vagueness may prove to have stood it in good stead relative to the Air Force and Army strategic scenarios, tightly focused on a general war in Central Europe, that crumbled so quickly in the path of *perestroika* in late 1989–90, and in the re-vectoring to southwest Asia in 1990–91. However, the Maritime Strategy was not able to stem the tides toward jointness that led to further service unification, or to maintain the much-enlarged Navy that many believed was its true goal as a "procurement strategy."

THE "NEW WEAPONRY"

In the early 1970s, as the United States withdrew from Southeast Asia, the complexity of tactics and doctrine was being heightened by the appearance of both air-delivered and ground-fired precision guided munitions. The dramatic effects of American "smart bombs" in Vietnam were first seen by the public on television in 1972, while a year later, a variety of such weapons yielded unexpectedly grave losses in the October/Yom Kippur/Ramadan War. A growing variety of "new weaponry," including cruise missiles and fuel-air explosives, raised the prospect of cheaper and more reliable non-nuclear networks of defense for Western Europe. Later in the 1970s and early 1980s, as the swelling arrays of Warsaw Pact tanks, troop carriers, and guns and refinements in Soviet doctrine and tactics raised anxieties in Western defense circles about sudden surprise and theater war, a growing concern about catalytic war was dramatized in Sir John Hackett's best-selling futuristic novel, *The Third World War*. While fears among military planners mounted that a Soviet surprise attack might be launched out of a maneuver format, and assumptions of warning time were scaled down consequently from weeks to days, public anxieties in Western Europe were increased by the Soviet build-up on the one hand, and the arrival of American-controlled cruise missiles and Pershing IIs on the other. As the Soviet naval "renaissance" and intervention in Afghanistan further jangled the nerves of many Western Europeans, U.S. deployment of enhanced radiation weapons— "neutron bombs"—in the late 1970s was thwarted by political demonstrations, as the rise of the nuclear freeze movement accelerated the search for new tactical counters to the rising Soviet mass of maneuver. Although the Soviets' shooting down of a Korean airliner in 1983 sharply reduced such activism, the political unacceptability in Western Germany of any phase-line or territorial defense scheme that accepted even transitory Soviet intrusion and occupation, or that relied on using nuclear weapons led to a military doctrine of launching a deep counter-attack against an Eastern Bloc assault as quickly as possible.

After the Vietnam War, U.S. Army doctrine was retooled toward the goal of winning such a "first battle" by in essence inverting Soviet "deep battle" doctrine, and relying on superior maneuver and precision-guided weapons, equipment, and quality of forces. While the U.S. Army and Air Force began to mesh their doctrines in the late 1970s toward the goal of launching a major non-nuclear counter-offensive deep in Warsaw Pact rear areas, to paralyze Soviet "follow-on forces," the range of weapons needed to implement such concepts as Airland Battle 2000 was not available until the mid–1980s. Overall, however, in spite of the "31 Initiatives," the fusion of air and ground elements and inter-Allied linkages fell well short of what had been hoped for at NATO's founding in

1949.[140] Prospects for effective orchestration in a major battle seemed no more likely at the end of the 1980s than at the beginning of the decade, despite advances and refinements in command-and-control technologies.[141] Kenneth Allard's *Command and Control, and the Common Defense*, published in the immediate wake of the Goldwater-Nichols Act, traced interservice frictions in the development of JTIDS—the Joint Tactical Information Distribution System—back to the disparate service subcultures, for example, the Navy's use of data bit transmission compared to the Air Force's preference for voice communication.[142]

JOINT CHIEFS OF STAFF REFORM IN EARNEST: THE GOLDWATER-NICHOLS ACT OF 1986

Throughout the early 1980s, the mischances and errors of Eagle Claw and Urgent Fury had been widely attributed to structural problems in the Joint Chiefs of Staff. As pressure for JCS reform mounted, with support from many quarters, the most ardent advocate was Air Force General David Jones, who spoke out while serving as chairman of the Joint Chiefs. The new spirit was evident in 1984, when an Air Force colonel, in proposing a unified command structure in any future theater operations, argued against the "focus on systems to fight a war and service orientation instead of the structure itself" and for "the delegation of responsibility by functional area."[143] The Goldwater-Nichols Act was passed by Congress in early May of 1986 and signed in late September. A month later, David Packard presented the report of the Blue Ribbon Committee on Defense Management, which underscored many of the points made earlier. The JCS structure now lay closer to models proposed a generation earlier, with the JCS chairman as the principal military adviser to the president and Secretary of Defense, and with a deputy. Eisenhower's concept of "Unified Action Armed Forces," central to the "Joint Perspective," was revitalized and promulgated through joint doctrinal publications.[144] Orchestration of jointness fell to the J-7 branch of the Joint Staff, the Directorate for Operational Plans and Interoperability, and a major product of its efforts, the Joint Doctrine Master Plan, became the "spearhead of the warfighting doctrine of the Commanders-in-Chief of Unified and Specified Commands."[145]

Major structures were altered as well. A Special Operations Command was created in 1986, and, in 1987, a Transportation Command was established to encompass elements of all three services, while Forces Command became a specified command. Rewards were built into the personnel system to reverse the long-standing aversion of military careerists to "purple-suit," that is, joint assignments. Formerly avoided, joint duty became career-enhancing under the Goldwater-Nichols Act. "Purple" became a more popular color, as officers were required to have 30 percent of their service in joint assignments to be considered for promotion to flag (i.e., general or admiral) rank.[146] However, that took time, and many contrary forces were at work, especially the unexpected shrinkage of the force structure that had many such "slots" in its upper tiers.

The Goldwater-Nichols Act had not specifically guaranteed that control of the American defense nexus would swing back toward uniformed military professionals. The recast role of the JCS chairman was a new tool for someone to wield, and the chairman of the Joint Chiefs, Admiral William Crowe, was the first to take it in hand. It appeared to be business as usual in 1987 when he was left in Washington during the Reagan-Gorbachev meetings in Rekjavik, Iceland, while his counterpart, Marshal Akhromeyev, sat at the Soviet premier's elbow, and major arms control cuts were made there without consulting Crowe or the JCS. Fate intervened at that point, however. Crowe had not favored the administration's creation of the Special Operations Command in October 1986, which, under the logic of William Casey's tenure as chief of the CIA, constituted a "black budget" private army sealed off from JCS, service and congressional scrutiny and fiscal control. Beyond that, assignment of key roles in the National Security Council to an admiral and a Marine colonel lay far from the spirit of jointness.

In the wake of the revelation of the Iran-Contra affair, the death of Casey, and the departure of Secretary of Defense Casper Weinberger, Crowe expanded his powers, naming the deputy provided for in the Goldwater-Nichols Act, while the Goldwater-Nichols Act's doctrinal and structural changes slowly and steadily infused jointness into service career dynamics. Other major and unexpected forces came to bear on the joint process. Defense budget reductions had been underway since 1986, and when Admiral Crowe retired in late 1989, euphoria emanating from political events in central and eastern Europe led to new proposals for retrenchment and a "peace dividend." Amid the greatest proportional shrinkage in the U.S. forces since the Korean War, Crowe's successor, Army General Colin Powell, further expanded the chairman of the Joint Chiefs' role.

The first test of the new jointness came in the U.S. attack on the Noriega regime in Panama at the end of 1989. The overall quality of planning, execution, and interservice linkage, especially in the realm of special operations, in Operation Just Cause was seen as markedly superior to Urgent Fury. Nevertheless, a major argument had erupted,[147] as planning began for the Panama incursion, over the operational control of an aircraft carrier by the designated non-naval commander. It lasted almost a year, the Navy hierarchy arguing that such authority only extended to broad definition of the mission. The Navy had not abandoned the tenet that their antecedents had adhered to in the Spanish-American War that all afloat was under Navy jurisdiction in respect to specific and detailed orders.[148] Crowe ultimately rejected that logic.

THROUGH A GLASS AND DARKLY: JOINTNESS IN DESERT SHIELD/DESERT STORM

Jointness was again tested in Desert Storm, along with collective security, and the use of international policing power by a coalition against an aggressor that underlaid the Covenant of the League of Nations and the Charter of the

United Nations. A principal question regarding jointness that some critics raised before fighting began, since it was implicit in the joint command structure, was whether campaign plans would aim at all services' sharing in the victory, rather than relying on attrition through air power. It was not easy to appraise that through the haze of battle and security classification at the time and immediately afterward. However anomalous it seemed on the surface, having Army General Colin Powell, the chairman of the U.S. Joint Chiefs of Staff, and Norman Schwarzkopf, Central Command commander in chief preside over an air offensive seemed the best tactic for avoiding a battle with the Iraqi army on its most favorable terms. Many, including commanders and planners on the spot, expected heavy losses if it came to pitched ground combat. Described as the fourth largest in the world, with vast amounts of armored vehicles and artillery and well dug-in, Iraq's army had displayed great facility in fortification in its long war against Iran, as well as skill in deception In the spirit of its Soviet tutors' *maskirovka* doctrine—camouflage, concealment, and deception.

As much as can be determined through the veil of secrecy, the Allied command structure seemed to function reasonably well, with only minor discontinuities and occasional contradictory statements evident. A broader spirit of jointness was visible, at least symbolically, in the Combined Operations shoulder patches worn by British briefing officers. Little specific data were forthcoming on such matters, however, since detailed description of command organization and process, and friction between coalition states, personalities, or between or within services would provide ammunition in the propaganda war, as well as intelligence. Yet it was apparent on the eve of Operation Desert Shield-Desert Storm that the old Army-Air Force tensions regarding direct battlefield control of close-air support versus routing through Air Force channels had not been put to rest, in spite of the co-locating of headquarters and improved rapport. In the immediate aftermath, the frequent assertion that "jointness worked" suggested that things had been more in hand than in Vietnam or Grenada. Nevertheless, during Operation Desert Shield, substantial problems with airlift and sealift became visible, both activities that the Air Force and Navy respectively viewed as marginal to their primary focus on war-fighting, but which they held onto nonetheless. Apparent successes in other provinces of jointness in Desert Storm included special operations, close-air support, air-sea-land rescue, and medical evacuation as well as other areas demarcated in the "31 Initiatives" and its amendments.

Beyond apparent maneuvering by each armed service for a piece of the operational action,[149] a number of interservice difficulties came into public view in the United States in the months following the Gulf War, including Air Force mistakes in estimates of Tomahawk missile effectiveness, excessive security compartmentalization that hampered intelligence diffusion, "incompatible communication links,"[150] and substantial confusion and turbulence in the medical system.[151] The most bitter "lesson learned" in regard to jointness emerged from behind the screen of tight secrecy in August 1991, when it was purported that almost a quarter of American casualties in Operation Desert Storm were due to friendly fire. Recognizing murky doctrine and inadequate practice as a cause of the problem, the U.S. Army's Training and Doctrine Command and the Air Force's Tactical Air Command entered into a formal agreement to "develop a common doctrine for air-land attacks," announced as part of a projected effort throughout the military, air, and naval hierarchies to draw upon "applicable" lessons from the Gulf War over the next few years.[152] That seemed to conform with General Holley's view, on the eve of the conflict, of "the tragedy" that in each recent American war, "the services . . . after much delay, constructed a solution," which was then "abandoned and largely forgotten almost as soon as the fighting stops," and then reconstituted it "in some form after much suffering and delay when the next war occurs."[153]

The Gulf War was followed by official plaudits for the many advantages gained from the refining of U.S. joint doctrine and the hard work done over the previous decade or so. The long list of lessons presented by the Office of the Secretary of Defense in mid–1992 included a number of "issues," or problems related to jointness.[154] The resemblance to the insights and lessons learned in other operations raises the dilemma that General Holley pointed out. How much will declining resources and human attitudes shape the nature of jointness henceforth? What will a review of that long list of "issues" show in the way of change and continuity in five, or ten, or fifty years? No reasonable observer would expect that all would be brought right, that everyone would agree as to what that meant, or that all contingencies could be anticipated. Nevertheless, those questions will prove vital to the extent that jointness continues to be a significant dimension of armed conflict.

NOTES

1. Vincent Davis, *The Admiral's Lobby* (Chapel Hill: University of North Carolina, 1967), p. 217.

2. For example, see Wesley Frank Craven and James Lea Cate, *The Army Air Forces in World War II: Men and Planes*, vol. 6 (Chicago: University of Chicago, 1955), p. 17; for a somewhat more temperate air force perspective on unification from 1921 to the end of the first Truman administration, see Harold B. Hinton, *Air Victory: The Men and Their Machines* (New York: Harper & Brothers, 1948), pp. 157ff, pp. 356–58.

3. See Table 6.1, "Wartime Studies Related to Unification," in Curtis William Tarr, *Unification of America's Armed Forces: A Century and a Half of Conflict, 1798–1947* (Stanford University Ph.D. Dissertation, 1981), p. 167.

4. For detailed surveys of the 1945–50 period, see Edgar F. Raines, Jr. and David R. Campbell, *The Army and Joint Chiefs of Staff: Evolution of Army Ideas on the Command, Control and Coordination of the U.S. Armed Forces, 1942–1985* (Washington, D.C.: Center of Military History, 1986); and Kenneth W. Condit, *The History of the Joint Chiefs of Staff*, vol. ii, *1947–49* (Washington, D.C.: Historical Division, Joint Secretariat, Joint Chiefs of Staff, 1978); Russell F. Weigley, *A History of the United States Army* (New York: Macmillan, 1967), Ch. 20, pp. 485–504; and C. Joseph Bernardo

and Eugene H. Bacon, *American Military Policy: Its Development Since 1775* (Harrisburg, Pa.: Stackpole Co., 1961), Ch. 20, pp. 442–61.

5. Demetrios Cavaley, *The Politics of Military Unification: A Study of the Conflict Process* (New York: Columbia University, 1966); Paolo Coletta, *The United States Navy and Defense Unification, 1947–1953* (Newark: University of Delaware Press, 1981).

6. Logan C. Ramsey, "The Aero-Amphibious Phase of the Present War," *U.S. Naval Institute Proceedings* 69 (May 1943): 702–3; and Thomas C. Hart, "Amphibious War Against Japan," *U.S. Naval Institute Proceedings* 69:5 (May 1943): 268.

7. Quoted in J. W. Perkins, "Use of Heavy Bombers on Tactical Missions," *Military Review* 26:2 (May 1946): 18–21.

8. For example, L. MacLean, "Air Power or Air Force," *Air University Quarterly* 24:6 (February 1948): 317–20.

9. George Fielding Eliot, *Strength We Need: A Military Program for America Pending Peace* (New York: Viking, 1946), p. 160.

10. For example, Vincent Davis, *Postwar Defense Policy and the United States Navy* (Durham, N.C.: University of North Carolina, 1966); Paul Y. Hammond, *Organizing for Defense: The American Military Establishment in the Twentieth Century* (Princeton: Princeton University Press, 1961); Gordon W. Keiser, *The U.S. Marine Corps and Defense Unification, 1944–47: The Politics of Survival* (Washington, D.C.: National Defense University, 1982); and Townsend Hoopes and Douglas Brinkley, *Driven Patriot: The Life and Times of James Forrestal* (New York: Knopf, 1992).

11. Raines and Campbell, *The Army and the Joint Chiefs of Staff*, vol. i, p. 48.

12. Henry Adams, *Witness to Power: The Life of Fleet Admiral William D. Leahy* (Annapolis: U.S. Naval Institute, 1985), p. 324.

13. Ernest J. King, *U.S. Navy at War, 1941–45: Official Reports to the Secretary of the Navy, 1941–45* (Washington, D.C.: U.S. Navy Department, 1946), p. 172.

14. Raines and Campbell, *Army and the Joint Chiefs*, p. 15.

15. Quoted in *Hearings, Subcommittee on the Armed Forces of the Committee on Armed Services*, 84th Congress, 2nd Session, June 25, 1956, pp. 1333–34.

16. In a memo to Lieutenant General Harold George, July 25, 1945, in Louis Galambos et al., eds., *The Eisenhower Papers*, vol. vi, *Occupation, 1945* (Baltimore: Johns Hopkins, 1978), pp. 214–15.

17. Ferdinand Eberstadt, *Report to the Hon. James V. Forrestal, Secretary of the Navy, Navy Department and Post War Organization for National Security* (Washington, D.C.: U.S. Government Printing Office, 1945).

18. Harry S. Truman, *Memoirs*, vol. ii, *Years of Trial and Hope* (Garden City, N.Y.: Doubleday, 1956), pp. 49–51.

19. For Vinson's philosophy on the value of separate services, see John C. Ries, *The Management of Defense: Organization and Control of the U.S. Armed Services* (Baltimore: Johns Hopkins, 1964), p. 210; for another view, see Peter Karsten, *The Naval Aristocracy* (New York: Free Press, 1972), p. 215.

20. Truman, *Memoirs*, vol. ii, p. 47.

21. Robert G. Albion and Robert H. Connery, *Forrestal and the Navy* (New York: Columbia University Press, 1962), pp. 29–30.

22. Frank H. Hough, *The Island War: The United States Marine Corps in the Pacific* (Philadelphia: Lippincott, 1947), pp. 10–11.

23. Harold B. Hinton, *Air Victory: The Men and the Machines* (New York: Harper and Brothers, 1948), p. 359.

24. William Bradford Huie, *The Case Against the Admirals: Why We Must Have a Unified Command* (New York: E. P. Dutton, 1946), p. 141.

25. Ibid., pp. 161–69, 174–79.

26. Ibid., p. 207. A major spokesman for the navy point of view at this point was Hanson W. Baldwin; cf. "What Air Power Can and Cannot Do. It Can Carry Huge Bombloads Great Distances, But Cannot Win a Major War Unaided," *New York Times*, May 30, 1948, pp. 5–7, 21.

27. John C. Ries, *The Management of Defense: Organization and Control of the U.S. Armed Services* (Baltimore: Johns Hopkins, 1964), pp. 58, 85–86.

28. For background and details of the National Security Act of 1947, see James F. Schnabel, *The History of the Joint Chiefs of Staff*, vol. i, *The Joint Chiefs of Staff and National Policy* (Washington, D.C.: Historical Division, Joint Secretariat, Joint Chiefs of Staff, 1979).

29. Herman S. Wolk, *Planning and Organizing the Postwar Air Force, 1943–1947* (Washington, D.C.: Office of Air Force History, 1984), p. 221.

30. For example, see Donald P. Booth, *The Joint Logistics Plans Committee of the Joint Chiefs of Staff and the Logistics Work of the Joint Staff* (Washington, D.C.: Joint Chiefs of Staff, 1949).

31. Herbert Hoover et al., *The Hoover Commission Report on Organization of the Executive Branch of Government* (New York: McGraw Hill, 1949), pp. 187, 190.

32. Ibid., p. 187.

33. Stuart W. Symington, "Our Air Force Policy," *Vital Speeches* 15 (July 1949): 567–70.

34. Wolk, *Planning and Organizing*, p. 129.

35. Galambos et al., *Eisenhower Papers*, vol. x, p. 483.

36. Armed Services Committee, House of Representatives, U.S. Congress, *Investigation of the B–36 Bomber Program: Hearings before the Committee on Armed Services on H.R. 248. 81st Congress, 1st Session* (Washington, D.C.: U.S. Government Printing Office, 1949).

37. A point that Clark Clifford made to Truman; cf. Coletta, *United States Navy and Defense Unification*, p. 330.

38. Galambos et al., *Eisenhower Papers*, vol. i, p. xi.

39. Paul Y. Hammond, "Super Carriers and B–36 Bombers: Appropriations, Strategy and Political Decision," in Harold Stein, ed., *American Civil-Military Decisions: A Book of Case Studies* (Tuscaloosa, Ala.: University of Alabama Press, 1963), pp. 465–564.

40. David Bolton, "Setting the Scene," *Royal United Services Institute Brassey's Defense Yearbook 1984* (London: RUSI/Brassey's, 1984), p. xx.

41. House Committee on Armed Services, *National Defense Program*, p. 525.

42. Ibid., p. 524. Halsey thought B–29s flew bombing missions with fighter escorts; cf. ibid., p. 239.

43. See Murray Green, "Hugh J. Knerr: The Pen and the Sword," in John L. Frisbee, ed., *Makers of the U.S. Air Force* (Washington, D.C.: Office of Air Force History, 1987), pp. 99–126.

44. Davis, *Admirals' Lobby*, pp. 225–26.

45. For a participant's perspective, see J. Lawton Collins, *War in Peacetime: The History and Lessons of Korea* (Boston: Houghton-Mifflin, 1969), pp. 370–78.

46. Lionel Max Chassin, *The Communist Conquest of China: A History of the Chinese*

Civil War, transl. Timothy Osato and Louis Gelat (Cambridge: Harvard University Press, 1965), p. 141.

47. Daniel E. Barbey, *MacArthur's Amphibious Navy: Seventh Amphibious Force Operations, 1943–1945* (Annapolis: U.S. Naval Institute Press, 1969), pp. 28, 346–47.

48. The following account draws heavily on Lynn Montross and Nicholas A. Canzona, *The Inchon-Seoul Operation—U.S. Marine Operations in Korea, 1950–1953* (Washington, D.C.: Headquarters U.S. Marine Corps, 1955).

49. Phillip S. Meilinger, *Hoyt S. Vandenberg: The Life of a General* (Bloomington: University of Indiana Press, 1989), pp. 167, 168, 171–73.

50. For example, see Charles L. Black, "The Truth About Air Support," *Flying* 48:2 (February 1951): 11–15.

51. N.a., "Front-line Air Force," *Flying* 48:5 (May 1951): 44–46, 178–79.

52. For a detailed analysis of U.S. Air Force and Marine Corps air support and the struggle for control of air elements in the Korean War, see Allan R. Millett, "Korea, 1950–1953," in B. Franklin Cooling, ed., *Case Studies in the Development of Close Air Support*, (Washington, D.C.: Office of Air Force History, 1990), pp. 345–410.

53. For various perspectives on the approval of Inchon, see Matthew B. Ridgway, *The Korean War* (Garden City, N.Y.: Doubleday, 1967), p. 40; Collins, *War in Peacetime*, p. 129; and Lawrence J. Korb, *The Joint Chiefs of Staff: The First Twenty-Five Years* (Bloomington: Indiana University Press, 1976), pp. 138–46.

54. Truman, *Memoirs*, vol. ii, p. 360.

55. Robert Futrell, *The United States Air Force in Korea, 1950–1953* (Washington, D.C.: Office of Air Force History, 1983), p. 44.

56. Ibid., p. 45.

57. Raines, *The Army and the Joint Chiefs*, p. 60.

58. Ibid., p. 30.

59. James F. Schnabel and Robert J. Watson, *History of the Joint Chiefs of Staff*, vol. iii, *The Korean War*, Part ii (Washington, D.C.: Historical Division, Joint Chiefs of Staff, 1979), p. 1063.

60. Dwight D. Eisenhower, *The White House Years: Waging Peace*, vol. 2 (Garden City, N.Y.: Doubleday, 1965), p. 246.

61. Joint Chiefs of Staff, *Unified Action Armed Forces* (Washington, D.C.: Office of the Joint Chiefs of Staff, 1959), pp. 4, 6.

62. For example, see Jack Shulimson, *Marines in Lebanon 1958* (Washington, D.C.: Headquarters U.S. Marine Corps, 1966), pp. 29–31.

63. Roger Spiller, *'Not War but Like War': The American Intervention in Lebanon* (Fort Leavenworth, Kan.: Combat Studies Institute, 1981), p. 37.

64. Ibid., p. 38.

65. For a post-Korean War perspective, see Department of the Air Force, *Air Operations in Conjunction with Amphibious Operations: Air Doctrine* (Washington, D.C.: Department of the Air Force, 1954).

66. U.S. Congress, Committee on Armed Services, 85th Congress, 1st Session, Doc. 29, *Air Power: Report of the Subcommittee on the Air Force of the Committee on Armed Services, U.S. Senate, 84th Congress* (Washington, D.C.: U.S. Government Printing Office, 1957), p. 8.

67. U.S. Congress subcommittee on the Air Force, Committee on Armed Services, *Report of the Subcommittee on the Air Force of the Committee on Armed Services, U.S.*

Senate, 84th Congress, 2nd Session (Washington, D.C.: U.S. Government Printing Office, 1957), pp. 74–79.

68. For a contemporaneous perspective on McNamara's tenure as secretary of defense, see C. W. Borklund, *The Department of Defense* (New York: Praeger, 1968); for a post-Vietnam War critique, see Gregory Palmer, *The McNamara Strategy and the Vietnam War: Program Budgeting in the Pentagon, 1960–1968* (Westport, Conn.: Greenwood, 1978).

69. William W. Kaufmann, *The McNamara Strategy* (New York: Harper and Row, 1964), p. 184.

70. Robert Art, *The TFX Decision: McNamara and the Military* (Boston: Little Brown, 1968), pp. 149, 155, 166. Some saw this decision, although defended on the basis of systems analysis, as a case of awarding a major contract to a firm in difficulty.

71. Paul Schratz, "The Ivy-Clad Man on Horseback," *United States Naval Institute Proceedings* 91:3 (March 1965): 47–48.

72. See Edward A. Kolodziej, *The Uncommon Defense and Congress, 1945–1962* (Bowling Green: Ohio State University, 1966), pp. 350–64.

73. For a controversial perspective, see Mark Perry, "The War of the Chiefs," *Four Stars* (Boston: Houghton-Mifflin, 1989), pp. 132–66.

74. Maxwell D. Taylor, *Uncertain Trumpet* (New York: Harper & Row, 1959), p. 176.

75. For a detailed litany of such problems, see Jonathan M. House, "Joint Operational Problems in the Cuban Missile Crisis," *Parameters* 21:1 (Spring 1991): 92–102. The destruction of key records in the early 1970s makes the role of the Joint Chiefs in the Cuban Missile Crisis and many other instances uncertain; for a summary of two sharply different views of McNamara's visit to the flag plot of October 24, 1964, and related matters, see Walter S. Poole, "How Well Did the JCS Work?" *U.S. Naval Institute Proceedings* 118:4 (April 1944): 19–21.

76. As evidenced by the single coordination dotted line on the organization chart between MACV and "Free World Forces," cf. U.S.G. Sharp and William Westmoreland, *Report on the War in Vietnam* (Washington, D.C.: U.S. Government Printing Office, 1968), p. 102. Even the model proposed at the end of American involvement in the U.S. Army's official study on command and control lacked designated coordination between major service field commands, even though its author urged a SHAEF-type unified theater command and a premium on liaison in any major future overseas command; cf. George S. Eckhardt [Maj. Gen.-U.S. Army], *Vietnam Studies: Command and Control, 1950–69* (Washington, D.C.: Department of the Army, 1974), pp. 86–88.

77. See n.a., *The Pentagon Papers, Senator Gravel Edition: The Department of Defense History of United States Decision Making on Vietnam* (Boston: Beacon Press, 1971), vol. ii, pp. 357–58, 413, 478–80.

78. Bruce Palmer Jr., *The 25-Year War: America's Military Role in Vietnam* (New York: Touchstone, 1984), p. 30.

79. See W. Scott Thompson and Donaldson D. Frizzell, *The Lessons of Vietnam* (New York: Crane & Russak, 1977), pp. 268–72.

80. For details of command of the air war, see Carl Berger, ed., *The United States Air Force in Southeast Asia, 1961–1973: An Illustrated Account* (Washington, D.C.: U.S. Government Printing Office, 1987).

81. Neil Sheehan, *A Bright Shining Lie: John Paul Vann and America in Vietnam* (New York: Random House, 1988), pp. 556–57.

82. Herbert Schandler, "JCS Strategic Planning and Vietnam: The Search for an Objective," *Military Planning in the Twentieth Century: Proceedings of the Eleventh Military History Symposium, U.S. Air Force Academy* (Washington, D.C.: U.S. Government Printing Office, 1984), p. 304.

83. David Hackworth and Julie Sherman, *About Face* (New York: Simon and Schuster, 1989), p. 524.

84. For example, see Douglas S. Blaufarb, *The Counterinsurgency Era: U.S. Doctrine and Performance, 1950 to the Present* (New York: Free Press, 1977).

85. Robert H. Whitlow, *U.S. Marine Corps in Vietnam: The Advisory and Combat Assistance Era, 1954–1964* (Washington, D.C.: Headquarters, United States Marine Corps, 1977), p. 62.

86. John D. Bergen, *Military Communications: A Test for Technology* (Washington, D.C.: Center for Military History, 1986), p. 56.

87. Donald J. Mrozek, *Air Power and the Ground War in Vietnam: Ideas and Actions* (Maxwell Air Force Base: Air University Press, 1988), pp. 23–26.

88. Ibid., p. 27.

89. Benjamin Schemmer, *The Raid* (New York: Harper & Row, 1976), pp. 57–58.

90. Ibid., p. 211.

91. George S. Eckhardt, *Vietnam Studies: Command and Control, 1950–1969* (Washington, D.C.: Department of the Army, 1974), p. 37.

92. For a detailed account, see John T. Sbrega, "Southeast Asia," in Cooling, *Close Air Support*, pp. 411–90.

93. Ibid., pp. 446.

94. As dramatized in attempts of Colonel Brink in the early 1950s and of General Lansdale in the mid–1960s to steer American doctrine away from a high firepower model.

95. A concise overview of tactical air operations in Vietnam is John Morocco et al., "The In-Country Air War," *Thunder from Above: Air War, 1941–1968* (Boston: Boston Publishing, 1984), pp. 72–95.

96. For a detailed survey of CAS in Vietnam, see John T. Sbrega, "Southeast Asia," in Cooling, *Close Air Support*, pp. 448–54.

97. So argued Townsend Hoopes in *The Limits of Intervention* (New York: Norton, 1978), pp. 161–62.

98. For a close consideration of this question, see Sbrega, "Southeast Asia," in Cooling, *Close Air Support*, pp. 470–73.

99. For example, see Robert McClintoch, "The River War in Indochina," *U.S. Naval Institute Proceedings* 80:12 (December 1954): 1303–11.

100. Thomas J. Cutler, *Brown Water, Black Berets* (Annapolis: Naval Institute Press, 1988), pp. 211–66.

101. Brent L. Gravatt, "Command and Control in Joint Riverine Operations," *Military Review* 64:5 (March 1984): 64.

102. Earl F. Tilford, *Setup: What the Air Force Did in Vietnam and Why* (Maxwell Air Force Base, Ala.: Air University Press, 1991), pp. 280–81.

103. Christopher John Lamb, *Belief Systems and Decision-Making in the Mayaguez Crisis* (Gainesville: University of Florida Press, 1989), p. 133.

104. For various perspectives along the way, see Korb, *The Joint Chiefs of Staff*; Vincent Davis and Samuel P. Huntington, *Reorganizing America's Defense: Leadership in War and Peace* (Washington, D.C.: Pergamon-Brassey's, 1985); Allan R. Millett, Mackubin Thomas Owens, Bernard E. Trainor, Edward C. Meyer and Robert Murray,

Reorganization of the Joint Chiefs of Staff: A Critical Analysis (Cambridge: Institute for Foreign Policy Analysis, 1986); Edgar F. Rains Jr. and David R. Campbell, *The Army and the Joint Chiefs of Staff: Evolution of Army Ideas on the Command, Control and Coordination of the U.S. Armed Forces, 1942–1985* (Washington, D.C.: Analysis Branch, U.S. Army Center of Military History, 1986); Lewis C. Sowell, Jr., *Base Development and the Rapid Deployment Forces* (Washington, D.C.: National Defense University, 1982); Gordon W. Keiser, *The U.S. Marine Corps and Defense Unification, 1944–1947* (Washington, D.C.: National Defense University, 1982); Archie D. Barrett, *Reappraising Defense Organization: An Analysis Based on the Defense Organization Study of 1977–1980* (Washington, D.C.: National Defense University, 1983); and Terry L. Heyns, *Understanding U.S. Strategy: A Reader Based on the Ninth National Security Conference, October 8–9, 1982* (Washington, D.C.: National Defense University, 1985).

105. Dean Rusk and Richard Rusk, *As I Saw It*, ed. Davis S. Papp (New York: W. W. Norton, 1990), p. 453.

106. See Robert A. Liston, Appendix 1, "Pueblo's Radio Transmissions," *The Pueblo Surrender* (New York: M. Evan, 1988), pp. 273–83.

107. See Trevor Armbrister, *A Matter of Accountability: The True Story of the Pueblo Affair* (New York: Coward McCann, 1970), pp. 210–13, 222, 228–29.

108. Franklyn A. Johnson, *Defence by Ministry: The British Ministry of Defence* (London: Duckworth, 1980), p. 182.

109. PRO ADM I/ 19643 [CAFO 403/ M. 3530/46—27 June 1946], *Future of Combined Operations in Peacetime*.

110. James Bellini and Geoffrey Peattie, *A New World Role for the Medium Powers: The British Opportunity* (London: Royal United Services Institute, 1977), pp. 109–10.

111. For example, see Philip Darby, *British Defense Policy East of Suez, 1947–1968* (London: Oxford, 1973), p. 142.

112. J.H.F. Eberle, "Defense Organization—The Future," in *The Management of Defence*, ed. Laurence Martin (London: Macmillan, 1976), pp. 105–23.

113. The standard account of the Suez campaign is Hugh Thomas, *Suez* (New York: Harper & Row, 1967).

114. For a detailed after-action report, see PRO DEF 2/2057, *Operation MUSKETEER*, Part 5, *Operation Reports*.

115. A perspective on the eve of the Thatcher revolution is Laurence Martin, ed., *The Management of Defence* (London: Macmillan, 1976).

116. Secretary of State for Defence, *The Way Forward* (London: Her Majesty's Stationery Office, 1981) [Cmd. 8288].

117. For various perspectives, see Secretary of State for Defence, *The Falklands Campaign: The Lessons* (London: Her Majesty's Stationery Office, 1982) [Cmd. 8758]; Martin Garrod, "Amphibious Warfare: Why?" *Royal United Services Institute Journal* 133:4 (Winter 1988): 25–30; and John Baylis, ed., *Alternative Approaches to British Defense Policy* (New York: St. Martin's Press, 1983).

118. For comments on Cmd. 9315, see Lawrence Freedman, "Economy Rules at M.O.D.," *Defense Attache* no. 4:13, 14, 17 (1984).

119. For an articulate statement of such skepticism regarding command and control in the Air-Land Battle, see Jeremy Saye, "Close Air Support in Modern Warfare," *Air University Review* 31:1 (January-February 1980): 11.

120. For example, see Committees on Government Operations, House of Representatives, U.S. Congress, *Hearings on Readiness of the Navy: Tactical Air Force* 98th

Congress, 1st Session, November 1983; Lane Pierrot and Bob Kornfeld, *Tactical Combat Forces of United States Air Force: Issues and Answers* (Washington, D.C.: U.S. Government Printing Office, 1985); Daniel P. Leaf, "The Future of Close Air Support," *Military Review* 69:3 (March 1989): 10.

121. M. A. Campbell, E. W. Downs, and L. V. Schnetta, *The Employment of Airpower in the Greek Civil War, 1947–1949* (Maxwell Air Force Base, Ala.: Air University, 1964), p. 50.

122. Noel Barber, *The War of the Running Dogs: The Malayan Emergency: 1948–1960* (New York: Weybright & Talley, 1971), pp. 98–99.

123. For the effect of Nifty Nugget on joint structure, see Robert P. Haffa Jr., *Rational Methods, Prudent Choices: Planning U.S. Forces* (Washington, D.C.: National Defense University Press, 1988), p. 97.

124. John G. Kester in *The JCS: A Better System?*, John G. Holloway, ed. (special issue of *AEI Foreign Policy and Defense Review*) 2:1 (1979): 13, 23.

125. Thomas C. Linn, "Amphibious Shipping Shortfall Undermines Maritime Strategy," *Armed Forces Journal International* 126:9 (April 1989): 54, 56, 58.

126. Paul B. Ryan, *Iran Rescue Mission: Why it Failed* (Annapolis: U.S. Naval Institute, 1985), p. 132.

127. For example, Frank Uhlig Jr., "Amphibious Aspects of the Grenada Episode," in *American Intervention in Grenada: The Implications of Operation "Urgent Fury"* (Boulder, Colo.: Westview, 1985), p. 96; Mark Adkin, *Urgent Fury: The Battle for Grenada* (Lexington: Lexington Books, 1989), p. 333; "Grenada: Tales of Things Gone Wrong," in n.a., *The New Face of War: Commando Operations* (Alexandria: Time-Life Books, 1991), pp. 63–67. A lack of logistical jointness was also evident in Urgent Fury; Gilbert S. Harper, "Logistics in Grenada: Supporting No-Plan Wars," *Parameters* 20:2 (June 1990): 54, 62.

128. For a succinct view of the development of issues see Lon Nordeen, "Close Air Support," *National Defense* 74/449 (July-August 1989): 26–30; for details, see Richard G. Davis, *The 31 Initiatives: A Study in Air Force-Army Cooperation* (Washington, D.C.: Joint Assistant and Initiatives Office, 1987).

129. See John Wickham, Address at the U.S. Training and Doctrine Command—Tactical Air Command—Association of the U.S. Army Symposium, in *Collected Works of the Thirtieth Chief of Staff* (Washington, D.C.: Department of the Army, 1987), pp. 104–7, 132, 140.

130. For example, see Terry C. Pierce, "The Tactical Strategic Link," pp. 66–69, and Sean Coughlin, "Maneuver or Victory?" pp. 70–71, both in *U.S. Naval Institute Proceedings* 116:9 (September 1990).

131. Ralph E. Williams Jr., "America's Moment of Truth," *United States Naval Institute Proceedings* 81:3 (March 1955): 252–54.

132. J. C. Wylie, "On Maritime Strategy," *United States Naval Institute Proceedings* 79:5 (May 1953): 471.

133. Samuel P. Huntington, "National Policy and the Transoceanic Navy," *United States Naval Institute Proceedings* 80:5 (May 1954): 483–93.

134. J. C. Wylie, "Why a Sailor Thinks Like a Sailor," *United States Naval Institute Proceedings* 83:8 (August 1957): 813.

135. For a comprehensive analysis, see Norman Friedman, *The U.S. Maritime Strategy* (London: Jane's, 1968).

136. For example, Alfred Thayer Mahan, Julian Corbett, Sir Herbert Richmond, Admiral Bradley Fiske, and Admiral Lord Fisher.

137. For example, George Fielding Eliot, Hanson Baldwin, Robert Komer, Bernard Brodie, Giuseppe Fioravanzo, Oskar Morgenstern, and Samuel P. Huntington. For a tracing of the Maritime Strategy's genealogy through Huntington and J. C. Wylie to Admiral Forrest P. Sherman, chief of Naval Operations, 1949–51, see Michael A. Palmer, *Origins of the Maritime Strategy: American Naval Strategy in the First Postwar Decade* (Washington, D.C.: Naval Historical Center, 1988).

138. For a succinct view of the Maritime Strategy, see Linton F. Brooks, "Naval Power and National Security: The Case for the Maritime Strategy," in Steven E. Miller and Stephen Van Evera, eds., *Naval Strategy and National Security* (Princeton: Princeton University Press, 1988); for a critique, see John Mearsheimer, "A Strategic Misstep: The Maritime Strategy and Deterrence in Europe," in the same work.

139. Seymour J. Deitchman, *New Technology and Military Power: General Purpose Military Forces for the 1980s and Beyond* (Boulder, Colo.: Westview, 1979), p. 175.

140. For example, see Robert E. Osgood, *NATO: The Entangling Alliance* (Chicago: University of Chicago Press, 1962), p. 348.

141. For example, see Jeremy G. Saye, "Close Air Support in Modern Warfare," *Air University Review* 31:2 (January-February 1980): 11; and Thomas H. Buchanan, *The TAC-Air Control System: Its Evolution and Its Need for Battle Management* (Maxwell Air Force Base, Ala.: Air University, 1987), pp. 51–58.

142. C. Kenneth Allard, *Command and Control, and the Common Defense* (New Haven: Yale University, 1990).

143. Thomas A. Cardwell, *Command Structure for Theater Warfare: The Quest for Unity of Command* (Maxwell Air Force Base, Ala.: Air University, 1984), p. 73.

144. For a perspective on the identified areas of jointness, see n.a., *Joint Publication System: Joint Doctrine and Joint Tactics, Techniques, and Procedures Development Program* (Washington, D.C.: Joint Chiefs of Staff, 1988), esp. Ch. 6.

145. N.a., *United States Military Posture, FY 1989* (Washington, D.C.: Joint Chiefs of Staff, 1988), pp. 83–86.

146. For example, for a perspective on the impact on the army, see the Joint/Combined Operations issue of *Military Review* 69:3 (March 1989): esp. Joseph J. Palastra, "The Forscom Role in the Joint Arena," pp. 3–9.

147. For example, see Malcolm McConnell, *Just Cause: The Real Story of America's High-Tech Invasion of Panama* (New York: St. Martin's Press, 1991); "An Auspicious Comeback in Panama," in n.a., *The New Face of War: Commando Operations* (Alexandria: Time-Life Books, 1991), pp. 111–53.

148. See Thomas Donnelly, Margaret Roth, and Caleb Baker, *Operation Just Cause: The Storming of Panama* (New York: Lexington Books, 1991), pp. 27–28.

149. On the eve of the ground phase of Desert Storm, a former congressman with fourteen years' service, held forth on the persistence of "military politics"; cf. Otis Pike, "Military Politics Make a Ground War Likely," *Houston Chronicle*, February 19, 1991, p. 13A.

150. Molly Moore, "Gulf War Exposed Snafus in Military Teamwork," *Houston Chronicle*, June 10, 1991, p. 8A.

151. Mark Thompson, "Audit Faults Army Medical System in War," *Houston Chronicle*, February 6, 1992, p. 16A.

152. Stewart M. Powell, "Joint Plan of Attack for Army, Air Force," *Houston Chronicle*, August 28, 1991, p. 3A.

153. I. B. Holley, "A Retrospect on Close Air Support," in Cooling, *Close Air Support*, p. 540.

154. For example, see Narrative Section, n.a., *Conduct of the Persian Gulf War: Final Report to the Congress* (Washington, D.C.: Office of the Secretary of Defense, 1992), pp. 59, 245–46, 309, 414, and Appendices, pp. C–18, 19, D–25, I–49, J–28, K47–51, N–9, R–4. For a description of joint structures and undertakings in the period immediately following the Gulf War, see John H. Cushman, "Joint, Jointer, Jointest," *U.S. Naval Institute Proceedings* 118:5 (May 1992): 78. For a post-Gulf War perspective on further reform, see Leslie H. Gelb, "Each Armed Service Duplicates Other," *Houston Chronicle*, July 28, 1991, p. 12.

_____ Chapter 6 _____

Patterns and Paradoxes: The Central Problem of Friction

A central paradox of jointness is the hostility that it has often generated. Of course, many social scientists and theorists have studied the conflict, social stratification, and territoriality visible in organizations around the world and throughout history. While such behavior may be normative in politics, sports, business, or street gangs, military and naval forces have much deeper needs for redundancy in communication for clear and layered authority and for discipline and shared values than any other type of organization. Armies, navies, and air forces must be able to restore and regenerate after major destruction and heavy losses. They function in the face of death, maiming, mutilation, capture, and punishment, conditions with no counterpart in civil life aside from, and then only briefly, major catastrophes. Many of the quirks, pathologies and anxieties among the military professionals who anticipate and endure the horrors of war have been mapped by such British practitioners of the "new military history" as Richard Holmes, John Ellis, and Norman Dixon. It is not surprising, then, given the hunger for strong, well-demarcated allegiances and identities found among warriors, that many have resisted cooperation, fusion, and jointness. Such impulses to turn inward are reflected in the fact that liaison between adjacent friendly units locked in combat, although vital, is very hard to establish and maintain.

Many of the structures and attitudes in military-naval organizations are products of historical momentum rather than deliberate design, and attempts at rational structuring have sometimes produced anomalies. For example, anti-aircraft development was assigned to the U.S. Army Coast Artillery on the basis that both shot at moving targets. In a similar vein, until the spring of 1916, defending Britain against air attack was seen as part of the Admiralty's responsibility for protecting the nation's coast.[1] Thus, jointness has often arisen in crisis and war from perceptions of a need to blend separate service elements to perform such functions as airlift, air base security, close-air support, reconnaissance, special operations, airborne operations, air defense and antisubmarine warfare, command and control, and logistics.

While more and more functional blending has arisen from accelerating technical evolution in the last two centuries, many have fought that trend tooth and nail. As a consequence, in the mid–1980s, interservice rivalry was seen as the foremost cause of mismanagement of defense procurement in the United States.[2] Such resistance, noted throughout this study, lies far from the assertion made in a post-mortem of Vietnam that "all students of the military art learn right off that one of the principles of war is unity of command—a single commander must have control of all forces in an operation."[3] Even though blending different weapons and systems and bending them away from the purposes that originally shaped their design and acquisition have been common in modern warfare, the "untoward influences of limited identifications" have persisted.[4] Of course, there have been many exceptions, as Admiral Richmond Kelly Turner noted in observing:

We found the most important technique of amphibious warfare to be the willingness and ability to cooperate in spite of differences of opinion or viewpoint between individuals, between branches in each service and between the different Services themselves, including Allied Services. . . . If they are any good, men of all those elements believe they are the particular group who will most contribute to success. . . . Conflicts between the different elements (which are inevitable) must be adjusted in order to produce a smooth working team.[5]

In much the same vein, Marine Corps General Pedro del Valle described the meshing of service efforts in the Pacific War as something "which mere command will seldom attain, a hearty and wholesome unity of spirit which seemed to say, 'This is an American force engaged in defeating an enemy. We have subordinated any thoughts of personal or 'unit' glory to the task at hand.' Such maturity of thought and action must be regarded as classical."[6] And General Mark Clark testified before the House Armed Services Committee, in October 1949, that: "There is more unification out in the field, sir, than there is in Washington."[7]

Trying to reduce jointness and opposition to it to rational, measurable terms matches the dilemma of the biologist who must kill to dissect, since the separate roots of this conflict rise from the common ground of intense human emotions. Thus, Richard Aliano saw the American officer corps politicized by budget dynamics and congressional processes, and military planning as a "social rather than an intellectual process" emanating from a "constellation of domestic forces."[8] Just as uncharted motives and complex processes lie behind policy and politics, such intangible factors as the "interplay of personalities," foibles, impulses, and idiosyncrasies often come to bear [in war and crisis].[9] That is often well out of sight, as the flat, impersonal language of military manuals and after-action reports, and, often, of even memoirs, biographies, and hearings fails to convey the passions behind such conflict. Yet in war, the impulses, reflexes, and decisions of key individuals become vitally important.

Appraising the influence of personality in war, Merrill Bartlett viewed U.S. Marine Corps assaults in the Pacific War, 1942–45, not as a product of peacetime theory and exercises but as a projection of the will of "the forceful and irascible Chief of Naval Operations, Fleet Admiral Ernest J. King."[10] Historians, journalists, and novelists from Tolstoy to Norman Mailer have grappled more with the less rational side of command process[11] than military historians, who have "paid little attention to pathologies such as conformity, faulty feedback, trust, careerism, dysfunctional selection and promotion values and unrealistic training."[12]

How much has inter-service friction and melding been the product of idiosyncratic factors? Many cases of jointness that hinged upon close rapport or lack of it have been noted: Wolfe and Saunders; Conner and Scott; Grant and Porter; Quesada, Kirk and Bradley; Eisenhower and Spaatz; Smith and Turner; Coningham and Montgomery; and Kenney, Barbey and MacArthur. In view of those, it is not surprising to find little difference in essence between John Ehrman's judgment that a late seventeenth-century British joint expedition failed due to "lack of cooperation between Army and Navy . . . and antagonism between them and local officials . . . leading to a heavy death-toll"[13] and James' and Wells' appraisal of the World War II Allied high command system as potentially "costly . . . [and] cumbersome" and producing "innumerable difficulties" by failing to adhere to "principles of successful warfare."[14]

Whatever those principles may be, some patterns are plainly visible. Jointness has tended to flourish more in war than in peace, and it has been more often at the "grass roots . . . [that] ambitions, doctrine and prejudice [have been subordinated to] the task of finding practical solutions."[15] In the European theater in World War II, for example, Army and Navy subelements often ignored the shoreline boundary that lay at the center of interservice "diplomacy" for generations. Navy bulldozers cleared obstacles inland, and the services' medical systems intermeshed in a spirit of function as opposed to form,[16] manifestations of what Lord Tedder labeled the "unities of war."[17]

Similar attitudes were evident in inter-Allied relations. Like the Byzantine strategist Maurice, Paul Kennedy noted that coalitions "require . . . much more than any unilateral campaign, substantial doses of tolerance, understanding and flexibility."[18] Looking at that problem, General Sir Frederick Morgan, a premier practitioner of both jointness and Allied cooperation, in SHAEF in World War II, proclaimed "any form of co-operation that is not based on absolute frankness is quite worthless." He also lamented "the incessant clashes of personality"[19] that marked the "great symphony of . . . the victorious armies."[20]

Another participant, lamenting such discordancy, noted:

We had great experience of High Commands in the field in the Second World War, and one outstanding feature is that no two Supreme Command Headquarters were organized alike. . . . Conditions varied. . . . There was no standard organization. . . . Commanders were given the greatest freedom in organizing their headquarters and command organizations as they wished. . . . It was not uncommon for this freedom to allow personality, dogma and whim to override the merit of the case.[21]

Sir Frederick Maurice, appraising inter-Allied cooperation in World War I, saw links between the armies as weakest, those between navies as relatively smooth, and the rapport of air forces as strongest,[22] a pattern that did not carry over to World War II, during which it also varied between theaters of operations.[23] Like jointness, alliance/coalition architecture and dynamics[24] lie from the realm of science.[25] The British, for example, preferred a triservice committee structure while Americans like the supreme commander model.[26]

In World War II, jointness in the British and U.S. armed forces took hold about half-way through their respective involvement in the war, a point when, in both cases, because of defeat and frustration, "the services began to pull together for victory," having "failed to do so when disaster could be avoided."[27] It was not until 1943, for example, that remedies were applied to the special problems of landing craft crews, such as lack of shipboard creature-comforts and exposure to harsh weather, constant detachment and reassignment, lack of higher command concern, poor discipline, low morale, and intense danger with minimal protection and armament. Hence Charles Shrader's judgment that, in Operation Torch, "inexperience, coupled with the lack of systematized internal procedures within the services and lack of an established system of coordination between them made the deficits of time and information even more profound."[28] Bernard Fergusson noted the litany of jealousies and "downright opposition and obstruction" that thwarted headquarters' Combined Operations attempts to disseminate hard-won lessons and methods to operational commands,[29] as "service parochialism . . . spilled over in the Second World War with disastrous results."[30]

The return of such divisiveness after 1945 and its effect on Suez and the Vietnam War can be traced to many factors, such as bureaucratic process, the clash of wills, the mindset implanted at service academies, anxieties arising from proposals for total service unification, reduced funding, the creation of the Air Force, nuclear weapons, basic human tribal impulses, and so on. But that does not mean that withdrawal into service fiefdoms would not have occurred under more placid circumstances. Perhaps only such sharp setbacks as Gallipoli and the Allied defeats and failures during the first half of World War II and in the opening phase of the Korean War generated enough energy to loosen the normative bonds of parochialism. If so, a corollary to any such law or effect is the transience of its effects. While the clear-cut disasters of 1939–42 served to overcome parochialism from 1943 to 1945 far more than the diffuse frustrations of Vietnam did, the traumas of World War II had relatively little permanent "bite." Yet some realignments of that conflict did take hold. For example, Pearl Harbor led the U.S. Navy to place air power at the center of its main battle-line doctrine, forging what the Italian naval theorist Admiral Giuseppe Fioravanzo

deemed "a single entity, which . . . can be called 'naval-air forces.' " For the
next half-century, the U.S. Navy held onto that pattern as tenaciously as the
"gun club" had built its tactical conceptions around battleships and cruisers
between the world wars.

In respect to other patterns, the vast increase in the frequency of amphibious
operations in the twentieth century reversed von Bernhardi's view in 1914 of
such undertakings as "exceptional."[31] As variants of jointness, caused by con-
fluences of ever more complex technology, frequently mixed once-exclusive
elements, a rebound effect was often visible. After Vietnam, a "warrior" ethic
emerged in each of the U.S. armed services, a byproduct of hostility toward
bureaucratization and a management ethic that critics ascribed to World War II
Army Chief of Staff George Marshall and others. Others saw it as having led
to stalemate in Korea, to defeat in Vietnam and arising from careerism based
on bureaucratic as opposed to martial values. At the same time, in the Nuclear
Age/Cold War, armies, navies, and air forces of the major and middle-range
powers became increasingly involved in constabulary, peace keeping, and advisory roles, special operations, and psychological warfare. The linking of services was implicit in each of those areas and was sometimes dramatically visible,
for example, the fusion of U.S. Air Force, Army Special Forces and Belgian
paratroops in the Stanleyville raid in the Congo in 1962.

The tension between structures and attitudes on the one hand and tasks and
missions on the other that has marked debates over jointness resembles the classic
polarity in management theory between scalar/hierarchical and functional/spe-
cialization. While some of that tension rises from military-naval discipline, it is
also fuelled by social and psychological forces that are no less powerful for
being unmeasurable or unclear. It is not clear at the time of this writing whether
the Goldwater-Nichols Act of 1986 will offset frictions among the armed services
that seem likely to intensify as shrinkage feeds parochialism, as it has in the
past. The persistence of such tension was underscored by the chairman of the
Joint Chiefs of Staff, General David Jones, on the eve of the Goldwater-Nichols
Act, when he spoke of a "facade of jointness," and half a decade later, by
Hedrick Smith, who saw "the Department of Defense . . . [as] a confederation
of bureaucratic tribes with celebrated rivalries and long established but less well-
known patterns of communal collusions."[32] Both of those observations were in
keeping with Vincent Davis' view of "interservice differences . . . [as] subcul-
tural differences."[33]

Like the service academies' football rivalry (not a trivial source of parochial
tension in itself), some roots of interservice friction run no less deep for not
being brought into open view. Bradley's "Fancy Dan" comment in 1949 touched
on several sore points, including the elitist style and bearing and social isolation
of the naval officer corps, traced out by Peter Karsten in *The Naval Aristocracy*.
Beyond such tribalism and the unchartable but pervasive clash of personalities
and cliques within and among the services lies the murky realm of special
interests. Vendors have influenced the shaping of doctrine, and the buying of

products has been justified by military professionals on the basis of best professional judgment. Thus, General James Gavin, after serving as the army chief of research and development in the late 1950s, observed that "interservice rivalry is fundamentally industrial rivalry." The fact that each service has done business with particular firms, in some cases for generations, is not an evil ipso facto, but it adds another layer of uncertainty to determining what is appropriate and ethical.

Another source of interservice friction lies in their differences in function. Under the most balanced and rational conditions, the varying tasks and environments in air, at sea, and in ground warfare would generate different expectations, reflexes, styles, and attitudes among those doing their separate "thing." Not surprisingly, as the weapons and systems of each service have meshed in modern military operations, many practices, values, and reflexes have remained separate, well beyond the level dictated by a division of labor. Just as differences, recruitment, and socialization have shaped style, certain habits and traditions have persisted, evidence that military-naval systems are subcultures that cannot be altered easily or quickly, and that formal obedience to edict may not be matched in essence.

It was, after all, witnessing the testiness and rudeness of strong-willed men facing death, fear, uncertainty, and the judgment of history that led von Clausewitz to lament the scarcity of tact, which he saw as an antidote to the friction of war. Sir Ian Hamilton saw service differences as being caused by both a gap in "basic technical principles"[34] and by frictions arising from the "little punctilios and etiquettes"[35] of each service. He devised a matrix demonstrating basic variances in respect to movement, firing, charging, and holding.[36] Such differences in mindset have sometime stood forth sharply, like the Marine who, after hearing a U.S. Navy officer's concerns for the thinness of the armor of a ship supporting a landing operation, leaned across the conference table, thrusting forward the lapel of his own uniform for comparison. Just after the Spanish-American War, Alfred Thayer Mahan threw the chasm between service mindsets into bold relief when he wrote, "If we lost ten thousand men, the country could replace them; if we lost a battleship, it could not be replaced."[37] Three generations later, Admiral James Watkins said, "I like interservice rivalries. In peacetime I could just never, never bring myself to do anything to help the Air Force or Army."[38]

It has been seen that such basic differences shaped in peacetime have often affected operations in war. Although all came right in the end, the departure of Admiral Halsey and the main carrier elements from the Leyte beachhead in 1944 to pursue what he believed to be the main Japanese carrier force was a variant in essence of the conflict between naval and landing force priorities seen at Dakar, in Torch and at Guadalcanal, and an attitude that has remained unchanged. The special authority of command at sea, bolstered by maritime and military law and tradition, has long permeated interservice relations. The idea of ships being controlled by commanders of other services is anathema to naval professionals. That attitude and reflex, visible on several occasions, was dramatized in the purported clash between Chief of Naval Operations Admiral George Anderson and Secretary of Defense Robert McNamara over the control of specific ship movements in the Pentagon during the Cuban missile crisis in October 1962.[39] Thus, Arthur Hadley judged the U.S. Army more inclined to smooth interservice and inter-Allied relations to the other services due to the fact that even its lowest echelons depended upon complex supporting systems and teamwork, while aircraft pilots and small ships' commanders' ideal was independent action. In spite of that, as so many of the cases in this study demonstrate, ground forces have often engaged in vigorous turf battles. Hadley also saw the Navy as more elitist and apathetic to functions aside from those related to being at sea in warships.[40] Some saw this attitude reflected in the Navy's reputation as the most poorly administered of the armed services, in the epidemic of accidents at sea in the late 1980s, sealift deficiencies revealed in the early phase of Operation Desert Shield, and the spate of personnel problems in the early 1990s.

What basic differences between the armed services lie beyond a specific focus on ships as opposed to planes or close ground combat? There tends to be rather greater concern in armies than in navies and air forces for cohesion and bonding, and for the effect of group structure on morale. Hence the British service aphorism that navies and air forces man equipment, while armies equip men. While sea battles have usually been less prolonged than combat ashore and have yielded fewer casualties than ground battles and sustained air operations, danger in sea battles is shared by all ranks aboard ship and there is no way to leave the zone of battle and hazard. Another differential, noted by David Hackworth, Hadley, and others, arises from the Air Force's psychic distance from the effects of its response and the blurring of the realities of war in aerial combat.[41] Beyond that, each service sets the pace and scale of operations against different references in time and space. Ground forces in combat may sit still for very long periods of time, and when they move, speed may range from yards and miles per hour, on foot, to dozens of miles in motorized vehicles, hundreds in helicopters, or even thousands, if air-landed or parachuted. The pace of ground operations ranges from sitting or crawling through the two miles per hour of infantry marching off roads to dozens of miles a day in an all-out advance or retreat. Navies almost always move when out of port, often several hundred miles a day, while air forces' operational frame of reference routinely encompasses thousands of miles per day and, sometimes, per hour; SDI has exponentially extended the Air Force's space-time gestalt. The speed of naval vessels ranges from dead-slow at a knot or two, through the classified flank speeds of nuclear vessels in excess of forty knots, to the higher speeds of hydrofoils, surface-effect machines, to naval fighters roughly matching those of the Air Force's.

Style and attitudes toward subtlety, artifice, and stratagem also vary from service to service and within each one. To some extent, the head-down American tactical and strategic style in the Civil War, the world wars, Korea after Inchon, and in Vietnam, such as, the amphibious and naval tactics in the Central Pacific in World War II, were shaped by geostrategic factors. Yet a senior naval intelligence officer found that some high-ranking naval officers in the Pacific War "regarded victories scored by psychological warfare as unworthy of naval tradition."[42] There has also been a strong predisposition to linear tactical and strategic forms in the Army and Air Force, for example, Grant's "I shall fight it out on this line if it takes all summer," Eisenhower's broad-front strategy, Operation Strangle, and Schweinfurt-Regensburg. Although such gestalts may have sprung from the bending of the proverbial twig of the officer corps by the heavily technological curriculum and extended disciplinary regimen of the service academies, there are many exceptions, including Jackson and Lee's tactical fluidity, MacArthur's "bypass" strategy and his "left hook" at Inchon, and the latter format's reappearance in Desert Storm as compared with the predisposition of civilian strategists for linearity reflected in the DEW Line and the McNamara line.

In major amphibious landings, the Army wanted large amounts of materiel landed early as a hedge against being cut off, while the Navy sought flexibility to counter such a move. The latter was sometimes insensitive about how its departure left those ashore without adequate logistical and gunfire and air support, either if the enemy ashore launched a major attack or if opportunity for exploitation developed, for example, the animosity of some U.S. Marines toward Admiral Ghormley's hesitancy at Guadalcanal and the Navy's scaling down of the bombardment program at Iwo Jima.[43] How much are such disparities irreduceable? Can a melding of styles and interests come only occasionally, or over a very long time? How much has the Goldwater-Nichols Act changed that? The outcome will doubtless conform to Mark Perry's and Sir Frederick Morgan's observations that ordaining structure does not guarantee the compliance of those upon whom it is imposed or a full or exact rendering of the intent of the designers.[44] With that in view, Bruce Blair cautioned: "Central authorities cannot reasonably expect military organizations simply to carry out orders, no matter how rational the orders may be. . . . Organizations are not that pliant."[45]

In a more theoretical vein, the complex dynamics of jointness offer a rich field for social scientists' delvings into "tribalism," structure, behavior in the face of a common threat,[46] semiotics, including such differentiating symbols as clothing, semantics, agonism,[47] rites of passage,[48] boundaries, roles, perceptions, and the vital but often ignored or rejected functions of coordination and liaison.[49] Whether or not analyses along those lines or a review of studies already done might lead to procedures that would reduce or eliminate the strong emotions so prevalent in jointness in the past, it has usually been personal experience and intuition that shaped proposals for reform. For example, Winston Churchill, among many others,[50] saw a "balanced force" system as an antidote to the unpleasant side-effects of overcentralization. John Ehrman, after carefully appraising the Allied high command structure in World War II, judged the committee system superior to a supreme command model because it stimulated the flow of information between the services and led to greater flexibility.[51]

Leaving the shaping of jointness to "ad hocing," muddling through, and crisis management, that is, to fate, is obviously risky. But so is depending on specific contingencies, on rigid models and/or doctrines. The Goldwater-Nichols Act's requirement that officers work extensively in joint roles to be considered for high rank was aimed at blunting parochialism. If reduced funding allows that to persist, only time will tell how much requiring of diverse experiences will offset such deep undercurrents of hostility to jointness as the intense parochialism arising from separate rites-of-passage in the training of officers and of various subelements and corps d'elite, and from other career dynamics,[52] or if it will merely replace one parochialism with another.

Although it does seem that momentum toward service fusion fell off because amphibious operations became a rarity after 1945, major tides ran toward jointness from other directions, and service autonomy was eroded by the blending pressures from logistics, communications, and tactical air power. Even during the bitter interservice battles of the late 1940s, aspects of jointness beyond amphibious operations were addressed in doctrine and practice, although, in spite of a number of incremental accords, service autonomy and turf-guarding lived on. Looking back at the services' "unpleasantly durable" rivalry and autonomy in the Vietnam War, Donald Mrozek observed that separate perceptions generated friction so that "issues of command having to do with precedence and authority proved to be more compelling than concern about maximizing effectiveness in actual operations."[53] So it had been at Rochefort in 1757.

It has been seen that the British and American paths to jointness that diverged in 1945 ended up at much the same place on parallel tracks by the mid-1980s. The functional command unification under a naval joint commander in the Falklands War, widely seen as contributing to the British victory, came just as American military professionals and defense intellectuals were debating jointness in earnest. In the early 1990s, however, in spite of the fusion mandated by the passage of the Goldwater-Nichols Act in 1986, problems that Admiral Logan examined in 1943 in the wake of defeats and frustrations were still in view in the American defense system. There was less than fully unified command, competition frequently prevailed over cooperation, and interservice communications were uneven.[54]

The effects upon Desert Storm of both British and American reforms of the 1980s will take time to appraise, as will the meshing of NATO members' forces. The Gulf deployment also demonstrated once again that when one service controls a low-preference, pan-service mission, like sea or air transport, that function tends to fall between the cracks, or at the very least, shortfalls in such functions are likely. The relief of Air Force Chief of Staff General Dugan, the Marines' pique at being denied a major assault, and tussles over close-air support control provided glimpses of services and branches still pushing to wage war in a way closest to their most dearly held images, ideals and roles, and to the raison d'etre of their respective structure and funding. Such tension between preference and function, in keeping with Toynbee's "concept of . . . [the] Nemesis of Creativity: Idolization of an Ephemeral Technique,"[55] was visible in the marginality of anti-submarine warfare in the Royal Navy, U.S. and Japanese navies in World War I and between the world wars, and in the relatively low status of mine warfare and sealift in the U.S. Navy, and of tactical aviation and airlift in the U.S. Air Force.

After tracing confusions arising from the interaction of three separate provisional command networks in the American incursion into Lebanon in 1958, Roger Spiller mused that service discontinuities might have been exploited by a "determined and professional enemy."[56] The Lebanon incursion took place as Army-Air Force friction mounted over rocketry in the wake of the Soviets' successful test of an intercontinental ballistic missile in September 1957, followed by the highly visible deployment of the Sputnik space satellite in early October. Stephen Ambrose noted that "backbiting and blame fixing had already begun the day after the latter went into orbit."[57] The persistence of service factionalism into the "space age" was visible a generation later, when the movement toward developing an anti-ICBM space-based system, Star Wars, led each service to create its own space command.

Given all these complex factors, constraints, and conditions, it may be expecting too much for humans to have done much better than they did in preparing for the uncertainties and hazards of war. The occasional eruption of public concern about "friendly-fire" casualties, command error, and so on reveals the great gap between popular expectations and the actual level of disorder and mischance in war, and the limits of perfectibility. After all, the lag between problem definition and response in the realm of jointness has been virtually glacial. Steps taken in the 1980s to strengthen jointness in the U.S. defense system were variants of models and plans first proposed almost three-quarters of a century earlier. Hence former Secretary of Defense Harold Brown's conclusion, much in the spirit of Eisenhower, that the main superstructure laid down in 1947 could be changed only incrementally and by "a departing or recently departed administration."[58] Since much is thus left to chance, to tradition, and to inertia, attainment of functional jointness is likely to remain elusive and situational.

The history of joint operations shows how often what was done was not all that could have been done, and how the price of tinkering and leaving matters to fate was often far higher than expected. Those who leave the matter of jointness to fate or proceed on the basis of best-case assumptions in this time of major retrenchment may fare better than those who did so before. Although jointness may not remain a central issue in policy debates, should it re-emerge as a matter of vital concern, as in 1915, 1940, 1950, 1956, 1972, and 1991, it is likely that the dictum of Admiral Harold Stark made on the eve of World War II will ring as true as it did then: "You can't buy yesterday with dollars."

NOTES

1. Douglas Robinson, *The Zeppelin in Combat* (London: G. T. Foulis, 1962), p. 128.

2. Herbert Stein, "Why Defense is Mismanaged?" *Fortune* 114:8 (October 1986): 178.

3. Dave Richard Palmer, *Summons of the Trumpet* (New York: Ballantine Books, 1978), p. 46.

4. Elting E. Morison, "A Case Study of Innovation," *Engineering and Science Magazine*, April 1950, p. 9.

5. George C. Dyer, *The Amphibians Came To Conquer: The Story of Admiral Richmond Kelly Turner* (Washington, D.C.: U.S. Government Printing Office, n.d., c. 1972), p. 930.

6. Pedro A. Del Valle, "Guam: The Classical Amphibious Operation," *Military Review* 27:1 (April 1947): 11.

7. House Committee on Armed Services, U.S. Congress, 81st Congress, 1st Session. *The National Defense Program: Unification and Strategy* (Washington, D.C.: U.S. Government Printing Office, 1949), p. 569.

8. Richard A. Aliano, *American Defense Policy from Eisenhower to Kennedy* (Athens, Ohio: Ohio State University, 1975), p. 265.

9. T. K. Derry, *The Campaign in Norway* (London: His Majesty's Stationery Office, 1953), p. 196; also see John A. Hixson, "Operation Shingle: Combined Planning and Preparation," *Military Review* 69:3 (March 1989): 63–77.

10. Merrill L. Bartlett, Foreword, *Assault from the Sea: Essays on the History of Amphibious Warfare* (Annapolis: U.S. Naval Institute Press, 1983), p. xix.

11. For example, see R. A. Hornell, "The Friction of War," *Naval Review* xvii:4 (November 1930): 635; and John Gooch, *The Plans of War: The General Staff and British Military Strategy, c. 1900–1916* (London: Routledge and Kegan Paul, 1974), p. 307.

12. R.A.D. Applegate, "Why Armies Lose in Battle: An Organic Approach to Military Analysis," *Journal of the Royal United Service Institute* 132:4 (December 1987): p. 53.

13. John Ehrman, *The Navy in the Wars of William III, 1689–1697* (Cambridge: Cambridge University Press, 1953), p. 609.

14. See D. Clayton James and Anne Sharp Wells, *A Time for Giants: Politics of the American High Command in World War II* (New York: Franklin Watts, 1987), pp. 171–81.

15. Kent Roberts Greenfield, *American Strategy in World War II: A Consideration* (Baltimore: Johns Hopkins, 1963), pp. 102–9.

16. Historical Section, *ETOUSA, Operation Report Neptune: Omaha Beach, 26 February–26 June 1941* (N. pl.: Provisional Engineer Special Brigade Group, 1944), p. 136.

17. Arthur W. Tedder, *Air Power in War* (London: Hodder and Stoughton, 1959), p. 19.

18. Paul Kennedy, "Military Coalitions and Coalition Warfare Over the Past Century," in Keith Neilson and Roy A. Prete, *Coalition Warfare* (Waterloo, Ont.: Wilfred Laurier Press, 1983), p. 146.

19. Frederick Morgan, *Overture to Overlord* (Garden City, N.Y.: Doubleday, 1950), p. 15.

20. Ibid., p. 41.

21. E. J. Kingston-McLoughry, *The Direction of War: A Critique of the Political Direction and High Command in War* (New York: Praeger, 1955), p. 252.

22. Frederick Maurice, *Lessons of Allied Cooperation, Naval, Military and Air, 1914–1918* (London: Oxford University Press, 1942), p. 24.

23. See Mark A. Stoler, *The Politics of the Second Front: American Military Planning and Diplomacy in Coalition Warfare, 1941–1943* (Westport, Conn.: Greenwood, 1977); for a Soviet perspective on "coalition war methods," see V. G. Kulikov, "Military Strategy," *Great Soviet Encyclopedia*, vol. 24 (New York: Macmillan, 1980), p. 164.

24. For perspectives on the additional complexities of alliance/coalition as an element or variant of jointness, see Archibald P. Wavell, "Allied Cooperation," in his *Soldiers and Soldiering* (London: Jonathan Cape, 1953), pp. 84–93.

25. For a tracing of the evolution of NATO's tangled web, see John W. Holmes, "Fearful Symmetry: The Dilemma of Consultation and Coordination in the North Atlantic Treaty Organization," *International Organization* 22:1 (Winter 1968): 820–21; James A. Huston, *One for All: NATO Strategy and Logistics through the Formative Period—1949–1969* (Newark: University of Delaware Press, 1984); and Augustus Richard Norton, Robert A. Friedlander, Martin H. Greenberg, and Dennis S. Rowe, *NATO: A Bibliography and Research Guide* (New York: Garland Publishing, 1985), pp. 164–80.

26. Kingston-McLoughry, *The Direction of War*, p. 253.

27. J. L. Moulton, *A Study of War in Three Dimension: The Norwegian Campaign of 1940* (Athens, Ohio: Ohio University Press, 1967), p. 297.

28. Charles R. Shrader, "BOBCAT: Rapid Deployment in 1942," *Military Review* 60:3 (March 1989): 36.

29. Bernard Fergusson, *The Watery Maze: The Story of Combined Operations* (New York: Holt, Rinehart and Winston, 1961), pp. 299, 298, 318, 322, *inter alia*.

30. Brian Bond and Williamson Murray, "The British Armed Forces, 1918–1939," in Alan R. Millett and Williamson Murray, eds., *Military Effectiveness*, vol. ii (Boston: Allen & Unwin, 1988).

31. Friedrich von Bernhardi, *On War of Today*, transl. Karl von Donat, vol. ii (New York: Dodd & Mead, 1914), pp. 419–20.

32. Hedrick Smith, *The Power Game: How Washington Works* (New York: Ballantine, 1988), p. 193.

33. Vincent Davis, *The Admiral's Lobby* (Chapel Hill, N.C.: University of North Carolina, 1967), p. 213.

34. Ian Hamilton, *The Soul and Body of an Army* (New York: Doran, 1921), p. 256.

35. Ibid.

36. Ibid., p. 257.

37. Alfred T. Mahan, *Lessons of the War with Spain and Other Articles* (Boston: Little Brown, 1899), p. 186.

38. Gregg Eastbrook, "Radio Free Watkins and the Crisis at Energy," *Washington Post Magazine*, February 18, 1990, p. 34.

39. Bruce Lambert, "Admiral George W. Anderson, 85: Was in Charge of Cuba Blockade," *New York Times*, March 22, 1992, pp. 1–17.

40. Arthur T. Hadley, *The Straw Giant: America's Armed Forces: Triumphs and Failures* (New York: Avon, 1987), p. 68.

41. David M. Hackworth and Julie Sherman, *About Face* (New York: Simon & Schuster, 1989), p. 54.

42. Ellis M. Zacharias, *Secret Missions: The Story of an Intelligence Office* (New York: Putnam's, 1946), pp. 302, 311.

43. For a discussion of the problem, see n.a., *Seventh Amphibious Force Command*

History, 10 January 1942–23 December 1945 (Shanghai: Seventh Amphibious Force, 1945), pp. II27–28.

44. Mark Perry, *Four Stars* (Boston: Houghton Mifflin, 1989), p. 338.

45. Bruce B. Blair, *Strategic Command and Control: Redefining the Nuclear Threat* (Washington, D.C.: Brookings Institution, 1985), p. 69.

46. For example, M. Sherif, "Group Conflict and Cooperation," in Peter Smith, ed., *Group Processes: Selected Readings* (Harmondsworth, England: Penguin Books, 1970), pp. 408–11.

47. For example, see Stephen Worchel, "The Role of Cooperation in Reducing Intergroup Conflict," in Stephen Worchel and William G. Austin, eds., *Psychology of Intergroup Relations*, 2nd edn. (Chicago: Nelson-Hall, 1986), pp. 296ff.

48. Elliot Aronson and Judson Mills, "The Effect of Severity of Initiation on Liking for a Group," in Dorwin Cartwright and Alvin Zander, eds., *Group Dynamics: Research and Theory*, 2nd edn. (Evanston, Ill.: Row & Peterson, 1960), pp. 95–103, esp. 102–3; John G. Holmes, John Ellard, and Helmet Lamm, "Boundary Roles and Inter-Group Conflict," in Worchel and Austin, eds., *Psychology of Intergroup Relations*, pp. 343–63.

49. Robert L. Kahn, Donald M. Wolfe, Robert P. Quinn, J. Diedrick Snoek, and Robert A. Rosenthal, eds., *Organizational Stress: Studies in Role Conflict and Ambiguity* (New York: John Wiley, 1964), esp. pp. 99–123.

50. For example, see Harold Brown, *Thinking about National Security: Defense and Foreign Policy in a Dangerous World* (Boulder, Colo.: Westview, 1983), p. 207; Alfred Vagts, *Landing Operations: Strategy, Psychology, Tactics, Politics from Antiquity to 1945* (Harrisburg: Military Service Publishing Co., 1952), pp. 4–5, 16; Donald MacIntyre, *The Naval War Against Hitler* (London: B. T. Batsford, 1971), p. 361; Curtis W. Tarr, *Unification of America's Armed Forces: A Century and a Half of Conflict, 1798–1947* (doctoral dissertation, Stanford University, 1961), p. 320; James L. Holloway III, "The Quality of Military Advice," *Foreign Policy and Defense Review* 2:1 (1979): 36; and PRO ADM 1/14897—Prime Minister to Hugh Molson, 3 April 1943, in *Unified Operational Control of the Anti-U-Boat Campaign*, p. 2.

51. John Ehrman, *Grand Strategy*, vol. vi, *October 1944–August 1945* (London: Her Majesty's Stationery Office, 1956), pp. 151–360.

52. Gregory D. Foster, "Why We Need a Joint Military Academy," *Houston Chronicle*, Feb. 18, 1986, p. A1. Charles Binford Gary, a General Motors executive and Naval Academy graduate, and who witnessed interservice hostility at close range in World War II in the Strategic Plans Division of the commander in chief of the U.S. fleet, wrote to Eisenhower in early 1949, arguing that the service academies were the seedbed of destructive rivalry, and that "if Waterloo was won on the playing fields of Eton, Pearl Harbor was lost on the Army-Navy football fields of Philadelphia and New York"; cf. Louis Galambos, ed., *Papers of Dwight D. Eisenhower*, vol. x (Baltimore, Md.: Johns Hopkins University Press, 1984), pp. 426–27. Eisenhower's interest in non-service specific training quickly faded as he confronted massive resistance.

53. Mrozek, *Air Power and the Ground War in Vietnam: Ideas and Actions* (Maxwell Air Force Base, Ala.: Air University, 1988), pp. 46 & 156.

54. Ramsey C. Logan, "The Aero-Amphibious Phase of the Present War," *U.S. Naval Institute Proceedings* 69:5 (May 1943): 702–3.

55. Arnold J. Toynbee, *A Study of History: Abridgment of Volumes I-VI*, ed. D. C. Somervell (Oxford: Oxford University Press, 1953), p. 581.

56. Roger Spiller, *'Not War But Like War': The American Intervention in Lebanon* (Fort Leavenworth, Kan.: Combat Studies Institute, 1981), p. 15.

57. Stephen Ambrose, *Eisenhower*, vol. II, *The President* (New York: Simon & Schuster, 1984), p. 427.

58. Harold Brown, *Thinking about National Security: Defense and Foreign Policy in a Dangerous World* (Boulder: Westview, 1983), p. 214.

Appendix 1

Principal Events Relating to Jointness in the U.S. Defense Nexus, 1943–1946

The question of effective direction and coordination of national defense, although a perennial topic for debate thereafter, was dealt with occasionally and in a spirit of grudging compromise. The following list is suggestive rather than exhaustive:

- Richardson Committee (1943) Joint Chiefs special study—navy dissent
- Bessell Committee (1943) Army Manpower Study
- Tompkins Plan (1944) Army Service Force plan for joint U.S. general staff
- McNarney Plan (1944) Army plan for Department of the Armed Forces and Common Supply Directorate
- Collins Plan (1945) Army plan for joint structure
- Eberstadt Report (1945) Navy plan for co-operative structure
- National Defense Act (1947) Created basic U.S. Cold War command structure, including JCS, Secretary of Defense, and joint agencies
- Key West and Newport agreements (1948) Service mission boundaries set by Forrestal amid squabbling
- Lutes Plan (1949) Army joint logistics plan
- Hoover Commission (1949) Suggested stronger Secretary of Defense role—included Eberstadt Committee Report
- Norstad-Sherman Plan (1949)—Army-Navy Compromise
- National Defense Act of 1947 amendments (1949–50) Strengthened Secretary of Defense role
- Collins proposal (1953) Army Chief of Staff proposed taking Joint Chiefs out of command loop without military staff
- Rockefeller Committee (1953) Led to Reorganization Plan No. 6

- Reorganization Plan No. 6 (1953) Eisenhower clarified role of chairman of JCS as adviser to president and secretary of defense and strengthened Joint Staff
- Coolidge Report (1957) Led to Amendments of 1947 Act
- Amendments of 1947 Act—ended "executive agent" system; services to training, administration, logistics; centralized research and development; chain of command tightened
- Eisenhower Reorganization Plan (1958)
- Symington Report (1960) Attacked service parochialism as a drag on central direction in crisis
- McNamara era at Defense Department (1961–68) Centralization; systems and analysis; program budgeting; little effective operational jointness among services
- Maxwell Taylor as chairman of JCS (1962) Close adviser to Kennedy; unique relationship; one-time only
- Joint Readiness Operations Center created after Bay of Pigs (1963)
- Fitzhugh "Blue Ribbon" Panel (1970) Saw JCS filtering and distorting command information flow; a hindrance to effective crisis management
- Ignatius, Rice and Steadman studies (1977–78) Attacked parochialism, ponderous staff process, lack of creativity, lack of relevance of JCS staff
- Rice Report (1978) On Defense Resource Management
- Odeen Report (1979) National Security Policy Integration Study
- Joint Planning and Execution Steering Committee Report
- Kerwin Group (1982) Assessed JCS staff process, low joint-assignment prestige, service competition; suggested range of reforms at all levels to strengthen cross-service co-operation
- Jones-Meyer proposals (1982–83) Called for JCS reform and led to Goldwater-Nichols Act
- "31 Initiatives" (1984) Air Force-Army compact
- Goldwater-Nichols Act (1986) Created vice chairman of JCS; made chairman chief adviser to president and secretary of defense; made joint assignments mandatory for promotion to high command
- Packard Report (1986) Reinforced Goldwater-Nichols Act

Some Official Definitions Related to Jointness

The official U.S. Department of Defense-NATO definition of "joint" is "activities, operations, organizations, etc. in which elements of more than one service of the same nation are involved,"[1] with subsequent recognition that nonmilitary agencies may be involved.[2] Some related terms are:

Specified command: has broad continuing mission and line of direct authority to president through secretary of defense, under one service's control.[3]

Unified command: same as above, but under two or more services' control.[4]

Integrated Staff: only one officer appointed to each staff position regardless of nationality or service.[5]

Parallel Staff: one officer from each nation or service working in parallel appointed to each staff position.[6]

Multiservice Doctrine: "fundamental principles" ratified by two or three services "that guide the employment of forces of two or three services of the same nation in coordination toward a common objective."[7]

NOTES

1. Joint Chiefs of Staff, *Official Dictionary of Military Terms* (Cambridge: Hemisphere Publishing Corp., 1988), p. 76.

2. Ibid., p. 197.

3. Ibid., p. 336.

4. Ibid., p. 380.

5. Ibid., p. 186.

6. Ibid., p. 268.

7. Ibid., 237.

Select Bibliography

This bibliography consists of English-language materials relating to jointness which those having access to a major public or university library or interlibrary loan facilities should find easily obtainable.

HISTORICAL OVERVIEWS

Merrill Bartlett, ed. *Assault from the Sea: Essays on the History of Amphibious Warfare* (Annapolis: U.S. Naval Institute Press, 1983).

P. H. Colomb. *Naval Warfare: Its Ruling Principles and Practice Historically Treated*, vol. 2 (Annapolis: Naval Institute Press, 1990 [orig. publ. 1891]).

John Creswell. *Generals and Admirals: The Story of Amphibious Command* (London: Longmans Green, 1952).

Bernard Fergusson. *The Watery Maze: The Story of Combined Operations* (New York: Holt, Rinehart and Winston, 1961).

Roger Keyes. *Amphibious Warfare and Combined Operations* (Cambridge: Cambridge University Press, 1943).

Thomas Molyneux. *Conjunct Expeditions: Or Expeditions that Have Been Carried on Jointly by the Fleet and Army with a Commentary on a Little War* (London: R. & J. Dodsley, 1759).

Chester W. Nimitz and E. B. Potter. *Sea Power: A Naval History* (Englewood Cliffs, N.J.: Prentice Hall, 1960).

Thomas G. Roe. *A History of Marine Corps Roles and Missions, 1775–1962* (Washington, D.C.: Historical Branch, G–3, Headquarters, 1962).

James L. Stokesbury. *Navy and Empire* (New York: William Morrow, 1983).

Alfred Vagts. *Landing Operations: Strategy, Psychology, Tactics, Politics, from Antiquity to 1945* (Harrisburg: Military Service Publishing Co., 1952).

TACTICAL AVIATION

Cajus Bekker. *The Luftwaffe War Diaries*, trans. and ed. Frank Ziegler (Garden City, N.Y.: Doubleday and Co., 1968).

Melrose M. Brant. *Air Support of the Close-In Battle* (Maxwell Air Force Base, Ala.: Air University Library, 1987).

B. Franklin Cooling, ed. *Case Studies in Close Air Support* (Washington, D.C.: Office of Air Force History, 1990).

Frank Wesley Craven and James Lea Cate. *U.S. Army Air Forces in World War II*, 6 vols. (Chicago: University of Chicago, 1949 ff).

Paul Deichmann, Noel F. Parrish, and Albert Simpson. *German Air Force Operations in Support of the Army*, edited by Littleton B. Atkins (New York: Arno, 1962).

Richard Hallion. *Strike from the Sky: The History of Battlefield Air Attack, 1941–1945* (Washington, D.C.: Smithsonian Institution Press, 1988).

Edward C. Johnson. *Marine Corps Aviation: The Early Years, 1912–1940*, edited by Graham A. Cosmas (Washington, D.C.: Headquarters United States Marine Corps, 1977).

H. A. Jones. *The War in the Air*, vols. iii and vi (Oxford, England: Clarendon Press, 1931).

John F. Kreis. *Air Warfare and Air Base Defense, 1914–1973* (Washington, D.C.: U.S. Air Force, 1988).

Elwood R. Quesada. "Tac Air Power," *Air University Review* 1, 4 (Spring 1949): 37–45.

Denis Richards and Hilary St. George Saunders. *Royal Air Force, 1939–1945*, vols. ii and iii (London: Her Majesty's Stationery Office, 1954).

James S. Santelli. *An Annotated Bibliography of the United States Marine Corps' Concept of Close Air Support* (Washington, D.C.: Historical Branch, G–3 Division, Headquarters, United States Marine Corps, 1968).

Robert Sherrod. *History of Marine Corps Aviation in World War II* (San Rafael, Calif.: Presidio Press, 1980).

John Terraine. *A Time for Courage: The Royal Air Force in the European War, 1939–1945* (New York: Macmillan, 1988).

J. R. Walker. *Air-to-Ground Operations* (London: Brassey's, 1987).

NAVAL GUNFIRE SUPPORT

Harold Bivins. *An Annotated Bibliography of Naval Gunfire Support* (Washington, D.C.: Historical Division, Headquarters, United States Marine Corps, 1971).

Walter Killilae. "Joint Operations of the Okinawa Campaign," three-part series in *Military Review* 27:3, 4, 5 (June, July, August 1947).

Donald W. Waller. "Salvo-Splash! The Development of Naval Gunfire Support in World War II," *U.S. Naval Institute Proceedings* 80, 8 (August 1954): 839–46 and 80, 9 (September 1954): 1011–21.

JOINTNESS AND COMMAND PROCESS

T. Armbruster. *A Matter of Accountability: The True Story of the Pueblo Affair* (New York: Coward McCann, 1970).

E. J. Kingston-McLoughry. *Defense Policy and Strategy* (New York: Preager, 1960).

Faris R. Kirkland. "The French Air Force in 1940: Was It Defeated by the Luftwaffe or by Politics?" *Air University Review* 36, 6 (September-October 1985).

Frederick Morgan. *Overture to Overlord* (Garden City, N.Y.: Doubleday and Co., 1950).

Williamson Murray. *Strategy for Defeat: The Luftwaffe 1933–1945* (Maxwell Air Force Base, Ala.: Air University Press, 1983).

Forrest Pogue. *The United States Army in World War II: The Supreme Command* (Washington, D.C.: Office of the Chief of Military History, 1954).

Paul B. Ryan. *Iran Rescue Mission: Why It Failed* (Annapolis: U.S. Naval Institute Press, 1985).

Herbert Y. Schandler. "JCS Strategic Planning and Vietnam: The Search for an Objective," in *Proceedings of the Eleventh U.S. Air Force Academy Military History Symposium* (Washington, D.C.: U.S. Government Printing Office, 1984).

Earl H. Tilford. *Set-Up: What the Air Force Did in Vietnam and Why* (Maxwell Air Force Base, Ala.: Air University Press, 1991).

Archibald P. Wavell. "Allied Cooperation," *Soldiers and Soldiering: Or Epithets of War* (London: Jonathan Cape, 1953), pp. 84–93.

JOINTNESS: DOCTRINE, STRUCTURE, AND POLITICS, 1945–90

Richard A. Aliano. *American Defense Policy From Eisenhower to Kennedy* (Athens, Ohio: Ohio State University Press, 1975).

Robert Greenhalgh Albion and Robert Howe Connery. *Forrestal and the Navy* (New York: Columbia University Press, 1962).

C. Kenneth Allard. *Command and Control and the Common Defense* (New Haven, Conn.: Yale University Press, 1990).

C. Joseph Bernardo and Eugene H. Bacon. "Demobilization and Unification," in *American Military Policy: Its Development since 1775* (Harrisburg, Pa.: Stackpole Co., 1961), pp. 442–61.

Brian Bond. *British Military Policy Between the World Wars* (Oxford, England: Clarendon Press, 1980).

Demetrios Cavaley. *The Politics of Military Unification: A Study of Conflict and the Policy Process* (New York: Columbia University Press, 1966).

Paolo Coletta. *The United States Navy and Defense Unification 1947–1953* (Newark: University of Delaware Press, 1981).

Kenneth W. Condit. *The History of the Joint Chiefs of Staff*, vol. ii, *1947–49* (Washington, D.C.: Historical Division, Joint Secretariat, Joint Chiefs of Staff, 1978).

Philip Darby. *British Defense Policy East of Suez, 1947–1968* (London: Oxford University Press, 1973).

Vincent Davis. *Postwar Defense Policy and the U.S. Navy 1942–1946* (Chapel Hill, N.C.: University of North Carolina, 1966).

———. *The Admirals' Lobby* (Chapel Hill: University of North Carolina Press, 1967).

N.a. *The Development of Air Doctrine in the Army Air Arm 1917–1941* (Maxwell Air Force Base, Ala.: Air University Press, 1967).

Ferdinand Eberstadt. *Report to the Honorable James Forrestal, Secretary of the Navy on Unification of the War and Navy Departments and Post War Organization for National Security* (Washington, D.C.: U.S. Government Printing Office, 1945).

Paul Y. Hammond. *Organizing for Defense: The American Military Establishment in the Twentieth Century* (Princeton: Princeton University Press, 1961).

————. "Super Carriers and B–36 Bombers: Appropriations, Strategy and Politics," in *American Civil-Military Decisions: A Book of Case Studies*, edited by Harold Stein (University: University of Alabama Press, 1963), pp. 465–564

Herbert Hoover et al. "The National Security Organization," in *Hoover Commission Report on Organization of the Executive Branch of Government* (New York: McGraw-Hill, 1949), pp. 183–98.

D. Clayton James and Anne Sharp Wells. *A Time for Giants: Politics of the American High Command in World War II* (New York: Franklin Watts, 1987).

Franklyn A. Johnson. *Defence by Ministry: The British Ministry of Defense* (London: Duckworth, 1980).

William W. Kaufman. *The McNamara Strategy* (New York: Harper and Row, 1964).

Gordon W. Keiser. *The U.S. Marine Corps and Defense Unification, 1944–1947: The Politics of Survival* (Washington, D.C.: National Defense University Press, 1982).

Lawrence Korb. *The Joint Chiefs of Staff: The First Twenty-Five Years* (Bloomington, Ind.: Indiana University Press, 1976).

Lawrence J. Legere. *Unification of the Armed Forces* (New York: Garland, 1988).

Julian Lider. *British Military Thought after World War II* (Aldershot, England: Gower, 1985).

Donald J. Mrozek. *Air Power and the Ground War in Vietnam: Ideas and Actions* (Maxwell Air Force Base, Ala.: Air University Press, 1988).

Gregory Palmer. *The McNamara Strategy and the Vietnam War: Program Budgeting in the Pentagon, 1960–1968* (Westport, Conn.: Greenwood, 1978).

Edgar F. Raines Jr. and David R. Campbell. *The Army and the Joint Chiefs-of-Staff: Evolution of Army Ideas on the Command, Control and Coordination of the U.S. Armed Forces, 1942–85* (Washington, D.C.: Analysis Branch, U.S. Army Center of Military History, 1986).

Steven L. Reardon. *History of the Office of the Secretary of Defense*, vol. i, *The Formative Years* (Washington, D.C.: Historical Office, Office of the Secretary of Defense, 1984).

John C. Ries. *The Management of Defense: Organization and Control of the U.S. Armed Services* (Baltimore: Johns Hopkins, 1964).

James F. Schnabel. *The History of the Joint Chiefs of Staff*, vol. iv, *The Joint Chiefs of Staff and National Policy* (Washington, D.C.: Historical Division, Joint Secretariat, Joint Chiefs of Staff, 1979).

James F. Schnabel and Robert J. Watson. *History of the Joint Chiefs of Staff*, vol. iii, *The Korean War*, Part i (Washington, D.C.: Historical Division, Joint Secretariat, Joint Chiefs of Staff, 1978).

Mark A. Stoler. *The Politics of the Second Front: American Military Planning and Diplomacy in Coalition Warfare, 1941–1943* (Westport, Conn.: Greenwood, 1977).

Curtis W. Tarr. *The Unification of America's Armed Forces: A Century-and-a-Half of Conflict, 1798–1947* (Stanford University, Ph.D. dissertation, 1961).

United States Congress, House of Representatives. *Statement of Louis L. Denfeld and Others Before the Armed Services Committee of the House of Representatives Investigating the B–36 and Related Matters* (Washington, D.C.: U.S. Government Printing Office, 1949).

United States Congress, House of Representatives, House Committee on the Armed Services. *The National Defense Program: Unification and Strategy* (Washington, D.C.: U.S. Government Printing Office, 1949).

United States Congress, Senate. *Air Power: Report of the Subcommittee on the Air Force of the Committee on Armed Services, U.S. Senate, 84th Congress with Minority Views* (Washington, D.C.: U.S. Government Printing Office, 1957).

Robert J. Watson. *History of the Joint Chiefs of Staff*, vol. v (Washington, D.C.: Historical Division, Joint Chiefs of Staff, 1986).

Russell F. Weigley. "Postwar and Cold War, 1945–1950," in *History of the United States Army* (New York: Macmillan, 1967), pp. 485–504.

Richard R. Weinert, Jr. *A History of Army Aviation, 1950–1962*, edited by Susan Canedy (Fort Monroe, Va.: Office of the Command Historian, 1991).

Richard I. Wolf. *The United States Air Force Basic Documents for Roles and Missions* (Washington, D.C.: Office of Air Force History, 1987).

Herman S. Wolk. *Planning and Organizing the Postwar Air Force 1943–1947* (Washington, D.C.: Office of Air Force History, 1984).

THEORY AND ANALYSIS

James B. Agnew. "From Where Did Our Amphibious Doctrine Come?" *Marine Corps Gazette* 63, 8 (August 1979): 52–59.

George Aston. *Sea, Land and Air Strategy: A Comparison* (London: John Murray, 1914).

Archie D. Barrett. *Reappraising Defense Reorganization: An Analysis Based on the Defense Organization Study of 1977–1980* (Washington, D.C.: National Defense University Press, 1983).

Gordon D. Batchellor. "The Eclipse of the Joint Chiefs of Staff." *Marine Corps Gazette* 74, 7 (July 1990): 32–34.

C. W. Borklund. *The Department of Defense* (New York: Praeger, 1967).

Bernard Brodie. "Land-Sea Operations," in *Sea Power in the Machine Age* (Princeton: Princeton University Press, 1943), pp. 148–63.

Harold Brown. *Thinking About National Security: Defense and Foreign Policy in a Dangerous World* (Boulder, Colo.: Westview, 1983).

Carl H. Builder. *The Masks of War: American Military Style in Strategy and Analysis* (Baltimore: Johns Hopkins, 1989).

Thomas A. Cardwell III. *Command Structure for Theater Warfare: The Quest for Unity of Command* (Maxwell Air Force Base, Ala.: Air University Press, 1984).

Julian S. Corbett. "Attack, Defence and Support of Military Expeditions," in *Some Principles of Maritime Strategy* (Annapolis: U.S. Naval Institute Press, 1911), pp. 280–304.

Reginald Custance. "On the Relations Between the Navy, Army and Aery," in *A Study of War* (Boston: Houghton Mifflin, n.d. [c. 1920]), pp. 86–93.

Norman Friedman. *The U.S. Maritime Strategy* (London: Jane's, 1988).

H. H. Frost. *The Conduct of an Overseas Naval Campaign* (Washington, D.C.: U.S. Government Printing Office, 1920).

George Armand Furse. *Military Expeditions Beyond the Seas*, vol. i. *Procedures*, vol. ii *Cases* (London: William Clowes, 1897).

Kent Roberts Greenfield. "Elements of Coalition Strategy," in *American Strategy in World War II: A Reconsideration* (Baltimore: Johns Hopkins, 1963), pp. 98–109.

Arthur T. Hadley. *The Straw Giant: America's Armed Forces Triumphs and Failures* (New York: Avon, 1987).

B. H. Liddell Hart. "Combined Defence," in *Europe in Arms* (London: Faber and Faber, 1937), pp. 185–211.

Robert Komer. *Bureaucracy at War: U.S. Performance in the Vietnam Conflict* (Boulder, Colo.: Westview, 1986).

Christopher Jon Lamb. *Belief Systems and Decision Making in the Mayaguez Crisis* (Gainesville, Fla.: University of Florida Press, 1959).

William Lynn. "The Wars Within: The Joint Military Structure and Its Critics," in *Reorganizing America's Defense: Leadership in War and Peace*, edited by Robert Art, Vincent Davis, and Samuel P. Huntington (Washington, D.C.: Pergamon-Brassey's, 1988), pp. 168–82.

Allan R. Millett, Mackubin Thomas Owens, Bernard E. Trainor, Edward C. Meyer, and Robert Murray. *Reorganization of the Joint Chiefs of Staff: A Critical Analysis* (Cambridge: Institute for Foreign Policy Analysis, 1986).

Louis J. Moses. *The Call for JCS Reform: Crucial Issues* (Washington, D.C.: National Defense University Press, 1985).

Michael A. Palmer. *Origins of the Maritime Strategy: American Naval Strategy in the First Postwar Decade* (Washington, D.C.: Naval Historical Center, 1988).

W. D. Puleston. *The Dardanelles Expedition: A Condensed Study* (Annapolis: U.S. Naval Institute Press, 1957).

Logan C. Ramsey. "The Aero-Amphibious Phase of the Present War," *U.S. Naval Institute Proceedings* 69, 5 (May 1943): 695–701.

James Schlesinger. "The Office of the Secretary of Defense," in *Reorganizing America's Defense: Leadership in War and Peace*, edited by Robert Art et al. (Washington, D.C.: Pergamon-Brassey's, 1985), pp. 255–74.

Maxwell D. Taylor. *Uncertain Trumpet* (New York: Harper and Row, 1959).

Jim Veksis, and Jim Toth. "The Color Purple," *Parameters* 19, 4 (December 1989): 110–11.

John P. Wisser. "Land and Naval Combined Operations," in *The Tactics of Coast Defense* (Kansas City: Franklin Hudson, 1908), pp. 157–210.

MEMOIRS AND BIOGRAPHIES OF PRACTITIONERS
OF JOINTNESS

Henry H. Adams. *Witness to Power: The Life of Fleet Admiral William D. Leahy* (Annapolis: U.S. Naval Institute Press, 1985).

Stephen Ambrose. *Eisenhower*, vol. ii, *The President* (New York: Simon and Schuster, 1984).

Cecil Aspinall-Oglander. *Roger Keyes: Being the Biography of Admiral of the Fleet Lord Keyes of Zeebrugge and Dover, G.C.B., K.C.V.O., C.M.G. and D.S.O.* (London: Hogarth Press, 1951).

Daniel Barbey. *MacArthur's Amphibious Navy: Seventh Amphibious Force Operations, 1943–1948* (Annapolis: U.S. Naval Institute Press, 1969).

C. W. Borklund. *Men of the Pentagon from Forrestal to McNamara* (New York: Praeger, 1966).

Lewis H. Brereton. *The Brereton Diaries* (New York: Morrow, 1946).

George C. Dyer. *The Amphibians Came to Conquer: The Story of Admiral Richmond Kelly Turner*, 2 vols. (Washington, D.C.: U.S. Government Printing Office, 1971).

Dwight D. Eisenhower. *The White House Years: Mandate for Change, 1953–1956* (Garden City, N.Y.: Doubleday, 1963).

———. *The White House Years: Waging Peace, 1956–61* (Garden City, N.Y.: Doubleday, 1963).

Richard Hough. *Mountbatten* (New York: Random House, 1981).

George Kenney. *Kenney Reports* (Washington, D.C.: Office of Air Force History, 1988).

Walter Millis, ed. *The Forrestal Diaries* (New York: Viking, 1951).

Bernard Law Montgomery. *The Memoirs of Field Marshal the Viscount Montgomery of Alamein, K. G.* (Cleveland: World Publishing, 1958).

Stephen Roskill. *Hankey: Man of Secrets*, 3 vols. (London: Collins, 1969).

John Schlicht. "Elwood R. Quesada: TAC Air Comes of Age," in *Makers of the United States Air Force*, edited by John Frisbee (Washington, D.C.: Office of Air Force History, 1987), pp. 177–203.

Holland M. Smith and Percy Finch. *Coral and Brass* (New York: Scribner's, 1948).

Richard S. West. *The Second Admiral: A Life of David Dixon Porter, 1813–1891* (New York: Coward-McCann, 1937).

F. E. Whitton. *Wolfe and North America* (Boston: Little Brown, 1929).

Rex Whitworth. *Field Marshal Lord Ligonier: The Story of the British Army, 1702–1770* (Oxford: Clarendon Press, 1958).

Basil Williams. *The Life of William Pitt Earl of Chatham*, vols. i and ii (London: Frank Cass, 1966).

Ronald Wingate. *Lord Ismay* (London: Hutchinson, 1970).

WARS, CAMPAIGNS, AND OPERATIONS: ANCIENT/CLASSICAL

F. E. Adcock. *The Greek and Macedonian Art of War* (Berkeley: University of California Press, 1957).

Norman Baynes. *The Byzantine Empire* (London: Oxford, 1962).

Pierre Ducrey. "Warfare at Sea," in *Warfare in Ancient Greece*, translated by Janet Lloyd (New York: Shocken Books, 1985), pp. 179–96.

Yvon Garlan. *War in the Ancient World: A Social History*, trans. Janet Lloyd (London: Chatto and Windus, 1975).

Romilly Jenkins. *Byzantium: The Imperial Centuries, A.D. 610–1071* (London: Weidenfeld and Nicolson, 1966).

Donald Kagan. *The Archidamian War* (Ithaca, N.Y.: Cornell University Press, 1974).

———. *The Fall of the Athenian Empire* (Ithaca, N.Y.: Cornell University Press, 1987).

William Ledyard Rodgers. *Greek and Roman Naval Warfare—4th to 16th Centuries: A Study of Strategy, Tactics and Ship Design* (Annapolis: U.S. Naval Institute Press, 1939).

John Van Duyn Southworth. *The Ancient Fleets: The Story of Naval Warfare under Oars, 1600 B.C.—1597 A.D.* (New York: Twayne Publishers, 1968).

Chester G. Starr. *The Roman Imperial Navy, 31 B.C.—A.D. 324* (New York: Barnes and Noble, 1960).

————. *The Influence of Seapower on Ancient History* (New York: Oxford University Press, 1989).

W. W. Tarn. *Hellenistic Military and Naval Developments* (Chicago: Ares Publishing, 1984).

Graham Webster. "The Navy," in *The Roman Imperial Fleet*, 3d ed. (Totowa, N.J.: Barnes and Noble, 1985), pp. 157–66.

J. B. Wilson. *Pylos 425 B.C.: A Historical and Topographic Study of Thucydides' Account of the Campaign* (Warminster, U.K.: Aris and Phillips, 1979).

MEDIEVAL/EARLY MODERN

John M. A. Ehrman. *The Navy in the War of William III, 1689–1697: Its State and Direction* (Cambridge: Cambridge University Press, 1953).

Winston Graham. *The Spanish Armadas* (New York: Doubleday, 1972).

John Francis Guilmartin, Jr. *Gunpowder and Galleys: Changing Technology and Medieval Warfare at Sea in the 16th Century* (Cambridge: Harvard University Press, 1974).

John Knox Laughton, ed. *State Papers Relating to the Defeat of the Spanish Armada Anno 1588* (London: Navy Records Society, 1894), 2 vols.

M. E. Mallett and J. R. Hale. *The Military Organization of a Renaissance State—Venice, c. 1400 to 1677* (Cambridge: Cambridge University Press, 1984).

George Ostrogorsky. *History of the Byzantine State*, trans. Joan Hussey (New Brunswick, N.J.: Rutgers University Press, 1969).

Steven Runciman. *Byzantine Civilization* (London: Edward Arnold, 1959).

Daniel Philip Waley. *Combined Operations in Sicily, A.D. 1060–78* (London: British School at Rome, Papers, vol. 22, [New Series, vol. 9, 1954]).

Alethea Weil. *The Navy of Venice* (London: John Murray, 1910).

EIGHTEENTH CENTURY

Christopher Duffy. *The Military Experience in the Age of Reason* (New York: Atheneum, 1988).

J. Christopher Herold. *Bonaparte in Egypt* (New York: Harper and Row, 1962).

William James. *The Naval History of Great Britain from the Declaration of War by France in 1793 to the Access of George IV* (London: Richard Bentley, 1859), 6 vols.

Gertrude Selwyn Kimball, ed. *Correspondence of William Pitt when Secretary of State with Colonial Governors and Military and Naval Commissioners in America* (New York: Kraus Reprints, 1969), vol. i and ii.

J. Robert Moskin. *The U.S. Marine Corps Story* (New York: McGraw-Hill, 1982).

J. L. Moulton. *The Royal Marines* (London: Leo Cooper, 1972).

Herbert Richmond. *The Navy in the War of 1739–48*, 3 vols. (Cambridge: Cambridge University Press, 1920).

J. Holland Rose. *William Pitt and the Great War* (London: G. Bell and Sons, 1914).

Davis Syrett. "British Amphibious Operations During the Seven Years and American Wars," in *Assault from the Sea: Essays on the History of Amphibious Warfare*, edited by Merrill L. Bartlett (Annapolis: U.S. Naval Institute Press, 1983).

NINETEENTH CENTURY

K. Jack Bauer. *Surfboats and Horsemarines: U.S. Naval Operations in the Mexican War, 1846–1848* (Annapolis: U.S. Naval Institute Press, 1969).

Wilburt S. Brown. *The Amphibious Campaign for Western Florida and Louisiana, 1814–1815: A Critical Review of Strategy and Tactics at New Orleans* (University: University of Alabama Press, 1969).

Byron Farwell. *Queen Victoria's Little Wars* (New York: W. W. Norton, 1973).

Frank Freidel. *The Splendid Little War* (Boston: Little Brown, 1958).

H. Allen Gosnell. *Guns on the Western Waters: The Story of River Gunboats in the Civil War* (Baton Rouge: Louisiana State University, 1949).

Rowena Reed. *Combined Operations in the Civil War* (Annapolis: U.S. Naval Institute Press, 1978).

Peter C. Smith. *Victoria's Victories* (New York: Hippocrene Books, 1987).

Richard S. West, Jr. *Mr. Lincoln's Navy* (New York: Longman's Green, 1957).

TWENTIETH CENTURY TO WORLD WAR I

William Felix Atwater. *The United States Army and Navy Development of Joint Landing Operations, 1898–1942* (Durham, N.C.: Duke University Press, 1986).

John Gooch. *The Plans of War: The General Staff and British Military Strategy, c. 1900–1916* (London: Routledge & Kegan Paul, 1974).

WORLD WAR I

A. J. Barker. *The Bastard War: The Mesopotamian Campaign of 1914–1918* (New York: Dial Press, 1967).

Maurice Hankey. *The Supreme Command*, 2 vols. (London: George Allen and Unwin, 1961).

Douglas Jerrold. *The Royal Naval Division* (London: Hutchinson, n.d. [1927]).

Sir Charles Lucas, ed. "The Cameroons Campaign," in *The Empire at War*, vol. iv., *Africa* (Humphrey Milford: Oxford University Press, 1924), pp. 62–120.

Charles Miller. *Battle for the Bundu: The First World War in East Africa* (New York: Macmillan, 1974).

Alan Moorehead. *Gallipoli* (New York: Harper and Row, 1956).

K. Von Tschischwitz. *The Army and Navy during the Conquest of the Baltic Islands in October 1917*, trans. Henry Hossfeld (Fort Leavenworth, Kan.: Command and General Staff College, 1931).

BETWEEN THE WORLD WARS

Kenneth J. Clifford. *Amphibious Warfare Development in Britain and America from 1920 to 1940* (Laurens, N.Y.: Edgewood, 1983).

Robert A. Doughty. *The Seeds of Disaster: The Development of French Army Doctrine* (Hamden, Conn.: Archon, 1988).

Walter Harris. *France, Spain and the RIF* (London: Edward Arnold, 1927).

A. D. Harvey. "The French *Armée de l'Air* in May-June–1940: A Failure of Conception," *Journal of Contemporary History* 25, 4 (1990): 447–65.

Robin Higham. *Armed Forces in Peacetime: Britain 1918–1940* (London: G. T. Foulis, 1962).

————. *The Military Intellectuals in Britain, 1918–1940* (New Brunswick, N.J.: Rutgers University Press, 1966).

Ronald Chalmers Hood III. *Royal Republicans: The French Naval Dynasties between the World Wars* (Baton Rouge: Louisiana State University, 1988).

Joint Board. *Joint Action of the Army and the Navy* (Washington, D.C.: U.S. Government Printing Office [series of editions throughout the 1920s and 1930s]).

Stephen Roskill. *Naval Policy between the Wars*, vol. 1 (New York: Walker & Co., 1968); vol. 2 (Annapolis: U.S. Naval Institute Press, 1976).

WORLD WAR II

A full list of official histories of American, Brazilian, British, Australian, Canadian, New Zealand, Soviet and other armed forces that encompasses jointness would run for several pages. Material on jointness can be found in each volume of the *U.S. Army in World War II* "Green Book" series, and especially in those focused on major amphibious operations. See Gordon Harrison's *Cross-Channel Attack* (1951), and Albert N. Garland and Howard McGaw Smith's *Sicily and the Surrender of Italy* (1965), the richest troves. Also useful are Craven and Cate's lengthy study, *The Army Air Forces in World War II*, and Samuel Eliot Morison's *U.S. Naval Operations in the Second World War* noted below, and Frank O. Hough, Verle E. Ludwig, and Henry I. Shaw, *History of U.S. Marine Corps Operations in World War II* (Washington, D.C.: Historical Division, Headquarters U.S. Marine Corps, 1958 and 1963), as well as such campaign studies as Charles S. Nichols' and Henry I. Shaw Jr.'s *Okinawa: Victory in the Pacific*. British official histories with substantial joint content include T. K. Derry's *The Campaign in Norway*, the *Grand Strategy* volumes by J. R. Butler, John Ehrman et al., S. Woodburn Kirby's *The War against Japan*, I.S.O. Playfair's *The Mediterranean and Middle East* and Lionel Ellis' *Victory in the West*, as well as Stephen Roskill's account of Royal Navy operations, and Richards' and Saunders' history of the Royal Air Force.

The following sources suggest the vast material on jointness in World War II, and some is also listed in other sections.

Martin Blumenson. *Anzio: The Gamble that Failed* (Philadelphia: J. B. Lippincott, 1965).

Saburo Hayashi and Alvin Cook. *Kogun: The Japanese Army in the Pacific War* (Quantico, Va.: The Marine Corps Association, 1959).

James Huston. *Out of the Blue* (Lafayette, Ind.: Purdue University Press, 1972).

J. D. Ladd. *Assault from the Sea, 1939–1945: The Craft, the Landings, the Men* (Newton Abbott, U.K.: David and Charles, 1976).

J. L. Moulton. *A Study of War in Three Dimensions: The Norwegian Campaign of 1940* (Athens, Ohio: Ohio University Press, 1967).

N.a., *Condensed Analysis of the Ninth Air Force in the European Theater of Operations* (Washington, D.C.: Office of Air Force History, 1984 [orig. publ. 1946]).

Friedrich Ruge. *Der Seekrieg: The German Navy's Story, 1939–45*, translated by M. G. Saunders (Annapolis: U.S. Naval Institute Press, 1965).

Hilary St. George Saunders. *Combined Operations: The Official Story of the Commandos* (New York: Macmillan, 1943).

Richard Suchenwirth. *Historical Turning Points in the German Air Force's War Effort* (New York: Arno Press, 1968).

Homer N. Wallin. *Pearl Harbor: Why, How, Fleet Salvage and Final Appraisal* (Washington, D.C.: Naval Historical Division, 1968).

THE KOREAN WAR

J. Lawton Collins. *War in Peacetime: The History and Lessons of Korea* (Boston: Houghton-Mifflin, 1969).

J. R. Fehrenbach. *This Kind of War* (New York: Macmillan, 1963).

James A. Field, Jr. *History of United States Naval Operations in Korea* (Washington, D.C.: U.S. Government Printing Office, 1962).

Robert F. Futtrell. *The United States Air Force in Korea* (Washington, D.C.: Office of Air Force History, 1983).

Richard Hallion. *The Naval Air War in Korea* (Annapolis: Naval Institute Press, 1986).

Max Hastings. *The Korean War* (New York: Simon and Schuster, 1987).

Robert Debs Heinl, Jr. *Victory at High Tide: The Inchon-Seoul Campaign* (Philadelphia: J. B. Lippincott, 1968).

The U.S. Army in the Korean War: vol. i, *South to the Naktong, North to the Yalu*, Roy E. Appleman (1961); vol. ii, *Truce-Tent and Fighting Front*, Walter G. Hermes (1966); vol. iii, *Policy and Direction: The First Year*, James F. Schnabel (1972) (Washington, D.C.: Office of the Chief of Military History/Center for Military History).

U.S. Marine Operations in Korea, 1950–1953, vol. i, *The Pusan Perimeter*, Lynn Montross and Nicholas Canzona (1954); vol. ii, *The Inchon-Seoul Operation*, L. Montross and N. Canzona (1955); vol. iii, *The Chosin Reservoir Campaign*, L. Montross and N. Canzona (1957); vol. iv, *The East-Central Front*, L. Montross (1962); vol. v, *Operations in West Korea*, Pat Meid and James M. Yingling (1972) (Arlington, Va.: Historical Branch, Headquarters, United States Marine Corps).

THE VIETNAM WAR

As in the case of World War II, this list only suggests the vast amount of material extant. Much of it lies in the official histories of the U.S. Army, Navy, Marine Corps and Air Force, and in Australia's and New Zealand's armed forces as well.

John D. Bergan. *Military Communications: A Test for Technology* (Washington, D.C.: Center for Military History, 1986).

Thomas J. Cutler. *Brown Water, Black Berets* (Annapolis: Naval Institute Press, 1988).

George S. Eckhardt. *Vietnam Studies: Command and Control, 1950–1969* (Washington, D.C.: Department of the Army, 1974).

Donald J. Mrozek. *Air Power and the Ground War in Vietnam: Ideas and Action* (Maxwell Air Force Base, Ala.: Air University Press, 1988).

N.a. *The Pentagon Papers: The Department of Defense History of U.S. Decision Making on Vietnam* (Boston: Beacon, 1971) [the Senator Gravel edition].

Bernard C. Nalty. *Air Power and the Fight for Khe Sanh* (Washington, D.C.: Office of Air Force History, 1973).

Bruce Palmer. *The 25-Year War: America's Military Role in Vietnam* (New York: Touchstone Books, 1984).

Mark Perry. *Four Stars* (Boston: Houghton-Mifflin, 1989).

Benjamin Schemmer. *The Raid* (New York: Harper and Row, 1976).

U.S. Grant Sharp and William Westmoreland. *Report on the War in Vietnam (as of 30 June 1968)* (Washington, D.C.: U.S. Government Printing Office, 1968).

Frank Uhlig, Jr. *Vietnam: The Naval Story* (Annapolis: Naval Institute Press, 1986).

OTHER JOINT OPERATIONS SINCE 1945

Ronald E. Berquist. *The Role of Airpower in the Iran-Iraq War* (Maxwell Air Force Base, Ala.: Air University Press, 1988).

Michael Carver. *War Since 1945* (London: Ashfield Press, 1990).

Thomas Donnelly, Margaret Roth, and Caleb Baker. *Operation Just Cause: The Storming of Panama* (New York: Lexington Books, 1991).

James F. Dunnigan and Austin Bay. *From Shield to Storm: High Tech Weapons, Military Strategy and Coalition Warfare in the Persian Gulf* (New York: William Morrow, 1992).

Robert A. Liston. *The Pueblo Surrender* (New York: M. Evans, 1988).

Martin Middlebrook. *The Falklands War, 1982* (London: Penguin, 1987).

Jack Shulimson. *Marines in Lebanon, 1958* (Washington, D.C.: Historical Branch, G–3 Division, Headquarters United States Marine Corps, 1966).

Roger Spiller. *'Not War but Like War': The American Intervention in Lebanon* (Fort Leavenworth, Kan.: Combat Studies Institute, 1981).

Hugh Thomas. *Suez* (New York: Harper and Row, 1967).

Frank Uhlig, Jr. "Amphibious Aspects of the Grenada Episode," in *American Intervention in Grenada: The Implications of Operation Urgent Fury*, edited by Peter W. Dunn and Bruce W. Watson (Boulder, Colo.: Westview, 1985).

Lawrence A. Yates. *Power Pack: U.S. Intervention in the Dominican Republic, 1968–1969* (Fort Leavenworth, Kan.: Combat Studies Institute, 1988).

Index

ABC–1 Agreement, 71, 88
Abd el Krim. *See* Krim, Abd el, Rif
   leader
ABDACOM (American-British-Dutch-
   Australian Command), 97
Abercromby, Ralph (General), 15
Aboukir, Anglo-Turkish amphibious
   landing at, 15
Abrams, Creighton (General): as head of
   MACV, 149; view of CAS, 153
Acadia, fall of, 10
Achaeans, 2, 44
Actium, Battle of, 5
Ad jir (Rif capital), 77; captured, 80
Admiralty (Br.), air defense role of, 185
Admiralty Islands campaign, World War
   II, tactical air support in, 114
Advanced Base Operations in Micronesia
   (Ellis), 68
Aegean Sea, 3; Byzantine control of, 6;
   in World War I, 44; in World War II,
   90
Aegetes Islands, 4
"aerial fire support" (U.S. Army), 151
"aero-amphibious war," concept of, 128
"Aery" concept, 73
Afghanistan, Soviet involvement in, 168,
   170

Agency for International Development
   (AID), in Vietnam War, 149, 151
agonism, and service friction, 192
Ainsworth, Frederick (Major-General), 31
air base security: and jointness, 186; in
   World War II, 89
"air control," as means of imperial
   policing, 73, 77
air control parties, U.S., 114
air defense: in "31 Initiatives," 168;
   U.S. Army role, in 1950s, 146
Air Force Association, 131
Air Force Headquarters (U.S.), 67
"Air-Land Battle" doctrine, 164, 168,
   170
air mobile units formed, 151
Air-Naval Gunfire Liaison Companies
   (ANGLICO), 143
Air Operations Centers (U.S. Air Force),
   151
"air policing," 73, 77
Air Power: Key to Survival (deSeversky),
   136
Air Support Control teams (Br.), 110
Air Support teams, U.S. Army-Army Air
   Forces, World War II, 115
airborne forces: decline of, 119; evolution
   of, 93–94; jointness and, 186; losses at

Gela, 82; operations after World War
    II, 95; in Rhine crossing, 93–94
aircraft, British; Battle, 107; BE 2C, 44;
    Harrier, 164; "Hurribomber," 110;
    Hurricane, 110; Lysander, 107;
    Typhoon, 112
aircraft, German: Focke Wulf 200
    Condor, 116–17; Junkers–87 Stuka
    dive bomber, 70, 106, 109; Junkers
    88C, 117
aircraft, Soviet, Ilyushin–2 Shturmovik,
    108
aircraft, U.S.: A–1 Skyraider, 152, 164,
    166; A–10, 164; B–24 Liberator, 117;
    B–25 Mitchell, 119; B–29
    Superfortress, 103, 116, 140; B–36
    Peacemaker, 134, 135–37; B–52
    Stratofortress, 208; Caribou, 151; F–
    14, 147; F–80 Shooting Star, 140; F–
    111, 147; Hawk, 70; Mohawk, 151; P–
    38 Lightning, 119; P–39 Airacobra,
    108, 114; P–400, 114; U–2, 157;
    Vengeance, 114
aircraft carriers: in nuclear war doctrine,
    134; reduction in Royal Navy and
    Falklands War, 162; Royal Navy-RAF
    wrangling, 75
airlift: in Gulf War, 193; and jointness,
    186; shortage of, in Suez Crisis, 158,
    161; U.S. Air Force role during 1950s,
    146; in Vietnam War, 149
"airpower and the modern army," as
    doctrinal rubric, 146
air-sea rescue, in Vietnam War, 149
air war, psychic distancing in, 191
Aitken, Arthur (Major-General), 42
Akhromeyer, Sergei (Marshal of the
    Soviet Union), 172
Aland Islands, landing by French in, 20
Alaska, 66
Alcazar Soreir, Morocco landing, 77
Aleutian Islands, Japanese landings in, 96
Alexander, Harold (Field Marshal), and
    close air support, 111
Alexandria, 30, 72; in Suez Crisis, 158
Algeria, 46; Algerian rebellion, 157;
    French conquest of, 17; as Suez base,
    158

Alhucemas, Franco-Spanish landing at,
    77–79; origin of concept, 83 n.34
Aliano, Richard, quoted, on U.S. officer
    corps, 186
Alison, John (Major General), 113
Allard, C. Kenneth, 171
Allied Tactical Air Forces, in North
    Africa, in 1943, 110
Allied Tactical Air Forces Commander,
    Air Marshal Coningham as, 111
Almond, Edward (Lieutenant General),
    and Inchon landing, 139
Amboina, Japanese landing at, 95
Ambrose, Stephen, quoted, on
    interservice wrangling after Sputnik,
    194
American-British-Dutch-Australian
    Command, 97
American Civil War, joint operations in,
    20–26, 43, 60
amphibious operations (see also under
    operational code names): in American
    Civil War, 25–27; in Chinese Civil
    War, 138; claims of conceptual
    preeminence by U.S. Marine Corps,
    67; in colonial wars of the late 19th
    Century, 27–28; in Dardanelles, 44–54;
    dominance of U.S. and Royal Navies
    in World War II, 93; in Egypt, 159–
    61; in Falklands/Malvinas War, 162;
    frequency of, in the 20th Century, 189;
    in Hundred Years' War, 8; in Korean
    War, 138–44; lack of Japanese doctrine
    for, 81; lack of resources for, in 1942,
    69, 72; lessons learned at Dieppe, 89;
    logistics in, 101–3; marginality in U.S.
    defense policy, during the 1970s and
    1980s, 167–68; in Maritime Strategy,
    169; Mediterranean and European
    Theaters, 89–95; in Napoleonic Wars,
    15–16; in Pacific Theaters, 95–101,
    103–5; post–World War II decline,
    119–20; resurgence of, in Korea, at
    Suez, and Falklands, 132; shaping
    factors, World War II, 192; in Sicily,
    7; at Vera Cruz, 17; in Vietnam War,
    153
Amsterdam, as imperial hub, 28

Anatolia, 2

Anderson, George (Admiral), in Cuban
missile crisis, 191

Anglo-French combined headquarters,
Suez expedition, 158

anti-aircraft: disaster at Gela, 92; need for
fire discipline, 89; origins of, 185

Anti-submarine warfare (ASW): in Battle
of the Atlantic, 115–17; jointness and,
186; low status of, 194; in Pacific
Theater, World War II, 118; post–
World War II, 119

Antony, Marc, 5

Antwerp: Anglo-Russian expedition, 15;
British expedition, 16

ANZAC Corps (Australia-New Zealand),
47, 48, 50, 51

Anzac Cove, 51–53

Anzio-Nettuno landings of, 1944, 90, 92

Apennines, 92

appeasement, effect on British defenses,
74

Arcadia Conference, 97

arditi, Italian elite troops, World War I,
118

Argentina: in Falklands/Malvinas War,
162–63; in War of the Triple Alliance,
17

Aristides, 3

Armée de l'Air: condition of, in 1940,
81, 107; creation of, 69; share of
budget, 1930s, 80

armored cars, 77

Army Air Corps. *See* U.S. Army Air
Corps

Army Air Forces. *See* U.S. Army Air
Forces

Army cooperation (Br.), 107

Army Ground Forces (U.S.), 115

Army National Guard (U.S.), 129

Army of the North (French), 14

Army of the Potomac, 25

Army of the Tennessee, 23

Arnold, Benedict, 13

Arnold, Henry H. (General of the Army):
on airborne operations, 94; favors
unification in 1945, 129; supports King
on Marianas landings, 103, 117

Arras, Battle of, 58

askaris, in World War I, 42, 43

Aspinall-Oglander, Cecil (Brigadier
General), 52

Asquith, Herbert Henry (Br. Prime
Minister), 41

Assistant Secretary of War, for
mobilization, 65

Assistant Secretary of War for Air, 67

Association of the United States Army,
131

Athens: forces in joint operations, 18–19,
21–22; as maritime power, 1, 2

Atlantic, Battle of, 111, 116, 117

Atlantic Charter, 71

Atlantic Fleet (U.S.), in Cuban Missile
Crisis, 148

attack aviation doctrine, U.S. Army Air
Corps, 69, 108, 165

Attila, 165

Attlee, Clement (Prime Minister),
dismantles joint structures after World
War II, 156

Atwater, William Felix, quoted, 97

Augustus Caesar (Octavian), 5

Australia, 97

Australian forces: close air support,
World War II, 114–15; in Dardanelles
campaign, 46; in Pacific theater, 99

Austria as Mediterranean sea power, 1

Axis powers: failure in jointness, 128;
victory of, feared, 109

back-channel communications, use of, in
Vietnam War, 151

Baker Board, 67

Baldwin, Stanley, 139

Balkan Wars of, 1908–13, 45, 48

Balkans, in World War II: cities in,
bombed, 133; strategic debate over, 93

Baltic Sea, 11, 20, 31, 54; Soviet landing
operations in, 93

Baltimore, 16

"Banana Wars," U.S. Marine Corps in,
68

Banks, Nathaniel (General), 54

Barbary pirates, 1, 6

Barber, Noel, quoted, on joint processes
  in Malaya, 166
Barbey, Daniel (Rear Admiral), 99, 104;
  on low status of amphibious duty in
  U.S. Navy, 138
Bartlett, Merrill (Lieutenant Colonel),
  quoted, on amphibious campaigns in
  World War II, 187
Bartz, Karl, quoted, on Battle of the
  Atlantic, 117
Bataan Campaign, 95
Battle of the Atlantic, 111, 116, 117
Battle of Britain, 195
Battle of the Bulge, air support hiatus in,
  112
The Battle of Dorking (Chesney), 29
"Battle of the Potomac," 129
"Battle of the Smiths," 100, 103
Battlefield air interdiction, 165
Bayonne, France, 16
beach reconnaissance, in amphibious
  operations, 92
Beatty, David (Admiral of the Fleet), as
  obstacle to jointness, 76
Beaufre, Andre (General), in Suez
  expedition, 158
Beauregard, P.G.T., 23
Belgian paratroops, in Congo, 95, 189
Belgium, 57, 75; Nazi airborne
  operations in, 93
Belisarius, 6
Belize, 162
bellum (rivercraft in Iraq, in World War
  I), 43
Berlin: as imperial hub, 28; plan for
  airborne capture of, 94
Berlin Airlift (1948–49), 134
"Big Bertha" gun, 57
Bikini Atoll, atomic bomb tests at, 130
Birdwood, William (Field Marshal), 48
biremes, 2
Bismarck, Otto von (Chancellor), 45
Bismarck Archipelago campaign, 100
"black" (covert) activities, 167, 172
Black Sea littoral, riverine warfare, 25;
  Soviet operations in World War II, 90,
  93; in World War I, 44

Blair, Bruce, quoted, on authority and
  compliance, 192
blitzkrieg, 70, 109
Bloch, Ivan, 41
blockship system, in World War II, 102
Blue Ribbon Committee on Defense
  Management (Packard Report), 171
"bluejackets," 27
Boer War (1899–1901), 29–31, 46
Bolivia, in War of the Pacific, 27, 29
Bolshevik Revolution, 35, 57
"bolt out of the blue," surprise attack,
  30
Bolton, David, quoted, on service
  specialization, 136
Bombay, 42
Bomber Command, Royal Air Force, 141
"bomber line," World War II, 101
Bonaparte, Joseph, 16
Bonaparte, Napoleon: on British strategy,
  12; defeat in Egypt, 15, 16
Bosphorus, Straits of, 45, 46
Bougainville, 99
Boyle, Dermot (Marshal of the RAF), in
  Suez Crisis, 157
Bradley, Omar (General of the Army): on
  airborne units, 94; on amphibious
  landings' obsolescence, 136; as
  Chairman, JCS, in Korean War, 144;
  close rapport with Navy, World War
  II, 127, 187; "Fancy Dan" comment
  of 1949, 189; memoirs, 111
The Brain of an Army (Wilkinson), 154
Brandenburgers, 118
Brazil, in War of Triple Alliance, 27
Brereton, Lewis H. (General), as
  commander of First Allied Airborne
  Army, 94
Briggs, Harold (General), and joint
  methods in Malaya, 166
Brink, Francis J. (Brigadier General), on
  Vietnam policy, 179 n.94
"brinkmanship," 145
Britain, Roman landings in, 4
British armed forces: "air control," 73;
  in colonial wars of the 1920s and
  1930s, 77; evacuation from Europe
  (1940), 86; in Falklands War, 161–63;

joint exercises (1938–39), 72; plans for Locarno War, 75; postwar plans for jointness confounded, 156; state of, in 1939, 85; in Suez War, 155–61

British Armed Forces units: Eighth Army, World War II, 90, 115; 1st Airborne Division, World War II, 94; King's African Rifles, World War I, 42; New Army divisions, World War II, 50; 9th Corps, 99; Royal Marine Commandos, at Suez, 1956, 159; Royal Naval Division, 44, 47, 52, 57; Third Army, World War I, 58; 21st Army Group, World War II, 169; 29th Infantry Division, World War I, 47, 51, 53

British Army-RAF radio links, 197

British capital, and U.S. defense build-up, 71

"British disease," 162

British Empire, 109

British Expeditionary Force (BEF): 1908–1914, 31; 1940, 107

British Intelligence, links with O.S.S., 71

"broken-backed war," 169

Brooke, Rupert (First Lieutenant), 44

Brookings Institution, 65

Brown, Harold (Secretary of Defense): and "horizontal escalation," 167; quoted, on difficulty of jointness reforms, 194

Brunei, 162

Bruneval raid, 87

Brussels, as imperial hub, 28

Buenos Aires, British attacks repulsed, 16

Bulgaria, 51

bureaucratic process, as friction source, 188

Burke, Arleigh (Admiral), quoted, on service rivalry, 147

Burma, riverine warfare: close air support in, in World War II, 113; in 1880s, 25

Burnside, Ambrose (General), 25

Butler, Benjamin (Major-General), 25–26

Byron, Lord, 1

Byzantine fleet, 2; renaissance and decline during 9th Century, 7, 44

Byzantium, as maritime power, 1, 5

"cab rank," close air support system, 112

Cadiz: British expedition to, 13; English raid on, 9–11

Caen, bombing of, 115

Caesar, Julius, 4

Cairo, Illinois, 21

Cairo conference, 103

Calabria, amphibious landing at, 16

Cambodia: holocaust, 165; seizure of SS Mayaguez, 154

Cameroons. See German Cameroons

Canada: British capture of, 11; enters ABC–1 agreement, 88

Canadian armed forces: amphibious operations in World War II, 90; losses of at Dieppe, 88–89

Cape Helles, 47, 50–51, 53

Cape Misenum, Roman naval base, 5

Carden, Sackville (Admiral), 45

Cardwell, Thomas A. (Colonel), quoted, on jointness, 171

Caribbean Sea, maneuvers in, 68

carpet-bombing, in Desert War, 115

Cartagena expedition, 10, 12

Carter, Jimmy (President), administration of, 167

Carthage, as maritime power, 1, 4

Cassino, Battle of, 115

The Case Against the Admirals (Huie), 131

Casey, William, as CIA director, 172

"cash-and-carry" policy, 71

catalytic war, 170

Caucasus front: World War I, 45; World War II, 115

Caucasus oil fields, 115

Cebadilla, Morocco, 78

Celebes, Japanese capture of, 95

Central Europe, 160

Central Intelligence Agency (CIA): created, 132; MacArthur hostile to, 144; in Vietnam War, 149–51; and William Casey, 172

Central Pacific Theater of Operations, World War II, 100, 105; style in, 192; tactical air support in, 114

Central Powers, World War I, 51, 97

Ceuta, Morocco landing at, 77
Chairman of the Joint Chiefs (U.S.),
    limits of power of, 137–38
Chamber of Deputies (Fr.), votes in Suez
    affair, 159
Chamberlain, Neville (Prime Minister),
    85
"Champagne Campaign," 93
Champion's Hill, Battle of, 23
Chanak Crisis, 74
Channel Dash, of Kriegsmarine, 109;
    lack of British jointness in, 128
Chapultapec, U.S. Marines at, 19
Charles II (King of England), 11
Charles V (Holy Roman Empire), 9
Charleston, South Carolina, British
    landings at: 1776 and 1780, 13; 1863,
    26
Charter of the United Nations, 172
Chatfield, Ernle (Admiral), chairs Chief
    of Staff Committee, 75, 85–86
Chief of the Defence Staff, British, 163–
    64
Chief of Naval Operations (U.S.):
    Arleigh Burke as, 147; role in setting
    service boundaries, 66, 137; staff, 65
Chief of Staff, U.S. Army, role in setting
    service boundaries, 66
Chief of Staff of National Defense (Fr.),
    81
Chiefs of Staff Committee (Br.), 74–75,
    86, 88; after World War II, 156; in
    Suez Crisis, 157–60
Chile, in War of the Pacific, 27–28
China: falls to Communists, 134; German
    marines in, 57, 60, 66; Japanese
    invasion of, 76, 81, 95; threats to U.S.
    B–29 bases in 1944, 103, 107; as war
    theater, World War II, 97; Western
    incursions in, 30
China Relief Expedition, 27
Chinese Civil War, 119; amphibious
    operations in, 138
Churchill, Winston: becomes Prime
    Minister and Minister of Defence, 86;
    blocks Iraq takeover in 1941, 87; calls
    for Naval War Staff, 31; and Greece in
    1940, 109; and jointness, 186; names

Keyes Director of Combined
    Operations, 58; 1940 strategy of, 12;
    proposes Dardanelles effort, 45, 47,
    50, 54; quoted, on centralization, 192;
    quoted, on D Day, 93; reappointed
    First Lord of Admiralty, 85; supports
    "air control," 73; supports
    international air force, 133; on War
    Council, 1914–15, 41
CIA. See Central Intelligence Agency
Cicilian pirates, 5
CINCPAC/POA, 132, 154
CINCs (U.S. Pacific Ocean Area
    Commanders-in-Chief), 147; jointness
    and war-fighting doctrine of, 171; in
    reform proposals, 166
Civil Air Patrol, 131
Civil Operations and Rural Development
    (CORDS), in Vietnam, 149
Civil War, American, 20–27, 60; U.S.
    style in, 191
Civil War, English, 11
Clark, Mark W. (General): on airborne
    units, 94; and Anzio, 92; quoted, on
    jointness, 186
Clarke, I. F., 29
Claudius, Roman Emperor: landing in
    Britain, 4; and Roman navy, 5
Clausewitz. See von Clausewitz, Karl
Cleoprtra, 5
Clifford, Clark (Secretary of Defense),
    153
close air support (CAS): decline after
    World War II, 119; in Desert Storm,
    193; in Falklands/Malvinas, 163; and
    jointness, 192; in Korean War, 147;
    post-Vietnam, 164–65, 168;
    psychological effects of, 106; in
    Vietnam War, 150–53; in World War
    I, 58–60; between World War I and II,
    69–71; in World War II, 105–15
close air support, Australian, 114
close air support, British, 58–60, 70–71,
    76, 81, 107
close air support, French, 67, 69, 81,
    107–13
close air support, German, 58, 67, 70,
    107

close air support, Japanese, 67, 107
close air support, Russian, 67, 69, 81,
    107–8
close air support, U.S., 60, 69–70, 81,
    108, 111, 113–15, 138, 140, 146,
    150–51, 168
"close support bombing," RAF doctrine,
    107
clothing, as source of interservice
    differences, 192
CNO. See Chief of Naval Operations
Coastal Command (RAF), in Battle of the
    Atlantic, 117
Cochran, Philip (Colonel), 113
COIN. See counterinsurgency doctrine
Cold War, 128, 131, 133–34, 139;
    limited utility of air power in, 165;
    thawing of, 163
collateral damage, in Vietnam War, 152
collective security, in Gulf War, 172
Collins, J. Lawton (General): on
    Rockefeller Committee, 145; visits
    Japan, 141, 144
Colonial Defence Committee (Br.), 30
"colossal cracking," 115–16
Columbus, Kentucky, 20–21
combat loading, 19, 101
combinaison de colones, French joint
    tactics, 77
combined arms tactics: World War I,
    110; World War II, 113
Combined Chiefs of Staff, World War II,
    97, 103
Combined Operations (Br.), 72, 86–87;
    Diego Suarez and Dieppe lessons, 88–
    89; doctrine, 100, 131, 163; insignia,
    in Gulf War, 173; lowered priority, 88
Combined Operations Staff: logistical
    problems defined by, 102; U.S.
    officers assigned to, 88
Combined U.S.-Vietnamese Command,
    opposition to, 149
Command Control, and the Common
    Defense (Allard), 171
Command Decision (film), 135
command ships, 86, 92, 100
command-and-control, 89, 100; Allard
    on, 171; in Cuban Missile Crisis, 178

n.75; hostility to systems, 165–66; and
    jointness, 186; in Liberty affair, 166;
    in Mayaguez affair, 154; nuclear war
    related, 148; in Pueblo affair, 155; in
    "31 Initiatives," 168; in Vietnam,
    152, 178 n.76
Commander-in-Chief Pacific Fleet/Pacific
    Ocean Area (CINCPAC/PAO), 132,
    154
Commandos (Br.), 118
Committee of Imperial Defence (CID):
    disbanded, 41; establishes ISTDC, 73;
    formed, 31; as model for NSC, 132; as
    source of jointness, 76; subcommittee
    of Chiefs of Staff Committee formed,
    74
Committee of National Defense, 67
Communists: Czechoslovak, in coup of
    1948, 134; French, against Rif war, 77
"Concept for Improved Joint Air-Ground
    Coordination," 151
Confederate States of America, armed
    forces of, 20–27
Congo River, as imperial conduit, 28
Coningham, Arthur (Air Marshal):
    argument with Patton on air support
    doctrine, 111; commands Desert Air
    Force, 110
Conjunct Expeditions (Molyneux), 12–13
Conner, David (Commodore), 19, 187
Connolly, R. L. (Admiral), 104
Conservative Party (Br.): defense
    policies, 162–63; post-World War II,
    155; in Suez Crisis, 158–60; support of
    air defense, 75
"consists," 102
constabulary role: of armed forces in
    Cold War, 189; of U.S. Marine Corps,
    68
Constantinople: British naval raid on, in
    1807, 16; in Dardanelles campaign,
    44–45; sack of, 7
containment policy, of Truman
    administration, 135
continental strategy, British, 11
convoys, Russia-bound, World War II,
    116; losses, 118, 169

Coordinating Committee for Staff Duties in Combined Operations (Br.), 74

Copenhagen, British amphibious landing at, 16

Coral Sea, Battle of, 96

CORDS, 149

Corinth, Mississippi, 21

Corps Franc, French elite troops, World War II, 118

Corregidor, Japanese capture of, 95

corvus, 4

Cot, Pierre, French Air Minister, 80

counterinsurgency, covert operations: air support of, 119; in Burma, 113; and jointness, 139, 167; in World War II, 90

counterinsurgency doctrine (COIN), 150, 152

Covenant of the League of Nations, 172

Cretan Revolt, 4

Crete: defeat of Navy by Byzantines, 7; as maritime power, 1, 2; Nazi airborne invasion, 93, 109; as pirate base, 5

Crimean War, 20, 30

Crowe, William (Admiral), as Chairman, Joint Chiefs of Staff, 172

cruise missile, 167, 170

Crusaders, as maritime power, 1, 44

Cuba, operations in, 24, 32

Cuban Missile Crisis of 1962: command authority unclear in, 178 n.75; jointness lack evident in, 148

Cumberland River, 21

Cunard-White Star liners, 52

Cunningham, Alfred A. (Colonel), 70

Cunningham, Andrew (Admiral of the Fleet Viscount), on Chiefs of Staff Committee after World War II, 156

Custance, Reginald (Admiral), defines "mutual dependence" principle and "Aery," 73

Cyprus: insurgency in, 157; as maritime power, 1; in 16th Century, 8; as Suez expedition base, 158

Czechoslovakia, Communist coup in, 134

D Day: Normandy invasion, 92, 94, 115; in Suez invasion of 1956, 159

Daiquiri: lack of combat loading at, 101; U.S. landing, 32

Dakar expedition: failure of, 87, 89, 90; lessons of, 100, 128, 190

Danube flotilla: Roman, 5; Soviet, 90

Dardanelles campaign, 13, 27, 41, 44–54; evacuation, 52, 60–61, 78, 141, 143

Dardanelles Commission, findings, 48

Dardanelles Committee, 50

Davis, Charles (Flag Officer), 23

Davis, Vincent, quoted: on interservice differences, 189; on interservice rivalry, 127, 137

de Gaulle, Charles (President), changes France's role in European defense, 162

de Rivera, Primo (General), 77, 83

de Robeck, John (Vice-Admiral), 4, 45–46, 50, 141

de Seversky, Alexander P. (Major), 69, 127–31, 136

"deep battle" doctrine, of Soviet army, 170

"deep penetration." See interdiction, air

Defence Committee (Br.), 86

Defence White Paper (Br.), 162

Defense Intelligence Agency (DIA): created, 147; in Vietnam, 149, 151

Defence Policy and Operational Staff (Br.), 163

Defense Supply Agency (U.S.), 147

defoliation, in Vietnam, 165. See also Operational code names, Ranch Hand

del Valle, Pedro (Major General), quoted, on jointness, 186

demobilization, of U.S. after World War II, 119, 131

Denmark, war with Sweden, 11

Department of the Armed Forces, McNarney proposal, 127

Department of Defense (U.S.), 132; and McNamara reforms, 147

Department of Defense Reorganization Act of 1958, 145

Department of National Defense: Proposals by Smoot, 65, 67; proposals by Truman, 130

Derry, T. K., quoted, 186
Desert Air Force (RAF), 108–11
The Desert Song (Romberg), 77
"Destroyer Deal," 71
DEW (Distant Early Warning) Line, 172
Dickson, William (Air Marshal), in Suez Crisis, 157
Diego Suarez, Madagascar, landing at, 88
Dien Bien Phu, Battle of, 165
Dieppe Raid, 87–89; lessons of, 100, 143
Direct Air Support Center (U.S. Air Force), in Vietnam War, 153
Director of Combined Operations (Br.), Keyes named as, 87
Director of Common Supply, McNarney proposal for, 127
Director of Plans, U.S. Air Force, 151
Disaster Through Air Power (Andrews), 136
dive bombing: U.S. Army, 108, 111; British lack, 109; U.S. Marine Corps, 70; in Pacific Theater, World War II, 114
"Dixie Station," Vietnam War, 152
Dixon, Norman, 185
doctrine, armed services, vendor influence on shaping of, 189–90
Don Juan of Austria, 8
Dönitz, Karl (Grand Admiral), quoted, 116
"Doolittle Raid," 119
Drake, Sir Francis, 10
drakkars, Viking ships, 6
dromons, Byzantine ships, 2, 7
Drum Board, 67
Du Pont, Samuel (Admiral), 26
Dugan, Thomas (General), as Air Force Chief of Staff, 193
Duke of Parma, 9
Duke of York, 14
DUKWs ("Ducks"), amphibious craft, 89
Dulles, John Foster (Secretary of State): and "massive retaliation," 145, 148; and Suez Crisis, 157, 161
Dumbarton Oaks Conference, international air force proposed at, 133

Dundas, Henry (Lord), 14
Dunkirk: British expedition at, in 1793, 14–15; Allied evacuation of, in 1940, 86
Dutch East Indies. *See* Indonesia
Dutch marines, 27
Dutch Navy, raids on England, 11

East Africa, 57
Eastern Europe, riverine warfare in, 25
Eastern Front, (World War I), 60
Eberstadt, Ferdinand, 129, 132
Eden, Anthony (Prime Minister), in Suez Crisis, 157–61
Edward III, 8
Egypt: Caesar's landing in, 5; defeat of fleet by Byzantines, 7; marines of, 2; as maritime power, 1; Napoleon's expedition to, 9; in 1973 Middle East War, 165; in Suez Crisis, 155–61; in World War I, 46; in World War II, 97, 109
Ehrman, John, quoted: on Army-Navy friction, 187; on committee system of command, 193
Eisenhower, Dwight D. (General of the Army), accord with Spaatz, 187; on airborne operations, 94; aids Forrestal, 134; broad-front strategy of, in World War II, 192; Navy Fleet carrier proposals and testimony in "Revolt of the Admirals," 135; "New Look" defense policy of, 145; 1958 reforms and McNamara policies, 147–48, 154; quoted, 136; restructuring of JCS, 146; and Suez Crisis, 160–61, 171; and unification in 1945, 128–29
El Alamein, Battle of, 110
El Caney, Battle of, 34
"Electronic Battlefield" concept, 167
Elgin Committee, 31
Eliot, George Fielding, defense reorganization proposals of: in 1938, 67; in 1945, 128
Ellis, Earl Hancock (Major), 67–68
Ellis, John, 185
England: Norman conquest of, 7; Viking settlement in, 7

English Channel, 57, 92
enhanced radiation weapons. *See* neutron
    bomb
Englightenment, French, 11
Enniskillen Castle, siege of, 9
Escadrille Chirifiénne, 83 n.34
Ethiopia: imperial penetration of, 27–28;
    Italian invasion of, 72, 76, 81, 109
Eurasia, 1; rimlands of, 134, 139, 168
European Theater of Operations (World
    War II), 90, 97, 105, 113
"executive agent" concept, 66
"expansible Army," 65

Falaise Gap, 112
Falklands/Malvinas War: amphibious
    warfare in, 132, 144, 156, 161; causes
    and events, 162–63, 168; joint
    command in, 193
Far East: British joint exercises in, 73,
    88; MacArthur as commander in, 139
Far East Air Force (FEAF), in Korean
    War, 144
Farragut, David (Admiral), 23, 25–26
FEAF, 144
Fergusson, Bernard (Brigadier): on
    interservice friction, World War II,
    188; on Wolfe and Saunders rapport,
    13
Fez, Morocco, 78
field artillery, in 1973 Middle East War,
    165
"Field of the Cloth of Gold," 92
Field Service Regulations, joint revisions
    of, 72
Fifth (U.S.) Air Force, in *Pueblo* affair,
    155
fighter-bomber, appears as aircraft type,
    110
fighter direction ships, 89
Finnish campaign, 115
Fioravanzo, Giuseppe (Admiral), quoted,
    on "naval-air force," 188–89
First Allied Airborne Army, 94
"first battle," U.S. Army doctrine of,
    170
First Indochina War, 154, 157
First Joint Training Force, 68

First Korean Marine Corps Regiment, at
    Inchon, 143
First Special Service Force (U.S.-
    Canadian), 118
1st U.S.-Canadian Special Service Force,
    160
Fisher, John (Admiral of the Fleet Lord),
    31, 44, 47, 50
Flanders, World War I, 58
Fleet Air Arm, Royal Navy,
    modernization retarded by service
    friction in, 76
Fleet Marine Force, 138; air doctrine of,
    70, 139
FLEXes (Fleet Landing Exercises), 68,
    100
Flushing, Netherlands, 16
flying boats, Japanese, in World War II,
    118
"follow-on-forces," Soviet, 170
Force "J," 89
Forces Command (U.S.), becomes
    specified command, 171
Ford Motor Company, McNamara as
    president of, 146
Forrestal, James V. (Secretary of
    Defense): as Secretary of Defense, and
    suicide, 134–36; as Secretary of the
    Navy and foe of unification, 128, 131–
    32
Fort Donelson, 21
Fort Fisher, 26
Fort Henry, 21
Fort McHenry, siege of, 13, 16
Fort St. Philip, 17
"Fortress Falklands," 163
Forts, key role in imperialism, 11
Forward Air Controllers (FACs): in
    Korea, 140; origins, 112; in Vietnam,
    153
Fourth Crusade, 7
H.M.S. *Fox*, 42
FPOT (forward position own troops), 164
France, Battle of, 107
France: British fear of air attack by, 75,
    109, 112; Dardanelles involvement,
    45, 53; defeated in 1940, 75, 86, 89;
    as imperial power, 9; as maritime

power in Mediterranean, 1; in Suez
Crisis, 157–61; Viking settlement in, 7
Franco, Francisco (Marshall), in Rif
Wars, 77–79
Free French forces: at Dakar, 87; at
Diego Suarez, 88
"Free-fire Zones," in Vietnam, 153
French armed forces: cooperation in
riverine warfare in Indo-China, 54;
Marine infantry in World War I, 57;
naval aviation in 1930s, 81; in Suez
crisis, 157–61. *See also* Armée de
l'Air
French armed forces, units: Corps Franc,
118; Marine Infantry, 27, 58; Navy,
78, 80
French Army, in Morocco and Syria, 77
French Army *nettoyers*, 118
French capital and U.S. defense buildup,
71
French Corps, at Dardanelles, 47
French high command, 80–81
friction. *See* interservice friction
friendly fire: in Gulf War, 174, 194; in
Okinawa, 115
Frobisher, Martin (Sir), 10
From Here to Eternity (Jones), as image
of military incompetence, 135
fuel-air explosives (FAE), 167, 170
Fuller, J.F.C. (Major General), 70;
derides "colossal cracking," 115
Futrell, Robert, quoted, on jointness in
Korean War, 144

Gaba Tepe, 47
Gaitskell, Hugh (Labour Party leader), in
Suez Crisis, 157, 159
Gallipoli, 29, 44–54, 57–58, 66, 72–73,
77–78, 86–87, 90, 92, 100–101, 141;
parallels with Suez, 161, 188
Gamelin, Henry (Marshal), 81
Garlan, Yvon, on Roman marines, 5
Gavin, James (Lieutenant-General): on
confusion in Sicily airborne operations,
94; quoted, on vendor influence on
service doctrine, 190; resigns as Army
R&D chief, 145
Gavutu, landing on, 99

Geiger, Roy (General), 115
Gela, Sicily, 92, 94
General Board, U.S. Navy, 34
General Staff: fear of, in U.S., 147;
Prussian, 31; U.S. proposals, 34–35,
65
Genghis Khan, 165
Genoa, as maritime power, 1, 7, 44
Georgia, 130
German armed forces, units: 42nd
Infantry Division, World War I, 54;
Sixth Army, World War II, 205; 7th
Army, 112; 8th Army, World War I,
54; Marines, 17; Marines in China and
East Africa, World War I, 57;
Sturmtruppen, World War I, 118
German Army: losses at Dieppe, 89;
operation in East Africa, (1914–18),
42–43; training in Russia, (1925–35),
81
German Cameroons, 44
German East Africa, World War I, 42
German Navy. *See Kriegsmarine*
German-Iraqi build-up (1941), 161
Germany: cities bombed, World War II,
133, 169; as imperial power, 10, 29,
31, 75; rise in Nazi era, 76, 93
Gettysburg, Battle of, 25
Ghormley, Robert L. (Admiral), at
Guadalcanal, 99, 192
Gibraltar, British capture of (1703), 11;
in World War II, 90
Gilbert, William Schwenk, 30
Gilbert Islands, 99, 119
Gladstone, William (Prime Minister), 30
gliders, 94, 113
Golan Heights, in 1973 Middle East War,
165
Goldsborough, Louis M. (Flag Officer),
25–26
Goldwater-Nichols Act: effects of, 172,
189, 192–93; passed, 171
Gorbachev, Mikhail (Premier), at
Rekjavik, 172
Göring, Hermann (Reichsmarshal),
quoted, on claims of authority, 117
Gorshkov, Sergei (Fleet Admiral), on
Nazi U-boat failure, 116

Granspaan, Battle of, 28
Grant, Ulysses S. (General), 21, 23, 25,
    187; quoted, on strategy, 192
Gravatt, Brent L., quoted, on riverine
    operations command-and-control, 154
Great Britain: air defense of, 76; in
    Dardanelles campaign, 45–54; enters
    ABC–1 Agreement, 88; fears of
    invasion before World War I, 28;
    French-British expedition against, 13;
    as imperial power, 29; imperial
    retrenchment of, 155; retrenchments
    after Suez, 162; in Suez affair, 157–60
Great Depression, 67–68; and defense
    spending, 74
Great Northern War, 11
Greece: and Dardanelles campaign, 45–
    46, 52; Nazi conquest of, 87, 97
"Greek fire," 2, 7
Greek mercenaries, in Punic Wars, 4
Greek Civil War, air power in, 166
Green Beret murder case, 167
Greenland, Viking settlement in, 7
Grenada invasion, airborne forces in, 95,
    168, 173. See also operational code-
    names, Urgent Fury
Grenville, Lord, 14
Guadalcanal, 99; naval support on, 192;
    tactical air support on, 114, 190
Guadeloupe, French expedition, 16
Guam, Japanese capture of, 95, 97
Guantanamo Bay, Cuba, 32
Guilmartin, John: on forts and galleys, 5;
    on putting guns aboard ships, 8
Gulf of Mexico, 19
Gulf of Riga, 54
Gulf of Tonkin, 152
Gulf War, 112; close air support in, 164;
    coalition in, 161; U.S. Army prime
    command authority in, 132; U.S. and
    British joint commands in, 162, 173
"gun-club," U.S. Navy faction, 189
Gustav Line, 92

Hackett, John (General), writes The Third
    World War, 170
Hackworth, David (Colonel): on air war

psychic distancing, 191; on elite forces
    in Vietnam War, 150
Hadley, Arthur, on service differences,
    191
Hadrian, Byzantine admiral, 7
Haiti, French expedition of, 15
Haldane, Richard (Secretary of State for
    War), for revitalized CID, 74
Haldane reforms, 31
Halleck, Henry Wager (General), 23
Hallion, Richard, quoted, 112
"Halls of Montezuma," 19
Halsey, William "Bull" (Fleet Admiral),
    101; at Leyte Gulf, 190; views on
    jointness reversed, 128
Hamilton, Ian (General): in Dardanelles
    campaign, 44, 46, 48, 50–53; proposed
    reforms, 72, 141; quoted, on service
    differences, 190
Hammond, Paul, quoted, on B–36
    hearings, 136
Han River (Korea), crossing of, 144
Hankey, Maurice (Lord): appointed
    Secretary to CID, 31; on Dardanelles,
    54; effect on jointness, 85; as key
    policy shaper, 74; on War Council, 41;
    on World War I plans, 72
Hanseatic League, 33
Hart, Thomas (Admiral), 128
Hartington, Spencer Cavendish (Lord),
    30
Harvey, A. D., quoted, 81
Hatteras Inlet, 25
Havana, Cuba, 12
Hawaii, 68; weak service links in, before
    World War II, 96
Hawkins, Sir John, 10
Hayson, David (Wing Commander), 112
Head, Anthony (Minister of Defence),
    158
Head of Elk, Maryland, British landing
    at, 13
Healey, Denis (Minister of Defence),
    162–63
Heartbreak House (George Bernard
    Shaw), 76
Heggen, Thomas, 103

Heinl, Robert (Colonel), on naval gunfire
  support problems, 104
Helena, Arkansas, 23
helicopters, in close air support, 151
Hellenes, 44
Henry V, 8
Herriot government (Fr.), air policy of,
  80
Heseltine, Michael (Minister of Defence),
  163
"Highway of Death," in Gulf War, 112
Hinton, Harold, quoted, 131
Hiroshima, atomic bombing of, 133, 165
Hitler, Adolf (Reichschancellor), 106,
  111, 157, 165
Hoglund Island, landing at, 93
Holland, as imperial power, 10
Holland, Nazi and Allied airborne
  operations in, 93
Holley, I. B. (Major-General), quoted,
  on "lessons learned" transience, 174
Holloway Committee, on Eagle Claw
  raid, 167
Holmes, Richard, 185
Hondschoote, 14
Hong Kong, Japanese capture of, 95, 97
Hoover, Herbert (President) and Hoover
  Commission: on centralization of
  defense, 133; reduces U.S. Marine
  Corps, 68
hoplites, 3
"horizontal escalation," 167
Houchard, Jean Nicolas (General), 14
House Committee on the Armed
  Services, hearings on B-36 bomber,
  135-36
Howe, William (General), 13
Huie, William Bradford, critiques U.S.
  Navy in World War II, 131
Hundred Years War, 8
Huntington, Samuel, 133
Hussein, King, in Suez Crisis, 158
hydrogen bomb, development of, 137
hydrological surveys, for amphibious
  operations, 89

ICBM. See intercontinental ballistic
  missile

Iceland: in Battle of the Atlantic, 116;
  Viking settlement, 7
Iliad, 44
Imperial Defence College (Br.), 75
Imperial General Staff (Br.), 31
imperial policing, R.A.F. role in, 73
Imperial Rescript of 1907 (Jap.), 96
Inchon, landing at. See operational code-
  names, Chromite
India: British conquest of, 11; joint
  exercises in, 73; Soviet threat to, 74
independent air services, proposals, 67
Indian Army: in China, 42; in
  Dardanelles campaign, 46, 51; in East
  Africa, 41, 43; 10th Infantry Division,
  161
Indian Mutiny of 1857-58, 27
Indochina, French occupation of, 28
Indochina War, First, 25; airborne
  operations in, 95
Indonesia: after World War II, 119;
  Australian operations in, in World War
  II, 90
Industrial Revolution, 11
Inskip, Thomas (Sir), named Minister for
  Coordination of Defence, 75, 86
intelligence fusion: in Gulf War, 173;
  lack of, in World War II and role of,
  in low-intensity conflict, 166
intercontinental ballistic missile (ICBM):
  Soviets test, 146; U.S. and U.S.S.R.
  deploy, 148
intercontinental bombers, U.S. Congress
  opposes, 67
interdiction, air, 111-12, 165
international air force French proposal
  for, 80
International Monetary Fund, 161
interoperability, lack of, in Suez
  expedition, 158
interservice diplomacy, cases of, 69, 108,
  134, 151, 168, 188
interservice friction, 185-94; in Battle of
  the Atlantic, 117-18; in Britain, 76; as
  central problem in jointness, 185; in
  Civil War, 25-26; in Cuba, 32, 34; in
  Cuban Missile Crisis, 148; and defense
  procurement, 186; during the 1960s,

147; effect on Japanese defenses on
Peleliu, 103; as factor in Pearl Harbor
debacle, 97; between Japanese Army
and Navy, 81, 95–96; at New Orleans,
17; over missile control, 146, 194;
post–World War II, 127, 194; in
Operations Desert Shield and Desert
Storm, 172–73; in Operation Urgent
Fury, 72; between U.S. field artillery
and air support on Saipan-Tinian, 103;
at Vera Cruz, 17; in Vietnam War,
148–54
Inter-services Training and Development
Center (ISTDC), 73, 87
The Invasion of 1910 (LeQueux), 29
Iran-Contra affair, 172
Iraq, 43; Nazi ploy thwarted in, 87, 109;
aids Jordan, 158
Iraqi army, 116, 161; in Gulf War, 173
Ireland, Viking settlement in, 7
Irrawaddy River, as imperial conduit, 28
"island hopping," U.S. strategy, Pacific
theater, World War II, 96
Island No. 10, 21
Israel: Egyptian commando raids against,
156; paratroops in Sinai, 158–61; post-
Suez policy shift, 162; tactics in 1973
War, 165
Italian East Africa, 97
Italian Front (World War I), 60
Italian Marines, 27
Italian Navy: motorboat and human
torpedo units, 18; special operations,
119; support of covert operations, 119
Italy: aggression of, 76, 92; Allied
invasions of, 90; Allied joint
operations in, in World War II, 132;
under Byzantine rule, 6; cities bombed,
133; invades Egypt, 109, 112, 115; as
Mediterranean Sea power, 1
Iwo Jima, landing on, 93, 103, 104;
close air support in, 114; naval gunfire
program scaled down for, 192

J–7 branch, U.S. Joint Staff, 306
Jackson, Andrew (Major-General), at
New Orleans, 16

Jackson, Thomas "Stonewall," (Major-
General), 192
Jackson, Mississippi, 20
Jamaica, 16
James, D. Clayton, and Anne Sharp
Wells, quoted, on interservice friction,
187
Japan: aggression during 1930s, 76; air
forces in China, 81; Allied plans for
invasion of, 104; cities bombed in,
1944–45, 133; competes for industrial
production, 96; imperial penetration
by, 28; as imperial power, 10;
operations in China in 1914, 42;
Pacific campaigns, 95–96; Soviet threat
to, in 1950, 139, 140; U.S. war plans
against, 34
Japanese attacks on Oahu, 71
Japanese aviation industry, 96
Japanese Navy: air units support Army in
China, 107; anti-submarine efforts
weak, 118; ASW, marginal in, 194;
competes with Army for industrial
production, 96; off Guadalcanal, 99;
lack of coherent amphibious doctrine,
81; at Leyte Gulf, 190; support of
covert operations, 119
Japanese 2nd Army, 27
Japanese War Ministry, 96
JCS. *See* Joint Chiefs of Staff
Jesuits, 151
jet development, by Luftwaffe, 109
Johnson, Franklyn, quoted, on British
defense policy, 155
Johnson, Louis (Secretary of Defense):
cancels supercarrier, 135; and Inchon
decision, 141; steps down, 144
Johnson, Lyndon B. (President), sends
Maxwell Taylor to Saigon in 1964,
148, 150
Joint Actions of the Army and Navy
(JAAN), 66, 72, 132
Joint Air Support Companies (JASCOs),
115
Joint Board (U.S.), 34, 65–67; less than
satisfactory interservice link, 71
Joint Chiefs of Staff (JDC), 69; in close
air support debate, 151; as Council of

War, 138; declining status in early 1970s, 154; after Goldwater-Nichols Act, 172; in Gulf War, 173, 189; formed, 97; and Forrestal, 134–35; and Inchon landing, 141; Korean War role, 137; in McNamara era, 147; Marine Corps representation on, 138; proposals for restructuring in 1950s, 145; in *Pueblo* Affair, 155, 164; reforms proposed, 166–67

joint committees (Br.), after World War II, 156

joint doctrinal publications, 171

Joint Doctrine Master Plan, 171

joint logistics, 145. *See also* amphibious operations; logistics, joint

Joint Munitions Board, 65

Joint Operations Center, 150

"Joint Perspective," 171

Joint Planning Committee to the Chiefs of Staff (Br.), 74

Joint Staff (U.S.): created, 132; marginality in 1960s, 147, 171

Joint Tactical Information Distribution System (JTIDS), 171

Jomini, Baron Antoine, 29

Jones, David (General): proposes JCS reforms, 171; quoted, on "facade of jointness," 189

Jordan, Israeli attack on, 158

Joy, C. Turner (Admiral), as Far East naval commander, 144

JTIDS, 171

"K" lighters, at Alhucemas, 77–78

Kagan, Donald, 3

Kahn, Herman, on accidental nuclear war, 148

kamikaze, 104

Kämpfgeschwader 40, 116–17

Kanghwa forts, amphibious operations at, 27

Karachi, Pakistan, 87

Karsten, Peter, 189

Kashmir border conflict, U.N. role in, 137

Kaufmann, William, quoted, on McNamara policies, 147

Keightley, Charles (General), as Supreme Commander, Suez expedition, 157–60

Kemal, Mustapha, 44, 48, 51

Kennedy, John F. (President), administration of: counter-insurgency doctrine of, 150; defense policies in, 146

Kennedy, Paul, on inter-allied relations, 187

Kenney, George (General), 101; and tactical air support, 114

Kent, Roman landing in, 4

Kenya, insurgency in, 157

Kerch, landing on, 93

Kesselring, Albert (Marshal), as joint/combined commander, 92

Kettle Hill, battle of, 34

Key West Agreement, 134–35

Keyes, Roger (Admiral of Fleet): in Dardanelles campaign, 48, 50–52, 58; dismissed, 88; named head of Combined Operations, 88

Khe Sanh, Battle of, 116, 164–65

Khmer Rouge, seizure of SS *Mayaguez* by, 154

Khrushchev, Nikita (Premier), in Suez crisis, 157

Kiev, as Viking outpost, 6

Killala Bay, Ireland, French landing at, 16

King, Ernest J. (Admiral of the Fleet): augments Overlord-Neptune fire support, 104; favors Pacific First strategy, 99; gains U.S. Navy control over amphibious operations, 69; Marianas campaign plans, 103; opposes unification, 129; and World War II assault landings, 187

Kingston-McCloughry, E. J., quoted, on headquarters insularity in World War II, 188

Kirk, Alan (Admiral), close rapport with Army, World War II, 127, 187

Kitchener, Herbert Horatio (Field Marshal), 42–43; and Dardanelles campaign, 45–47, 52

"Kitchener Army," 51
kleine kriege, 118
Knerr, Hugh (Brigadier General), in
    Revolt of the Admirals, 136
Knights of Malta and Rhodes, as
    Mediterranean powers, 1
Knox, Frank (Secretary of the Navy),
    death of, 128
Kobe, 141
Kom Tang Island, Cambodia, 154
Komer, Robert, on Vietnam War
    command structure, 149, 164
Korea: airliner shot down by U.S.S.R.,
    170; Japanese occupation of, 28;
    western incursions in, 30, 146
Korean War: air power in, 140; airborne
    drops in, 95; British forces in, 147,
    162, 165, 172; cause of stalemate,
    189; ends, 14–15, 149, 151–52; FACs
    in, 153; Inchon landing, 139–44;
    jointness in, 188; resurgence of
    amphibious tactics in, 132; strategic
    bombing in, 116; Truman
    administration budget limits and, 136–
    45; U.S. style in, 191
Kriegsmarine: Baltic Fleet of, in Oesel
    landing, 54–55; in Channel Dash, 128;
    links with Luftwaffe, 116–17
Krim, Abd el, Rif leader, 77–80
Krueger, Walter (General), praises
    Marine close air support, 114
Kum Kale landing, 47
Kursk, Battle of, 108
Kut-el-Amara, siege of, 43–44
Kuwait, Iraqi takeover of, thwarted in,
    1961, 161
Kwantung Army, 107

La Chambre, Guy, French air minister,
    80–81
Labour Party (Br.): anti-military views,
    74; post-World War II, 155; in Suez
    Crisis, 157; support of RAF, 75
Labrador, Viking settlements in, 6
Lae-Salamaua, 99
Lake Champlain, as British invasion
    route, 13
Landing craft: crews, special problems
    of, 188; cruciality in World War II,

99; design, 73; at Inchon, 143; in
    Norway and at Dunkirk, 86; reserve
    force needs noted, 89; shortage in Suez
    Crisis, 158, 161
landing craft gun, 89
Landing Operations Doctrine, 68
landing ship medium (rocket), 143
landing ship tank (LST), 89, 99, 143
Langenboom guns, 57
Lansdale, Edward G. (General), 179
Latin America, U.S. incursions in, 66–67
"law of the situation," 66
Lawrence, T. E., (Lieutenant-Colonel):
    advocates "air control," 73; in special
    operations, 118
Le Clerc, Jacque Philippe (General), 15
League of Nations, 76; Covenant of, 172
Leahy, William (Fleet Admiral): opposes
    unification in 1945, 129; as personal
    chief of staff to F.D.R., 128; to
    Truman, 131
Lebanon: jointness lack in, 194; jointness
    shortfalls in, 146; incursion in, 145
Lee, Robert E., at Vera Cruz, 19
Legere, Lawrence, quoted, 71
Lehman, John (Secretary of the Navy),
    and Maritime Strategy, 169
LeMay, Curtis (General), as U.S. Air
    Force Chief of Staff, 150
Lemnos, 46–47
Lend-Lease Act of 1941, 71, 108, 155
Lepanto, Battle of, 8
Leros, landing in, 92
Levant, British amphibious operations
    plans at, 31, 47
levée en masse, 14
Leyte: Halsey leaves beachhead at, 190;
    landing on, 29, 99
Libau, 54–55
Liberty incident, 166
Libyan raid, 161
LIC. *See* low-intensity conflict
Liddell Hart, B. H. (Captain), 70, 75;
    proposes Ministry of Defence, 76, 165
light bombardment concept, U.S. Army
    Air Corps, 69
light-gas guns, 167
Ligonier, Sir John, 11–12, 14
limited war, 137

Limon Bay, Japanese landing at, 95
Lincoln, Abraham, 25
Lingayen Gulf: Japanese landing at, 95;
    U.S. landing at, 99
Linn, Brian, quoted, on jointness in
    Philippine insurrection, 29
Lisbon, 9; as imperial hub, 28
Lloyd George, David (Prime Minister),
    considers joint command structure, 74
Locarno War: in British war plans, 75–
    76; in French war plans, 80
Loföten Islands, Commando raid on, 87
Logan, Ramsey C., (Vice Admiral), 128,
    193
logistics, joint: and jointness, 186, 192;
    in Korea, 141; in World War II, 101–3
London: as imperial hub, 28;
    vulnerability to invasion, 30
Long, John (Secretary of the Navy), 32
long-range escort fighters, 213
long-range penetration forces, 113
Louis XIV, military reforms under, 10
Louis XVI, death of, 14
Louisbourg, fall of, 10
Louisiana, operations in Civil War, 25
Lovett, Robert (Secretary of Defense),
    144
Low Countries, Nazis overrun, 86
low-intensity conflict (LIC), 152;
    jointness in, 166
LSMR. See landing ship medium (rocket)
Luftwaffe: airborne drops, 94, 107; in
    Channel dash, 128; created, 69; links
    with Kriegsmarine, 116–17; loses
    initiative in 1943, 111; losses at
    Dieppe, 89; in North Africa, 109;
    Rotterdam bombing, 115
Luzon, Japanese invasion of, 95
Lyautey, Louis (Marshal), 83

MAAG. See Military Assistance and
    Advisory Group
MacArthur, Douglas (General of the
    Army): as Army Chief of Staff, 66; as
    commander in Philippines (1941–42),
    88, 101; favors unification in 1945,
    129; ignores JCS directives, 144; and
    Inchon landing, 138–45; Marine Corps'

animus toward, 103; tactical fluidity,
    192
MacArthur-Pratt Agreement, 66
McClellan, George B. (General), 25
McElroy, Neil (Secretary of Defense),
    asks JCS to review budget, 147
McKinley, William (President), 34
McNair, Lesley J. (General), 115
McNamara, Robert S.: orders close air
    support studies, 151, 153; in Cuban
    Missile Crisis, 191; as Secretary of
    Defense, 146; on Vietnam War
    command structure, 149–50
McNamara line, Vietnam War, 192
McNarney, Joseph T. (General), 127
MACV. See Military Assistance
    Command Vietnam
Madagascar, 88
Madden Report, 134
Madrid, as imperial hub, 28
Magdala, Ethiopia, 27
Mahan, Alfred Thayer (Rear Admiral),
    29, 32; quoted, on service difference
    of perspective, 190
Maida, Battle of, 16
Mailer, Norman, 187
Makin Island, landings on, 104, 191
"Malay Barrier," 97
Malaya: Communist insurgency in, 157,
    166; Japanese invasion of, 95, 97
Malta: siege of, 8–9; as Suez expedition
    base, 158
Malvern Hill, Battle of, 21
management theory, 189
Manchuria, role of Japanese army air
    elements in, 107
maneuver warfare concept, 168–69
Manhattan Project, 71
Manila, British expedition to, 12
Mao Zedong, conquers China, 134
Marathon, Battle of, 3
Marianas Islands, 103
Marine Corps Expeditionary Force, 68
Marine Corps Gazette, 70
marines: Athenian, 3; Byzantine, 2;
    Egyptian, 2; Rhodian, 2; Roman, 2;
    Venetian, 2
Marines' Hymn (U.S.), 20

maritime strategy (Br.), 31, 75
maritime strategy (U.S.), 168–70
Marmorice, 15
Marshall, George C. (General of the
    Army): agrees to U.S. Navy control
    over amphibious operations, 69;
    advocates dive-bombing, 108; on
    airborne operations, 94; as Secretary of
    Defense, 144; seen as source of
    management ethic, 189
Marshall Plan, 155
maskirovka doctrine (U.S.S.R.), 173
"massive retaliation" policy, 145–46,
    148
Maund, L.E.H. (Captain), heads
    I.S.T.D.C., 73, 87
Maurice (Byzantine strategist), 187
Maurice, Frederick (General), on World
    War I interservice dynamics, 188
Mayaguez incident, 154–55, 166–67
medical evacuation, in Gulf War, 173
medical units, cooperation of, in World
    War II, 103
Mediterranean Sea: British operations in,
    in World War II, 90; Cold War, 137,
    139, 141; galley warfare in, 16, 86, 89
Mediterranean Theater of Operations
    (World War II), 90, 97, 100, 105
Meiji Restoration, 96
Mekong River, as imperial conduit, 28
Melilla, Morocco, 78
Memphis, Tennessee, 21
Memphis, Battle of, 23
mercantilism, rise of, 9–10
Merrimac. See *Virginia*
Mesopotamian campaign of 1915–1917,
    25, 43–44
Messina, Straits of, 90
Mexican War, 17, 19
Mexico, U.S. invasion of, in 1847, 17
Mexico City, 19
Middle East: British imperial presence in,
    77; in Byzantine era, 6; Soviet threat
    seen by British, 75
Midway, Battle of, 96
Miksche, F. O., on low-intensity conflict,
    165
Miles, Nelson (Major General), 32, 34

Military Assistance and Advisory Group
    (MAAG): coordination problems of,
    178 n.77; in Vietnam, 149–50, 153–54
Military Assistance Command Vietnam
    (MACV), 149, 152
military Coordinating Committee (Br.),
    86
Military Staff Committee (United
    Nations), 133
The Mind of an Army (Shaposhnikov),
    154
mine/anti-warfare: low status in U.S.
    Navy, 194; in maritime strategy, 169
minesweepers, at Inchon, 143
Minister for Coordination of Defence
    (Br.): Admiral Chatfield as, 85, 156;
    Sir Thomas Inskip as, 75
Minister of Defence (MOD): Churchill
    becomes, 86; separated from Prime
    Minister, 156
Ministry of Aviation (Fr.), 107
Ministry of Defence (Br.), proposal for,
    30–31, 74, 76
Minorca, British expedition to, 13
Mississippi River, 20–21, 23
Missouri, 129
Mister Roberts (Heggen), 103; as image
    of military incompetence, 135
Mitchell, William "Billy" (Brigadier
    General), 69; and bombing tests, 73
Mitla Pass, Israel: airborne capture of,
    158; tanks into, 159
Mobile Bay, Battle of, 20, 26
Molyneux, Thomas, 12–13, 19, 101
Monckton, Walter (Minister of Defence):
    resigns, 158; in Suez Crisis, 157
Mondego Bay, 15
Mond-Weir Committee, 74
Monro, Charles (General Sir), 52–54
Monte Cassino Abbey, bombing of, 115
Montgomery, Bernard (Field Marshal
    Viscount): on Arnhem defeat, 94; on
    Chiefs of Staff Committee, 156; and
    close air support, 110; Rhine crossing
    in 1945, 116; for unification after
    World War II, 155
Moon Island, 54
Moore, John (Major General), 15

Moore, Joseph H. (General), in Vietnam, 150, 152
Moore, Molly, quoted, 173
Moorehead, Alan, on Gallipoli, 54
Morgan, Frederick (Lieutenant General): on compliance, 192; quoted, on inter-allied relations, World War II, 187
Morison, Elting, quoted, on "limited identifications," 186
Morison, Samuel Eliot (Rear-Admiral), on interservice friction in Battle of the Atlantic, 117
"morning prayers," joint meetings in Malaya, 166
Morocco, 77
Morro forts, Cuba, 67
Morrow Board, 67
Moscow: as imperial hub, 25; reaction to Suez affair in, 159
Moskin, Robert, quoted, on Marine Corps close air support, 114
Mosul, 87
Moulton, J. L., quoted, on jointness in World War II, 188
Mount Kilimanjaro, 42
Mountbatten, Louis (Admiral of the Fleet Lord): fights for unification, 163; named head of Combined Operations, 88; in Suez Crisis, 157; visit to Oahu, 71
Mrozek, Donald, quoted, 193
Mudros, 47
Munich Agreement of 1938, 71, 81
Mussolini, Benito (Duce): forces routed in North Africa, in 1940, 108, 157; invasion of Ethiopia, 72
mutual cooperation, principle of, 66

Nadzab, 99
Nagasaki, atomic bombing of, 133
The Naked and the Dead (Mailer), as image of military incompetence, 135
naplam: in Greek Civil War, 166; use in Vietnam, 152, 165
Naples, 5
Napoleonic Wars, amphibious operations in, 15–16
Narvik, joint operations at, 85

Nashville, Tennessee, 21
Nasser, Gamel Abdel (President), seizes Suez Canal, 156–60
National Defense Act of 1920, 65
National Defense Committee, 147
National Defense Ministry (Fr.), proposal for, 80
National Guard Bureau, 131
National Military Establishment (NME), 132
National Security Act of 1947, 131–32, 134, 136; amendments of 1949, 137; Eisenhower revision of, 145
National Security Council (NSC), 132, 154, 172
National Service (Br.), 161
Nationalists, Chinese, 138
NATO. See North Atlantic Treaty Organization
The Naval Aristocracy (Karsten), 189
Naval gunfire support/control: at Alhucemas, 78, 80; at Dardanelles, 46–48, 54; and jointness, 192; in Korean War, 140; at Salerno, 92; shortage of, at Iwo Jima, 103–4; and Suez Crisis, 161
Naval Industrial Association, founded by Forrestal, 131
Naval War College, U.S., 32, 35
Naval War Staff (Br.): created, in World War I, 58; proposed, 31
Navy League, U.S., 131
Nazar, Byzantine admiral, 7
Nelson, Horatio (Admiral Lord), 11, 16, 61
neo-colonialism, U.S. fears of, in Vietnam War, 149
Netherlands Marines, 27
nettoyers, 118
Neutral Zone, Tangier, 77
Neutrality Acts of 1936–37, U.S., 71
neutron bomb, 170
New Britain Campaign, 99, 139
New Deal, 67
New Georgia, 99
New Guinea, 99, 101, 114
"New Look," Eisenhower defense policy, 145–46, 148

"new military history," 185
New Orleans, Battle of: 1815, 13, 16–17;
  1862, 20, 23, 26
"new weaponry," 170
New Zealand, forces in Pacific Theater,
  99
Newfoundland, 71
Newport, 134
Nicaragua, U.S. Marine Corps air
  operations during 1920s and 1930s in,
  70
Nicephorus Phocas, Byzantine emperor, 7
Niger River, as imperial conduit, 28
Nile River: as imperial conduit, 28, 52;
  riverine warfare on, 25, 27, 43
Nimitz, Chester W. (Fleet Admiral):
  direct liaison with industry, 102; views
  on jointness reversed, 128
Nixon, Richard (President), 167
Norfolk, Virginia, 26
Noriega, Manuel, 172
Normandy: Allied landings in, and
  campaign, 90, 92–94, 112; Luftwaffe
  losses, 117. See also operational code
  names, Neptune; operational code
  names, Overload
Normans: conquest of England, 7; as
  maritime power in the Mediterranean,
  1
North Africa: airborne operations in, 93,
  101; close air support in, 109–11, 113;
  invasion of, by Allies in 1942, 69, 89–
  90; joint operations in, in World War
  II, 132; in Punic Wars, 4
North African Tactical Air Force, 111
North America, colonial war in, 10
North American Air Defence Command
  (NORAD), in nuclear war scheme, 146
North Atlantic Blockading Squadron,
  U.S. Navy, 25
North Atlantic Treaty Organization
  (NATO): Britain's role in, 156;
  members, in Gulf War, 193; "out-of-
  area" dilemma, 161, 164; precedent in
  SHAEF, 132, 137; war plans of, 169–
  70
North Cape, in maritime strategy, 169
North Korea, 140; navy of, 155

North Korean People's Army (NKPA),
  116, 138–45
North Vietnam, 147; Son Tay POW
  camp in, 166
northwest frontier of India, air operations
  in, 71, 77
Norway: as base in Battle of the Atlantic,
  115; effect on Allied doctrine, 86, 92,
  101, 128; German invasion of, in
  1940, 85
Norwegian bastion, of German forces, in
  World War II, 116
Nuclear Age, 189
nuclear diplomacy, in Iran crisis of 1946,
  133
nuclear weapons: British, French, Israeli
  post-Suez development of, 162; effect
  of Korean War on utility, 137, 148;
  effect on U.S. Air Force doctrine, 150;
  implications for centralization, 133;
  add to interservice friction, 128; as
  nemesis of warfare, 119; as source of
  interservice friction, 188; Soviet
  acquisition of, 134

Oahu, 71, 132
"oceanic deterrent" concept, 137
Ocotal, siege of, 70
Octavian (Augustus Caesar), 5
October/Yom Kippur/Ramadan War, 165,
  170
Odyssey, 44
Oesel landing, 54–56, 77
Office of Strategic Services (O.S.S.):
  links with British intelligence, 71;
  MacArthur hostile to, in World War II,
  144
Okinawa campaign, 29, 104; close air
  support in, 115, 163
Omaha Beach, 92
Omdurman campaign, 28
Ooryphus, Byzantine admiral, 7
"operational art," 1, 166
operational code names: Anvil-Dragoon,
  93; Arclight, 165–72, 116; Avalanche,
  90; Boathook, 158; Cartwheel, 100;
  Chromite, 136, 138–39, 141–43, 191;
  Cobra, 115–16; Crossroads, 130;

Desert Shield, 172, 191; Desert Storm, 104, 116, 165, 173, 192, 193; Detachment, 103; Eagle Claw, 167, 171; Farm Gate, 150; Goodwood, 115; Husky, 90, 92, 100; 111; Just Cause, 66, 132; Market Garden, 93–94; Merkur, 93; Musketeer, 157–61; Neptune, 186; Nifty Nugget, 166; Overlord, 92–93, 104; Overlord-Neptune, 128; Queen, 115; Ranch Hand, 152; Sealion, 32; Strangle, 192; Torch, 69, 89, 90, 99, 100, 190; Urgent Fury, 168, 171–72; Varsity, 116
"Orange" war plan, 34
Ostend raid, 58

pace of operations, service differences, 191
Pacific Ocean, 130
Pacific Ocean Area, 97
pacifism, effects on defense between World Wars, 74–75
Packard, David, 171
Painlevé, Paul (Prime Minister), 77
Pakenham, Edward (Major-General), 16
Palestine, U.N. role in, 137
Palmer, Bruce (General), on lack of jointness in Vietnam War, 149
Panama, 66, 68
Panama invasion, by U.S., (1989). *See* operational code names, Just Cause
pan-Arabism, 156
Panzerarmee Afrika, 109
"paramount interest," principle of, defined, 66
paras (Fr. airborne forces), in Indochina and at Suez, 95
Paris: as imperial hub, 28; plan for airborne drop in 1944, 94
"Paris Gun," 57
Parliament (Br.), votes in Suez affair, 159
Patterson, Robert (Assistant Secretary of War), favors unification in 1945, 129
Patton, George S., Jr. (General), 111
Patton (film), 110
Patuxent River, 16

"peace dividend," 172
Pearl Harbor: effect on naval doctrine, 188; hearings, 97, 100, 128, 132; lack of jointness at, 129–30; U.S public anger over, 88, 96
Pei-Tang, landing at, 27
Peleliu: assault landing, 103; naval gunfire support of, 104
Peloponnesian War, 3
Pemberton, John C. (General), 23
Peninsula Campaign, American Civil War, 20–21, 25
Pentagon Papers, 154
pentakonters, 2
perestroika, 169
Perry, Mark, 192
Perry, Matthew (Commodore), 19
Pershing II missile, 170
Persian Gulf, 43
Persian Wars, 3
Persians, as maritime power, 1, 3
Peru, in War of the Pacific, 27–28
Petain, Henri (Marshal), 77
Petrograd, 55
Philippine Insurrection, 32, 34
Philippine Islands, 29; Japanese invasion of, in 1941, 95; plight of U.S. forces in, during 1941–42, 88, 132; tactical air support in, during 1944–45, 114–15; U.S. landings in, during 1944–45, 99
Phoenicians, as maritime power, 1, 4
Phoenix program, Vietnam War, 167
Pisa, as maritime power, 7
Pitt, William, the Elder, 11
Pitt, William, the Younger, 14, 16
Plains of Abraham, Battle of, 13
planning-programming-budgeting system (PPBS), 146
Plataea, 2
Pohang-dong, Korea, landing at, 140
Poitou, landing at, 15
Poland, campaign of, 107
Polaris, nuclear submarine, 148
police, role in low-intensity conflict, 166
Polk, James K., 19
Pompey, 5
Pompey Sextus, 5

Pope, John (General), 21
Port Arthur, 27
Port Fuad, French landing at, 159
Port Hudson, Mississippi, 23, 25
Port Royal, South Carolina, 26
Port Said, in Suez Crisis, 158–59
Porter, David Dixon (Flag Officer), 23, 25, 187
Portugal, as imperial power, 10
Powell, Colin (General): as Chairman, JCS, 172; and Gulf War, 173
PPBS. *See* planning-programming-budgeting system
Praetorianism, 135
Pratt, William Veazie (Admiral), as Chief of Naval Operations, 66
precision-guided munitions (PGM). *See* "smart weapons"
president of the United States, role in setting service boundaries, 66
prisoners of war, repatriation, post-World War II, 119, 170
privateers, 27
"procurement strategy," of U.S. Navy, 169
propaganda, role in low-intensity conflict, 166
Prussian General Staff, 30
Prussianism, 135
psychological warfare: aversion to, in U.S. Navy, in World War II, 192; in Cold War, 189; in low-intensity conflict, 155; marginality of, in Vietnam War, 152; in Suez Crisis, 159
Ptolemy, 2
Pueblo incident, 154–55, 167
Puerto Rico, 34
Puleston, John (Captain), quoted, 54
Punic Wars, 23
"purple-suit," 171
Pusan, Korea, 116; breakout, 144; perimeter battles, 138–39, 141
Pylos, 3

Quantico, Virginia, 68
quasi-war, U.S.-German (1941), 71
Quebec, British campaign against, 12–13
Quebec Conference, 103

Quesada, Elwood "Pete" (General), leaves Air Force, 140, 187
Quiberon expedition, 15
quinqueremes, 2
Quintus Metullus, 4

Rabaul, reduction of, 101
racism, as factor in Pacific war, 99
radar, in Hawaii, 96
Radford, Arthur (Admiral), critique of B–36 bomber, 135
rail guns, 167
railway guns, of U.S. Navy, in France, 57
Ramsey, Logan (Vice Admiral), on jointness, 128
Rangers, 118
Ravenal, Earl, 149
Ravenna, Roman naval base, 5
Rawson, Wyatt (Lieutenant), 28
Reagan, Ronald (President): administration of, 161, 167; and Beirut incident (1983), 168
Reagan-Gorbachev meetings in Rekjavik (1987), 172
reconnaissance, 186
Red Army: close air support in, 108; landing operations in World War II, 92; 1941 defeats of, 88; victory at Kursk, 111
Red River expedition, 26
reform movement (U.S.), 167
Regia Aeronautic: formed, 69, 107; in North Africa, 109
regional commands (U.S.), 132
Reign of Terror, 14
Rekjavik, Iceland, 172
Republic of Vietnam, 149; Air Force of, 166; approval on air and artillery strike required, 153
Republican Guard, Iraq, 1991 bombing of, 116
Republican Party (U.S.), right wing favors "Pacific First" strategy, World War II, 88
request-delivery lag, 110
"Revolt of the Admirals," 135–37
Rex (Italian liner), 66

Rhine, crossing of, in 1945, 93, 116
Rhine Flotilla (Roman Navy), 5
Rhode Island, Benedict Arnold's raids on, 13
Rhodes, siege of, 8
Richardson, F. O. (Admiral), and unification, 127
The Riddle of the Sands, 29
Rif insurgency, 77–80; U.S. volunteers in, 83 n.34
Riga, 55
"rimlands," as geopolitical concept, 134–39, 168
rites of passage, and service differences, 192
River Clyde (steamer), 48, 52
riverine warfare, 2, 25; in 1st Indochina War, 154; in Mesopotamia, 43–44; in Vietnam, 149
Roanoke, Virginia, capture of, 25–26
Rochefort expedition, 112–13, 193
Rockefeller Committee, 145
"roles and missions," 164
Romberg, Sigmund, 77
Rome: Civil Wars, 4–5; fall of, to Allies in 1944, 92; founding of Empire, 5; as imperial hub in modern era, 28; landings in Britain, 4; marines, 2; as maritime power, 1–5; navy, 5, 44
Rommel, Erwin (Field Marshal): arrives in North Africa in 1941, 109; in North Africa in 1941, 88; wounded by British fighter-bomber, 106
Roosevelt, Franklin D. (President): attempts to restructure military, 67; death of, 128–29; meets with Churchill, 71
Roosevelt, Theodore (President), 34
Root, Elihu (Secretary of War), 31
Root Reforms, 34
"rope of coordination," 166
Ross, Robert (Major-General), 16
R.O.T.C. (Reserve Officers Training Corps), 65
"Rover David," 112
"Rover Frank," 112
"Rover Joe," 112
"Rover Paddy," 112

Royal Air Force: and airborne drops, 94; in Battle of the Atlantic, 117; close air support evolution, 108–13; created, 69; effect on jointness, 73; plans for "Locarno War," 75; strategic bombing in 1941, 88; support of covert operations, 118; tactical doctrine of, 107, 192
Royal Australian Air Force, 115
Royal Flying Corps, 58
Royal Marines, 27; in imperial role, 72; in late 19th Century imperial wars, 28
Royal Navy: aircraft carriers reduced, 162; amphibious plans before 1914, 31; and anti-submarine warfare, 117, 194; in Falklands campaign, 162–63; Far East concerns, 75; in German Cameroons, 44; inability to save Crete, 93; joint exercises, 72; joint plans for Dardanelles landings, 46; operations in Mesopotamia, 43; opposes air control, 73; raid into Bosphorus, 45; as "Senior Service," 30; supports covert operations, 119, 128; in Zeebrugge raid, 57
Rusk, Dean (Secretary of State), on lack of jointness in Vietnam War, 154
Russia: and Dardanelles campaign, 45–47; as imperial power, 10; as Mediterranean power, 1; site of clandestine German training, 70; state in 1939 and cooperation with Germany, 81; Viking settlements in, 7; wars with Sweden, 11
Russian Navy, 58
Russo-Japanese War of 1904–05, 60
Russo-Turkish War of 1878, 30

"S" beach, Gallipoli, 48
S.A.C. *See* Strategic Air Command
SAFU (self-adjusting foul-up), 94
Saigon, 148–50
Saipan, 29; fire support problems on, 103–4
Salamis, Battle of, 3
Salerno, Allied landing on, 29, 90, 92, 103

Salisbury Committee, recommends CIP formation, 74
Salonika Front, 51–52, 60
Samar, 29
Sampson, William (Admiral), 32, 34
samurai spirit, impairs jointness, 95
San Diego, California, 138
San Juan de Ulloa, fortress, 19
San Juan Hill, Battle of, 34
Sandino, Augusto, 70
Sanjurjo, Sacanell (General), 77
Santiago, Cuba, 32
Santo Domingo, Battle of, 16
Saronic Gulf, 3
Saunders, Charles (Admiral), 12, 187
Savannah, capture of, 13
Savo Island, 99
Scarpe River, 58
Scheldt estuary, 16
Schemmer, Benjamin, quoted, on Son Tay raid, 151
Schlachstaffein, World War I, 58
Schmidt, Karl (Vice Admiral), 55
Schwarzkopf, Norman (General), as Central Command CINC in Gulf War, 173
Schweinfurt-Regensburg, raid on, 192
Scott, Percy (Admiral), quoted, on "unity of control," 57
Scott, Winfield (Major General), 17, 19, 34
SDI. *See* Strategic Defense Initiative
"sea dogs," 9–10
Sea of Marmora, 44
sealift: deficiencies of, in Desert Shield, 191, 193; low status in U.S. Navy, 194; in Vietnam War, 149
"Second Front," Soviet demands for, 88–89
Secretary of the Air Force, quoted, 133
Secretary of Defence: created, 132; post-Gulf War, "issue" list, 174; in *Pueblo* affair, 155; role strengthened, 136, 148; in Vietnam War, 149; weak powers, 135
Secretary of the Navy, role in setting service boundaries, 66

Secretary of War, role in setting service boundaries, 66
Select Committee on Postwar Military Policy, U.S. House of Representatives, 127; final report, 128
Seljuk Turks, 7
semantics, and service differences, 192
semiotics, and service differences, 192
"Senior Service," Royal Navy as, 30
Seoul, Korea, capture of, 141
Serbia, in World War I, 51
service academies: as source of interservice friction, 188–89; and tactical linearity, 192
service doctrine, vendor influence on shaping of, 189–90
Service Secretariats (Br.), eliminated by Thatcher government, 163
Sevastapol, Siege of, 20
Shafter, William (Major General), 32, 34
Shanghai, Royal Marines at, 72–73
The Shape of Things to Come (Wells), 141
Shaposhnikov, Boris (Marshal), 154
Sharm-el-Sheikh, captured by Israelis, 159
Sharp, U. S. Grant (Admiral): as CINCPAC/POA during Vietnam War, 149; on close air support, 152
Shaw, George Bernard, 76
Shepherd, Lemuel (General), as Inchon concept, 139
Sherman, Forrest P. (Admiral): death of, 144; eases interservice friction, 137
Sherman, Thomas (General), 26
Sherman, William T. (General), 23
Shikiuso, China, landing at, 138
Shiloh, Battle of, 21
shore parties, amphibious, 89
Shrader, Charles, quoted, on shortfalls in Torch planning, 188
Sicily: Allied invasion of, 29, 90, 93, 111–12; as pirate lair, 5–6; in Punic Wars, 4; Viking settlement in, 7
Sims, William (Admiral), as advocate of air power, 73
Sinai: in 1856, 158; in 1973, 165
Singapore: defense of, as British priority

in 1920s and 1930s, 73, 75; fall of, in 1942, 97

Sino-Japanese War of 1937–45, 76, 81

Six Day War, Israeli attack on USS *Liberty* in, 166

Slim, William (Field Marshal): on "air-mindedness," 105; quoted, 106, 113

"small wars," 68, 118

Smart, H. B. (Air Vice Marshal), in Iraq, 87

"smart weapons," 167, 170

Smith, Hedrick, quoted, on DoD tribalism, 189

Smith, Holland M. (General), 68, 99–100, 187

Smith, Julian (General), quoted, on Tarawa, 100

Smith, Ralph (Major General), 100

Smith, Walter A., quoted, 113

Smoot, Reed (Congressman), proposes Department of National Defense, 65

Snow, Charles (Sir), on landing craft role in World War II, 99

Sokol, A. B., quoted, 116

Solomon Islands, U.S. landings in, 99, 101

Son Tay raid, 166–67

Sophocles, 2

Soult, Nicholas (Marshal), 16

South America, riverine war in, 25

South Atlantic Blockade Squadron, 26

South Korean Constabulary: in Pusan perimeter, 138; routed, 137

South Vietnam (SVN), 149; dilemmas of allegiance, 153, 166; fall of, 150; joint U.S.-SVN structures, 150

Southeast Area Command (Br.), 89

Southeast Asia, 113, 119, 128; joint operations in, in World War II, 132, 152, 170

Southeast Asia Theater, in World War II, 163

Southwest Pacific Theater, in World War II, 86, 97, 100, 104, 114–15

Soviet Air Force. *See* Voyenno-Vozdushnoye Sily

Soviet Navy: expansion of, 162, 164; in U.S. Maritime strategy, 169

Soviet Union: concept of "operational art," 166; ICBM-Sputnik launches, 146; 1970s build-up in Eastern Europe, 167; proposes "Second Front," 88; in Suez Crisis, 157–61; support for Iraq, 173

Spaatz, Carl (General of the Army), favors close air support for Army, 130, 134, 140

Spain: as imperial power, 10; as Mediterranean power, 1; in Punic War, 4

Spanish-American War, 32, 34, 42, 172, 190

Spanish Armadas: 1588, 8–9; 1596 and 1597, 9

Spanish Army, in Morocco, 77

Spanish Civil War, 60; air war images, 76, 81; German participation in, 70

Spanish Foreign Legion, 77–79

Sparta, as maritime power, 1, 3–4

Special Branch (Br.), in Malaya, 166

Special Committee Investigating the National Defense Program, U.S. Senate (Truman Committee), 130

special operations ("special ops"): in Cold War, 189; conventional forces in, 119; and jointness, 186; Son Tay raid, 151; in "31 Initiatives," 168; in Vietnam War, 150; in World War II, 90, 118

Special Operations Command: as covert enclave, 172; created, 171

Special Planning Division, U.S. Army General Staff, devises unification plan, 127

Special Service Force (Br.). *See* Commandos

Specified Command, 171

"Specified Strike Zones," in Vietnam War, 153

"spectrum of response," 148

Speer, Albert (Minister of Production), 111

Sphacteria landing, 3

Spiller, Roger, quoted, on Lebanon, 145, 158, 194

"splits," U.S. Joint Chiefs, 138, 154

Sputnik, 146
Spykman, Nicholas, geopolitical
    prognostications of, 139
SS *Mayaguez*. See *Mayaguez* incident
SS *Virginia/Merrimac*, 56
St. Lô, breakout, 115
Stalin, Josef (Premier), supports
    international air force, 113, 165
Stanleyville raid, 189
Stanton, Edwin (Secretary of War), 26,
    146
Star Wars. *See* Strategic Defense
    Initiative
Stark, Harold R. (Admiral), quoted, 194
Starr, Chester, quoted, 4
State Department, 66; in Vietnam War,
    151
Sterling crisis, 161
Stockwell, Hugh (General), in Suez
    expedition, 158
Stopford, Frederick (General), 51
Straits of Messina, 90
Strategic Air Command (SAC), 133, 135,
    137; as mainstay of U.S. defense
    policy during 1950s, 145
strategic air power, 69
strategic bombers: in Cold War, 133–34;
    in Korean War, 140–41; in nuclear war
    schema, 146; in tactical role during
    World War II, 115–16
strategic bombing offensive, in World
    War II, 88
Strategic Defense Initiative (Star Wars),
    167, 191, 194
Stratemeyer, George (General), as Far
    East air commander in Korean War,
    140,144
Strike Command (U.S.), 147
Stringham, Silas (Admiral), 25
Sturmtruppen, World War I, 118
Sudan campaign, 27
Suez Canal: Axis threat to, 109; Egyptian
    seizure of, 156; lessons and results of,
    161–62; in Suez War, 159–61
Suez Crisis (1956): amphibious warfare
    in, 132, 144, 156; lessons of, 161,
    188; main events of, 156–61
Sullivan, Arthur (Sir), 30

Sullivan, John L. (Secretary of the
    Navy), 135
Sumatra, Japanese capture of, 95
The Supreme Command (Hankey), 54
supreme command model, 97
Supreme Headquarters Allied Power in
    Europe (SHAPE), in World War II,
    178 n.76, 187
Supreme Military Council, Maxwell
    Taylor's proposal for, 148
surprise attack, NATO concerns for, 170
Suvla Bay, 52–53
Sweden: ascendancy in Baltic, 11; iron
    mines of, 85
Sword of Honour (Waugh), 87
Symington, Stuart (Secretary of the Air
    Force): false accusations of, 135;
    quoted, on unification, 133
Syracuse, Athenian expedition to, 4
Syria: under Byzantine rule, 6; defeat of
    fleet by Byzantines, 7; failed coup in
    1956, 158; French occupations of, 77;
    in 1973 Middle East War, 165;
    pipelines cut during Suez Crisis, 159

tact and jointness, 190
Tactical Air Command (TAC):
    downgraded by General Vandenberg,
    134; post-Gulf War friendly fire study,
    174
Tactical Air Control Center (U.S. Air
    Force), at MMV Headquarters, 153
tactical air support/tactical aviation/close
    air support, 106; low status in U.S. Air
    Force, 194. *See also* close air support
tactical use of strategic bombers, 115–56;
    in Korea, 140; in Vietnam War, 150–
    51
Tagga Bay, landing at, 55–56
Taku forts, 27
Tampa, Florida, 34
Tanga, German East Africa, landing at,
    42–43
Tangier, Rif threat to, 77
Tarakan, Japanese capture of, 95
Taranto, 90
Tarawa, 78, 90, 103; assault landing at,

99–100; inadequacy of gunfire support at, 104; in 1943, 90, 99

Taylor, Maxwell (General): reform attempts, 148; resigns as Army chief of staff, 145

Taylor, Zachary, 17, 19

Technological change: effect on special operations, 118; source of jointness, 189

Tedder, Arthur (Air Chief Marshal), as member of Chiefs of Staff Committee, 156

Teheran, Iran, 167

Tel-el-Kebir, Battle of, 28, 30

Tennessee River, 21

"tentacles," RAF close air support elements, 107

Tentative Landing Operations Manual, U.S. Navy, 68

"Ten-Year Rule," 74–75

Teplov, Boris, Russian psychologist, 59

Terceira, Spanish expedition, 9

Terraine, John, quoted: on RAF-Army rapport, 109; on RAF-Royal Navy rapport, 117

Territorial Army (Br.), 86

terrorism, 165

Terry, Alfred (Major-General), 26

Tetuan, Morocco, 78

Texas, operations in Civil War, 25

TFX fighter controversy, 147

Thailand, Japanese invasion of, 97

Thatcher, Margaret (Prime Minister): defense policies of, 161–62; relation with services, 164

Thermopylae, Battle of, 2

Things to Come (Wells), 76

Third World, reactions to Suez affair in, 159

The Third World War (Hackett), 170

Thirty Years' War, 10

"thirty-one initiatives," 168, 170, 173

Thompson, Robert (Sir), and joint methods in Malaya, 166

Thompson, W. Scott and Donaldson D. Frizzell, quoted, on Vietnam command fragmentation, 149

Tigris-Euphrates Valley, 43–44

Tilford, Earl F., quoted, on *Mayaguez* affair, 154

Tinian, 103

Tizard Mission, 71

Tojo, Hideki, as Premier of Japan, 96

Tokyo, as imperial hub, 28

Tolstoy, Leo, 187

Tomahawk missile, 173

Tompkins Plan, 127

Tonambogo landing, 99

Toulouse, Battle of, 16

Toynbee, Arnold, quoted, 194

Trafalgar, Battle of, 16, 67

Training and Doctrine Command, U.S. Army, 174

Trajan's Column, 5

Transportation Command (U.S.), 171

transporter submarines: Japanese, in World War II, 96; U.S., and Makin raid, 119

Trenchard, Hugh (Air Chief Marshal): as obstacle to jointness, 76; propounds "air control," 73; on Singapore defense, 75

"tribalism," of armed services, 189, 192

triremes, 2

Trojan Wars, 44

Trojans, 44

Truman, Harry S. (President): administration of, 128; budget squeeze and containment, 135; derides Marine Corps, 139; favors unification, 129–31, 133; and Korean War, 137–45; praises from, after Inchon, 144, 154

Truscott, Lucian (Major General), 92

Tsingtao, China: in 1914, 42; in 1947, 138

Tunis, sieges of, 8, 9

Tunisia, 110

Turkey, 45

Turkish Army: in Dardanelles campaign, 44–54, 77; operations in Mesopotamia, 43–44

Turkish Army units, 19th Infantry Division, 51

Turks, as maritime power, 1

Turner, Richmond Kelly "Terrible"

(Vice-Admiral), 99; quoted, on jointness, 186–87
Twelve O'Clock High (Lay), as image of military incompetence, 135
"twelve points," 131

U-boats, in World War II, 88, 116–17
Udet, Ernst (General), 70
Ukraine, in World War II, 93
Ulster, 162
Uncertain Trumpet (Taylor), 148
Underwater Demolition Team (UDT), 102
unification of high command: in Britain, 72; in France, 81; in Germany, 81; proposed, in U.S., 65, 67; proposed by Maxwell Taylor, 148; as source of interservice friction, 188
unification plan, U.S. General Staff (Joint) Plan, 127
Unified Action Armed Forces, 171
uniforms, and service differences, 192
United Nations (UN): Charter of, 172–73; founding of, 119; in Korean War, 140–41; military role, 133, 137; in Suez Crisis, 158–61
United Services General Staff, 72
United States: enters ABC–1 Agreement, 88; as imperial power, 10, 29; as Mediterranean sea power, 1; state of naval aviation, 76; in Suez Crisis, 157–60
"unities of war," 187
unity of command: principle of, 66; as principle of war, 186
Uruguay, in War of the Triple Alliance, 27
U.S. Air Force: air support doctrine assailed, 140; created, 128, 132; in Cold War, 189; creation causes friction, 188; dominant role in nuclear war, 133, 146, 148; fears Army role in COIN, 151, 168–69; Fifth Air Force, in *Pueblo* affair, 155; in interservice wrangling, 130; Navy doubts role, 137; Navy opposes creation, 130; and nuclear role, 133; in Pusan battles,

139; before Vietnam, 146; in Vietnam War, 147–55
U.S. Armed Forces Far East (USAFFE), 137
U.S. Armed Forces, joint units: 1st Amphibious Task Force, 99; First Joint Training Force, 68; Joint Assault Signal Companies (JASCO), 102
U.S. Army: and close air support, 151; doctrine linked to U.S. Air Force, 170; interservice friction and "31 initiatives," 168–69; Kennedy budget favors, 148; linearity of tactics, 192; reduction under "New Look," 145; in Vietnam, 149–55. *See also* U.S. Army units
U.S. Army Air Corps: MATS created, 132; state of tactical aviation in 1939, 66–67, 81
U.S. Army Air Forces (USAAF): and airborne forces, 94; close air support doctrine, 111; 1st Air Commandos formed, 113; friction with U.S. Navy in Battle of the Atlantic, 117; supports covert operations, 119; tactical air state-of-the-art, 114
U.S. Army Air Service, 60
U.S. Army Aviation branch, 165
U.S. Army units: 1st Air Commandos, 113; First Army, 116; Third Army, 93; Fifth Army, 92, 115; Sixth Army, 114; Eighth Army, 155; 1st Cavalry Division, 139–40, 144; Coast Artillery Corps, 66, 185; V Corps, 32; VI Corps, 92; X Corps, 143; Engineer Special Brigades (ESB), 102, 144; General Staff, 127; Ground Forces, 115; 1st Infantry Division, 68; 7th Infantry Division, 143–44; 27th Infantry Division, 100; Special Forces, 150, 189
U.S. Army-U.S. Air Force links, in World War II, 109–15
U.S.-British cooperation in 1940–41, 71
U.S. Congress: and CIA, 172; opposes intercontinental bomber, 67; shapes National Security Act of 1947, 131–32, 136, 148; unification proposals,

65–66; *versus* Hoover and Roosevelt reforms, 67

U.S. Department of Defense. *See* Department of Defense

U.S. Department of State. *See* State Department

U.S. General Staff (Joint) Plan, 127

U.S. Joint Chiefs of Staff. *See* Joint Chiefs of Staff

U.S. Marine Corps: amphibious assaults, in World War II, 95–115; ASW in, 194; in Beirut, 168; at Chapultapec, 48; claims of conceptual eminence in amphibious warfare, 67; close air support, 70, 108, 114–16; congressional support, 139; denied major role in Desert Storm, 193; dive bombers, in World War II, 114; at Fort Fisher, 26; at Khe Sanh, 164; in maritime strategy, 169; post-World War II reduction of, 119; reduction of proposed, 130, 138; retains close air support elements, 152; role in "Banana Wars," 27, 34; stagnation after Vietnam, 167; in trench warfare, 57

U.S. Marine Corps air wings: Army and Air Force seek, 138; support sought in Korean War, 140, 143

U.S. Marine Corps Expeditionary Force, 68

U.S. Marine Corps Staff College (Quantico), 68

U.S. Marine Corps units: Air-Naval Gunfire Liaison Companies (ANGLICO), 143; 1st Division, 68, 99, 139, 141, 143; 1st Provisional Brigade, 138, 141; 2nd Raider Battalion, 119; 5th Regiment, 143, 258; V Amphibious Force, 99; Fleet Marine Force, 138

U.S. Naval Institute, 131

U.S. Naval War College, 68

U.S. Navy: and air support, in World War II, 108; in Civil War, 20–27; claims of interservice rivalry, 127–37; disdain for jointness, 147; friction with U.S. Army Air Forces in Battle of the Atlantic, 117; growth in Reagan administration, 168; gunfire support problems, 103–4; in Korean War, 139–45; low status of amphibious duty, 138–39; naval guns in France, 57; favors "Pacific First" strategy in World War II, 88; Polaris deployed by, 148; post-World War II reduction of, 119–20, 127; public views of, after World War II, 130–31; support of convert operations, 119; in Vietnam War, 147–55; creates War College, 32; war plans versus Japan, 68; between World Wars, 66

U.S. Navy units: Asiatic Fleet, 128; Seventh Amphibious Force, 99, 104, 138; Supply Corps, 101; Underwater Demolition Teams (UDS), 102

U.S. Neutrality Acts, 131

U.S. Senate, air power hearings, 146

U.S. Strategic Bombing Survey, 131

U.S.M.C. Advanced Base Force, 68

USS *Hornet*, in Doolittle raid, 119

USS *Liberty*, 166

USS *Mount McKinley*, at Kobe, 141

USS *Pueblo. See Pueblo* incident

U.S.S.R., aid to Egypt, 158–61

V Amphibious Task Force, U.S. Marine Corps, 177

"V" beach, Gallipoli, 48

Väägso, Commando raid on, 87

Vandegrift, Arthur W. (General), opposes unification, 129

Vandenberg, Hoyt (General): downgrades tactical aviation, 134; in Korean War, 140; retirement of, 144

Vella Lavella, 99

Vendée Revolt, 15

vendor influence, on shaping of service doctrine, 189–90

Venice, as maritime power, 1, 7, 44

Venizelos, Eleutherios (Prime Minister), 52

Vera Cruz, U.S. landing at, 34

Versailles Treaty, 70

very long range aircraft (VLR): in Battle of Atlantic, 116–18; in Hawaii, 96; role in sea control, 76

Vicksburg, Mississippi, siege of, 23–25
Victoria Cross, 87
Viet Cong, 151
Vietnam, Republic of, 122; U.S. forces
  depart from, 149
Vietnam War: air power orchestration in,
  164; Anglo-French detachment in, 162;
  CAS in, 152–54; CINCPAC/POA
  command in, 132, 140, 146–47;
  command channels in, 178 n.76, 186,
  188–89; jointness and interservice
  friction in, 148–54, 193; uncertain
  utility of air power in, 165, 170, 173;
  U.S. style in, 192
"Vietnamization," deferral of, 152
Vikings, 2, 6
Vinson, Carl (Congressman), as
  champion of Navy, 130
Virginia, 26
Voices Prophesying War (Clarke), 29
von Bernhardi, Frederick (General), view
  of amphibious operations, 189
von Clausewitz, Karl, 168, 190
von Hutier, Oskar (General), 54
von Kluge, Günther (Field Marshal), on
  impact of air power, 106
von Lettow-Vorbeck, Paul (Major-
  General), 42–43, 118
von Sanders, Liman (General), 47, 51,
  53
Voyenno-Vozdushnoye Sily (VVS)
  (Soviet Air Force), 107–8; support
  covert operations, 119; use of strategic
  bombers in tactical role in World War
  II, 115
V-weapons sites, Holland, 94

Wainwright, Jonathan (Lieutenant
  General), 95
Wake Island, Japanese landing at, 95, 97
Walcheren expedition, 16
Walker, Walton (Lieutenant General),
  commands in Pusan battle, 139, 143
Walsingham, Francis (Sir), intelligence
  service of, 151
War Cabinet (Br.), 42; in World War II,
  86
War Council (Br.), 41–42, 46, 50

war councils in Malaya, 166
War Office (Br.), opposition to
  amphibious schemes before 1914, 31
War of the Pacific, 27
war plans (Br.), "Locarno War," 75–76;
  versus Italy and Japan, 72
war plans (U.S.): "Gray," 68;
  "Orange," 34, 68
War Plans Division, U.S. Army General
  Staff, 65
War of the Triple Alliance, 27
"warrior" ethic, in post-Vietnam U.S.
  force, 189
"wars of national liberation," Soviet
  concept of, 157
Warsaw Pact, 164, 170
Washington, George (General/President),
  38
Washington, Lawrence, 12
Washington, D.C.: capture of, 13, 16; as
  imperial hub, 28, 141; reaction to Suez
  affair, 159
Washington Naval Conference, effects of,
  74
"water gap," bridging devices for, 89
Watkins, James (Admiral), on
  interservice rivalry, 190
Waugh, Evelyn, as Commando officer,
  87
Wavell, Archibald (Field Marshal): in
  North Africa, 109; as Supreme
  Commander, ABDACOM, 97
"Way Forward," (Br. Defence White
  Paper), 162
Wehrmacht: airborne force, 93; in
  invasion of Norway, 85; as joint
  command model, 81; lack of reserves,
  112, 131; losses at Dieppe, 89; uneven
  interservice relations in, 92
Wehrmacht close air support system, 107
Weihaiwei, China, 138
Weimar Republic, 70
Weinberger, Casper (Secretary of
  Defense), resignation of, 172
Weinberger Doctrine, 147
Welles, Gideon (Secretary of the Navy),
  21, 26
Wellesley, Arthur, 15–17

Wellington, Duke of, 15–17
Wells, H. G., 76
Wemyss, Wester (Admiral of the Fleet), 54
West, Richard, quoted, 75
West Africa, riverine warfare, in 19th and 20th centuries, 25
West Indies, as prize in imperial wars, 12
Western Europe, 138
Western Flotilla, U.S. Navy, in Civil War, 13, 21
Western Front, 48, 50, 57; air operations on, 58, 60
Westmoreland, William (General): and "Electronic Battlefield" concept, 167; as head of MACV, 149, 150, 152
Wheeler, Earl (General), as Chairman, JCS, 154
White, Brudenell (Lieutenant-Colonel), 52
White Conference, 129
White House, situation room, 155
White House meeting of May 1946, 131
Wilhelm II (Kaiser), 31, 159
Wilkinson, Spenser, 154
William of Normandy, 7
William, Ralph, quoted, 169
Willoughby, W. F., concept of unified defense, 65
Wilmington, North Carolina, 26
Wilmont, Chester, on landing craft role in World War II, 99
Wilson, Arthur (Admiral), 65
Wilson, Bertram (Captain), suggests ISTDC, 73
Wilson, Charles E., 144
Wilson, Henry (Field Marshal), 31

Wilson, Woodrow (President), 34
Wilt, Alan, on quality of U.S. air support, in World War II, 111
Wingate, Ronald (Sir), quoted, 76
"wolf packs," 116–17
Wolfe, James (Major-General), 12, 141, 187
Wolmi-do, South Korea, in Inchon landing, 143
Wolseley, Garnet (Field Marshal), calls for Ministry of Defence, 30
The World Crisis (Churchill), 54
World War II, U.S. entry in, 68
Worth, William J. (General), 19
Wylie, J. C. (Captain), quoted, 169

"X" beach, Gallipoli, 48
Xenophon, 1

"Y" beach, Gallipoli, 47–48
Yamamoto, Isoroku (Admiral), 119
Yamamoto mission, 119
"Yankee Station," Vietnam War, 152
York, Ontario, Canada, U.S. troops' exercises at, 13
Yorktown, 26
Ypacarai, Battle of, 27
Yugoslavia, Nazi conquest of, 87

"Z"Day, Dardanelles, 53
Zacharias, Ellis M., quoted, on psychological warfare, in World War II, 192
zaibatsu, 96
Zeebrugge raid, 57, 86
Zeppelins, in World War I, 57

About the Author

ROGER A. BEAUMONT, Professor of History, Texas A&M University, has specialized in the study of command and control and of special operations and elite units. His books include *Special Operations Elite Units: A Reference Guide, 1939–1988* (Greenwood Press, 1988), *The Nerves of War: Emerging Issues in and References to Command and Control* (1986), and *Horizontal Escalation* (1983), among others.